War Through Italian Ey

There is a popular notion that the Italian armed forces of the Second World War were an inferior fighting force. Despite the vast numbers taken as prisoners, detailed studies of the experiences of these soldiers remain relatively uncommon and the value of this group to furthering our understanding of the Italian experience of war under Fascism is also rarely acknowledged. The existence in the National Archives of hundreds of pages of transcripts of covert British surveillance of Italian POWs has made it possible to engage with their experiences and opinions in much greater depth. The euphemistically termed 'Special Reports' present historians with a unique insight into how all levels of Italian soldiery viewed Fascist Italy's experience of war, 1940–1943. This book examines reactions to Italian political leadership, the progress of the war as well as Italian soldiers' 'everyday' views on sex, war, the enemy, death, food, their allies, bravery, race and killing. These fascinating documents reveal the complexity of the outlook of these men, which persistent – and influential – national stereotypes and historiographical trends fail to acknowledge.

Dr Alexander Henry is a historian of the Second World War with particular research interests in the conflict fought between the Allies and Fascist Italy, 1940–1943. Alex completed his PhD, MA and BA in the Department of History at the University of Nottingham between 2010 and 2018.

Routledge Studies in Second World War History

The Second World War remains today the most seismic political event of the past hundred years, an unimaginable upheaval that impacted upon every country on earth and is fully ingrained in the consciousness of the world's citizens. Traditional narratives of the conflict are entrenched to such a degree that new research takes on an ever-important role in helping us make sense of Second World War. Aiming to bring to light the results of new archival research and exploring notions of memory, propaganda, genocide, empire and culture, Routledge Studies in Second World War History sheds new light on the events and legacy of global war.
Recent titles in this series

Unknown Conflicts of the Second World War
Forgotten Fronts
Chris Murray

A New Nationalist Europe Under Hitler
Concepts of Europe and Transnational Networks in the National Socialist Sphere of Influence, 1933–1945
Edited by Johannes Dafinger and Dieter Pohl

The Swedish Jews and the Holocaust
Pontus Rudberg

Mussolini's Army against Greece
October 1940–April 1941
Richard Carrier

Sweden, Japan, and the Long Second World War
1931–1945
Pascal Lottaz and Ingemar Ottosson with an Essay by Bert Edström

War Through Italian Eyes
Fighting for Mussolini, 1940–1943
Alexander Henry

For more information about this series, please visit: https://www.routledge.com/Routledge-Studies-in-Second-World-War-History/book-series/WWII

War Through Italian Eyes
Fighting for Mussolini, 1940–1943

Alexander Henry

Routledge
Taylor & Francis Group

LONDON AND NEW YORK

First published 2021
by Routledge
2 Park Square, Milton Park, Abingdon, Oxon OX14 4RN

and by Routledge
605 Third Avenue, New York, NY 10158

Routledge is an imprint of the Taylor & Francis Group, an informa business

© 2021 Alexander Henry

The right of Alexander Henry to be identified as author of this work has been asserted by him in accordance with sections 77 and 78 of the Copyright, Designs and Patents Act 1988.

All rights reserved. No part of this book may be reprinted or reproduced or utilised in any form or by any electronic, mechanical, or other means, now known or hereafter invented, including photocopying and recording, or in any information storage or retrieval system, without permission in writing from the publishers.

Trademark notice: Product or corporate names may be trademarks or registered trademarks, and are used only for identification and explanation without intent to infringe.

British Library Cataloguing-in-Publication Data
A catalogue record for this book is available from the British Library

Library of Congress Cataloging-in-Publication Data
Names: Henry, Alexander, 1992- author.
Title: War through Italian eyes : fighting for Mussolini, 1940-1943 / Alexander Henry.
Description: Abingdon, Oxon ; New York : Routledge, 2021. | Series: Routledge studies in Second World War history | Includes bibliographical references and index. |
Identifiers: LCCN 2021002485 (print) | LCCN 2021002486 (ebook) |
Subjects: LCSH: Great Britain. Combined Services Interrogation Centre. | Italy. Regio Esercito--History--World War, 1939-1945--Sources. | Soldiers--Italy--Attitudes--History--20th century. | Soldiers--Italy--Psychology--History--20th century. | Prisoners of war--Italy. | Prisoners of war--Great Britain. | World War, 1939-1945--Prisoners and prisons, British. | World War, 1939-1945--Prisoners and prisons--Italy. | Military interrogation--Great Britain--History--20th century. | World War, 1939-1945--Military intelligence--Great Britain.
Classification: LCC D810.S7 H44 2021 (print) | LCC D810.S7 (ebook) | DDC 940.54/0945--dc23
LC record available at https://lccn.loc.gov/2021002485
LC ebook record available at https://lccn.loc.gov/2021002486

ISBN: 978-0-367-51561-4 (hbk)
ISBN: 978-1-032-03847-6 (pbk)
ISBN: 978-1-003-05442-9 (ebk)

Typeset in Bembo
by MPS Limited, Dehradun

Contents

	Acknowledgements	vi
	Introduction	1
1	CSDIC (UK) and the protocols	15
2	Reading the sources	42
3	Friends and foes	62
4	Occupation, war crimes and antisemitism	90
5	Warriors of land, sea and air	116
6	Attitudes towards Italian political leadership	148
7	Winning and losing the war	176
	Conclusion: A hopeful future?	192
	Bibliography	199
	Index	218

Acknowledgements

The process of writing a book is not one taken alone, and I have built up a debt of gratitude to many. I would firstly like to thank the Department of History at the University of Nottingham and the family of John Robinson. Without the award of the John Robinson Studentship, it would have been impossible for me to study for the PhD and write the thesis which forms the backbone of this book. For that, I will be eternally grateful.

I would not be where I am today without the inspirational teaching of Jon Wale, Martin Parham and Stuart Dalley. Many thanks are also due to Anna Greenwood, Anna Walas, Joe Merton, Nick Thomas, [...] Andrew Stewart, Amedeo Osti Guerrazzi and Karen Adler. Karen Adler who have all provided invaluable feedback and guidance over the years. Special thanks are owed to David Laven for his generosity, good-humour and sage advice on all matters relating to this project and beyond.

This book would have been impossible to complete without the love and support of my friends and family. Thank you, Mum, Dad, Abi, Buster, Barney and Pheobe. Likewise, I am much obliged to my PhD compatriots Mark Anderson, Katie Griffiths, Katie Harrison, Harriet Lander, Esther Lewis, Tim McManus, Hannah Nicholson, Jon Rowson, Freddie Stephenson, Emma Vosper and Scott Weightman. Without your excellent company and friendship, the journey of the past few years would have been far harder. Many thanks are also due to Jonni Shepard, Jozef Doyle, Matt Light, Max Ogden and Jacob Youngs for their mental and physical support. To Hannah Jeffery, thank you for Seinfeld, Sunny and unending encouragement.

I remain indebted to Martin Feighan for converting me to the trials and tribulations of supporting Gloucester Rugby. Without which this book may have been finished earlier, and at far less expense, but would have been a much less enjoyable experience. A debt of gratitude is also owed to John Robins, [...] Elis James, Dave Masterman, Mike Bubbins [...] Steff Garrero and the Crown Inn (Beeston, Notts). All masters of their art.

I would like to thank everyone at Routledge, and the *British Journal of Military History* and the British Commission for Military History for permission to make reproductions from my article, 'Everybody to be Armed': Italian Naval Personnel and the Axis Occupation of Bordeaux, 1940-1943.'

This book is dedicated to the memory of Alfred Cole and Arthur Henry, for the role they played in fighting the 'Italian War.'

Introduction

Ordinary Seaman Stefanni was an Italian sailor and survivor of the submarine *Baracca*. In November 1941, he spoke of his experiences on board a *Regia Marina* submarine during the early stages of the Second World War,

> When we came back from that cruise, everybody had scabies and lice, from the commander downwards [...] all of us were covered with lice and scabies [...] I can't tell you how many there were in that green jersey of mine. I soaked it in paraffin and then hung it up. It was swarming with them. We used to amuse ourselves in the evenings hunting them with an electric torch.[1]

> The first cruise was a jazz affair! There were at least fifteen people on the bridge all the time, enjoying themselves as if they were on a pleasure cruise. Standing there smoking. Suddenly there was an alarm; an aircraft appeared. It was a Spanish aircraft however. But what a scene! The men all made a dash for the conning-tower, and the *capo di silurista*, an idiot who was afterwards sent home (in disgrace), came on deck in his underpants trembling like a virgin on her wedding night.[2]

Dirt, squalor, bonhomie and cowardice. These snapshots offer two contrasting memories of Stefanni's war. They are memories that give the reader a sharp insight into the daily life of an Italian submariner. You can almost feel Stefanni's jersey crawling with lice, and you can imagine the fear when an aircraft is spotted from the bridge of the *Baracca*. Alongside these episodes in Stefanni's short-lived war, we also have a record of his thoughts on subjects such as Italo-German relations, POW interrogations, provisions at sea and empire.[3]

Stefanni's words are of enormous historical value, yet they were not originally preserved for the interests of historians, but for wartime intelligence personnel. More specifically, they were recorded by staff of the British-run Combined Services Detailed Interrogation Centre (United Kingdom) – or CSDIC (UK). Between September 1939 and October 1945, the Centre monitored, recorded, transcribed and translated the private conversations of thousands of Axis prisoners of war at specialised POW camps in southern England.[4] In all, over 500 Italian soldiers, sailors and airmen passed through these camps between 1940 and 1943; close to 2000 transcripts – variously described as 'reports,' 'protocols,' 'special reports,' 'listening reports' and 'SR reports' at the time – were made of their conversations.[5] So secret that they were withheld even from the Allied prosecution teams at the Nuremberg War Crimes trials,[6] these documents remained out of the public eye until their declassification in 1996.[7] There was a request to use the protocols in the trials, to which CSDIC (UK) responded in the negative, arguing, 'it is not merely a question of the nature of information contained in the report but the methods used for obtaining it and, even more important possibly, the amount and value of the information so obtained.'[8]

Although several works have been published on the conversations between German prisoners,[9] no English-language work has systematically engaged with the sources pertaining to Italian personnel. This book seeks to rectify this imbalance. Its central question is to ask how the CSDIC (UK) sources shape our understandings of Italian servicemen in the period 1940–1943. A great effort has been put into including representative examples from the Italian Army, Navy and Air Force wherever possible. However, the nature of the sources means that there is much greater material on naval personnel, and this has led to a corresponding imbalance towards the men of the *Regia Marina* throughout the book. I expand further on this in Chapter Two. The chronological scope of this study is defined for two reasons. First, it corresponds to the era when a politically united and independent Fascist Italy was at war with the Western Allies. This period will be referred to as 'the Italian War.' Second, it is dictated by the simple fact that Italian POWs were not handled by the Centre before 1940 or after 1943.

Each chapter has its own specific focus, but two strands of argument run through many of them. The first is to reject many stereotypes about the character of Italian soldiers during this period. These are stereotypes that variously cast Italian servicemen as harmless nice guys (*Italiani brava gente*), cunning (*furbo*) and devotees of *l'arte di arrangiarsi* (the art of 'getting along' by any means).[10] The second is to dispel the myth surrounding the war fought between Fascist Italy and the Western Allies between 1940 and 1943. In both historiography and popular culture, it is not unusual to see the conflict involving the Italians as little more than a 'sideshow,' characterised by less military determination and by a good-natured, even hedonistic, world view.[11] I shall argue that the transcripts reveal the Italian War to have been tough and brutal, and to have resulted in a very high human cost. The fighting was much more than a good-natured warm-up to the operations in North-West Europe in 1944–1945 and demands greater analysis. The CSDIC (UK) transcripts are an excellent source to tackle both issues. In this, I build on the work of historians such as Schlemmer and Rodogno who have demonstrated the degree to which Italian soldiers were 'invaders, not victims.'[12]

Chapter One offers a detailed contextualisation of CSDIC (UK) and the transcripts that they produced, through an examination of the protocol totals, their presentation and format, how the transcripts were made and a brief organisational history of the Centre. Chapter Two explores the protocols as historical sources, their language and translation, how they are shaped by the prisoner of war experience, their contemporary usage and historical significance from a British intelligence perspective. While comparatively little-known, the work of CSDIC (UK) was a highly valuable part of the wartime British intelligence gathering system. Approaching these sources in such a methodologically rigorous fashion allows for a deeper engagement with the content of the CSDIC (UK) protocols in Chapters Three to Seven, each of which discusses a specific theme.

Chapter Three looks at how the Italian POWs viewed other nationalities and is divided into sections on perceptions of Americans, the British, the French, the Soviets and Germans. These views subvert the simple divide between 'friend' and 'foe.' Disdain towards Americans, British and French could be more than matched with animosity towards their German allies, while there was a considerable warmth towards the Soviets. Chapter Four considers the topics of Italian atrocities and antisemitism, alongside their related role as occupiers in the Balkans and the southwestern French city of Bordeaux. The Centre protocols provide clear evidence of Italian complicity in serious war crimes as well as a range of racist, corrupt and exploitative behaviour at home and abroad.

Chapter Five engages with how the prisoners talked about their experiences of actually fighting the war with sub-chapters devoted to: 'Combat on Land and in the Air,' 'The War at Sea,' 'On Equipment and Supplies,' 'On Leadership at the Front' and 'The Home Front.' All of which supports a view of Italian soldiery that is complex and nuanced. Chapter Six considers the dominant attitudes towards Italian political leadership. Amongst the transcripts is an unyielding vein of criticism for virtually all Italian political leaders, but there can be little doubt that the most ferocious verbal attacks are made against the Fascist party and Benito Mussolini. Finally, Chapter Seven charts the fluctuating views about victory and defeat. The descent from confidence in an Axis victory to near-universal defeatism takes some time amongst the Italian POWs but becomes unstoppable from the summer and autumn of 1942 onwards.

This book is not intended to be a comprehensive analysis of every subject discussed in the protocols. Rather, these topics reflect on the aspects of the war that recur most frequently in the transcripts. It would undoubtedly have been fascinating to have explored attitudes towards the Roman Catholic Church. However, references to it were too few to do so to any meaningful extent.[13] They are also themes chosen because they were of interest to a range of cohort members. The years between 1940 and 1943 were a pivotal period in Italian history and ones that greatly impacted all levels of Italian society. As a result, this study is not just interested in the perspectives of high-ranking officers and commanders, but the experience of war at all levels of the Italian military. The thoughts of Generals and Field-Marshals are found alongside those of private soldiers and ordinary seamen in the transcripts themselves. It is only right to reflect that variety here.

Resisting the temptation to turn this project into an edited collection of the source material, a deliberate effort has nonetheless been made to include as much of the content of the transcripts as possible. One of the great values of the CSDIC (UK) protocols is how they have preserved the private conversations of Italian servicemen during the war itself. In this way, they offer a unique perspective on this historical period when compared to wartime service records, diaries and letters, or post-war interviews and memoirs which are often used in histories of Italy's involvement in the Second World War.[14] As such this will assist in correcting another historiographical imbalance – while the 'voices' of British, American, Japanese and Soviet veterans abound in published works of the period, those of Italian servicemen remain largely absent.[15]

Historiography – CSDIC (UK)

No work on the Italian CSDIC (UK) protocols can ignore the research undertaken on the German transcripts by the social psychologist Harald Welzer and the historian Sönke Neitzel.[16] In many ways, the genesis of my research project can be traced back to reading *Soldaten* over the summer of 2013. It was not the case that these two researchers 'discovered' the transcripts in the National Archives, the work of Centre and some of their reports had been mentioned in previous works, for example, those of Hinsley, Gannon, Moore and Fedorowich.[17] Mallett also offered a perspective on American involvement with the CSDIC (UK) programme.[18] However, these works prioritized CSDIC (UK)'s policies and organisational structures more than the content of the transcripts. Neitzel and Welzer were the first researchers to dedicate entire monographs to the content of the transcripts.

The findings of Neitzel and Welzer offer fascinating insights into the mentality of the German armed forces at many levels, from prolonged discussion of the 20 July 1944 'Valkyrie' plot amongst captured Generals to detailed consideration of technical topics by *Wehrmacht* rank-and-file.[19] Both *Tapping Hitler's Generals* and *Soldaten* reveal an 'internal world' where you can practically hear the soldiers talking, gesticulating, and arguing among themselves.'[20] Neitzel and Welzer argue that the 'reference frame of German soldiers firmly anchored the virtues of following orders, doing one's duty, and fighting bravely to the last.'[21] This research has been well received. *Tapping Hitler's Generals* was translated into five languages from the original German and *Soldaten* into an even more impressive nineteen. Further research into these sources was also undertaken by the project 'Reference Frames for War.' Headed by Neitzel and Welzer, this had led to the publication of five additional monographs by 2013.[22]

Osti Guerrazzi's *Noi non sappiamo odiare* (*We Do Not Know Hate*) is the only work of the 'Reference Frames for War' project to focus on the Italian protocols. The title itself comes from a statement of one of the Centre's prisoners, Field-Marshal Giovanni Messe: 'We are generous […] we do not know how to hate. Our souls are made like this, so I have always maintained that we are not a warrior people.'[23] This is reflective of a wider attitude of denial and self-justification that resounds throughout the words of the Italian senior officers that make up the majority of Osti Guerrazzi's material base. On topics such as war-planning, foreign policy and military operations, criticisms of the Fascist regime are damning, but made with the benefit of hindsight.[24] It is a work that rails against the myth of the *italiani brava gente* but by focusing on one small proportion of the CSDIC cohort – Italian army generals – the opinions of naval and air force personnel are shut out. This is an important point given that, non-Army personnel made up the vast majority of the CSDIC (UK) Italian cohort.[25] Osti Guerrazzi's is a hugely useful work in gaining a better understanding of Italian elites that would become so influential in the political transition to democracy. However, its scope is narrow, which prevents it from providing a more representative reflection of the rich content of the Italian transcripts.

It would be incorrect to assume that 'Reference Frames for War' was the only outlet for research concerning CSDIC (UK). One former PhD student of Neitzel – who nevertheless appears distinct from the 'Reference Frames' team – has also written about the organisation. Falko Bell's 2016 article gives a succinct and well-researched overview of the structure, methods and importance of CSDIC (UK),[26] particularly concerning German prisoners in the run-up to the 1944 D-Day landings – the moment it reached 'its greatest expanse.'[27] Bell's work gives an excellent overview of Centre as an organisation, but little consideration of the protocols themselves. Understandably given that his specific focus on the D-Day landings, no attention is given to the Italians.

A not dissimilar dynamic can be observed in the works of Helen Fry.[28] Fry is the first to pay considerable attention to the intelligence personnel – the 'secret listeners' – who monitored the microphones at the CSDIC (UK) sites, a number of whom were German-speaking refugees who had fled Nazi-occupied Europe. Her book *The M Room* is movingly dedicated to 'the Secret Listeners who fled Hitler and worked for MI19' and who had to keep silent about their wartime work for over sixty years.[29] Fry devotes much time to the structures in place, the dynamics amongst the Trent Park Generals, and engages with some protocols, especially those that relate to German war crimes and the Holocaust.[30] Like Bell, Fry gives very little consideration to the Italian POWs present at CSDIC (UK) facilities, stating that beyond a handful of unfavourable references to their intelligence value, 'Italian prisoners and intelligence will not be explored further.'[31] However, Fry's works remain a highly useful contribution to the literature on the Centre and Neitzel's criticism that *The M Room* 'does not meet scholarly standards' and 'the evaluation of the knowledge gained from the tapping programme is just as naïve as the analysis of selected transcripts' is harsh.[32]

There is a small but well-formed body of work on CSDIC (UK). Admittedly there has been some previous research into the Italian protocols, but most of the historiographical attention has been given to either the German transcripts or the organisational histories. There is a distinct gap in the historiography for a broader examination of the Italian sources that also fully explores the context in which they were created. This is where this book positions itself.

Historiography – Italian stereotypes

In her 'historical genealogy' of the perceived national characteristics of Italians, Patriarca outlines several which are relevant to a reading of the CSDIC protocols. For example, the idea of the Italians as *brava gente*, 'a good humane people, basically untainted by fascism, including its shameful racist policies, and in fact a victim of fascism and the war itself.'[33] For all of Italy's 'political, economic and social flaws' the argument goes, the nation remained a 'human and civilised bedrock,' with a redeeming 'ancient and ancestral kindness.'[34] This is, however, a post-war construct, a deliberately self-absolutory and sentimental view of the Italian national character intended to help in the political transition of Italy from Fascist enemy to an ally of the democratic West. Whilst also aiding in attracting post-war mass tourism to the land of the *dolce vita*.[35]

Often couched in terms of comparing 'good Italians' with 'bad Germans' and the ways in which Italian Fascism was an aberration from the long durée of Italian history while Nazism was supposedly the logical apex of German history, it is a troubling phenomenon that lumped all responsibility for the evils of the war on the Nazis while impeding a thorough probing of Italian atrocities.[36] As the CSDIC reports demonstrate, the Italians were perfectly capable of callousness, racism, hatred and killing. There are few signs of an Italian 'ancient and ancestral kindness' in accounts of counter-insurgency in the Balkans or submarine warfare in the Atlantic.[37] The Italian armed forces were not all monsters, but neither were they all 'nice guys.' The reality is a shade of darker grey.

The concept of '*furberia*' or '*furbo*' (shrewdness or cunning) is a cliché of the Italian national character initially associated with the self-serving Neapolitan bourgeoisie of the nineteenth century, growing to become a preferred trait of wider Italian society in the twentieth.[38] It is a concept that put individual success and loyalty to family well above duty to the state, and also one that exalted corruption and economic profiteering.[39] In the words of the Italian writer Giorgio Faletti, 'an intelligent man gives the world more than he receives, a shrewd man tries to take as much as possible and gives the bare minimum in return.'[40] *Furberia* is connected to *l'arte di arrangiarsi*, a concept variously translated as the art of 'getting along,' or 'living by one's wits.'[41] It is another expression of an 'Italian' mentality that puts considerable faith on the individual or the family network during times of trouble and crisis. Amongst the cohort, there is some evidence of the admiration of such qualities, but they are by no means universal. For every opportunist POW 'on the make,' there were plenty of critics of *furberia* and *l'arte di arrangiarsi*. The protocols certainly demonstrate examples of cunning and corruption. For instance, the conversations between Sub-Lieutenant Budini (I/N 373) and Lieutenant Francesali

(I/N 377) in Chapter Four. However, they do not appear often enough to be indicative of an essential aspect of the Italian 'national character.' That Fascism was a regime riddled with corruption does not mean the same was so for this group as a whole.[42] It also bears considering if there was any army of the Second World War that did not have members who were 'on the make.'[43]

It is striking how often popular culture is supportive of the ideas of *furberia*, *l'arte di arrangiarsi* and *Italiani brava gente*. Films such as *Mediterraneo*, *Captain Corelli's Mandolin*, *La linea del fuoco*, *Italiani brava gente* and *The Secret of Santa Vittoria* all support an image of Italian soldiery as amateurish, convivial and libidinous.[44] These are films where Italian soldiers are often far more interested in sex and football than fighting, precisely because they are 'Italian.' Films that offer an unfavourable view of the Italian military do exist, for example, 1981s *Lion of the Desert*,[45] but they are harder to find and lack the financial and critical success of their less censorious counterparts. Bankrolled by the regime of Colonel Gaddafi, *Lion of the Desert* made only $1 million back from its budget of $35 million, whereas *Mediterraneo* walked away from the 1992 Academy Awards as Best Foreign Language Film. These are impressions also echoed in literature, such as in Linklater's *Private Angelo* where the title character is decidedly lacking in 'the gift of courage.'[46] Linklater's work has today slipped into relative obscurity, but was viewed at the time as typical of Italians at war. The influence of his ideas was given even greater impetus by his status as an official historian of the Italian campaign.[47]

The problem with – especially Anglophone – understandings of the 'Italian character' is that all too often we let such simple 'characteristics' shape how we view Italian history, rather than letting a dispassionate analysis of the past allow us to build a multi-layered understanding of outlooks and mentalities of Italian people on a wide variety of war-related topics; careful reading of the CSDIC (UK) enables this. In recent years, as the forces of Italian nationalism and xenophobic apologism for Fascism once again assume control of Italian politics, with their own entrenched views of what is and is not 'Italian,' it becomes even more important for historians to consider how ideas of 'Italianness' have been expressed themselves in the past.

Historiography – the 'Italian War'

The label of the campaign in the Western Desert as a 'war without hate' is said to have come from the words of Field Marshal Erwin Rommel himself.[48] Bierman and Smith both acknowledge that such a romantic view of the fighting is a 'self-deception' of many veterans that remember their experiences in those terms. And yet, they still chose it as the title of their account of the Battle of El Alamein.[49] As the many accounts of fighting in the CSDIC (UK) transcripts show, to view the 'Italian War' as one fought 'without hate' is disingenuous. As a group, the Italian POWs were perfectly capable of malice towards their enemies. Between 1940 and 1943 the 'Italian War' was a major military undertaking by the forces of Fascist Italy, and the Western Allies.

In the waters of the Mediterranean and Atlantic, in the skies above southern England and Malta, across the sand dunes of the Western Desert, and on the scrubby hillsides of East Africa the militaries of both sides devoted considerable effort in killing each other's young servicemen and women. These were undeniably clashes which lacked the scale of suffering of Luzon, Stalingrad and Cassino, but such a quantitative perspective would have been of little comfort to those soldiers in their foxholes for whom a bullet could kill just as easily whether it came from a German Mauser, British Lee-Enfield or an Italian Carcano rifle. We should not lose sight of this.

When you observe the historiography of the 'Italian War' several problematic trends emerge. It is often overlooked entirely, or when it is engaged with misunderstood as soft or unimportant, as a distraction from the 'real show' against the Germans. Such viewpoints overlook the fact that the 'Italian War' was an important element of the fighting in the West between 1940 and 1943, and that it was fought with hardness, especially by Italians. Liddell Hart makes no direct mention of the Italian Air Force in the otherwise detailed index of *A History of the Second World War*. This is surely an oversight given the entries for subjects as comparatively niche as the German air-sea rescue service and Japanese optical instruments.[50] There are only a handful of references to the Italian Navy, of which contempt is the overarching feeling. According to Liddell Hart, 'the Italian Navy's contribution to the struggle [in the Battle of the Atlantic] proved negligible' with its submarines achieving 'virtually nothing.'[51] The evaluation of the Army is little better, portrayed as a feeble force effortlessly brushed aside by Allied forces.[52]

These are statements that grossly simplify the Italian contribution to, and experience of, the war fought between 1940 and 1943, and yet they are reflective of how the Italian wartime performance was viewed in the post-war era. Morison described the *Regia Marina* as the 'Dago Navy,' long regarded as a 'huge joke.'[53] In Duff Cooper's famous – and widely cited – diaries, the only mention of the Italian military is a fleeting glimpse of the Italian prisoners who were his manservants in Algiers in 1944.[54] Even Churchill largely ignored the role of Italian naval forces in the Mediterranean after the Battle of Taranto in his history of the Second World War,[55] overlooking how during the conflict itself he had complained that the Admiralty was unable to bring the Italian surface fleet to battle and to cut Axis supply lines.[56]

Even when British efforts in the Mediterranean are engaged with, the Italian presence can be overshadowed. Allport's *Browned Off and Bloody Minded* is an excellent portrait of the British Army in the Second World War that expertly bridges the gap between military and social history. However, it overlooks that British soldiers spent three years engaged in a serious shooting war with their Italian counterparts. Aside from brief mentions of the 'routing' of Italian forces at Bardia in January 1941 and the surrender of Italo-German forces in North Africa in May 1943, you could be forgiven for forgetting that the British fought the Italians at all.[57] The ecology of the Western Desert is presented as more of an enemy than the *Regio Esercito* itself.[58] Allport devotes time to the meaning of the Western Desert campaign to the Germans and the British, but not to the Italians, the instigators of the fighting there.[59] Rome is considered more for its post-liberation role as a hub for British soldiers on leave rather than as the capital of a major Axis power.[60] None of this should devalue Allport's worth to historians seeking to better understand the personnel of the British army between 1939 and 1945, but it does serve as another example of a major academic work on the Second World War that bypasses meaningful engagement with the 'Italian War.'

Throughout the fighting in North Africa, most Axis forces were Italian. On the eve of the Second Battle of El Alamein, the Axis line consisted of nine Italian divisions and four full German divisions – with the addition of the Ramcke Parachute Brigade.[61] Even accounting for the smaller size of two-infantry regiment *binario* Italian divisions, this is a clear imbalance towards the *Regio Esercito*. Yet, this is as overlooked now as it was during the war itself by British audiences. As Holland states, most of the British Eighth Army instinctively thought of their enemy as 'German,' even when the units directly facing them were Italian.[62] This is a trend identified by Holland, and yet one he does relatively little to contest in this work. Throughout, the Italian armed forces in the theatre are glimpsed but scarcely engaged with.[63] There is little to challenge the stereotypical and pre-conceived image of Italians as 'hopeless, charming, loquacious, dirty and puzzled.'[64]

In Jackson's *The Fall of France,* the entirety of the Italian invasion of France is consigned to 'on 10 June Italy declared war on France. Mussolini's late entry into the war won him a tiny zone of occupation in south-east France.' No mention is made of Italian attacks along the *Petite Ligne Maginot* in the Southern Alps in otherwise detailed accounts of the fighting. Priority is instead given to clashes such as the 13 May Battle of Hannut, the collapse of the 55th and 77th *Divisions d'Infanterie* on 13 and 14 May, and the sacrifice of the 12th *Division d'Infantrie Motorisée* at Dunkirk.[65] Similarly fleeting glimpses of Italian involvement in the invasion and occupation of France are offered by Burrin, Ousby and Paxton.[66] It is not just in accounts of clashes with British and Commonwealth forces that Italian participation is overlooked.

In Keegan's *The Second World War,* the 'tenacity and courage' with which the Italians fought in the First World War is contrasted with the 'lethargy' with which they fought in the Second.[67] He argues that between 1940 and 1943, 'Italy would never be an equal partner' to their German Allies. The Italian armed forces were hamstrung by organisational and structural problems that they were not given the time or resources to correct. The fundamental failing of Italians as fighters, according to Keegan, was the fact that the 'Italians harboured little or no hostility towards the enemies Hitler had chosen for them.' He argues that aside from a 'mild Francophobia,' most Italians simply did not regard their enemies with any sort of hostility: 'the Italian upper class is notably Anglophile, while Italy's peasants and artisans have high regard for the United States.' Thus, 'it was a half-hearted Italian army which crossed swords with the British in 1940-41.'[68] Keegan also makes the point that by May 1943 over 350000 Italians had been captured, as if the Italians should only be known for how many found their way into Allied POW camps. What Keegan says about structural problems is valid, but his analysis loses sight of the experience of war for Italian military personnel. Just because their equipment was 'antediluvian' did not mean they were left to experience the war from the side-lines.

Such has been the historiographical influence of works that denigrate Italian involvement in the Second World War that Knox states that the idea that the war was fought by Italians 'lethargically' and uselessly is one that has become widely accepted.[69] He is not wrong. For example, Macksey compares the Italians to chickens, an undeniably stinging criticism, evoking strong images of cowardice and faint-heartedness, especially given his hailing of the German 'eagle.'[70] Similar ideas have been carried on by Bishop and Warner, who say that most Italian army units could only be relied on to 'fold like a house of cards,' with no real substance behind their 'dash and élan.'[71] Nor is such an image one that has been shaped entirely after 1945. In Mussolini's own writings, he lamented the total collapse of the Italian war machine, blaming it on 'congenital deficiencies in Italians' will and temperament.'[72] In April 1943, the famed US war correspondent Ernie Pyle, concluded that the Italians in Tunisia, 'are almost unanimously happy to be captured.'[73] According to such accounts, there is very little indeed which can be said in defence of the showing of Italian forces in the Second World War – they fought poorly and surrendered accordingly.

Sadkovich summarises this image of the Italian armed forces during Second World War,

> The greasy Eyeties, at the mercy of that bombastic fool and master of bluff and braggadocio Mussolini, made only an occasional appearance to throw down their arms and be meekly led away to a POW camp, or to lose their ships to superior British seamen and their aircraft to superior British pilots [… most Anglophone works] agreed that the Italians had been totally incompetent, and the war in the Mediterranean a lark – save, of course, for the Germans, who had proven the only worthy opponents in a decidedly second-rate theatre.[74]

Whilst Sadkovich perhaps goes a little far in his lambasting of 'Anglo-American authors,' accusing them of being 'racist' and 'ethnocentrically convoluted,'[75] he does make some valid points. His idea of a 'tunnel vision attitude' as a result of historians using only a handful of rather biased sources to make sweeping generalisations of the Italian war effort as a whole, does have support.[76] Mackenzie, writing an official history of the British Indian Army, noted that despite the fact that Italian units in East Africa were some of the best that Indian soldiers came up against, Italian soldiers were presented as 'comic warriors' for the benefit of wartime propaganda.[77] Walker corroborates this, stating that a biased view was created in British propaganda as a result of the defeat of Italian 10th Army in North Africa in 1940. This view, understandable at the time, where it was used to improve British morale at an otherwise dark part of the war, then went on to inform wider perspectives after 1945.[78]

Such a historiographical 'tunnel vision' is demonstrated further in accounts of the 1940-1941 East African campaign. In many general Anglophone accounts of the conflict, it is portrayed as a simple open and shut case. Here, Italian forces fought poorly and swiftly surrendered to an Allied force that they outnumbered significantly.[79] However, the reality is far more complicated. Such an impression ignores the fact that preceding the eventual surrender the Italians were a thorn in the side of the British. Despite the fact that these Italian forces were cut off from resupply and reinforcement they fought effectively for 18 months – forcing the surrender of British Somaliland and at clashes such as the Battles for Keren and Gondar.[80] In addition to this, the guerrilla campaign fought by Italian forces who declined to stop fighting after the surrender of November 1941 is virtually ignored in Anglophone historiography, despite there being works by numerous Italian authors.[81] Del Boca, Segre and Di Lalla deal with issues that have been barely touched upon in Anglophone writings; issues which should be taken into consideration before writers such as Liddell Hart, Keegan and Macksey, so readily dismiss the performance of Italian fighting men.

Notes

1 I/SRN 251 – 18 November 1941, WO 208/4189, The National Archives (TNA).
2 I/SRN 248 – 17 November 1941, WO 208/4189, TNA.
3 I/SRN 290 – 28 November 1941, WO 208/4189, TNA; I/SRN 255 – 18 November 1941, WO 208/4189, TNA; I/SRN 159 – 16 October 1941, WO 208/4189, TNA; I/SRN 145 – 15 October 1941, WO 208/4189, TNA.
4 These being Trent Park (Cockfosters, London), Latimer House (Latimer, Buckinghamshire) and Wilton Park (Beaconsfield, Buckinghamshire).
5 There is some debate around the precise numbers of Italian CSDIC (UK) POWs and transcripts. This will be examined at length in Chapter One.
6 Sönke Neitzel and Harald Welzer, *Soldaten: On Fighting, Killing and Dying* (London: Simon & Schuster, 2013), 351.
7 Every report is headed with, 'This report is most secret. If further circulation is necessary, it must be paraphrased so that neither the source of the information nor the means by which it has been obtained is apparent.' (SRIG 217 – 10 August 1943, WO 208/4186, TNA).
8 Memo from MI19 (a) to GSO1 MI19, 4 December 1945, WO 311/632, TNA.
9 Foremost amongst these are Sönke Neitzel, *Tapping Hitler's Generals: Transcripts of Secret Conversations, 1942–45* (Barnsley: Frontline Books, 2007); Neitzel and Welzer, *Soldaten*.
10 Silvana Patriarca, *Italian Vices: Nation and Character from the Risorgimento to the Republic* (Cambridge: Cambridge University Press, 2010), 85, 175, 189.
11 James Sadkovich, 'Anglo-American Bias and the Italo-Greek War of 1940–1941', *The Journal of Military History*, 58/4 (1994), 617–642; James Sadkovich, 'Re-evaluating Who Won the Italo-British Naval Conflict, 1940–42', *European History Quarterly*, xvii (1988), 455–471; Max Hastings, *Chastise: The Dambusters Story, 1943* (London: William Collins, 2019), 15.

12 Introduction

12 Thomas Schlemmer, *Invasori, non vittime. La campagna italiana di Russia 1941–1943* (Rome: Laterza, 2009); Davide Rodogno, *Fascism's European Empire: Italian Occupation during the Second World War* (Cambridge: Cambridge University Press, 2006).
13 Only two instances were found during my research. In January 1943, Naval Lieutenant Paladini (I/N 298) said critically: 'The Vatican does nothing at all. They are really against us.' At the same time, Midshipman Devescovi (I/N 334) said: 'Yes. When you know that ships are carrying contraband you can't be expected not to sink them. We're not such fools as all that. We'd sink them even if they were sailing under the flag of the Vatican City.' See: I/SRN 832 – 6 January 1943, WO 208/4191, TNA; I/SRN 925 – 18 January 1943, WO 208/4191, TNA.
14 For example: Carlo Ferroni, *Italian POWs Speak Out at Last: Prisoners of War Break their Silence* (London: Teneo Press, 2013); Eugenio Corti, *Few Returned: 28 Days on the Russian Front, Winter 1942–43* (Missouri: University of Missouri Press, 1997); Nuto Revelli, *Mussolini's Death March: Eyewitness Accounts of Italian Soldiers on the Eastern Front* (Lawrence: University Press of Kansas, 2013).
15 See: Catherine Merridale, *Ivan's War: The Red Army, 1939–1945* (London: Faber & Faber, 2005); Richard Aldrich, *Witness to War: Diaries of the Second World War in Europe and the Middle East* (London: Corgi, 2005); Svetlana Alexievich, *The Unwomanly Face of War: An Oral History of Women in WWII* (London: Penguin Classics, 2017); Laurence Rees, *Their Darkest Hour: People Tested to the Extreme in World War Two* (London: Ebury Press, 2011).
16 Neitzel, *Tapping*; Neitzel and Welzer, *Soldaten*.
17 Francis Hinsley, *British Intelligence in the Second World War: Its Influence on Strategy and Operations, Volume One* (London: HMSO, 1979), 282–283; Francis Hinsley, *British Intelligence in the Second World War: Its Influence on Strategy and Operations, Volume Two* (London: HMSO, 1981), 32–34; Michael Gannon, *Black May: The Epic Story of the Allies' Defeat of the German U-Boats in May 1943* (New York: Naval Institute Press, 1989), 1-49; Bob Moore and Kent Fedorowich, *The British Empire and its Italian Prisoners of War, 1940–1947* (Basingstoke: Palgrave Macmillan, 2002), 97–106.
18 Derek Mallett, *Hitler's Generals in America: Nazi POWs and Allied Military Intelligence* (Lexington: University Press of Kentucky, 2013), 1–2, 21–30.
19 Neitzel, *Tapping*, 237-280; Neitzel and Welzer, *Soldaten*, 176–192.
20 Neitzel and Welzer, *Soldaten*, viii.
21 Neitzel and Welzer, *Soldaten*, 266.
22 Amedeo Osti Guerrazzi, *Noi non sappiamo odiare: L'esercito italiano tra fascism e democrazia* (Milan: UTET, 2010); Harald Welzer, Sönke Neitzel and Christian Gudehus, eds., *Der Führer war wieder viel zu human, viel zu gefühlvoll: Der Zweite Weltkrieg aus der Sicht deutscher und italienischer Soldaten* (Frankfurt/Main: Fischer, 2011); Felix Römer, *Kameraden: Die Wehrmacht von innen* (Munich: Piper, 2012); Sebastian Groß, *Gefangem im Krieg Frontsoldaten der Wehrmacht und ihre Welsicht* (Berlin: Be.Bra, 2012); Tobias Seidl, *Führerpersönlichkeiten: Deutungen und Interpretationen deutscher Wehrmachtgeneräle in britischer Kriegsgefangenschaft* (Paderborn: Schöningh Ferdinand, 2012); Frederik Müllers, *Elite des Führers: Mentalitäten im subalternen Führungspersonal von Waffen-SS und Fallschirmjägertruppe 1944/45* (Berlin: Be.Bra, 2012).
23 'Noi siamo generosi [...] non sappiamo odiare. La nostra anima è fatta così perciò io ho sempre sostenuto che noi non siamo un popolo guerriero.' Osti Guerrazzi, *odiare*, 232.
24 Osti Guerrazzi, *odiare*, 50–111, 112–130, 131–176, 177–200.
25 See 'Exact Numbers' in Chapter One for more on this.
26 Falko Bell, ''One of our Most Valuable Sources of Intelligence': British Intelligence and the Prisoner of War System in 1944', *Intelligence and National Security*, 31/4 (2016), 556–578.
27 Bell, 'Valuable', 557.

28 Helen Fry, *The M Room: Secret Listeners Who Bugged the Nazis in WW2* (London: CreateSpace, 2012); Helen Fry, *The Walls Have Ears: The Greatest Intelligence Operation of World War II* (New Haven: Yale University Press, 2019).
29 Fry, *M Room*, 3, 13, 275–278.
30 Fry, *M Room*, 273.
31 Fry, *Ears*, 99–120, 210–231.
32 Neitzel, *Tapping*, 9.
33 Patriarca, *Vices*, 189.
34 Patriarca, *Vices*, 215, 232.
35 Patriarca, *Vices*, 189, 215.
36 Filippo Focardi, *Il cattivo Tedesco e il bravo italiano: a rimozione delle colpe della seconda guerra mondiale* (Bari: Laterza, 2013); Benedetto Croce, *Il dissidio spirituale della Germania con l'Europa* (Bari: Laterza, 1944), 21; Michele Battini, *The Missing Italian Nuremberg: Cultural Amnesia and Postwar Politics* (Basingstoke: Palgrave, 2007); Filippo Focardi, 'Italy's Amnesia over War Guilt: The "Evil Germans" Alibi', *Mediterranean Quarterly*, 25/4 (2014), 5–26.
37 See Chapters Four and Five.
38 Patriarca, *Vices*, 85, 175.
39 Patriarca, *Vices*, 85, 199.
40 'Un uomo intelligente a volte dà al mondo più di quanto riceve, uno furbo cerca di prendere il più possibile e dare in cambio in minimo indispensabile.' Giorgio Faletti, *Io uccido* (Milan: Baldini & Castoldi, 2014), Chapter 1
41 Natalia Ribas-Mateos, *The Mediterranean in the Age of Globalisation: Migration, Welfare and Borders* (New Brunswick: Transaction Publishers, 2005), 184.
42 Richard Bosworth, '*Per necessità famigliare*: Hypocrisy and Corruption in Fascist Italy', *European History Quarterly*, 30/3 (2000), 357–387.
43 For American and British examples, see, respectively: Kenneth Alford, *Allied Looting in World War II: Thefts of Art, Manuscripts, Stamps and Jewelry in Europe* (Jefferson: McFarland & Co, 2011); Isobel Williams, *Allies and Italians under Occupation: Sicily and Southern Italy, 1943–45* (London: Palgrave Macmillan, 2013), 169–194.
44 *Mediterraneo* (Dir: Gabriele Salvatores, 1991); *Captain Corelli's Mandolin* (Dir: John Madden, 2001); *La linea del fuoco* (Dir: Enzo Monteleone, 2002); *Italiani brava gente* (Dir: Giuseppe de Santis, 1965); *The Secret of Santa Vittoria* (Dir: Stanley Kramer, 1969).
45 *Lion of the Desert* (Dir: Moustapha Akkad, 1981).
46 Eric Linklater, *Private Angelo* (London: Jonathan Cape, 1946).
47 Eric Linklater, *The Campaign in Italy* (London: HMSO, 1959).
48 John Bierman and Colin Smith, *Alamein: War Without Hate* (London: Penguin, 2002), 2.
49 Bierman and Smith, *Alamein*, 2.
50 Basil Liddell Hart, *A History of the Second World War* (London: Pan, 2014), 918, 930.
51 Liddell Hart, *History*, 447.
52 Liddell Hart, *History*, 362–363, 907.
53 Samuel Morison, *Operations in North African Waters, 1942 – June 1943* (Boston: Naval Institute Press, 1984), 189.
54 John Julius Norwich, ed., *The Duff Cooper Diaries: 1915–1951* (London: Pheonix, 2006), 286.
55 Winston Churchill, *The Second World War, Volume II: Their Finest Hour* (Boston: Houghton Mifflin, 1949), 440; Winston Churchill, *The Second World War, Volume III: The Grand Alliance* (Boston: Houghton Mifflin, 1950), 211.
56 Alberto Santoni, *Il vero traditore: Il ruolo documentato di ULTRA nella Guerra del Mediterraneo* (Milan: Mursia, 1981), 110–111.
57 Alan Allport, *Browned Off and Bloody-Minded: The British Soldier Goes to War, 1939–1945* (New Haven: Yale University Press, 2015), 88, 199.
58 Allport, *Bloody-Minded*, 42–43, 141.

14 *Introduction*

59 Allport, *Bloody-Minded*, 139.
60 Allport, *Bloody-Minded*, 135.
61 Bryn Hammond, *El Alamein: The Battle that Turned the Tide of the Second World War* (Oxford: Osprey, 2012), 280–294.
62 James Holland, *Together We Stand: Turning the Tide in the West, North Africa, 1942–1943* (London: HarperCollins, 2006), 87.
63 Holland, *Together*, 89–90, 147, 220.
64 Holland, *Together*, 605, 37.
65 Julian Jackson, *The Fall of France: The Nazi invasion of 1940* (Oxford: Oxford University Press, 2004), 161–182, 236.
66 Philippe Burrin, *France under the Germans: Collaboration and Compromise* (New York: WW Norton, 1996), 166; Ian Ousby, *Occupation: The Ordeal of France, 1940–1944* (London: Pimlico, 1999), 103, 241; Robert Paxton, *Vichy France: Old Guard and New Order, 1940–1944* (New York: Columbia University Press, 2001), 82, 182–183, 372.
67 John Keegan, *The Second World War* (London: Pimlico, 1997), 285, 116.
68 Keegan, *Second*, 286–287.
69 MacGregor Knox, *Hitler's Italian Allies: Royal Armed Forces, Fascist Regime, and the War of 1940-43* (Cambridge: Cambridge University Press, 2000), 169.
70 Kenneth Macksey, *Tank Warfare: A History of Tanks in Battle* (New York: Stein and Day, 1972), 163.
71 Chris Bishop and Adam Warner, *German Campaigns of World War II* (London: Grange, 2001), 72.
72 Philip Morgan, *The Fall of Mussolini: Italy, the Italians and the Second World War* (Oxford: Oxford University Press, 2007), 3.
73 Quoted in Ferroni, *Italian POWs*, 150.
74 James Sadkovich, *The Italian Navy in World War II* (Westport: Greenwood Press, 1994), xiv-xv.
75 James Sadkovich in Robert Mallett, 'The Fascist Challenge Dissected', *The Historical Journal*, 44/3 (2001), 860.
76 James Sadkovich, 'Of Myths and Men: Rommel and the Italians in North Africa', *The International History Review*, 13/2 (1991), 311.
77 Compton Mackenzie, *Eastern Epic* (London: Chatto & Windus, 1951), 64.
78 Ian Walker, *Iron Hulls, Iron Hearts; Mussolini's Elite Armoured Divisions in North Africa* (Ramsbury: Crowood, 2003), 68.
79 For an overview of the limited literature on the East African campaign, see: Andrew Stewart, *The First Victory: The Second World War and the East Africa Campaign* (New Haven: Yale University Press, 2016), xiii-xiv.
80 Stewart, *First Victory*, 71–94, 195–190, 228–231.
81 See: Angelo Del Boca, *Gli Italiani in Africa Orientale La caduta dell'Impero* (Rome: Laterza, 1982); Vittorio Segre, *La guerra private del tenente Guillet* (Milan: Corbaccio, 1993); Fabrizio Di Lalla, *Sotto due bandiere. Lotta di liberazione etiopica e resistenza italiana in Africa Orientale* (Chieti: Solfanelli, 2016).

1 CSDIC (UK) and the protocols

Introduction

At the heart of this book are the intelligence protocols themselves, the transcripts of secretly recorded conversations between Italian POWs that were committed to paper by CSDIC (UK). Their role in this research project is central, and as both the transcripts and this centre will be unfamiliar to many readers, the nature of these sources is discussed at length. Fully establishing the context of CSDIC (UK) enables a more rounded reading of the transcripts themselves in later chapters. The documents themselves will be addressed as a source and the following questions asked of them – how many were produced in total? Between what dates were they collected? How were they created? How were the protocols presented and formatted? What was the process by which hushed conversations or boisterous arguments were transformed into neatly typed sides of paper? Who was responsible for their creation and dissemination? How and when was the Centre formed? How did it function as an organisation? How did it evolve and develop with the progress of the war? What, indeed, was its fate after hostilities ended?

Exact numbers

The exact number of CSDIC (UK) transcripts that pertain to Italian prisoners of war is a murky issue. Neitzel has claimed that 'CSDIC prepared 16,960 protocols from German and 18,903 from Italian personnel.'[1] However, the figure relating to the Italians is revised in *Soldaten* to 1943.[2] The number of protocols from CSDIC camps outside the United Kingdom is given as 538,[3] although there is no indication as to how many of these are 'Italian' transcripts. In the February 1945 table entitled 'CSDIC (UK), Yearly Comparison of SR Output'[4] (see Table I), the total number of transcripts from Italian prisoners is 1943.[5] This corroborates the figure from *Soldaten*. In contrast, in the National Archives subseries 'Interrogation reports on Italian prisoners of war' by adding the record numbers, one arrives at a figure of 1959 listening reports for Italian POWs.[6]

16 CSDIC (UK) and the protocols

Table I Appendix II – CSDIC (UK), Yearly Comparison of SR Output, WO 208/3451, TNA

Year	PW	Records	Drafts	SRN	SRM	SRA	SRX	SRGG	GRGG	I/SRN	I/SRM	I/SRA	I/SRX	SRIG	Extracts etc.	Total
1939 (4 mths)	169			3											29	29
1940	1119			116	13	1081	152			42		22	18		141	1635
1941	1138	5328	3853	572	1	1320	456			270		2	9		85	2715
1942	864	9008	6244	653	142	1061	755			453		27			283	3374
1943	1493	18060	10702	1143	258	1274	442	732	109	539	64	2	115	380	499	5557
1944	3823	21003	16037	1954	725	890	191	376	129						171	4436
Total	8606			4491	1139	5636	2012	1108	238	1304	64	53	142	380	1179	**17746**

Author's Note: This and all the Pictures, Tables and Diagrams that follow, have been reproduced for reasons of practicality from the original archival documents. No fundamental changes to the wording or data have been made, however certain changes to presentation were unavoidable.

My research suggests that, despite some minor statistical disparity between individual sources, the number of complete 'Italian' protocols from CSDIC (UK) is approximately 1950. As Table II makes clear, this started with the collection of 82 reports in 1940, 281 in 1941, 480 in 1942 and 1100 in 1943. Further complicating the numerical complexity, Table II also mentions 1177 'Extracts Etc.' There is no way of telling how many of these concern Italian personnel and whether any contain totally 'new' information not found anywhere else, although it is possible they have been preserved as the series 'Special extracts from interrogation reports on German and Italian prisoners of war,' which are also held in the National Archives.[7] The National Archives also contains at least 581 reports relating to both German and Italian prisoners from the CSDICs 'Central Mediterranean Forces,' 'Africa' and 'Middle East.'[8] The actual number collected at these sites is likely to have been higher than this. The reason for this is that the protocol serial numbers accessible in the archive are not in an uninterrupted sequence. For example, we only have at Kew, ME 359-599, while the whereabouts of ME 1-359 – or existence of ME 600 and beyond – are unknown.

Another important question is that of the exact number of Italian POWs who passed through the Centre. In the table 'CSDIC (UK) analysis of PW interrogated at CSDIC (UK) up to 31 December 1944' dated 4 February 1945 (see Table III), a figure of 517 Italians and 8089 Germans is given. But different figures can be found elsewhere. For example, in Table II, the total number of Italian prisoners 'handled' by CSDIC (UK) is given as 563, with 10195 Germans. It is not altogether clear why there are two different figures. The compilers of Table II may have benefitted from the most up-to-date information, given that the subsuming report was produced several months after the report containing Table III. Or it could be that there was a difference between those subjected to bugging and those from whom information was actually recorded and transcribed. What is indisputable is that the information found in Table II is much more detailed. From this, we can see that the Italian cohort was made of up 465 naval, 55 army and 43 air force personnel. The numbers of Italian prisoners handled by CSDIC (UK) each year grew steadily from 36 in 1940 to 158 in 1941, 164 in 1942 and 205 in 1943 after which no more additional prisoners passed through the UK centres. This was presumably a result of the 3 September 1943 Armistice of Cassibile.

Presentation and format

The protocols vary in length from single sides of paper to files dozens of pages long. However, there is a consistency in many elements of presentation and format, regardless of whether they relate to Italian or German prisoners of war. Each protocol has a unique serial number, a date, details concerning the different bodies to which the report was distributed and coded designations for the individuals under observation – including their rank, unit, date and location of capture. In some files, the names of the individuals have been added

18 CSDIC (UK) and the protocols

Table II Appendix C – Analysis of Prisoners Handled and Reports Issued by CSDIC (UK) – September 1939–October 1945, WO 208/4970, TNA

Prisoners handled

	German				Italian				Grand total
	Naval	Military	Air force	Total	Naval	Military	Air force	Total	
Sep-Dec 1939	142	–	27	169	–	–	–	–	169
1940	310	113	660	1083	31	–	5	36	1119
1941	635	3	342	980	145	–	13	158	1138
1942	436	52	212	700	146	1	17	164	864
1943	645	255	388	1288	143	54	8	205	1493
1944	1154	1686	1167	4007	–	–	–	–	4007
Jan-Nov 1945	516	639	813	1968	–	–	–	–	1968
Total	3838	2748	3609	10195	465	55	43	563	10758

Records out S.R. reports

	German							Italian							Grand total
	SRN	SRM	SRA	SRX	SRGG	GRGG	Extracts	Total	I/SRN	I/SRM	I/SRA	I/SRX	I/SRGG	Total	
Sep-Dec 1939	–x	3	–	16	–	–	–	29	–	–	–	–	–	29	29
1940	–x	13	10	152	–	–	141	1553	42	–	22	18	–	82	1635
1941	166	–	1081	456	–	–	85	2434	270	–	2	9	–	281	2715
1942	572	142	1330	755	–	–	283	2894	453	–	27	–	–	480	3374
1943	5328	258	1061	442	732	109	499	4457	539	64	2	115	380	1100	5557
1944	9008	725	1274	191	376	129	171	4436	–	–	–	–	–	–	4436
Jan-Nov 1945	21003	115	890	64	197	88	199	1157	–	–	–	–	–	–	1157
	11028	335	159												
Total	( )64427	1254	5795	2076	1305	326	1378	16960	1304	64	53	142	380	1943	18903

Army interrogation reports

	Operational				Non-operational		
	SIR	IRM	IR	IRA IRN	GRX	P/W paper	Total
Sep-Dec 1939	–	–	–	–	–	–	–
1940	–	109	–	–	–	–	109
1941	–	4	–	–	9	–	13
1942	4	41	–	29	12	–	86
1943	92	70	11	25	5	–	203
1944	1154	–	20	–	–	46	1220
Jan-Nov 1945	478	–	–	–	–	91	569
Total	1728	224	31	54	26	137	2200

x = No figures available
(.) = This figure does not include records out Sep 1939 to Dec 1940
S.R. Reports = Listening Reports
Extracts = Listening reports given only restricted circulation due to limited interest

SRN = Listening Reports on Naval Ps/W
SRM = Listening Reports on Military Ps/W
SRA = Listening Reports on Air Force Ps/W
SRX = Listening Reports on Ps/W from Navy, Military and/or Air Force mixed.
SRGG = Listening Reports on Senior Officer Ps/W
GRGG = Omnibus Report on Senior Officer Ps/W combining material obtained by direct and indirect means

Table III Appendix 3 – CSDIC (UK) Analysis of PW Interrogated at CSDIC (UK) up to 31 December 1944, WO 208/3451, TNA

	Prior to 'D' day	'D' day to 31 July 44	Aug-44	Sep-44	Oct-44	Nov-44	Dec-44	Total since 'D' day	Grand total
GERMAN PW									
By N.I.D.	2581	112	122	95	122	65	84	680	3261
By Army Int.	584	570	268	204	164	189	116	1511	2095
By A.D.I.(K)	1720	317	168	175	151	89	113	1013	2733
	4885	1079	558	474	437	343	313	3204	8089
ITALIAN PW									
By N.I.D.	420								
By Army Int.	55								
By A.D.I.(K)	42								
	517								517
Grand Total German and Italian									8606

in pencil. Very rarely additional background information such as age, civilian profession and hometown is included.[9] If the conversations were in foreign language, the transcript comes with a copy of the original text, along with the English translation.

Conversations that took place in a language other than Italian are admittedly rare, but Italian and German prisoners did have a tendency to use English or French when they were mixed together.[10] If the meaning of the original text remained indecipherable or uncertain in any of the reports, the protocol could be accompanied by a note, such as, 'the Italian text of this report is very obscure, but an attempt has been made to translate it.'[11] Editorial notes of a similar nature can be found on transcripts where conversations became heated or muddled, which made individual utterances or speakers challenging to identify.[12] Picture I is a good example of a transcript that demonstrates many of these properties.

Gathering information

The route by which POWs found themselves at CSDIC (UK) camps was long but well-developed. Having been captured and identified by an Allied unit, the prisoners would be passed over to a 'Forward Intelligence Centre' for a preliminary interrogation by intelligence officers operating at a divisional level. After this, designated POWs would move into 'Rear Intelligence Centres' for a more detailed examination at the hands of officers from the Prisoner of War Interrogation Section (PWIS) operating out of General Headquarters (GHQ) or Allied Force Headquarters (AFHQ). The majority of POWs at these stages would be directed to conventional POW camps, however those of particular intelligence interest would be held in the GHQ or AFHQ 'cages' – as these prisoner processing facilities were known colloquially – before being moved onto the CSDICs. Theatre-level CSDICs – such as CSDIC 'Mediterranean Forces,' 'Africa' and 'Middle East' noted earlier – could act as an additional level before POWs were processed through to CSDIC (UK) (Diagram I).

A 1943 report explained the system,

> The various stages can best be compared to a series of 'sieves' or ever-narrowing meshes which will produce, at each appropriate stage, the information-bearing requirements of that stage and, at the final sifting [i.e. CSDIC (UK)] the selected Ps/W potentially most interesting for long-term detailed interrogation [would be isolated.] [13]

CSDIC (UK) operated at a War Office or War Department level for 'long-term strategic and technical examination of selected Ps/W.'[14] This was a system that could process Italian prisoners of war rapidly. For example, having been captured in May 1943 in Tunisia, Lieutenant-Colonel Pedala (I/M 13) and Second Lieutenant Rizzi (I/M 14) found themselves in a Centre camp by mid-June.[15] It only took seven days after their capture on 11 November 1940

File

MOST SECRET

I/S.R.N. 263

THIS REPORT IS MOST SECRET. IF FURTHER CIRCULATION IS
NECESSARY, IT MUST BE PARAPHRASED SO THAT NEITHER THE
SOURCE OF THE INFORMATION NOR THE MEANS BY WHICH IT HAS
BEEN OBTAINED IS APPARENT.

Poli ✓   I/N 102 - Sottotenente di Vascello (Sub. Lt. in s/m BARACCA) Captured 8.9.41

Costanzi ✓ I/N 136 - Sottotenente di Vascello (Sub. Lt. in s/m FERRARIS) Captured 25.10.41

Sistini ✓   I/N 137 - Sottotenente di Vascello (Engine-room Midshipman in s/m FERRARIS) Captured 25.10.41

TRANSLATION:

?   We're accustomed to danger and if we went back to ITALY now, we wouldn't be able to settle down quietly.
When I put BORDEAUX behind me, whether I was going on leave or on a cruise, I was genuinely glad.
(Re leaving BORDEAUX). We went along together, then you turned to the left and we to the right. The escort left us at sundown.

?   But why do you say one went to the left and one to the right?

?   Why, because at night you don't want to be near each other.

ITALIAN TEXT

?   Siamo abituati al pericolo e se adesso ritornassimo in ITALIA, noi non potrommo adessor star tranquilli.
Quando mettevo di poppa BORDEAUX se andavo in licenza o se andavo in missione mi faceva veramente piacere.
(RE leaving BORDEAUX). Abbiamo fatto la strada insieme, poi voi avete girato alla sinistra e noi alla dritta. La scorta ci ha lasciati al tramonte.

?   Ma perché dite uno andava a sinistra, l'altro dritta?

?   Eh, perché di note non sis ta insieme volontiori.

C.S.D.C: (U.K.)
Information received: 20.11.41

DISTRIBUTION:
M.I.9.a.   (21 Copies)
Admiralty (4 Copies)
N.I.D.XI   (1 Copy)
A.I.1.k.   (4 Copies)

Picture I I/SRN 263 – 20.11.41, WO 208/4189, TNA.

for two *Regia Aeronautica* pilots to start being monitored in a CSDIC (UK) facility.[16] This was a rapidity that reflects both the impressive efficiency of the British POW processing system and the value of the work of CSDIC (UK) to the wartime authorities.

22 CSDIC (UK) and the protocols

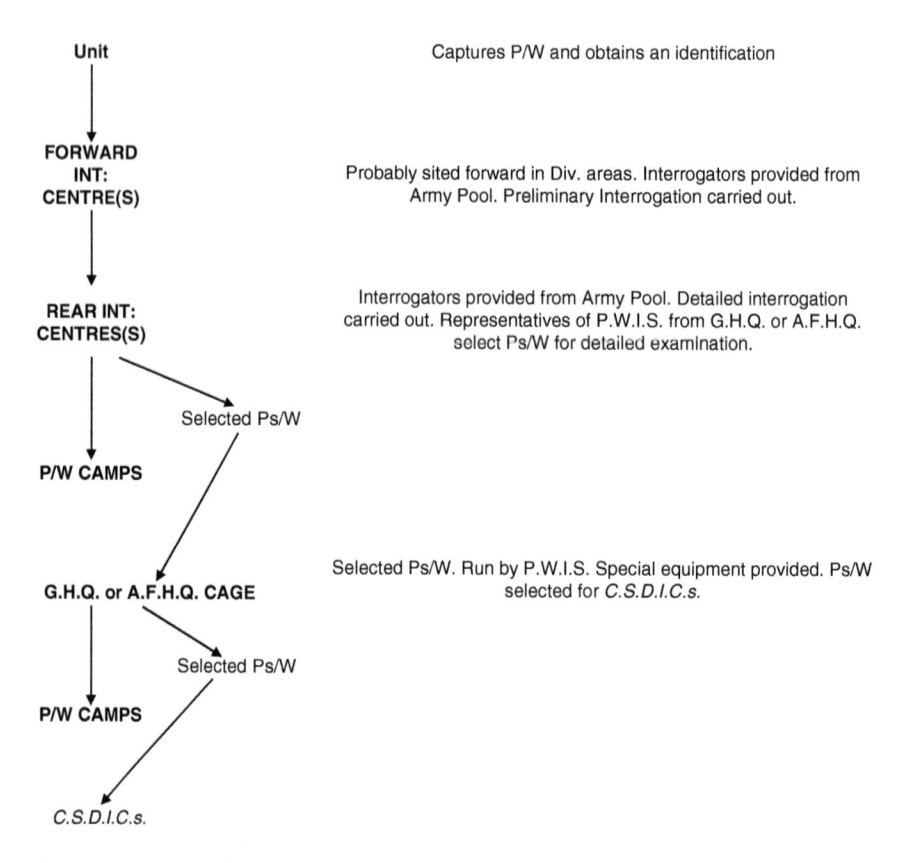

```
Unit                              Captures P/W and obtains an identification
  │
  ▼
FORWARD
INT:                              Probably sited forward in Div. areas. Interrogators provided from
CENTRE(S)                         Army Pool. Preliminary Interrogation carried out.
  │
  ▼
REAR INT:                         Interrogators provided from Army Pool. Detailed interrogation
CENTRES(S)                        carried out. Representatives of P.W.I.S. from G.H.Q. or A.F.H.Q.
                                  select Ps/W for detailed examination.
  │        ╲ Selected Ps/W
  ▼         ╲
P/W CAMPS    ╲
              ╲
               ╲
G.H.Q. or A.F.H.Q. CAGE           Selected Ps/W. Run by P.W.I.S. Special equipment provided. Ps/W
                                  selected for C.S.D.I.C.s.
  │        ╲ Selected Ps/W
  ▼         ╲
P/W CAMPS    ╲
              ╲
               ▼
C.S.D.I.C.s.
```

Diagram I Appendix A – Interrogation and Routing of Prisoners of War, WO 208/4970, TNA. Author's Note: This is a (slightly modified) copy of a diagram from TNA file WO 208/4970. Words in bold and italic are my own modifications.

On arrival at CSDIC (UK) facilities, the POWs were enmeshed in an extensive and technically sophisticated network of electronic listening and recording equipment. Both Wilton Park and Latimer House had six interrogation rooms and thirty other 'bugged' rooms equipped with microphones, while Trent Park had 12 bugged rooms including the common room.[17] Lamp fittings were the preferred – but not exclusive – location for the microphones themselves. In the common room at Trent Park used by captured German Generals, there was a bugging device concealed within the billiard table.[18] The 'listening apparatuses' were initially supplied by the Radio Corporation of America (RCA), a commercial firm. Supply was soon shifted to the Post Office Research Station (PORS), 'in view of security requirements.'[19] Even though RCA had previously worked for the Secret Intelligence Service (SIS),[20] evidently no chances could be taken with a project of the Centre's importance. RCA being both a commercial firm and American. There seem to have been few objections to this change of procurement. Indeed, a 1943 report claimed that,

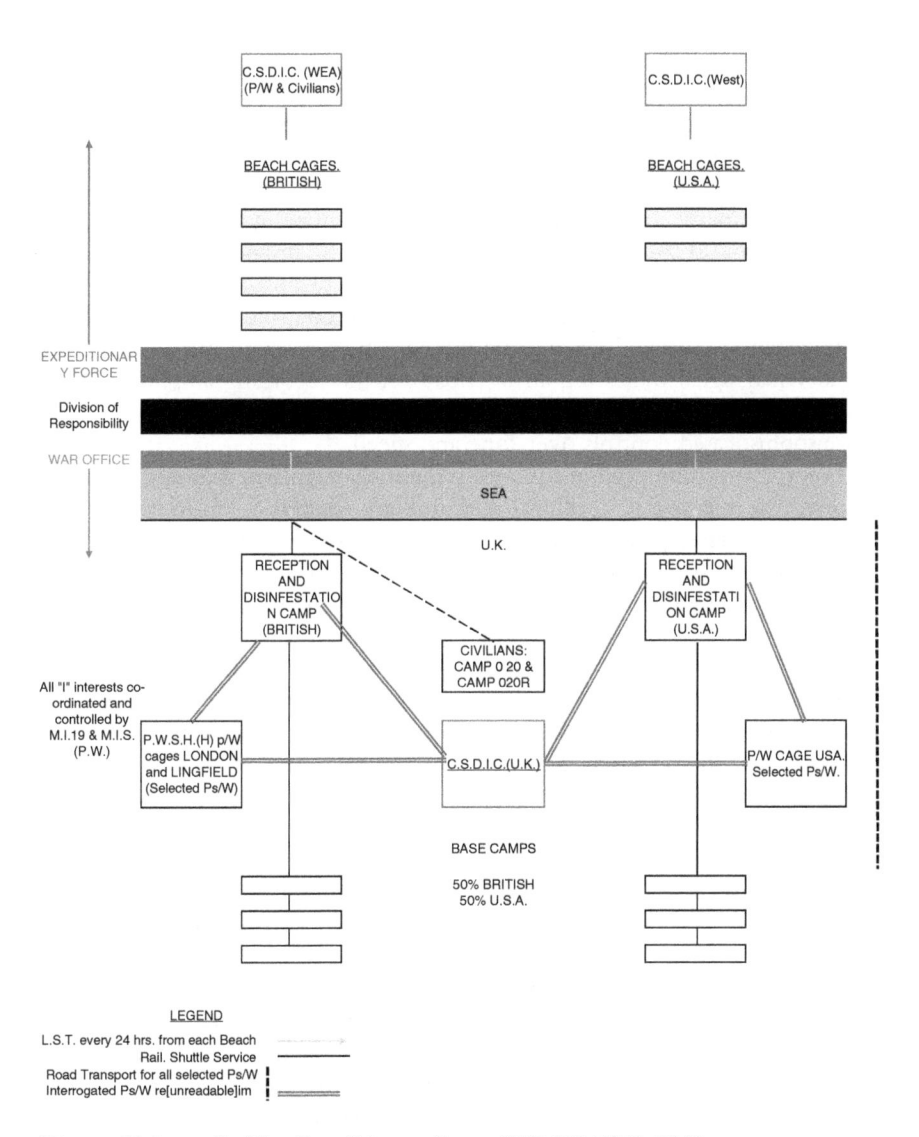

Diagram II Appendix 'F' – Expeditionary Force, WO 208/4970, TNA.
Author's Note: This is a (slightly modified) copy of a diagram from TNA file WO 208/4970.

The static listening and recording equipment in use by C.S.D.I.C.s. has been brought by the Post Office Research Station to a very high state of efficiency. New equipment and replacement parts are being provided continually and at very short notice for despatch to C.S.D.I.C.s. in all theatres of war where they are giving universal satisfaction.[21]

Such was the reliability of the easily concealed 'moving coil' microphones used at CSDIC (UK) that there were only two recorded instances of their failing over a three-year period. Similarly, the loudspeakers and headphones used were described as 'equally satisfactory.'[22] Headphones were especially favoured, as their use did not require the installation of specialist sound-proofing in the listening position room. This saved a huge amount of time, effort and expense to the CSDIC (UK) programme when one considers anything from 20 to 30 listening positions could be provided in a single installation. Given that most of the operators were to be language rather than technical specialists, wherever possible equipment controls were kept 'as little complicated as possible,' leaving the listener operators with just volume and 'some visual signal indicating an overload on the recording amplifier.' That said, it was found profitable to equip those transcribing the protocols with more sophisticated controls over tone and speed.[23]

Recording commenced as soon as 'something important was said' – above all anything relating to 'political and military matters' – from which the protocol was subsequently made.[24] As even a cursory glance at the listening reports makes clear, information was gathered on a vast array of subjects. For example, intelligence on submarines, human torpedoes, surface ships, codes and ciphers, gunnery, mines, orders of battle, unit organisation, tanks, rockets, character studies of senior officers, aerial combat tactics, navigational methods, aircraft, armament types, the bombing of UK cities, morale of the German and Italian people, oil supplies, military headquarters, bomb damage to Axis cities, the state of domestic Fascist and Nazi politics, the status of both neutral and occupied countries, political 'personalities' and the structure of civil administration and local government.[25] It is impossible to know what was said and went undocumented, but it seems that many aspects of the POWs' personal and emotional lives were not considered important enough to record. References to subjects such as family can be found, but only as they relate to political and military affairs. For instance, prisoners who talked about an anti-Fascist father or a mother who was struggling with scarce rations.[26]

The recordings themselves were made using the 'revolving disc method.' This reliable system allowed transcribers to 'repeat sentences and even words over and over again with no effort or delay.' This was crucial in allowing accurate transcription, as even if there were perfect acoustics and effective equipment, there were always passages that could only be understood after numerous repeats.[27] The discs themselves could accommodate a conversation of up to seven minutes in length. As many conversations lasted much longer than this – the average individual recording was said to last 90 minutes – long conversations were divided up over a number of discs.[28] The processes of listening, recording and transcribing recordings were achieved by the personnel of the 'M' Room, the central CSDIC (UK) switchboard. 'M' Room – 'M' for 'miked' – then passed on the products of their work to the personnel of the 'Editorial Section' who saw to it that the protocols were properly translated, edited and published (see Diagram III). Due to the problems of

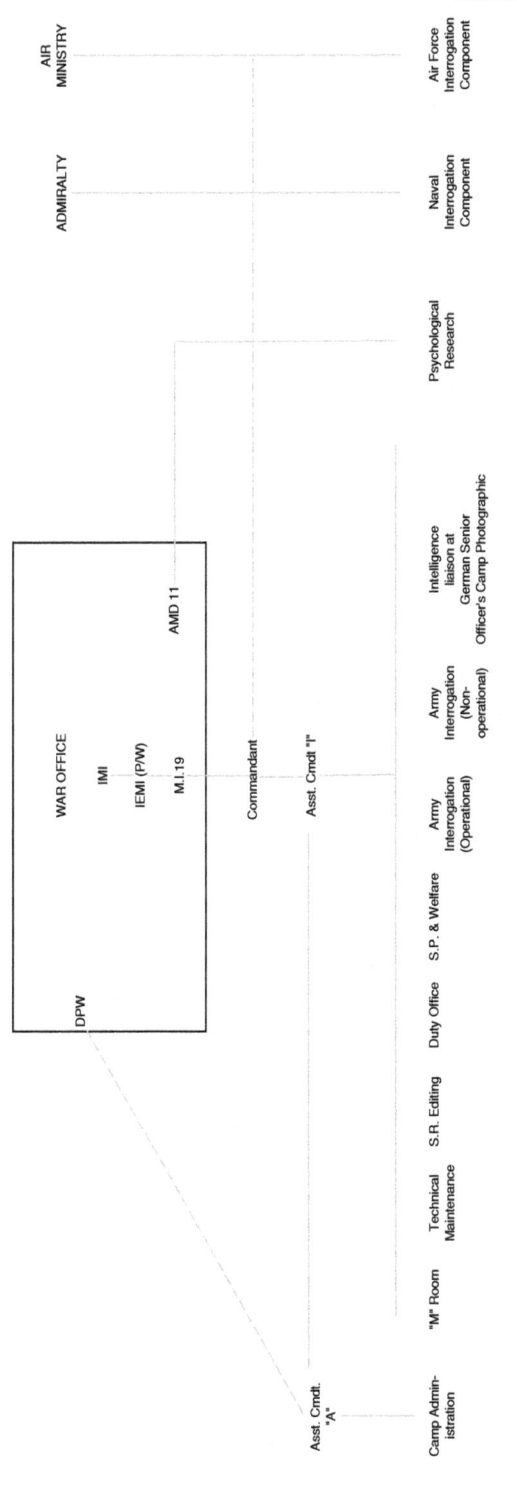

Diagram III Appendix D – CSDIC (UK) – Chart of Organisation, WO 208/4970, TNA.

recruiting enough British-born intelligence officers with the 'necessary linguistic qualifications,' permission was eventually given for the recruitment – often from the Pioneer Corps – of 'alien refugees' to use the microphones.[29] Some of those who had fled their homes in the face of Fascist and Nazi tyranny were now an invaluable part of an intelligence system bent on those very regimes' destruction.

The systems implemented at the CSDIC (UK) sites regarding the work of the 'M' Room and the Editorial Section were highly sophisticated. For example, accommodation at the camps was organised so that no more than three prisoners of war were allocated to a single room. This was to allow 'M' Room operators to easily differentiate their voices. Additionally, only a 'minimum' amount of reading material was permitted to the prisoners in the hope of encouraging them to converse. They were also allowed out of their rooms as little as possible to limit the time they could speak beyond the range of the microphones. The 'M' Room operators were organised into squads of 12. These squads were then divided into two shifts – early and late – that covered respectively the hours of 0800–1600 and 1600–2300 (or later). It was always intended that 'one particular set of Ps/W would always be covered by the same squad' to encourage familiarity with the prisoners' voices, personalities and behaviours. It was also 'found by experience to be preferable to "cover" a limited number of selected rooms [continuously] rather than to switch from room to room in the hope of picking something up.'[30]

Practice also showed that secrecy was better protected, and POWs more likely to speak candidly, if they had a sense of isolation within the wider spatial geography of the camp. As a result, their own accommodation was as far away from the listening posts as practicable. Constructing the camps so that there were clearly discernible gaps between rooms was said to foster this 'feeling of isolation.' Having a separate equipment building out of the prisoners' sightlines also made it easier for the operators to come and go. In all, it was felt that the 'ideal layout' was a 'P/S block completely surrounded by exercise pens, this giving a feeling of isolation to the Ps/W.'[31] Developing a better understanding of the spatial geography of the camps is however inhibited by the fact that 'certain drawings' held by the Office of Works and the Post Office – possibly planning drawings – were destroyed for security purposes during the war.[32] These methods, with their reliance on cunning and guile over brute force, help to explain how no reports of POW abuse were filed against any of the CSDIC (UK) sites.[33]

Once a recording had been transcribed, it was rigorously vetted and scrutinized. There was little appetite to pass on inaccurate or unreliable intelligence resulting from translation problems. The manuscript was then passed to the draft room to be typed. The typescript itself was analysed by an additional party for typing errors.[34] It was only after this lengthy process that transcripts were handed to the Editorial Section for registration, editing, translation, checking, typing, dispatch and filing.[35] On average, 80 copies were made of each report.[36] By February 1945, the Centre was working closely with MI5, MI6, MI8, MI10,

MI14, MI15,[37] the Military Intelligence Research Section (MIRS), the Joint Intelligence Staff (JIS), 21st Army Group, Supreme Headquarters Allied Expeditionary Force (SHAEF),[38] the Special Operations Executive (SOE), the Foreign Office Political Intelligence Division (PID), the Ministry of Economic Warfare (MEW), the Control Commission for Germany, Allied Commission Austria, the General Staff of US Army Headquarters in Europe (HQ ETOUSA), Allied Force Headquarters (AFHQ)[39] and the Military Intelligence Service (MIS) Washington.[40] By 1944, the officer and NCO staff of the CSDIC (UK) 'M' Rooms was around 100. These were personnel who possessed superb 'academic' language skills, coupled with an excellent grasp of the 'colloquial idiom' as well as near 'perfect hearing.' They also had to be 'very alert and adaptable' during their long shifts, and have 'an extensive knowledge of service slang, conditions and technical gadgets.' In all, it never took less than three months to train a listening room operator – an emblem of the wider culture of thoroughness that contributed to the Centre's impressive intelligence regime.[41]

The use of specialised listening equipment to eavesdrop on private conversations was just one of the three ways that information was gathered at CSDIC (UK). It was combined from the very beginning both with 'interrogation proper,' and from the end of 1940 with the use of informers, or 'stool pigeons' – often abbreviated to 'SPs.' Initially four were selected from 'some eighty refugees; who had been interviewed by the intelligence services,'[42] and during the course of the war a total of 49 were chosen. The all-important 'Special Fund' was used to reimburse 'professional' stool pigeons, as well as to reward 'those recruited from amongst the prisoners' with 'preferential treatment and outings, etc.' At Trent Park, a British intelligence officer stool pigeon was employed 'in the guise of a welfare officer' who effectively won the POWs' trust, which enabled him to seamlessly ingratiate himself amongst the group. Such was his perceived success that a similar stool pigeon system was implemented amongst high-ranking Italian prisoners during 1943 and 1944 at the Wilton Park facility.[43] All three methods had their limitations. For instance, direct interrogation depended on the cooperation of the prisoners themselves, as well as relying upon highly knowledgeable and well-briefed intelligence officers. Stool pigeons worked under a huge amount of psychological stress and strain. Eavesdropping allowed for no 'stage management' of the nature of the conversations.[44] However, by bringing all three methods together, CSDIC (UK) was able to glean the maximum amount of good quality intelligence from their prisoners.

A history of CSDIC (UK)

The history of military intelligence is as long as the history of warfare itself, with spies and intelligence gathering even mentioned in the Bible.[45] As Sun Tzu wrote in his renowned *Art of War*, 'he who knows both sides has nothing to fear in a hundred fights; he who is ignorant of the enemy, and fixes his eyes only on his own side, conquers, and the next time is defeated.'[46] That prisoners of war could offer a vital inroad into 'knowing your enemy' is hardly something that the British discovered in the Second World War. The questioning of captured enemy personnel is permitted under the 1929 Geneva Convention, although prisoners were 'not required to provide more than a minimum of information about their identity' and 'harsh interrogation' methods were strictly forbidden.[47] Yet a case can be made that the British very much led the way in the use of electronic eavesdropping as a means to acquire crucial military intelligence from prisoners of war.[48]

It was during the winter of 1917-1918 that the British intelligence services found it 'necessary to develop long-term detailed interrogation of selected Ps/W.'[49] This would be done as part of a joint programme between the Army and Navy, with a particular emphasis on German submariners and pilots. With the creation of the RAF in April 1918, the collection of 'bombing target intelligence' also became of paramount importance. A site was originally established at Cromwell Road, London, but as the scope of operations expanded, it was required to move to a larger site at Wimbledon, 'which was fitted with special technical apparatus.' Despite all this hard work, its official opening coincided exactly with the armistice of 11 November 1918. As a result, not a single POW passed through its doors.[50] It was only with the approach of a new war in the summer of 1939 that the Air Force, Army and Admiralty agreed to form a 'Combined Services Detailed Interrogation Centre' that could be fully operational within 24 hours of the outbreak of hostilities. The object of the CSDIC as set out in its 26 October 1939 charter was 'to submit selected P of W, either Naval, Military or Air Force or internees to a comprehensive interrogation by specially qualified officers.'[51]

These plans worked so well that a core team was operational by 2 September 1939, the day before the declaration of war. Initially operating under the title 'MI1H,' it was officially renamed as 'CSDIC (UK)' on 26 October 1939. Its commander was Captain (later Colonel) Thomas Kendrick, a hugely experienced intelligence officer – a veteran of the Boer War and the Western Front who had overseen interwar spy networks across Austria, Germany, Czechoslovakia, Hungary and Italy.[52] The Centre was initially installed in the Tower of London, with a staff of one naval officer accompanied by two from the RAF and three from the Army. The PORS had ensconced listening apparatuses in just two rooms.[53] From these humble beginnings, the CSDIC (UK) programme would go on to become an integral part of British intelligence's framework.[54]

For all its rich heritage, the Tower proved unsuited to a large intelligence operation of this type and CSDIC (UK) was moved to Trent Park in North London in December 1939. For security reasons, the site was often referred to as the Cockfosters Camp.[55] Whilst lacking the Tower of London's prestige, it was by no means a drab locale. The estate itself dated back to the Enfield Chase Royal hunting grounds and featured a handsome country mansion, complete with renaissance statues, swimming pool, terrace and nine-hole golf course. Indeed, Churchill's later Assistant Private Secretary, Jock Colville would play a round of golf at Trent Park with his brother on 3 September 1939, the first afternoon of the war.[56] The POWs in residence at Trent Park could add their names to a guest book that had featured George Bernard Shaw, T.E. Lawrence, the King and Queen of Belgium, Charlie Chaplin and Winston Churchill.[57]

The growth of CSDIC (UK)'s activities meant that even Trent Park was soon stretched to the limit. The need for further expansion was both an issue of sufficient space for growing numbers of prisoners and military staff, and because of the mounting risks of aerial bombing. So that a single stick of enemy bombs would not derail the entire CSDIC (UK) programme, in autumn 1940 British intelligence chiefs planned two new CSDIC sites. Latimer House, Buckinghamshire and Wilton Park, Beaconsfield, Buckinghamshire, were duly requisitioned and adapted by the Office of Works and the PORS. Alongside this, '4 semi-mobile units, mounted in 32 seater coaches' were allocated for the joint purposes of acting as a tactical reserve in the event of a catastrophic *Luftwaffe* raid, and to allow an operational flexibility should their services be required at other locations in the British Isles.[58]

It was not until 15 July 1942 and 13 December 1942 that operations were formally transferred from Trent Park to what was termed 'No. 1 Distribution Centre (D.C.) Latimer' and 'No. 2 Distribution Centre Beaconsfield' respectively.[59] It was the Beaconsfield site that became the central hub for Italian prisoners. Before the December 1942 move and after the July evacuation of Cockfosters, Italian prisoners of war had been processed by a mobile unit at Newmarket, near an Italian prisoner of war camp.[60] At Wilton Park, Italian senior officers were accommodated in the estate's grand mansion – the 'White House.' There they amused themselves with a diet of Italian and British radio, newspapers, books and sport. Tennis, croquet and darts were particularly popular.[61] By March 1945, the three camps could accommodate a maximum of 396 prisoners at any one time, although in the interests of not stretching resources too far – and therefore compromising the information gathered – the actual working total of prisoners in residence was much lower at 265.[62]

Parallel to the dramatic physical transformation of CSDIC (UK) were a series of profound organisational shifts. From March 1940 CSDIC (UK) came under the jurisdiction of MI9, the Directorate of Military Intelligence founded 'to help British prisoners of war escape and to interrogate those who succeeded.' In July of the same year, the Prisoners of War Interrogation Service (PWIS) Home was established. In addition to providing translators for commando raids, PWIS Home 'formed an important link between the CSDIC and field units' (see Diagram II).[63] January 1941 saw the Home Office established the London Reception Centre at the Royal Victoria Patriotic Schools, London for 'the reception and interrogation of alien escapees and refugees.' By the end of the same year, it was deemed necessary by intelligence chiefs for CSDIC (UK), PWIS (Home) and the LRC to have their own independent branch of Military Intelligence, and so MI19 was established on 10 December 1941.[64]

These advances came with teething problems. The difficulties stemming from proper controls over the remits of the three services involved in the CSDIC can be traced back to the organisation's charter. After all, whilst the War Office took on all administrative affairs, 'it had no control over Naval and Air Force intelligence matters.' On top of this, the War Office themselves split 'responsibility' between the Senior Army Officer – who oversaw intelligence matters – and the Camp Commandant – who oversaw the day-to-day running of the camp.[65] However, as the official history of British Intelligence in the Second World War makes clear, this was a time 'in which while difficulties persisted, inter-Service and other conflicts were steadily reduced by the expansion of resources and the accumulation of experience.' So much so that when all three service sections moved to Latimer in 1942, they were more than capable of working 'in comparative harmony despite some divergences about methods.'[66]

The growing numbers of people working as part of CSDIC (UK) – or to use the correct military parlance, the CSDIC (UK) 'war establishment' (WE) – reflects its dynamic wartime history. The six-strong officer staff of September 1939 had grown by October 1940 to a 97 strong intelligence staff with further administrative and guard officers. The total war establishment of all ranks was 515. In December 1942, this had expanded again to 843 officers and other ranks. By January 1944, in a 'Revised Single W.E.,' CSDIC (UK) is recorded as comprising of 991 all ranks.[67] A 11 February 1945 report shows that CSDIC (UK) was employing some 976 personnel, which was broken down to 220 intelligence personnel, 397 devoted to administration, 10 to 'services' and 319 guards (see Table IV). The scale of the CSDIC (UK)'s workforce commitment is put into stark relief when you consider that the *Luftwaffe*'s foremost interrogation camp, Dulag Luft, only employed 303 people.[68]

In a War Establishments Investigation Committee (WEIC) report from March 1945, the total war establishment figure is 967. As this report makes clear, these numbers cannot always be taken at face value. The official war establishments are 'apt to give a false impression' as they only show the Army personnel, and 'the fact that there are three separate camps, two with annexes, means that there have to be considerably more administrative personnel than if there were one camp only.' The actual total of people 'wholly or partially administered by C.S.D.I.C. (U.K.)' at that time was 1102 officers and other ranks, the equivalent of a regiment in the British Army. This figure consisted of 1004 from the Army and ATS, 18 from the Navy, 63 from the Royal Air Force and 17 American servicemen. This 1102 was accompanied by some 265 prisoners of war.[69] One of the most detailed breakdowns of the numbers employed at CSDIC (UK) is the war establishment of 18 February 1944. Here the total figure of 967 is divided by rank, job title and department. From Table V, we can now see that CSDIC (UK) had on its books four motorcyclists, six groundsmen, an armourer, one hairdresser and fifty cooks. To a much greater degree than the grand WE totals, these figures give a fascinating glimpse into the inner workings of the – predominately male – community of hundreds of people that the Centre became.[70]

Table IV Army Personnel in CSDIC's, 'Personnel for 'CSDIC', Note on JIC/185/45 dated 11 February, 1945, WO 208/3451, TNA

	Offrs.	O.Rs.	ATS Offrs.	ATS O.Rs.	Total all ranks
1. U.K.					
Int. Personnel	69	101	30	20	220
Adm"	6	223	4	164	397
Services"	3	37			10
Guards"	9	310			319
TOTALS	87	671	34	184	976
2. M.E.					
Int. Personnel	32	52		11	95
Adm"	3	72	1	42	118
Services"	1	24		3	28
Guards"	4	50			54
TOTALS	40	198	1	56	295
3. N.A.					
Int. Personnel	53	77		14	144
Adm"	3	174			177
Services"		40			40
TOTALS	56	291		14	361
4. Italian Increment of C.S.D.I.C., N.A.	18	145			163
TOTALS	18	145			163
GRAND TOTAL ALL Ranks all C.S.D.I.C's =					**1795**

The efforts of the CSDIC programme as a whole constitute an interesting case study of the military and diplomatic collaboration which was instrumental to the eventual Allied victory.[71] As Hinsley writes, 'by the summer of 1943 a US POW section was working alongside MI9, a USAAF officer had joined ADI (K) and US interrogators had been attached to CSDIC (UK).'[72] This relationship was mutual, as evidenced by the secondment of a British Navy interrogator to the American prisoner of war centre in Washington. It became especially pronounced in the run-up to Operation Overlord in 1944 when CSDIC (UK) opened its doors again to a 'large number' of American Army interrogators.[73] Additionally, the Combined Services Detailed Interrogation Centre at Algiers was 'inter-allied' in its approach from the outset.[74] Furthermore, a significant number of the listening reports themselves form a testament to this partnership, being stamped with the 'secret and top secret designations of the UK and USA.'[75] Alongside the key role of the refugee 'secret listeners,' this adds a significant international dimension to the character of the Centre.

This book is not the place to give a detailed consideration to the Combined Services Detailed Interrogation Centres formed outside the United Kingdom. Nevertheless, some brief discussion of their role offers valuable context. There is evidence to suggest the existence of CSDIC Middle East (ME),

Table V Appendix I – Combined Services Detailed Interrogation Centre (UK) Home War Establishment, 18 February 1944, WO 208/3451, TNA

Detail	Officers	Warrant Officers, class I	Warrant Officers, class II	Staff-serjeants and serjeants	Corporals	Lance-Corporals	Privates	Civilians	Total, Combined Services Detailed Interrogation Centre (U.K.)
STAFF									
Commandant (colonel)	1								1
Assistant commandant (intelligence) (intelligence officer, lieutenant-colonel)	1								1
Assistant commandant (administration and local centre commandant) (lieutenant-colonel)	1								1
Senior commander, A.T.S.	1								1
Regimental serjeant-major		1							1
Regimental quarter-master-serjeant			1						1
Total, staff	4	1	1						6
INTELLIGENCE STAFF									
Intelligence officers -									
Majors	7								7
Captains or lieutenants	60								60
Junior commanders or subalterns, A.T.S.	30								30
Intelligence Corps personnel		10	20	68					98
Draughtsman, mechanical, R.E.				1					1

Clerks (special intelligence duties), A.T.S. (a)		2	4	14			20
Total, intelligence staff	97	12	24	85			218
ADMINISTRATIVE STAFF							
Centre commandant (major)	1						1
Administrative officers (captains)	2						2
Interpreters (captains)	2						2
Company serjeant-major			1				1
Company quarter-master-serjeant				1			1
Clerks (includes one staff serjeant)				2	2	12	16
General dutymen				3	2	9	126	140
Motor-cyclists						4	4
Tota, administrative staff	5		1	6	4	9	142	167
MAINTENANCE –					(b) 4	43		7
Stokers, stationary engine			1	1				33
Fitters, R.E.								4
Electricians, maintenance							1	2
Electricians, (power or wiremen)								2
Carpenters and joiners								2
Painter and decorator								1
Bricklayer								1
Plumbers and pipefitters								4
Pioneers, R.E.								4
Groundsmen							6	6
Total, maintenance				1	4	4	43	7	59

(Continued)

Table V (Continued)

Detail	Officers	Warrant Officers, class I	Warrant Officers, class II	Staff-serjeants and serjeants	Corporals	Lance-Corporals	Privates	Civilians	**Total**, Combined Services Detailed Interrogation Centre (U.K.)
WARDERS -									
Warders			1	22			95		118
Total, warders			1	22			95		118
GUARDS -									
Commanders (captains)	2								2
Subalterns	7								7
Guards			1	10	19	18	135		183
Total, guards	9		1	10	19	18	135		192
R. SIGNALS -									
Captain	1								1
Instrument mechanics			3	6	3	2	9		23
Linemen						2	4		6
Total, R. Signals	1		3	6	3	4	13		30
R.A.M.C. -									
Medical officers (majors, captains or lieutenants)	2								2
Serjeants (dispensers)				2	2				2
Nursing orderlies					2		4		6
Total, R.A.M.C.	2			2	2		4		10
R.A.P.C. -									
Clerk				1					1
Total, R.A.P.C.				1					1
R.E.M.E. -									
Armourer				1					1
Total, R.E.M.E.				1					1

A.T.S. –					
Junior commanders	2				2
Subaltern or second subaltern	1				1
Company serjeant-major		1			1
Clerks		1	1	1	3
Officers' messes –					
Stewards		2			2
Cooks			2	4	6	12
Orderlies			1	2	23	26
Serjeants' messes –					
Cooks			1	3	5	9
Orderlies				2	10	12
Rank and file messes –					
Cooks		1	6	4	18	29
Orderlies		1	1		20	22
General dutywomen		2	1	3	23	29
Nursing orderlies			2		4	6
Hairdresser					1	1
Telephone orderlies			2	2	8	12
Total A.T.S.	3	7	17	20	119	167
Total, combined services detailed interrogation centre (U.K.)	**121**	**13**	**30**	**138**	**53**	**54**	**575**	**7**	**967**

(a) If A.T.S. linguists are not available, male linguists (of any nationalist) may be employed in lieu.
(b) Includes one lance-serjeant.
Author's Note: This is a (slightly modified) copy of a diagram from TNA file WO 208/3451.

Mediterranean (Med.), India, Paiforce, Australia, Algiers (as distinct from CSDIC (ME) and in France and Germany (CSDIC West) from 1944 onwards.[76] Indeed, there appear to have been few theatres of war in which British forces operated that had not have links to a CSDIC in some capacity. CSDIC Middle East offers a useful insight into the nature of such 'satellite' centres. The order to found CSDIC (ME) came early in the war, in August 1940. By December, conveniently located near General Headquarters Middle East, it had the capacity to handle 60 prisoners of war at a time.[77] By spring 1942, there was a specialist Naval Unit at C-in-C Mediterranean. There was also an Army Mobile Unit based in the Western Desert. The function of CSDIC (ME) was the acquisition of intelligence of a more immediate operational or tactical nature than CSDIC (UK). The most high-profile prisoners were ultimately transferred to the United Kingdom, 'where the more long-term and technical results of interrogation were collated with other intelligence before being disseminated to the Commands.'[78] Thus, we add a further layer to the overall picture of a broad and multifaceted intelligence network in operation at this time, of which the CSDICs were a key part.

By 1942-1943, the era of site expansion and structural reorganisation for CSDIC (UK) had ended, bringing in its stead a time of consolidation. The period from 1943 to eventual victory in Europe in 1945 is when CSDIC (UK) emerged as an effective body that could be left largely to its own devices in gathering important military intelligence.[79] Another defining feature of this period of CSDIC (UK)'s history was that with the mounting success of Allied forces in Europe and North Africa, the sheer numbers of prisoners of war who could be selected for further interrogation was becoming hard to manage. Archival documents tell of 'the increase of work caused by the large numbers of Ps/W captured during the campaigns in North Africa and Southern Italy,' so that as early as July 1942 it could be said that 'the problem of Italian Ps/W had now assumed serious proportions.'[80] This situation was further exacerbated by the successful D-Day landings and by the subsequent campaigns across Western Europe. Not only did more and more Axis prisoners of war come under Allied control,[81] as the land forces advanced it became possible to hold these prisoners in the liberated territories themselves, instead of ferrying them across the English Channel. As a result it 'became impossible for a U.K. organisation [CSDIC (UK)] to guarantee the best results, in that they were no longer selecting from 100 percent [of the] Ps/W.'[82] From this point onwards, the slow but steady decline of CSDIC (UK) had begun in earnest.

By March 1945, discussions concerning the reductions of personnel employed as part of CSDIC (UK) had reached a critical point.[83] A meeting of the Chiefs of Staff Committee on 1 March had 'invited' the War Office to see whether a reduction of a fifth of CSDIC (UK)'s Administrative personnel was feasible; it was then recommended by the War Establishments Investigation Committee (WEIC) that a cut of 11.5 percent would be more appropriate.[84] The WEIC report itself stated that the demands for both the operational and non-operational intelligence furnished by CSDIC (UK) had not diminished;

indeed, in a number of respects, these had actually increased. Furthermore, unless the personnel situation became critical, the levels of Intelligence Staff should remain constant. The report continued to argue that cutting any more of the 95 positions identified would compromise the efficiency and effectiveness of CSDIC (UK), and even these losses would cause many problems.[85] The Centre's Commandant certainly did not remain silent, warning the Chief of Staff of MI19 that 'whilst we quite appreciate the necessity for economising in manpower to the fullest extent [...] if implemented in full [it] might have repercussions on the Intelligence work of the centre.'[86]

It was in the wake of the unconditional surrender of Nazi Germany that the dissolution of CSDIC (UK) quickened. By August 1945, a statement from Deputy Director Military Intelligence (P/W) made clear that 'in view of the reductions that have to be effected in Home War Establishments, it will shortly become necessary to cease all Interrogation of Ps/W in the UK.' The baton was now passed to the British Liberation Army (BLA) in the British zone of occupied Germany. The planned cuts were drastic. From 1 September 1945 – almost six years to the day since CSDIC (UK) had been formed in the Tower of London – the war establishment was halved as CSDIC (WEA) was set-up as part of 21st Army Group. 1 October was suggested as the day from which 'it will no longer be necessary for CSDIC (U.K.) to continue production of reports.'[87] This was the same date suggested in advance of the 42nd meeting of the Joint Intelligence Committee on 27 August.[88] It was only just over a month later on 8 November that MI19 as a whole 'ceased to exist.' Emotions are often hard to detect in the records of British military bureaucracy in the Second World War. Yet it is not unthinkable to read a level of genuine sadness from the intelligence officer who finishes the 'Story of MI19' simply with 'Requiescat in Pace.'[89]

Notes

1 Neitzel, *Tapping*, 19.
2 Neitzel and Welzer, *Soldaten*, 346. It seems likely that the much larger number in *Tapping Hitler's Generals* stems from simple human error in reading a poorly laid-out table in 'The Story of M.I.19', WO 208/4970, TNA.
3 Neitzel and Welzer, *Soldaten*, 346.
4 S.R. Reports = Listening Reports.
5 The 'Italian' designations being: I/SRN, I/SRM, I/SRA, I/SRX and SRIG.
6 See: CSDIC (UK) – Interrogation reports on Italian prisoners of war, I/SRA 1–53, November 1940–January 1943, WO 208/4184, TNA; CSDIC (UK) – Interrogation reports on Italian prisoners of war, SRIG 1–130, May-July 1943, WO 208/4185, TNA; CSDIC (UK) – Interrogation reports on Italian prisoners of war, SRIG 131–260, July-September 1943, WO 208/4186, TNA; CSDIC (UK) – Interrogation reports on Italian prisoners of war, SRIG 261–379, September 1943–February 1944, WO 208/4187, TNA; CSDIC (UK) – Interrogation reports on Italian prisoners of war, I/SRM 1–67, June-August 1943, WO 208/4188, TNA; CSDIC (UK) – Interrogation reports on Italian prisoners of war; I/SRN 1–400, October 1940-July 1942, WO 208/4189, TNA; CSDIC (UK) – Interrogation reports on Italian prisoners of war, I/SRN 401–769, August-December 1942, WO 208/4190, TNA; CSDIC (UK) – Interrogation reports on Italian prisoners of war, I/SRN 770–1130, December 1942-April 1943, WO 208/

4191, TNA; CSDIC (UK) – Interrogation reports on Italian prisoners of war, I/SRN 1131–1313, 1 April-31 October 1943, WO 208/4192, TNA; CSDIC (UK) – Interrogation reports on Italia n prisoners of war, I/SRX 1–139, 1 November 1940–31 August 1943, WO 208/4193, TNA; CSDIC (UK) – Interrogation reports on Italian prisoners of war, X/SRX 1–8, November 1940-August 1941, WO 208/4194, TNA.

7 See: CSDIC (UK) – Special extracts from interrogation reports on German and Italian prisoners of war, January 1941-August 1945, WO 208/4198, TNA; CSDIC (UK) – Special extracts from interrogation reports on German and Italian prisoners of war, December 1941-May 1944, WO 208/4199, TNA; CSDIC (UK) – Special extracts from interrogation reports on German and Italian prisoners of war, December 1942-March 1945, WO 208/4200, TNA; CSDIC (UK) – Special extracts from interrogation reports on German and Italian prisoners of war, February 1943–March 1944, WO 208/4205, TNA; CSDIC (UK); Special extracts from interrogation reports on German and Italian prisoners of war, August 1943–May 1945, WO 208/4206, TNA. Research shows that just over a dozen protocols in WO 208/4198, WO 208/4200 and WO 208/4205 concern Italian POWs.

8 See: CSDIC (Middle East) – Interrogation reports on German and Italian prisoners of war: ME 359–599, 3 December 1941–19 October 1942, WO 208/5518, TNA; CSDIC (Middle East) – Interrogation reports on German and Italian prisoners of war: ME/X 822–825, 26 October 1944–28 October 1944, WO 208/5519, TNA; CSDIC (Africa) – Interrogation reports on German and Italian prisoners of war: Middle East and North Africa; MU/3/1-25, 15 April 1943–21 August 1943, WO 208/5507, TNA; CSDIC (Africa) – Interrogation reports on German and Italian prisoners of war: AFHQ 1–107, 30 May 1943–27 March 1944, WO 208/5508, TNA; CSDIC (Africa) – Interrogation reports on German and Italian prisoners of war: naval and air personnel; AFHQ/X 105–123, WO 208/5509, TNA; CSDIC (Central Mediterranean Forces) – Interrogation reports on German and Italian prisoners of war: CMF/X 1–151, 13 March 1944–9 April 1945, WO 208/5513, TNA; CSDIC (Central Mediterranean Forces) – Interrogation reports on German and Italian prisoners of war: CMF/Y 3–6 and 10, 24 July 1944–7 November 1944, WO 208/5514, TNA; CSDIC (Central Mediterranean Forces) – Interrogation reports on German and Italian prisoners of war: CMF (MAIN)/X 81–114, 28 October 1944–5 January 1945, WO 208/5516, TNA.

9 I/SRA 39 – 6 July 1942, WO 208/4184, TNA; I/SRA 30 – 3 July 1943, WO 208/4184, TNA; I/SRA 24 – 28 June 1942, WO 208/4184, TNA.

10 For example: X/SRX 2 – 28 November 1940, WO 208/4194, TNA and X/SRX 5 – 20 August 1941, WO 208/4194, TNA.

11 I/SRN 381 – 6 August 1942, WO 208/4189, TNA.

12 I/SRA 22 – 12 August 1941, WO 208/4184, TNA; I/SRA 7 – 23 November, 1940, WO 208/4184, TNA.

13 'Appendix D – The Interrogation of Prisoners of War (1943)', WO 208/4970, TNA.

14 'Appendix D', WO 208/4970, TNA.

15 I/SRM 2 – 15 June 1943, WO 208/4188, TNA.

16 I/SRA 2 – 18 November 1940, WO 208/4184, TNA. It is highly likely that these were survivors of the 11 November 1940 raid by the *Corpo Aereo Italiano* on RAF targets in southern England.

17 Bell, 'Valuable', 563.

18 Fry, *M Room*, 86, 124.

19 'The Story of M.I.19', WO 208/4970, TNA, 3.

20 Fry, *M Room*, 17.

21 'Appendix D – The Interrogation of Prisoners of War (1943)', WO 208/4970, TNA, 4.

22 'Appendix G – Installation and Use of Microphones at CSDIC (UK) P/W Camps 1939–1945', WO 208/4970, TNA.

23 'Appendix G – Installation and Use of Microphones', WO 208/4970, TNA.

24 Neitzel, *Tapping*, 20–21.
25 'Appendix F – Editorial Section', WO 208/4970, TNA.
26 I/SRN 517 – 30 August 1942, WO 208/4190, TNA; I/SRN 300 – 30 November 1941, WO 208/4189, TNA.
27 'Appendix G – Installation and Use of Microphones at CSDIC (UK) P/W Camps 1939–1945', WO 208/4970, TNA.
28 Neitzel, *Tapping*, 21.
29 'Enclosure I – The History of C.S.D.I.C. (U.K.)', WO 208/4970, TNA, 5, 8. See also, Fry, *M Room*, 20–29, 118–124.
30 'Appendix E – The 'M' Room', WO 208/4970, TNA, 1–2.
31 'Appendix G – Installation and Use of Microphones at CSDIC (UK) P/W Camps 1939–1945', WO 208/4970, TNA.
32 Fry, *M Room*, 18.
33 Helen Fry, *The London Cage: The Secret History of Britain's World War II Interrogation Centre* (Yale University Press: New Haven, 2017), 20.
34 'Appendix E – The 'M' Room', WO 208/4970, TNA, 1–2.
35 'Appendix F – Editorial Section', WO 208/4970, 1–2.
36 'Appendix F – Editorial Section', WO 208/4970, 1–2.
37 The branches of British military intelligence (MI) which dealt with intelligence operations in Britain (MI5), intelligence operations abroad (MI6), signals intelligence (MI8), German intelligence post-1940 (MI14) and aerial photoreconnaissance (MI15). See, Alan Stripp, *Codebreaker in the Far East* (Oxford: Oxford University Press, 1989), 147–148.
38 General Eisenhower's headquarters of Allied forces in North West Europe 1943–1945.
39 The headquarters that coordinated all Allied operations in the Mediterranean from 1942 to 1945.
40 M.I.19(a)/DIS/1818, Letter from S. Comd, G.S., M.I.19(a) to G.S.O.1., 1 February 1945, WO 208/3451, TNA.
41 'Appendix E – The 'M' Room', WO 208/4970, TNA, 2–3.
42 'Enclosure I – The History of C.S.D.I.C. (U.K.)', WO 208/4970, TNA, 5–6, 8.
43 'Enclosure I – The History of C.S.D.I.C. (U.K.)', WO 208/4970, TNA, 5–6, 8. Intelligence officers masquerading as welfare officers are referred to as 'BAO' in the transcripts. See: SR 95, 22 May 1943, WO 208/4197, TNA; Osti Guerrazzi, *odiare*, p. 19. However, the identities and exact numbers of the stool pigeons used at Wilton Park are unclear.
44 Hinsley, *Volume One*, 282–283. See also, Fry, *Ears*, 38–39.
45 Christopher Andrew, *Secret World: A History of Intelligence* (New Haven: Yale University Press, 2018), 13–26.
46 Sun Tzu, *The Art of War* (Chichester: Capstone, 2010), 24.
47 John Hickman, 'What is a Prisoner of War for?', *Scientia Militaria*, 36/2 (2008), 28.
48 Neitzel, *Tapping*, 17.
49 'The Story of M.I.19', WO 208/4970, TNA, 2–3.
50 'The Story of M.I.19', WO 208/4970, TNA, 2–3.
51 'Enclosure I – The History of C.S.D.I.C. (U.K.)', WO 208/4970, TNA, 1.
52 Fry, *Ears*, 2–5.
53 'The Story of M.I.19', WO 208/4970, TNA, 3.
54 Hinsley, *Volume One*, 90.
55 'Enclosure I – The History of C.S.D.I.C.(U.K.)', WO 208/4970, TNA, 3
56 James Holland, *The War in the West: A New History, Volume I: Germany Ascendant, 1939–1941* (London: Bantam, 2015), 58.
57 Patrick Campbell, *Trent Park: A History* (London: Middlesex University Press, 1997), 36–43.
58 'The Story of M.I.19', WO 208/4970, TNA, 6.

40 CSDIC (UK) and the protocols

59 The label of 'Distribution Centre' was used as an attempt to obscure the camps' true – and top-secret – purpose; Bell, 'Valuable', 570.
60 'Enclosure I – The History of C.S.D.I.C. (U.K.)', WO 208/4970, TNA, 4.
61 Osti Guerrazzi, *odiare*, 34–35.
62 W.E.I.C. (W). No. 66., War Establishments Committee Investigating Section Report on Combined Services Detailed Interrogation Centre (U.K.), W.E. No. VIII/418/2, 19 March 1945, WO 208/3451, TNA, 2.
63 Hinsley, *Volume One*, 90, 283.
64 Hinsley, *Volume Two*, 32.
65 'Enclosure I – The History of C.S.D.I.C. (U.K.)', WO 208/4970, TNA, 2.
66 Hinsley, *Volume Two*, 31–33.
67 'Enclosure I – The History of C.S.D.I.C. (U.K.)', WO 208/4970, 3–5.
68 Bell, 'Valuable', 563.
69 W.E.I.C. (W). No. 66., War Establishments Committee Investigating Section Report on Combined Services Detailed Interrogation Centre (U.K.), W.E. No. VIII/418/2, 19 March 1945, WO 208/3451, TNA, 3.
70 Female staff of the Auxiliary Territorial Service (ATS) made up just 22.5 percent of the war establishment in Table I. These 218 women fulfilled a variety of roles on the intelligence staff, in the messes, as nursing orderlies, as clerks and as the CSDIC (UK)'s officers. Nonetheless, it bears reminding that it was a masculine-dominated environment – the POWs were all men, the war establishment was predominately male and the transcripts were produced for a patriarchal military intelligence system. This was not an organisation that privileged the female voice.
71 Gerhard Weinberg, *World War II: A Very Short Introduction* (Oxford: Oxford University Press, 2014), 97.
72 Hinsley, *Volume II*, 51.
73 Francis Hinsley, *British Intelligence in the Second World War: Its Influence on Strategy and Operations, Volume Three, Part One* (London: HMSO, 1984), 467–468.
74 'Appendix D – The Interrogation of Prisoners of War (1943)', WO 208/4970, 3.
75 Mallett, *Hitler's Generals*, 6.
76 Neitzel, *Tapping*, 17 and 'The Story of M.I.19', WO 208/4970, TNA, 5, 11.
77 Hinsley, *Volume I*, 205.
78 Hinsley, *Volume II*, 32.
79 See: Hinsley, *Volume II*, 32–33, Hinsley, *Volume III, Part I*, 362–366, 450, 467–468, and Francis Hinsley, *British Intelligence in the Second World War: Its Influence on Strategy and Operations, Volume Three, Part Two* (London: HMSO, 1988).
80 'The Story of M.I.19', WO 208/4970, TNA, 7–9.
81 In the Battle of the Falaise Pocket (12–21 August 1944) alone, the Western Allies were able to capture 50000 survivors of *Wehrmacht* Army Group B. See Carlo D'Este, *Decision in Normandy: The Real Story of Montgomery and the Allied Campaign*, (London: Penguin, 2004), 430–431.
82 'The Story of M.I.19', WO 208/4970, TNA, 11.
83 This debate presumably formed part of the broader efforts to find replacement forces for the losses during the North-West Europe Campaign and in anticipation of a much-expanded presence in East Asia and the Pacific. For more on the issue of manpower shortages in the British Army see: David French, *Raising Churchill's Army: The British Army and the War against Germany, 1919–1945* (Oxford: Oxford University Press, 2000), 244–245.
84 MI19 (a)/2308, SUBJECT: Investigation into the numbers of personnel employed in CSDIC (UK), 24 March 1945, WO 208/3451, TNA.
85 W.E.I.C. (W). No. 66., War Establishments Committee Investigating Section Report on Combined Services Detailed Interrogation Centre (U.K.), W.E. No. VIII/418/2, 19 March 1945, WO 208/3451, TNA, 2–7.

86 S.C.1/7, Letter from Commandant of CSDIC to G.S.O.1. of M.I.19., 22 March 1945, WO 208/3451, TNA.
87 MI19 (a)/2372, Statement from D.D.M.I. (P/W), 12 August 1945, WO 208/3451, TNA.
88 Note on J.I.C. (45) 42nd Meeting, Item 4: Future Policy Regarding Interrogation Centres, 27 August 1945, WO 208/3451, TNA.
89 'The Story of M.I.19', WO 208/4970, TNA, 13.

2 Reading the sources

Introduction

The focus of this chapter is a close reading of the transcript sources themselves, which have been described as deeply 'ambivalent.'[1] Captivating and fascinating as they undoubtedly are, they present important questions of representation, selection, reliability, accuracy, agenda and language. An additional layer is how the very act of becoming and 'being' a prisoner of war in this context shapes these sources. I do not intend to hide the potential pitfalls of dealing principally with a single type of source material. Rather I shall argue that, while the material needs to be dealt with in a methodologically rigorous fashion, it offers a wealth of unique insights into a range of political, social and military issues. This is as true now as it was during the war, where the work of CSDIC (UK) was viewed as a highly valuable part of Britain's military intelligence network. This chapter will help to bridge a gap in the historiography between works by Neitzel, Welzer and Osti Guerrazzi that primarily engage with the content of the transcripts, and those of Bell and Fry that focus on the institutional context that led to their creation.[2]

Limitations

The Italian and German prisoners of war transferred through the British surveillance camps were certainly not representative 'in any scientific fashion.'[3] It was never the case that all those who passed through the ranks of the Italian armed forces from 1940 to 1943 stood an equal chance of falling within the purview of CSDIC (UK). For example, very few veterans of the 235000 strong *Armata Italiana in Russia* can be found in these sources. Those who were captured in the great retreat from the Don in the winter of 1942-1943 were destined to languish in Soviet prison camps.[4] A prominent exception to this rule was Field-Marshal Giovanni Messe (I/M 2) who had commanded the Italian forces on the Eastern Front from June 1941 until November 1942. After this, he was transferred to Tunisia where he served until his capture on 13 May 1943.[5]

In contrast, as Table V demonstrates, personnel from the *Regia Marina* are over-represented, outnumbering the combined number of Army and Air

Force personnel by four times. This is possibly a symptom of practicality – these POWs were often captured in the seas in and around the British Isles – and of the importance of naval matters to the domestic British intelligence services, who were concerned with gathering information to ensure supremacy and survival in the Atlantic and Mediterranean. In all, the 563 selected Italian POWs made up just 0.4 percent of the 157000 servicemen who were interned in the United Kingdom during the Second World War.[6] It also bears considering that not all of the CSDIC (UK) cohort were necessarily included in the protocols, while some POWs appear in the transcripts more than others. For example, Corporal Gigante (I/M 32) and Private Acquaviva (I/M 33) are only present in a handful of protocols,[7] while Ordinary Seaman Stefanni (I/N 131) alone speaks at length in dozens of transcripts.[8]

British intelligence officers had no qualms about cherry-picking those POWs whom they thought possessed the most meaningful militarily information. This selection mechanism was at the very heart of the CSDIC (UK) project. Furthermore, the POWs were to a certain degree self-selecting. This is not a simple question of bravery versus cowardice and should not be conflated with any moral judgement. But, surrendering to the enemy is in a great number of cases, a rational choice based on several inter-linked probabilities. The first being, the 'likelihood of one's being killed if one continues fighting.' The second being, 'the likelihood of one's being killed by one's own side if one attempts to surrender.' The third and last being, 'the differential between the recent quality of life as a fighting soldier as compared with the anticipated quality of life as a prisoner.'[9] For those fighting in the Second World War, surrendering to the enemy was just one of the five 'alternatives' of action each man faced. The others were to stand and fight, to desert, to mutiny or to acquire a self-inflicted wound.[10]

Naturally, the Italians killed in the heat of battle are excluded from the CSDIC (UK) group.[11] There can be no doubt that many Italian soldiers did fight to the bitter end. As an account from an Australian Battery Sergeant Major shows, 'the Italian artillery [in North Africa] was definitely good at their trade [...] The Italians fought their guns to the last, many were found dead in their gun emplacements.'[12] The Second Battle of El Alamein alone cost an estimated 971 Italian lives – and this is a conservative evaluation.[13] The transcripts themselves make clear that many Italians were not prepared to surrender or to be taken prisoner. For example, Petty Officer Marghetta (I/N 179) related how Captain Primo Longobardo of the submarine *Pietro Calvi*, alongside many of his men, died in a lethal combination of machine-gun fire and depth charges when their vessel was sunk on the night of 14/15 July 1942.[14]

Nevertheless, despite the prevalence of naval personnel, the absence of the dead, the lack of veterans of the Eastern Front and the selective practices of British intelligence officers, the men under observation came from all service arms, were drawn from all ranks, came from many and diverse units and had experience of numerous campaigns. They *do* represent a remarkable cross-section of Italian military personnel: from field-marshals and corps commanders to midshipmen and bomber-gunners.[15]

The frankness with which many prisoners of war related some of the events they had witnessed and in which they had participated is striking. 'It landed on one wheel, and the moment it touched the ground, the one wheel retracted as well – the aircraft bounced and crashed – only one man got out, the W/T operator. The mechanic, the gunner and one of the pilots were dead, while the first pilot had a bullet in his lungs and was in a pretty bad way.'[16] So begins one man's recollection of the aftermath of an Allied bombing raid on the Italian air base at Rhodes. *Primo Aviere Motorista* Vanicelli's (I/A (Am) 3) account goes on to relay the human cost of that day in September 1940 as plane after plane returned carrying severely wounded and dead Italian airmen.[17] Regarding his colleagues in the Fascist militia (MVSN), Lieutenant-Colonel Pedala (I/M 13) exclaimed, 'those damned militia people! Talk about the Germans being offensive, they were worse than the Germans! Revolting ignorant lumps of filth! That's the militia, the English ought to send them to the stake everyday.'[18] A crucial question is whether this candour is emblematic of an attitude amongst the prisoners that their conversations were going to remain private, or whether the Italian and German POWs under observation did in fact know their conversations were being bugged.

It is the opinion of Mallett in his discussions of German officer POWs that, despite all they revealed to Allied intelligence officers, 'it is difficult not to conclude that the generals suspected their conversations were being monitored' and, as a result, they self-censored their conversations to mislead the British. After all, Berlin had specifically highlighted the probable use of stool pigeons and secretly hidden microphones if they fell into British hands. On 11 June 1941, the *Ausland-Abwehr* – the German Military Intelligence Service – issued such warnings in their instructions pertaining to the behaviour of German military personnel in the event of capture by the British. Likewise, in the officially produced propaganda film *Kämpfer hinter Stacheldraht* ('Warriors Behind Barbed Wire'), the danger of careless talk is repeatedly stressed.[19] In Mallett's view, the captured German general officers orchestrated an elaborate ruse throughout the war by which 'small amounts of useful intelligence about the Eastern Front' would 'convince the British eavesdroppers to trust the veracity of their information' on other subjects, primarily how the *Wehrmacht* High Command and – above all – Adolf Hitler bore sole responsibility for the outbreak, progress and consequences of the war. This was done to 'absolve themselves of any responsibility for their part in the war.' Mallett goes on to suggest that 'the origins of the myth of the clean Wehrmacht began at Trent Park.'[20]

For all the interesting points that Mallett raises, other evidence suggests that those under observation did not know their conversations were bugged or changed their behaviour accordingly. There is only a single case where prisoners are known to have uncovered hidden recording equipment.[21] This is a remarkably low figure if the activities of CSDIC (UK) were so transparent in the eyes of the Axis prisoners of war who experienced them. Bell writes that there was a growing 'security consciousness' amongst *some* of the German prisoners from the spring of 1941. But this did not present an existential threat to the work of the Centre as this was 'effectively overcome by careful planning in the choice of companions and providing proper incentives to speech.'[22]

It is also important when considering the effectiveness of centrally issued directives to examine their implementation, especially when the directives are the only evidence that Mallett offers to support his claims. Just because the German authorities instructed that something should happen, did not guarantee universal obedience. In a 1943 report to *Wehrmacht* supreme command it was revealed that the German officers interned at Trent Park 'were too open and cavalier in their mutual conversations, neglecting the need for caution.'[23] Likewise, repeated references to 'Warriors Behind the Wire' are found in the exchanges between NCOs and enlisted men, however 'in the same breath, the speakers would then discuss matters they had concealed during interrogations.'[24] Mallett's is a significant claim to make on the basis of what appears to be very little supporting evidence.

Another point to be made against Mallett's argument is that the German POWs did not merely offer a harmless 'trail of breadcrumbs' to British intelligence to divert attention away from their own complicity in war crimes. They frequently implicated themselves in the most heinous of wartime crimes.[25] For example, a conversation of December 1944 between two Army privates, revealed the practice of 'bumping off' dozens of randomly-selected Italian civilian men in order to pacify the villages in which they were stationed. Similarly a prolonged discussion between two Luftwaffe officers who detailed the deliberate machine-gunning of civilians during the invasion of Poland.[26]

There is next to no evidence to suggest that Italian prisoners had a greater awareness of the fact that they were being bugged when compared to their German colleagues. That Italian prisoners of war were observed on several occasions in the listening reports secretively discussing how best to mislead their interrogators strengthens this point. On 10 July 1943 Second Lieutenant Rizzi (I/M 14) stated, 'I must be careful what I say about the Lake of Vico [...] even if I only say a little, they won't hesitate to go and bomb it.'[27] Likewise, having returned from an interrogation session on 24 November 1940, a Bomber-Gunner (I/A 4) told his cell-mate many details which he had explicitly denied knowledge of to the British intelligence interrogator; including the workings of his chronometer, training manuals, aerodrome set-ups and bomb types.[28] On 12 August 1941 an Observer from a Cant. Z. 506 seaplane (I/A 14) congratulated himself on misleading his intelligence officer on the subject of aircraft armaments, going on to say 'if they interrogate me again I shall spin some good yarns.'[29] We can be confident that the Italians were recorded without their knowledge. Especially as unlike their German counterparts – Italian airmen received little training on what to do in the event of capture. As one captured bomber-gunner (I/A 4) lamented, 'certainly Headquarters ought to tell us what we are to say when they take us prisoner.'[30]

The British intelligence officers stationed at CSDIC (UK), employed many sophisticated methods to 'trick' and encourage inmates to divulge as much information as possible. Not only was accommodation at the camps arranged to facilitate ease of recording and to encourage conversation amongst the prisoners, but a wide array of other tools were also mobilised at CSDIC (UK) against them.[31] 'Interrogation proper,' listening devices and stool pigeons were all part of a coordinated and symbiotic intelligence gathering operation.[32] The 'careful mixing of prisoners in the cells' was also an important aspect of CSDIC (UK)'s approach.[33] For example, prisoners of a similar rank or standing but from separate units, or with experiences of different regions and campaigns, were mixed, which encouraged the swapping of war stories to which they could all relate and which were of general interest.[34]

This is not to say that absolutely none of the Italian cohort had their reservations. Lieutenant Colacicchi (I/M 5), Field-Marshal Messe's Aide-de-Camp, wrote in his post-war memoirs that he suspected the British welfare officers he encountered were really intelligence personnel. Colacicchi was used as a liaison between senior Italian officers and the camp authorities, so he would have spent more time than most alongside the 'welfare' officers. But, whatever his suspicions, it did not take long before he began to openly gossip with them about his superiors.[35] Midshipman Manisco (I/N 297) had been suspicious of British attempts to monitor him when interned at Gibraltar, 'they put me there [in an allegedly bugged cell] because they wanted to listen to everything I said. But I spotted the trick and said nothing.'[36] An attached memo to this extract shows how three copies were forwarded on to higher ranks.[37] This was evidently of concern to the British intelligence services and they were pushing it through the chain of command. However, his concerns did not stop Manisco speaking at length once he got to CSDIC (UK), where he engaged in discussions about commando raids on Algiers, Italian naval missions to Japan and his own 10th *Flotilla MAS* training.[38] These discussions on sensitive issues suggest that any concerns Manisco may have held in Gibraltar were not carried into his time at CSDIC (UK). That he also boasted of misleading interrogators about Italian submarine numbers also strengthens the idea that he did not suspect he was under surveillance.[39]

In another instance, Commander Spezialetti (I/N (Am) 2) harboured specific concerns about the CSDIC (UK) camp, 'you must be very careful what you say here. They may be listening to us, [...] we are here because they want us to talk about certain things.'[40] That Spezialetti voiced such concerns, and encouraged his cellmates to be similarly worried, may explain why he was not a longstanding presence in the protocols. There is only one more protocol that includes him, also dated to 16 December 1942.[41] It is possible that Spezialetti was rotated out of CSDIC (UK) as a result of this conversation, so that his ideas did not spread further. Both these examples demonstrate that the British intelligence services were conscious of the problem of microphone awareness and took steps to address it, but also that the problem was not a huge one. These three instances form but a tiny proportion of hundreds of Italian transcripts.

When considering the reliability and authenticity of the transcripts, it is worth bearing in mind the limitations of other sources which can be used by historians in a similar way. There are few other sources that bring us as close to the actual conversations of Italian servicemen during the war. Certainly, there is evidence that the Italian intelligence services (SIM) and secret police (OVRA and POLPOL) used bugging devices to record some military conversations; however it was denunciation that remained their primary weapon of choice.[42] It also bears remembering that – unlike the Centre's files – only a residue of surveillance records have survived in the Central Police Records in Rome, with tens of thousands of files deliberately removed, destroyed or not made public.[43]

To be as productive as possible, direct interrogation – and the reports that stemmed from it – required a highly skilled team of intelligence officers and a cooperative and honest prisoner. This was not always possible. It was a substantial stumbling block to the work of the Prisoner of War Interrogation Service Home (PWIS Home) for several years following the outbreak of hostilities. In this context it was often found that 'Nazi Youth' and other radicalised diehards could 'not be made to give information by direct interrogation.'[44] Even when a prisoner was willing to talk, their statements have to be seen through a prism of 'self-preservation' – protecting the regime they fought for or themselves from any post-war judicial proceedings.[45] Many of these issues were readily acknowledged by the British authorities themselves who claimed that in contrast to secret listening, direct interrogation made it much harder to detect partisan opinions and 'as a general rule [cannot] reasonably be expected to provide the same insight into the prisoners' mind' as the use of microphones and recording equipment.[46]

The writing and receiving of letters from home was a defining preoccupation for many soldiers – and particularly prisoners of war – during the Second World War. There can be little doubt that they offer an immensely useful insight into the private thoughts and relationships of the men and women involved. But in many ways, they are a far less useful source than the CSDIC (UK) protocols. A fixation on letter writers, for instance, over-represents the voices of the best-educated and the most eloquent. When you consider that Italy was a nation where even as late as 1921 illiteracy rates in the southern regions could be as high as 50 percent, and 25 percent in the central zones, this is hardly an insignificant issue.[47] One must also acknowledge that the very act of letter writing can easily become wrapped-up in highly ritualised and performative terms. As Spitzer has highlighted in his research into the Great War correspondence of Southern Italian soldiers, writers could spend many of their precious letters asking for the blessing of their family or venerating their parents.[48] In contrast, not only do the CSDIC (UK) documents 'feature the voices of soldiers of whom no other documentary evidence has survived,'[49] they are also devoid of pandering to audiences on the home front. Ultimately, that the British authorities went to such lengths and incurred such costs to obtain this information, and then jealously guarded it for so long into the post-war period, suggests that the CSDIC (UK) protocols are indeed reliable and have high value as historical sources.

Language and translation issues

The language employed in the transcripts comes in the form of free-flowing conversations. Like all everyday exchanges, the speakers shift focus, change the subject and explore tangents. The sentences were formulated and articulated in an instant and were 'uttered in a single breath.'[50] As a direct result of this, 'they were not intended to be well rounded, consistent or logical,' rather 'they were told to create excitement, elicit interest, or provide space and opportunity for the speaker to add commentary or stories of his own.' The information exchanged as part of these conversations is done, as a result, to build relationships between peers. This certainly does not make these conversations devoid of 'bias.' They feature more than their fair share of boasting and chest-puffing, what was said *was* done with an audience in mind, yet they do have an organic naturalness rarely found in other sources.[51]

As with all translated documents, the protocols were subject to the 'autonomy' of the translator who would have made numerous judgement calls that would distinguish the translation from the original text.[52] Translation is never 'communicated in an untroubled fashion because the translator negotiates the linguistic and cultural differences of the foreign text by reducing them and supplying another set of differences [...] drawn from the receiving language and culture to enable the foreign to be received there.'[53] But, the context of the protocol translation is fundamentally different from the translation of literary works which have been a dominant interest in the field of translation studies.[54] Translation of the transcripts did not rely on any one translator, but was a collaborative, and repeatedly scrutinised, process across the CSDIC 'M' Room and Editorial Section. They also diverge from 'technical' or 'pragmatic' translations which serve to harbour the 'utopian dream of a common understanding between foreign and domestic cultures.'[55] Moulded by the pressures of war, the motivation of the translation of the Centre's transcripts was ultimately to aid in the destruction of the forces of Italian-speaking Fascism.

It is interesting the degree to which all the conversations reported appear to have taken place in remarkably good Italian, at a time when significant sections of the population – notwithstanding the policies of both the Liberal and the Fascist governments – would normally have spoken dialect or at the very least some version of 'italiano regionale.'[56] The remarkably standardised nature of much of the Italian that is transcribed and translated –albeit littered with vernacular expressions and the occasional obscenity[57] – begs the question of why the Italian is so consistent and generally grammatically correct. One possibility is that standardised Italian was being used as a *lingua franca* between POWs from different parts of the peninsula. Another is that those 'transcribing' were actually 'Italianising' what was at least 'italiano regionale' or chose only to report conversations that took place in Italian rather than, for example, Venetian or Palermitano. Nevertheless, even if there was some intervention on the part of those transcribing that privileged the 'national' language, 'sanitised' grammatical errors or ignored exchanges in dialect, the freshness and immediacy of the conversations attests to their fundamental authenticity.

Discussion of the POW experience

One of the most striking aspects of the POW experience throughout the many wars fought in the modern era is just how low humanity could sink in its treatment of captured enemy personnel.[58] However, despite the widespread barbarism manifest in the treatment of prisoners of war in the historic record, this was rarely the experience of Italian POWs held by the British. In this case at least, there is considerable evidence that the military and civilian authorities went to great lengths to follow the spirit of the Geneva Convention.[59] This is worthy of consideration. First, care must be taken in avoiding any unsubstantiated comparisons with other POW experiences. Second, it is important that discussion of British treatment of Italian POWs does not itself turn into an exercise in partisan self-congratulation. While admittedly never on the same institutionalised scale as the worst excesses of Axis or Red Army forces, it should never be overlooked that the British in the Second World War were perfectly capable of inflicting cruelty on captured enemy soldiers, as the well-documented accusations of institutionalised torture at interrogation centres such as the MI19 run 'London Cage' make all too clear.[60] Likewise, as recollections of Italian POWs in Ferroni's oral history attest, it was not uncommon for British and American camp guards to shoot prisoners for crossing camp lines, whether by mistake or when attempting escape.[61]

One thing that is immediately striking when reading sources relating to the British administration of Axis prisoners of war is the sheer energy and effort made by the authorities to provide for those in their care. From guidelines on 'the Administration and Safeguarding of Prisoners of War whilst on board ships proceeding from the Middle East,'[62] to detailed instructions pertaining to the 'correct' provision and distribution of items and services as diverse as canteens, pay, uniforms, beer, bugles, dentures, soap and wills.[63] Evidently the influx of thousands of Italian and German POWs was of huge political, social and economic significance to the British war effort. Enemy prisoners of war and interned civilians were also often the subject of prolonged and highly detailed discussions amongst Winston Churchill's War Cabinet.[64] It is telling that even at crucial moments of the war, when the continuation of hostilities by the British was not a foregone conclusion, the highest levels of government found time to consider the best interests of prisoners of war.

Nor does this attitude appear to have been the sole preserve of high-ranking war planners and administrators. The number of times 'fraternisation' or the 'mismanagement' of relations with enemy prisoners of war are mentioned in these documents makes it clear that tangible and friendly relations existed between prisoners and members of British civilian and military society. A Major-General D.A.C. – in a letter distributed throughout Middle East Command – lamented lax treatment towards enemy prisoners by Allied personnel, which manifested itself in 'overfamiliarity' with guards, poor discipline on trains and some Prisoners being taken on trips to the seaside.[65] Outside this active warzone, moratoriums on fraternisation were repeatedly issued in the United Kingdom.[66] Given all this attention from the British authorities there were evidently many who fraternised with the prisoner of war contingent at this time.[67]

Even under comparatively humane confinement however, prisoners of war remained vulnerable to periods of severe mental hardship. For one Italian artilleryman captured at Sidi El Barrani in January 1941, his time as a POW saw him imprisoned in Egypt, South Africa and the UK – he spent six days at sea in a lifeboat after the ship taking him to England was torpedoed. It was not until April 1946 that he made it back home to Italy. But his mental health had then deteriorated to such an extent that he was admitted to a mental hospital in early 1947. His depression and schizophrenia were diagnosed as a direct result of his prolonged imprisonment.[68] Felice Benuzzi wrote of the British-run internment camps he passed through in East Africa that 'people in prison camps do not live. They only vegetate,' and that it was 'torture' to glimpse people going about their daily lives from his side of the wire. In short, he stated, 'it was easy to understand how people go mad' when placed in a prison camp.[69] Benuzzi is far from alone in describing such a situation. Porter Halyburton and John McCain, two veterans of the US Naval Air Force captured in the Vietnam war remember that the shame of being forced to 'confess' to their interrogators was much harder to bear than any physical torture they experienced.[70] In the Korean War, United Nations prisoners described how the deadliest force at play in their camps was 'giveup-itis' where POWs simply gave up the will to live and eat and any allegiance to nation or comrades simply dissolved.[71] The mental strains of wartime captivity are repeatedly explored by Makepeace in her recent study of British POWs.[72]

There are numerous reasons for this. The mental health implications of long-term incarceration, even in a civilian setting are well documented.[73] When mixed with the possibility of psychological damage stemming from a prisoner's wartime experiences, we are confronted with a recipe for a highly toxic cognitive environment. In becoming a prisoner of war a serviceman or woman becomes trapped in a 'limbo world,' where they are robbed of 'the relative security of political or social membership' and 'cannot expect effective help from any organised society; they do not know when, if ever, they will be "at home" again [and] they are compelled to reconstruct or redefine their obligations without clear-cut reference, to authoritative laws and commands.'[74] Being forced into a relationship not dissimilar to that of 'slave and master' would be humiliating for anyone.[75]

This shock was even greater for wartime service personnel who, as soldiers, occupied a highly exalted position at the pinnacle of masculine ideals of agency and potency. The Italian POWs were products of a highly militarised society that had spent twenty years glorifying the 'masculine experience' of modern warfare and made heroes of its fallen soldiers.[76] Italian political culture did not have a good record of viewing their POWs with kindness. In the First World War the Liberal Government uniquely refused to provide provisions for their captured soldiers, leaving thousands to starve to death in Austro-Hungarian and German camps. The influential proto-Fascist writer Gabriele D'Annunzio had labelled the prisoners, 'sinners against the Fatherland, the Spirit and Heaven.'[77]

Moore and Fedorowich give an excellent overview of some of the emotional burdens facing Italian POWs in British captivity,

> If capture had been interpreted by prisoners as a humiliation and a slur on their masculinity, then the reports from home merely served to heighten such feelings of inadequacy and impotence. Incarcerated in foreign lands, miles from home with no immediate prospect of repatriation, they were unable to fulfil traditional patriarchal functions as breadwinner, protector of the family or role model for children.[78]

The Italian cohort operated under several psychological stresses and emotional pressures in their role as prisoners of war. But, several CSDIC (UK) POWs were evidently happy to be prisoners of the British. Amongst this number, Second Lieutenant Rizzo (I/M 45) appreciated that it was a relatively easy choice in the minds of many Italian service personnel to give themselves up to the British. According to Rizzo, there was little competition between the dangers of the battlefield and well-provisioned POW camps.[79] A Midshipman from the submarine *Tritone* (I/N 340) shared Rizzo's perspective. He maintained that he was 'jolly glad to see so many Italian prisoners with smiling faces [in British newspapers]. It really gives me great pleasure.'[80] He also agreed with Midshipman Gridelli (I/N 378) that he would 'sooner do fourteen months as a P/W than seven months at the Naval Academy – in fact I'd rather do twenty-one months.'[81]

Not all Italian POWs who passed through the Centre were happy to wait out the war behind the wire. Several enthusiastically entertained the idea of escape, with some making advanced plans to break free. Lieutenant Cristini (I/N 361) and Lieutenant Morone (I/N 375) discussed this at length. Cristini imagined that the British kept a 'strict watch on the trains here.' Whilst Morrone speculated that 'if I could only get hold of a suit of civilian clothes and get to London' there might have been some chance of getting home, however small.[82] A descriptive comment left by a member of the intelligence staff on another protocol noted how, in the winter of 1940, a W/T Petty Officer (I/N 25) and a captured Fighter Pilot (I/A 1), 'discussed wild plans for escaping.'[83]

A similar feature on a transcript of a conversation between two naval POWs (I/N 17 and I/N 18) described how, in the middle of an air raid, 'I/N 18 expressed the hope that a bomb would fall on the house so that they might have a chance to escape in the confusion. Discussion followed [...] P/Ws concluded regretfully that this would be very difficult.'[84] No evidence has yet come to light to suggest that escape attempts – successful or otherwise – were made by Italian POWs at CSDIC (UK) facilities. Given the heightened level of surveillance and security at these sites this is hardly a great surprise.

Nevertheless, that such ideas were even discussed does suggest that ideas of resistance endured for some Italian captives. The exchanges serve as a reminder that not all Italian POWs meekly acquiesced to their captors once surrendered.

Whether they were contentedly waiting out the war, discussing grand plans to escape or consumed by unspoken turmoil, we cannot stereotype responses to the POW experience. While they were all prisoners, there is no 'single, easily identifiable prisoner-of-war story.'[85] Each prisoner of war rationalised their status in their own way. Their emotions were conditioned by unique factors such as, 'their military service, the nature and competence of their leaders, their commitment to the Fascist cause, or the strength of their desire to be put out of the war.'[86] They remained individuals, but individuals shaped by their ongoing wartime experiences when we encounter them in the transcripts.

How did the British view and utilise the CSDIC (UK) sources?

The gathering of military, political, social and economic information from prisoners of war was an instrumental facet of British intelligence gathering. CSDIC officer Lieutenant-Colonel G.L. Harrison, stated in a discussion with New Zealand intelligence chiefs on 22 June 1942 that 'POW interrogation' accounted for *at least* 40 percent of British intelligence and that the 'most essential confirmation of that obtained from other sources had also been acquired from this source.'[87] There can be little doubt that the role played by Italian prisoners of war in this was extensive. Between 1940 and 1943, they were numerically the biggest group of enemy personnel held by the forces of the British Empire and Commonwealth.[88] By May 1943 and the end of the various African campaigns, over 350000 Italian service personnel shared this fate.[89] This gave the appropriate intelligence agencies not only a vast pool of potential sources but also an excellent opportunity to develop strategies which could then be applied to prisoners of war of other nationalities.[90] The operations of CSDIC (UK) were key part of this, both in general and specifically relating to Italian POWs.

As Moore and Fedorowich have argued, 'the types of information divulged by Britain's Italian captives were many and varied' and for all the intense pressures under which the staff of CSDIC (UK) operated, the information they unlocked proved 'very revealing for Britain and her allies.'[91] This is a position corroborated by the official historian of British intelligence in the Second World War, Sir Harry Hinsley, who wrote that, by 1942, the work of the Centre 'came to be classed among the most reliable [and respected] sources of intelligence' by the military establishment.[92] This offers one possible explanation as to why the dissolution of CSDIC (UK) as European hostilities drew to a close was such a protracted and drawn-out process.[93] As stated in a February 1945 War Cabinet Report, CSDIC was perceived from the very outset as 'one of our most valuable sources of intelligence,' providing both operational and non-operational intelligence on subjects such as 'banking, education, propaganda, religion, law, social insurance [and] industry.'[94] Concerns about the 'repercussions on intelligence work' if the proposed manpower cuts were not handled with care were more than justified.[95]

The Centre's protocols were a crucial tool to support or refute information that had been gathered from other sources. Even as early as 1939, the monitoring and interrogation of POWs was paired with analysis of seized enemy documents and downed aircraft to reveal details about Axis submarine locations, aerial unit identification and enemy technological developments.[96] Reciprocity and cooperation between intelligence organisations in this instance was able to corroborate and provide useful 'cover' for 'ULTRA' designated intelligence material gathered from highly secret signal intelligence (SIGINT).[97] Additionally, the facts collated by SIGINT could be passed onto interrogation officers in order for their own activities to be more effective.[98] CSDIC (UK) intelligence reports designated as 'P.W. Reports (Conversations)' made their way to the Government Code and Cipher School (GC&CS) at Bletchley Park on a daily basis.[99]

It is true that these were just one of 27 reports, summaries and lists received at Bletchley. Nonetheless, it does suggest that the transcripts were held in high regard by top-flight British intelligence operations. It also reveals an important character trait of this wartime network: the ability of its various branches to work together towards a set of common goals. This stands in stark contrast to the internecine power struggles that compromised, for example, so much of the German intelligence services which were deliberately and competitively split between organisations such as Canaris's *Abwehr*, Kaltenbrunner's RSHA, branches within Ribbentrop's Foreign Ministry, the economic intelligence gathered by the WiRuAmt and the separate codebreaking operations of the *Luftwaffe*, *Kriegsmarine* and *Wehrmacht*.[100]

In addition to Bletchley Park, the Combined Services Detailed Interrogation Centre (UK) could count amongst its supporters Field Marshal Bernard Montgomery, who, by early 1945, was requesting his 21 Army Group have its own CSDIC.[101] Montgomery was – in this instance at least – not alone. There were many others who held the work of the CSDICs in high esteem. In February 1941, MI6 chief Stewart Menzies argued that, 'from my point of view, the [CSDIC] reports are of distinct value, and I trust the work will be maintained and every possible assistance given to the Centre.'[102] The success of the Centre's three camps was further recognised when its head, Colonel Thomas Kendrick, was awarded an OBE in 1943 and the US Legion of Merit in 1947 for services to Allied intelligence.[103]

During discussions concerning the addition of the Wilton Park site to the CSDIC (UK) portfolio between December 1940 and January 1941, then Vice Chief of the Imperial General Staff, Lieutenant-General Sir Robert Haining, stated 'I am satisfied that the works to be carried out at Wilton Park and Latimer House are vital to the needs of the three fighting services and that it is a matter of great urgency that the sites be brought into operation as soon as possible,' going on to give it '1A priority.'[104] Likewise, during the same discussions, the Director of Naval Intelligence, J.H. Godfrey, saw the expansion of the CSDIC (UK) as 'vital,' owing to the high level of 'operational importance' of its reports. It was in his opinion 'as of such importance as to override normal considerations of cost.'[105]

Air Commodore A.R. Boyle was of the same opinion, writing to the Director of Military Intelligence that 'experience has fully justified this [CSDIC] method, since the value of the information obtained has been inestimable, and at all costs must continue to be obtained to the fullest possible extent.'[106] The funds allocated for the Wilton Park and Latimer House expansion were considerable – well over £400000, equivalent to almost £16 million today.[107] The development was deemed so important as to curtail the building of nearby aerodromes. Too noisy for the microphones, this decision was made even though hundreds of thousands of pounds had already been spent on the airfield expansions.[108]

These declarations suggest that Hinsley may have been overly pessimistic in his statement that it took until 1942 for prisoner of war interrogations to become well-regarded as intelligence sources by the Air Ministry and Admiralty.[109] It is clear that there were several highly influential figures coming to that conclusion months, if not years, beforehand. The Wilton Park discussions are of particular relevance to the scope of this book as this site (also known as No. 2 DC Beaconsfield) was from the very outset focused on the surveillance of Italian prisoners of war.[110] This is strong evidence to suggest that the intelligence gathered on Italian matters was of the highest interest to those in the driving seat of British wartime intelligence operations. This is in some respects unsurprising. Had the work of CSDIC (UK) not been so valued, it is arguable that the development of CSDIC (UK) as outlined in Chapter Two would not have been so rapid.

The importance of the intelligence work done by CSDIC (UK) in an Italian context is made even clearer when one considers the lack of success in other arenas. Whether in the operations before 1943 to gain reliable intelligence from direct interrogation of prisoners of war and internees, in mainland Italy by the Secret Intelligence Service (SIS), the Special Operations Executive (SOE) or through specifically Italian oriented SIGINT programmes. Even those that did were often incredibly hard-won. Moreover, the list of abject and costly failures was extensive. In contrast to this, as we have seen, the work of CSDIC (UK) was lauded by a host of influential players throughout the war.

Direct interrogation certainly provided valuable insights into the outlook of Italian soldiery. For example, in revealing how a great many of those captured in the isolated and overlooked campaign in East Africa became rapidly disillusioned with the war and wanted an end to the conflict at almost any cost. Additionally, such methods repeatedly stressed the 'gulf in confidence' in an eventual Italian victory between commissioned officers and the enlisted men that they led.[111] However, these useful excerpts had to be separated from the useless in a gruelling, tiresome and fraught process. In a great many cases when being grilled by intelligence officers prisoners of war simply 'invented stories,' played dumb or politely but directly refused to share any information.[112]

A not dissimilar tale can be told of efforts to acquire intelligence through the censoring of Italian prisoner of war correspondence. Initially undertaken by the War Office before being delegated to the Postal and Telegraph Censorship Department in Liverpool in May 1940, it fulfilled a 'vital supplement to POW interrogations.'[113] Nevertheless, it was also beset by important structural and practical issues. While in early 1941 only one hundred letters were available for analysis in Merseyside, by 1942 this had expanded to between 25000 and 30000 items, two thirds of which pertained to Italian prisoners.[114] This was a huge volume of correspondence that swamped the Italian and German linguists.[115]

If the British intelligence services struggled to directly interrogate prisoners of war, their efforts to recruit enthusiastic and reliable collaborators from civilian internee or military prisoner of war camps failed utterly. SOE scoured civilian internee camps on the Isle of Man, POW camps in the Middle East and Italian immigrant communities in the Americas, and only recruited a handful of volunteers, most of whom were totally unsuited to such operations.[116] Many of the candidates had confirmed unflattering Italian national stereotypes. As SOE assessor Lance-Corporal John Macalister wrote of two internee volunteers he encountered, they were undeniably 'hard working' but at the same time 'extremely docile' and 'completely lacking in heroic qualities.'[117] A high proportion of the Italians who volunteered to SOE were deemed of more use to the war effort as cooks or stokers.[118]

The distinctly unimpressive performance of SOE in recruiting Italian agents is not an isolated example of deficiency in its work in Italy between 1940 and 1943. As SOE Chief Hugh Dalton outlined in 15 October 1941, 'it is, I imagine, hardly necessary for me to say that no one is better aware than I am of the complete failure which we have so far made in Italy [...] we have no Italians under training; we have no lines into Italy [...] and we have so far entirely failed to recruit any suitable type of Italian in this country, the Middle East or Malta.'[119] Of the ten agents SOE inserted into mainland Italy, Sicily and Sardinia up to the Armistice of Cassibile,[120] half were killed on active service.[121] Others who avoided the firing squad could find themselves nevertheless promptly captured and facing violence and torture at the hands of the Fascist secret police, the OVRA or the *Servizio Informazione Militare* (SIM). Even where the SOE sincerely believed they had been successful in undermining Fascist Italy through espionage efforts – for example through the work of its desk in Switzerland – later revelations revealed this to be a complete fiction. Working together with SIM officers after the Italian surrender, SOE personnel soon realised that all their agents reporting back to Berne had in fact been 'turned' by the Italians and had been feeding the British false intelligence.[122]

SOE's operations in Italy did improve significantly in the wake of Allied landings on Sicily and mainland Italy, and in the aftermath of the September 1943 armistice. However, these developments came too late to make a substantial difference to the progress of the war against an Italy united under Mussolini. The bravery and heroism of SOE agents in Italy between 1940 and 1943 cannot be disputed, but they are isolated and singular examples, too few and too far between. The reality is that until 1943, 'the principle Allied force engaging in encouraging resistance inside Italy' was largely unable to fulfil its own professed aims to 'assist the [Allied] armed forces to bring about the defeat or withdrawal from the war' of Fascist Italy, the supposed 'weak link in the Axis.'[123] This SOE case study not only inverts the traditional wartime image of Italian military inferiority in the face of effortless British accomplishment,[124] but again adds to the strength of the transcripts as one of the relatively few success stories in the human intelligence war waged against Mussolini's Italy.

A similar trend towards misadventure and ultimate failure can also be observed in the work of the Secret Intelligence Service (SIS) – more commonly known as MI6. High-ranking officer Frederick Winterbotham stated that the position regarding Italy preceding its entry into the war was 'lamentable,' expressing his incredulity that SIS had been unable to approach Italian officers, businessmen or engineers then employed across Eastern Europe and the Balkans.[125] The SIS failed in its attempts to plant agents in Libya through their Cairo office, recruit from POW camps à la SOE, attract 'the right people' from Italian immigrant communities in Latin America, exploit the presence of foreign musicians visiting an International Musical Congress in Venice in September 1942, and set up a false film company in Portugal, which would be used to tour Italy visiting film production sites.[126] One SIS officer wrote that 'Italians make very bad agents, and although many of them dislike the Fascist regime yet they love their country and dislike danger.' He went on to express concern than inserting 'turned' Italians into Fortress Europe would likely merely serve as a glorified and costly 'repatriation scheme.' In January 1941, when the station in Athens was asked what progress had been made in inserting personnel into the southern regions of Italy, one anonymous official bluntly wrote across the minute, 'None.'[127]

Not only does the work of CSDIC (UK) on Italian matters compare favourably with the endeavours of SOE and SIS, a case can also be made to say that it stands up rather well against the work of Bletchley Park. The codes of Mussolini's armed services were, by all accounts, 'exceptionally secure.'[128] There can be no doubt that there were breakthroughs against Fascist Italy at Bletchley; for example, in the build-up to the Battle of Cape Matapan, invaluable information was provided about Italian naval plans.[129] But overall between 1940 and 1942, the Italians were able to achieve considerable successes in their cryptanalysis engagements with the British.[130] Between Autumn 1941 and June 1942, the Italians were able to decode the 'far from discreet' messages sent by the American military attache in Egypt. An Italian radio interception unit was even able to give hours of warning to the opening of the Second Battle of El Alamein. However, despite the best efforts of the unit's commander – Captain Giacomo Guiglia – to warn his comrades, this vital intelligence was ignored, and Guiglia dismissed as 'another jumpy Italian.'[131]

Given these struggles, the value of the intelligence provided by CSDIC (UK) is even more pronounced. It is also crucial to appreciate that, when it comes to intelligence matters, having two or more reliable sources is a win-win situation. Given the necessity of verification, corroboration and even constructive dissent, intelligence is rarely zero-sum. Triangulation of particular facts from several sources is indispensable. Considerable weight of evidence points towards the work of the Centre as an instrumental part of Britain's human intelligence war against Fascist Italy. Both in comparison to other human intelligence gathering efforts, and when CSDIC (UK) is placed alongside the signals intelligence (SIGINT) work done at Bletchley Park. Throughout the war, the output of the CSDIC camps was lauded by high-ranking field commanders, the Imperial General Staff and intelligence chiefs. It seems likely that this already impressive list would have been even greater had the intelligence not been kept so top-secret. Like a spider's web, the British intelligence services of the Second World War formed a vast mutually-supporting network of different agencies and departments.[132] As such, to treat each strand in isolation fails to appreciate fully their true significance, strength and importance. It is key not to overstate the individual importance of CSDIC (UK) on Italian matters. It was, after all, only ever one part of a much bigger operation set up to undermine the expansionist aspirations of Mussolini's regime. But there can be no doubt that it was a sophisticated and advanced programme that proved a very real asset to the British war effort.

Notes

1 Neitzel, *Tapping*, 8.
2 Neitzel and Welzer, *Soldaten*; Osti Guerrazzi, *odiare*; Bell, 'Valuable', 556–578; Fry, *M Room*.
3 I. Kershaw, 'Foreword' in Neitzel, *Tapping*, 3.
4 For the experiences of these men, see: Maria Giusti, *I prigionieri Italiani in Russia* (Bologna: Il Mulino, 2014).
5 SRIG 214 – 20 August 1943, WO 208/4186, TNA.
6 The 10195 Germans who passed through the hands of CSDIC (UK) make up 2.5 percent of their own 402000 total. For both, see: J. Anthony Hellen, 'Temporary Settlements and Transient Populations: The Legacy of Britain's Prisoner of War Camps: 1940–1948', *Erdkunde*, 53/3 (1999), 191.
7 I/SRM 21 – 23 June 1943, WO 208/4188, TNA; I/SRM 22–23 June 1943, WO 208/4188, TNA; I/SRM 24–26 June 1943, WO 208/4188, TNA.
8 My own notes reveal 46 protocols involving Stefanni. These include: I/SRN 180 – 19 October 1941, WO 208/4189, TNA; I/SRN 290 – 28 November 1941, WO 208/4189, TNA; I/SRN 302 – 1 December 1941, WO 208/4189, TNA.
9 Niall Ferguson, 'Prisoner Taking and Prisoner Killing in the Age of Total War: Towards a Political Economy of Military Defeat', *War In History*, 11/2 (2000), 152.
10 Ferguson, 'Prisoner Taking', 152. See also: Michael Walzer, 'Prisoners of War: Does the Fight Continue After the Battle?', *American Political Science Review*, 63 (1969), 778.
11 Those fallen on the field of battle could still offer vital intelligence to their enemies from the personal letters and writings, official documents, reports and even written orders.
12 Quoted in Francis Joseph, *Mussolini's War: Fascist Italy's Military Struggles from Africa and Western Europe to the Mediterranean and Soviet Union 1935–1945* (Solihull: Helion, 2010).

13 Niall Barr, *Pendulum of War: The Three Battles of El Alamein* (Woodstock: Overlook, 2005), 404.
14 I/SRN 345 – 1 August 1942, WO 208/4189, TNA.
15 SRIG 217 – 10 August 1943, WO 208/4186, TNA; I/SRN 398 – 9 August 1942, WO 208/4189, TNA; I/SRA 5 – 20 November 1940, WO 208/4184, TNA.
16 I/SRM 50 – 21 December 1942, WO 208/4188, TNA.
17 I/SRM 50 – 21 December 1942, WO 208/4188, TNA.
18 I/SRM 13 – 19 June 1943, WO 208/4188, TNA.
19 Neitzel and Welzer, *Soldaten*, 349–350.
20 Mallett, *Hitler's Generals*, 25–27.
21 Neitzel, *Tapping*, 25–26.
22 Colonel T. Kendrick quoted in F. Bell, 'Valuable', 570.
23 Neitzel and Welzer, *Soldaten*, 349–350.
24 Neitzel and Welzer, *Soldaten*, 349–350.
25 Fry, *M Room*, 195–213.
26 Neitzel and Welzer, *Soldaten*, 85–86, 45–49.
27 I/SRM 44 – 10 July 1943, WO 208/4188, TNA.
28 I/SRA 12 – 12 November 1940, WO 208/4184, TNA.
29 I/SRA 23 – 12 August 1941, WO 208/4184, TNA.
30 I/SRA 11 – 21 November 1940, WO 208/4184, TNA.
31 'Appendix E – The "M" Room', WO 208/4970, TNA, 1–2.
32 'Enclosure I – The History of C.S.D.I.C. (U.K.)', WO 208/4970, TNA, 5–6.
33 'Enclosure I – The History of C.S.D.I.C. (U.K.)', WO 208/4970, TNA, 6.
34 For example: SRIG 210 – 6 August 1943, WO 208/4186, TNA; I/SRA 15 – 10 December 1940, WO 208/4184, TNA; I/SRM 1 – 17 June 1943, WO 208/4188, TNA.
35 GRIG 81, 22 August 1943, WO 208/4197, TNA; Osti Guerrazzi, *odiare*, 19, 35–36.
36 Extract from S.R. Draft No. 6165 C – 21 December 1942, WO 208/4200, TNA.
37 Memo from Captain for Lt. Col., G.S., to GSOII MI19a, CSDIC (UK), 30 December 1942, WO 208/4200, TNA.
38 I/SRN 813 – 8 January 1943, WO 208/4191, TNA; I/SRN 755 – 21 December 1942, WO 208/4190, TNA; I/SRN 767 – 21 December 1942, WO 208/4190, TNA.
39 I/SRN 899 – 12 January 1943, WO 208/4191, TNA.
40 Extract from S.R. Draft Nos. 5915 & 5895 – 16 December 1942, WO 208/4200, TNA.
41 I/SRN 719 – 16 December 1942, WO 208/4190, TNA.
42 It is also worth mentioning the Gestapo counter-intelligence bugging of the 'Salon Kitty' brothel in Berlin, and the numerous schemes by the NKVD to bug conversations of captured German generals, the Western delegations at Yalta and Marshal Zhukov's *dacha*. Anthony Beevor, *Berlin: The Downfall, 1945* (London: Penguin, 2007), 68, 78, 346, 427.
43 TNA WO 208/4193, I/SRX 7 – 6 December 1940; Chiara Fonio, 'Surveillance under Mussolini's Regime', *Surveillance and Society*, 9/1/2 (2011), 83, 90; Jonathan Dunnage, 'Surveillance and Denunciation in Fascist Siena, 1927–1943', *European History Quarterly*, 38/3 (2008), 244–265.
44 'Enclosure II – The History of P.W.I.S. (H)', WO 208/4970, TNA, 4.
45 The *Memoirs of Field Marshal Kesselring* are a well-preserved example of such an approach by a prisoner of war. Written from memory during his time in prison under charges of War Crimes and a commuted death sentence, they became an extension of his courtroom defence, especially regarding the treatment of partisans and civilian reprisals against Italians. James Holland, 'Foreword', in Albert Kesselring, ed., *The Memoirs of Field Marshal Kesselring* (London: The History Press, 2007), xiv.
46 'Enclosure I – The History of C.S.D.I.C. (U.K.)', WO 208/4970, TNA, 6.
47 Mabel Berezin, *Making the Fascist Self: The Political Culture of Interwar Italy* (Ithaca: Cornell University Press, 1997), 46. Poor education infrastructures were compounded

by the use of strong regional dialects. The numbers of letter writers are likely to have been further decreased by soldiers who felt ill-at-ease using a literary, bureaucratic and 'foreign' official Italian language for their deeply personal letters.

48 Leo Spitzer, *Lettere di prigionieri di Guerra italiani, 1915–1918* (Turin: Boringhieri, 2014), 52, 55–58. See also: Aribert Reimann, *Der Große Krieg der Sprachen* (Essen: Klartext, 2000); Vanda Wilcox, '"Weeping Tears of Blood": Exploring Italian Soldiers' Emotions in the First World War', *Modern Italy*, 15/2 (2012), 171–184.
49 Neitzel and Welzer, *Soldaten*, 349.
50 Neitzel and Welzer, *Soldaten*, 85–86, 45-49.
51 Neitzel and Welzer, *Soldaten*, 85–86, 45-49.
52 Lawrence Venuti, ed., *The Translation Studies Reader* (London: Psychology Press, 2000), 5.
53 Lawrence Venuti, 'Translation, Community, Utopia' (2000), in Venuti, *Reader*, 468.
54 For example: Ezra Pound, 'Guido's Relations' (1929), in Venuti, *Reader*, 26–33.
55 Venuti, 'Translation', in Venuti, *Reader*, 486.
56 http://www.treccani.it/enciclopedia/lingua-del-novecento_%28Enciclopedia-dell%27Italiano%29/, accessed 1 October 2018. See also: Bruno Migliorini, *Storia della lingua Italiana* (Milan: RCS Libri, 1994); Tullio De Mauro, *Storia linguistica dell'Italia unita* (Rome: Laterza, 2003); Richard Bosworth, *Mussolini's Italy: Life under the Dictatorship, 1915–1945* (London: Penguin, 2006), 411–412, 562; Martin Clark, *Modern Italy: 1871–1995* (London: Longman, 1996), 34–35, 74, 369.
57 I/SRN 337 – 30 July 1942, WO 208/4189, TNA; I/SRN 247 – 16 November 1941, WO 208/4189, TNA; I/SRN 169 – 18 October 1941, WO 208/4189, TNA.
58 See: James Robertson Jr., *Soldiers Blue and Gray* (Columbia: University of South Carolina Press, 1998), 190–204, 212–213; Orlando Figes, *A People's Tragedy: The Russian Revolution, 1891–1924* (London: Pimlico, 1997), 645–647, 576–577; Hugh Thomas, *The Spanish Civil War* (London: Penguin, 2012), 250–251, 308, 897; Ferguson, 'Prisoner Taking', 148–192; Christian Appy, *Vietnam: The Definitive Oral History told from all sides* (London: Ebury, 2008), 94–97, 221–231, 470–481; Ronald Bailey, *Prisoners of War* (New York: Time-Life, 1981).
59 Bob Moore, 'Enforced Diaspora: The Fate of Italian Prisoners of War during the Second World War', *War in History*, 22/2 (2014), 176.
60 For more on the 'London Cage', see: Daniel Lomas, 'A Tale of Torture? Alexander Scotland, The London Cage and Post-War British Secrecy', in Christopher Moran and Christopher Murphy, eds., *Intelligence Studies in Britain and the US: Historiography since 1945* (Edinburgh: Edinburgh University Press, 2013), 251–262; Fry, *London Cage*.
61 Ferroni, *Italian POWs*, 75, 222, 236, 311.
62 Middle East Forces; General Headquarters; Orders for the Administration and Safeguarding of Prisoners of War Whilst onboard ships proceeding from the Middle East, October 1942, K12/451, IWM.
63 Home Office; Internment, General Files; Regulations and Enactments; Prisoner of War Camps in the UK: List of Locations and Copies of Administrative Instructions, 1945, HO 215/201, TNA and Middle East Forces; General Headquarters; Administration of Prisoners of War, 1st May 1942, K12/225, IWM.
64 See, for example: 'ARANDORA STAR' and Huyton Camp Enquiries, July-December 1940, PREM 3/49, TNA; Italian Prisoners, December 1940–May 1941 PREM 3/363/1, TNA; Japanese Prisoners, March–October 1943, PREM 3/363/5, TNA; Italian Prisoners of War in India, PREM 3/364/6, TNA.
65 Middle East Forces; General Headquarters; Treatment of Enemy Prisoners of War, 15 December 1941, K12/1550, IWM.
66 Home Office; Internment, General Files; Regulations and Enactments; Prisoner of War Camps in the UK: List of Locations and Copies of Administrative Instructions, 1945, HO 215/201, TNA.

67 See also: Sophie Jackson, *Churchill's Unexpected Guests: Prisoners of War in Britain in World War II* (Cheltenham: The History Press, 2010); *Orkney's Italian Chapel*, Chapel Preservation Committee, K12/744, IWM.
68 Morgan, *Fall*, 103.
69 Felice Benuzzi, *No Picnic on Mount Kenya* (London: Kimber, 1952), 10–12, 17–18. For more on life in the East African camps, see: Elena Bellina, 'Theatre and Gender Performance: WWII Italian POW Camps in East Africa', *PAJ: A Journal of Performance and Art*, 40/3 (2018), 80–91.
70 Appy, *Vietnam*, 222–226, 481.
71 Max Hastings, *The Korean War* (London: Pan Macmillan, 2010), 404, 423.
72 Clare Makepeace, *Captives of War: British Prisoners of War in Europe in the Second World War* (Cambridge: Cambridge University Press, 2017).
73 Jan Chabalala, 'Mental Health in Prisons', *Mental Health Matters*, 4/3 (2017), 38–40; Jane Senior, 'Mental Health in Prisons', *Trends in Urology & Men'*, 6/1 (2015), 9–11.
74 Walzer, 'Prisoners of War', 777.
75 Walzer, 'Prisoners of War', 778.
76 Simonetta Falasca-Zamponi, *Fascist Spectacle: The Aesthetics of Power in Mussolini's Italy* (Berkeley: University of California Press, 2000), 119, 148, 162–182.
77 Mark Thompson, *The White War: Life and Death on the Italian Front, 1915–1919* (London: Faber & Faber, 2009), 351–353.
78 Moore and Fedorowich, *British Empire*, 6.
79 I/SRX 130 – 7 August 1943, WO 208/4193, TNA.
80 I/SRN 1164 – 21 April 1943, WO 208/4192, TNA.
81 I/SRN 1179 – 23 April 1943, WO 208/4192, TNA.
82 Extract from Draft No. W 587 – 13 April 1943, WO 208/4200, TNA.
83 I/SRX 8 – 7 December 1940, WO 208/4193, TNA.
84 I/SRN 3 – 30 October 1940, WO 208/4189, TNA.
85 Moore and Fedorowich, *British Empire*, 3.
86 Moore and Fedorowich, *British Empire*, 3.
87 Lieutenant-Colonel G.L. Harrison in Moore and Fedorowich, *British Empire*, 92
88 Moore and Fedorowich, *British Empire*, 92.
89 Keegan, *Second*, 287.
90 Moore and Fedorowich, *British Empire*, 92.
91 Moore and Fedorowich, *British Empire*, 101–103.
92 Hinsley, *Volume Two*, 32–34.
93 See Chapter Two.
94 Personnel for the Combined Services Detailed Interrogation Centre, War Cabinet Report, 11 February 1945, WO 208/3451, TNA, 1, 5.
95 S.C.1/7, Letter from Commandant of CSDIC to G.S.O.1. of M.I.19., 22 March 1945, WO 208/3451, TNA.
96 Hinsley, *Volume One*, 282.
97 Hinsley, *Volume One*, 282.
98 Hinsley, *Volume One*, 282.
99 Memo on 'List of Summaries, Reports, etc. Received in Hut 3', 28 November 1940, HW 14/8, TNA; Memo from Director of GC&CS to Washington DC, 31 December 1944, HW 57/35, TNA.
100 See: Gerhard Weinberg, 'Aspects of World War II German Intelligence', *Journal of Intelligence History*, 4/1 (2004), 1–6.
101 Personnel for the Combined Services Detailed Interrogation Centre, War Cabinet Report, 11 February 1945, WO 208/3451, TNA, 5.
102 Letter from Stewart Menzies (MI6) to Norman Crockatt (MI9), 21 February 1941, WO 208/4970, TNA.
103 Fry, *Ears*, 150, 270.

104 Minute: M.I.9.a./624/2, V.C.I.G.S., 28 January 1941, WO 208/5621, TNA.
105 Letter from Director of Naval Intelligence J.H. Godrey to Director of Military Intelligence Major General F.H.N. Davidson, 7 January 1941, WO 208/5621, TNA.
106 Letter from Air Commodore A.R. Boyle to Director of Military Intelligence Major General F.H.N. Davidson, 19 December 1940, WO 208/5621, TNA.
107 Memorandum, 7 October 1941, CAB 121/236, TNA.
108 Joint Intelligence Committee, 5 November 1941, CAB 121/236, TNA.
109 Hinsley, *Volume Two*, 33.
110 'Enclosure I – The History of C.S.D.I.C. (U.K.)', WO 208/4970, TNA, 4.
111 Moore and Fedorowich, *British Empire*, 105–106.
112 Moore and Fedorowich, *British Empire*, 105.
113 Moore and Fedorowich, *British Empire*, 96.
114 Moore and Fedorowich, *British Empire*, 96.
115 Moore and Fedorowich, *British Empire*, 96.
116 Roderick Bailey, *Target Italy: The Secret War against Mussolini, 1940–1943* (London: Faber & Faber, 2014), 56–58, 83–88, 102.
117 Bailey, *Target Italy*, 58. The Canadian-born former Rhodes Scholar Macalister would himself later be parachuted into occupied France as a radio operator in June 1943. His fate, however, was not a happy one. Captured at a German checkpoint and viciously interrogated by the Gestapo, he was executed at Buchenwald Concentration Camp on 14 September 1944. See: Jonathan Vance, *Unlikely Soldiers: How Two Canadians Fought the Secret War Against Nazi Occupation* (Toronto: HarperCollins, 2008).
118 Bailey, *Target Italy*, 83.
119 Extracts from letter from Executive Director of SOE to S.O., 15 October 1941, HS 7/58, TNA.
120 This is a truly tiny figure when one considers that despite operating at the *absolute* operational range of the RAF's Whitley, Halifax and Liberator bombers, SOE was able to insert 346 parachutists into occupied Poland. Moreover, over 100 were dropped into Belgium. More men – 11 in total – were sent into Norway to blow up the Norsk Hydro heavy water plant in February 1943. Finally, just one of the six sections of SOE that operated in France had 118 *missing* agents on its books at the end of the war. See: Michael R.D. Foot, *SOE.: An Outline History of the Special Operations Executive, 1940–46* (London: Bodley Head, 2014), 212, 239, 240, 243, 285.
121 Bailey, *Target Italy*, 8.
122 Bailey, *Target Italy*, 1–3, 354–355.
123 Bailey, *Target Italy*, 4.
124 Bailey, *Target Italy*, 354–355.
125 Keith Jeffery, *MI6: The History of the Secret Intelligence Service, 1909–1949* (London: Penguin, 2011), 423.
126 Jeffery, *MI6*, 424–426.
127 Jeffery, *MI6*, 425–424.
128 Keegan, *Second*, 419.
129 Hugh Sebag-Montefiore, *Enigma: The Battle for the Code* (London: Cassell Military, 2004), 120–121, 127.
130 Maria Robson, 'Signals in the Sea: The Value of Ultra Intelligence in the Mediterranean in World War II', *Journal of Intelligence History*, 13/2 (2014), 176–188.
131 Stephen Bungay, *Alamein* (London: Aurum, 2002), 36–37, 159.
132 Hastings uses the pleasing metaphor of a bureaucratic and central command 'threshing machine' which amassed and processed all the elements of intelligence procured into its 'golden harvest.' See: Max Hastings, *The Secret War: Spies, Codes and Guerrillas, 1939–1945* (London: HarperCollins, 2015), 200.

3 Friends and foes

Introduction

In September 1943, as the 1st Battalion Kensington Regiment advanced from Taranto to Bari, the unit's official history recorded how,

> The streets in all the towns and villages were lined with the cheering populace. The [Bren Gun] Carriers were bedecked with flowers, and it was hard to decide whether this was a mobile force seeking the enemy or a wedding procession. The one thing which was never in doubt was the direction which we should take. The onlookers steadfastly foiled any attempt to take any side turning which would not bring us speedily into the enemy's lines.[1]

This was a rapturous reception for a military unit that was, after all, invading Italy. Troops from what had been an enemy power were now greeted as liberators. This was a dramatic about-face, but hardly an isolated incident. As well as crowds greeting Allied troops, many Italians also gave shelter and support to escaping Allied POWs in the aftermath of the Italian Armistice.[2] Such accounts complicate traditional ideas of 'friends' and 'foes' during wartime, and raise important questions of who, in a war of complex and shifting alliances, did the prisoners view as their primary antagonists and which nationalities did the POWs view with sympathy and fraternity?

The September 1943 armistice was a highly influential moment in the history of the Second World War, but what were the attitudes of Italian service personnel before that point? This chapter will focus on Italian attitudes towards 'Friends and Foes' in the years 1940–1943: How did Italian soldiers, sailors and airmen conceptualise the United States, Britain, the Soviet Union, France and Germany? What the CSDIC (UK) sources reveal in this regard is that, while Italian POWs entertained a wide range of, sometimes contradictory, perspectives – not least of all in regards to the armed forces of the Third Reich – where their opinions most often aligned was that 'their war' was above all against the old European empires of Britain and France. Plutocratic imperialism, not Stalinist communism or New-World capitalism, was Italy's true enemy. To argue that all Italian attitudes towards the Western Allies were as warm as accounts by Origo and Newby suggest is undermined by the CSDIC (UK) protocols which reveal considerable hostility towards the British and French, as well as contempt for the Americans. This existed alongside a surprising admiration for the Soviets and an uneasy relationship with the Germans. In this way, the transcripts undermine an image of Italy's war as one fought without animosity towards its enemies.

The foreign policy of Fascist Italy stands as a field of considerable historic interest.[3] Drawing upon the significant literature, it is possible to build ideas of what major Italian political figures said, did and felt about other powers. However, in these works of diplomatic history, we can lose sight of how ordinary Italians engaged with these geopolitical events – how outlooks can reflect both distant proceedings on the world stage, and deeply personal encounters. The protocols cannot speak for all Italians, but they do provide a valuable 'bottom-up' perspective on the end-results of Mussolini's foreign policy decisions. This will be done by individually examining views of Italy's four main wartime enemies – the USA, Britain, France and the USSR – before considering opinions of Italy's closest ally, Nazi Germany.

Gli Americani

Given the glut of popular narratives that stress the primacy of the USA in bringing about the defeat of European fascism, it might be expected that the 11 December 1941 Italo-American declaration of war would have greatly alarmed those under CSDIC (UK) observation.[4] What hope existed for the Axis cause now that the full economic, political and military might of the United States could be brought to bear? In Bologna, police reports showed, at best, an indifference amongst the assembled crowds as news of this was announced. War with the nation that generations of Italian economic migrants had viewed as a land of plenty was surely foolhardy.[5]

Within the CSDIC documents there is plenty of evidence that Italians recognised the value of the USA's economic strength, with its capacity to produce huge amounts of good quality weapons, tanks, planes and other vital war materiel.[6] One *Tenente di Vascello* (I/N 23) – a naval rank equivalent to Lieutenant – said on 9 January 1941 that 'in mechanical production America leads the world' due to the abundance of natural resources in North America.[7] The disparity in armaments production between the United States and the other wartime powers was huge. Between 1940 and 1943 the USSR produced 35000 aeroplanes, Britain 26000, Germany 25000 and Italy 11000. Meanwhile, the USA – the 'Great Arsenal of Democracy' – manufactured 86000 in 1943 alone.[8]

Petty Officer Boschin (I/N 176) connected this economic prowess to Allied military strength, observing in July 1942 how much the British war effort was aided by a conveyor belt of American supplies.[9] Bomber Pilot Ravazzoni (I/A 32) grimly predicted that, in the event of an Axis defeat, Italian businesses and workers would be crushed by powerful American firms. In response Italians would be forced to 'go back to the land and live as peasants and open the gates of our cities to the American tourists.'[10] The war enabled a striking growth in the US economy. Its gross national product grew from $88.6 billion in 1939 to $135 billion in 1944. Through the 'Lend-Lease' programme the US exported some $13.8 billion worth of goods to the United Kingdom and $9.5 billion to the Soviet Union. By 1945, 'the foundations of the United States' economic domination over the next quarter century had been secured.'[11] Through these assessments of US industrial prowess, the CSDIC (UK) POWs confirmed an unavoidable economic reality.

Examples can be found where the US Navy was praised and respected by Italian naval officers. On 8 February 1943 Chief Engine-Room Petty Officer De Guigan (I/N 342) stated that 'the American fleet has got to be reckoned with now.'[12] In a similar vein, on 6 January 1943, Lieutenant Badezzi (I/N 321), a veteran of the elite 10th *Flotilla MAS*, described the US Pacific Fleet as 'very strong now.'[13] While the tone of these remarks suggests that the Italians had not always considered the US Navy to be a formidable fighting force, by early 1943 it had earned a certain level of respect in the eyes of some Italian naval personnel. Despite early reverses in the Pacific, by mid-1942 it had begun to strike back, culminating in the brilliant success of the Battle of Midway.[14] It was also expanding rapidly: while from 1942 to 1944 the Japanese Navy built six fleet carriers the Americans constructed 14 fleet carriers, nine light carriers and 66 escort carriers.[15] The resolve and power of the Americans at sea had become obvious. This is reflected in the assessment of men such as Torpedo Petty Officer Villosio (I/N 188) who praised America for her tenacity, stating that 'even if we beat England, America won't give in.'[16]

But if some Italian servicemen recognised the vigour and strength of American forces, many others were contemptuous. In late November 1940 a captured submarine second-in-command (I/N 22) declared 'it is impossible for us to lose, even if the Americans join the English,'[17] a comment that says just as much about Italian belief in victory as perceptions of the military prowess of the USA. Lieutenant Cristini (I/N 361) stated on 2 March 1943 that 'the Americans were good for increasing the population, but they're no use in war.'[18] While the costly – if ultimately successful – 'English' raid on St Nazaire in March 1942 was hailed for its 'great courage,' the Americans were branded as 'fools' for failing to stand up to the dramatic advances of Imperial Japan in the Pacific.[19] In a remarkable outburst in June 1943 Second Lieutenant Izzi (I/M 22) exclaimed 'they ought to make a comic film out of it if the Americans land [in Greece]. The landing of the Americans, blacks, reds, yellows, Italians, Neapolitans! Oh! Poor Roosevelt, what a life!'[20] The great American 'melting pot' – which Italians, ironically were a key part – is clearly seen as a significant stumbling-block to success on the battlefield. Both these examples show how Fascist anti-American propaganda – expressed in posters, newspapers, radio, film and even slogans daubed on walls – that focused on the

USA's supposedly poor leadership, consumerist avarice, degenerate 'soulless materialism' and naivety, reflected opinion within sections of the Italian military.[21]

Given the sheer volume of anti-Italian prejudice prevalent within American society into the twentieth century – it was Italians, after all, who had been the victims of the largest mass-lynching in US history[22] – it is hardly surprising that when mobilised for total war there were many in Italian society who were ready to take a more negative view of America. This is an idea addressed directly by a captured submarine diver (I/N 21) who expressed an intense anger at the racial slurs used by Americans which equated Italians with African-Americans: 'the Americans, who call us [...] niggers!'[23] A similar impression is given in conversations between *Capitano di Corvetta* Bartolomei (I/N (Am) 1) and *Sottotenente di Vascello* Mazzinghi (I/N 249), where American camp guards are accused of insolence, theft, incompetence and are described as 'absolutely uncivilised,' 'gangsters' and a people existing 'in a state of semi-barbarism.'[24] Likewise, American soldiers encountered by Lieutenant Cristini (I/N 361) at Moreton POW camp in Gloucestershire are described as 'damned swine!'[25]

These comments may also reflect that for all the great successes of American arms later in the war – the dramatic breakout from the Normandy beachheads, the dogged defence of the Ardennes in the Battle of the Bulge, or the heroic, if not uncontroversial, efforts of the aircrews of the 'Mighty Eighth' Air Force – the initial showing of many American Army units in North Africa left much to be desired. The humiliation of U.S. II Corps in January 1943 at the Kasserine Pass, which saw thousands of American troops fleeing for their lives in the face of both German and Italian armoured thrusts, was not forgotten quickly by either side.[26] This was not lost on a number of those who passed through CSDIC (UK). In describing the fighting that took place on the advance to Tebessa in the aftermath of the breakthrough, Staff Officer Captain Pirola (I/M 8) recalled that 'the Americans were running away; in two days we took 2500 American prisoners [...] the whole plain was an orgy of burnt-out American tanks, there must have been at least 120; it was an orgy of victory.'[27] The Commander of the *Pistoia* Infantry Division (I/M 15) remarked in July 1943 of the marked difference in fighting quality between poorly-trained North American troops and the experienced British Eighth Army.[28] Derision for the US Army is palpable in the protocols.

Smyth has argued that the Italian declaration of war against the USA was not a free choice but was 'clearly dictated by the exigencies of [the] wartime alliance with Germany.'[29] This might imply that Mussolini's soldiers were reluctant to view America as an enemy, and may even have been reluctant participants in the war against the United States. As the transcripts demonstrate, this was not the case. The POWs may have struggled to respect the armed forces of the USA, but they did not have a problem conceptualising them as an adversary.

L'inglese

If these sources reveal a markedly Italian perspective on the fortitude of the USA, they also dwell repeatedly on the value of 'the English' as effective war-makers.[30] They are variously described as dogged, stubborn and confident of victory to the point of arrogance, a quality that irritated the Italian prisoners in question.[31] A captured seaplane observer (I/A 14) remarked in August 1941 that with his 'great and fine history of colonial conquest,' the 'English soldier is good – cool, level headed and stubborn.'[32] In a similar vein Petty Officer Boschin (I/N 176) said on 2 August 1942 that 'the English are not like the Indians or the Russians, you know. When they fight, they're tough.'[33] Boatswain Losi (I/N 239) said, that 'no nation is a phlegmatic as the English. When an Englishman sees a man killed beside him, he just looks at him like this and says: "He's dead. Cheerioh!"' but Italians 'are not like that.'[34] Another submariner (I/N 6) captured on 18 October 1940, and speaking on 2 January 1941, described the English sailors he had encountered as 'extraordinary' because 'they told us they were really enjoying the war. For them it is sport.'[35]

The Royal Navy is described as 'formidable' by Lieutenant Badezzi (I/N 321) in January 1943,[36] and there are several cases were the Royal Air Force is also extolled. During the Battle of Britain, Fighter Command was noted both for its potency – 'I have never seen an A.A. barrage like the one over Dover the other day. There they have got some guns' – and the skill of its personnel – 'Those [Hurricane pilots] who attacked us were very, very good.'[37] When in November 1940 two British pilots were killed in the skies above Turin, they were given a 'magnificent funeral, with full military honours' which was attended by a large crowd of the very people they had been bombing.[38] By the summer of 1943 it was clear to Second Lieutenant Izzi (I/M 22) that 'the English have now got supremacy in the air.'[39] Izzi also hailed the Spitfire for its ability to outclass both the C.R.42 fighter and the S.M.79 bomber, two workhorses of the *Regia Aeronautica*.[40]

Izzi was not alone in noting British material strength. In late January 1943 both Chief Boatswain Pontone (I/N 254) and Chief Sick-Berth Petty Officer Botti (I/N 318) were in awe of the quantity of British foodstuffs even after four years of war, including unrationed white bread, butter, shops stocked with consumer goods and 'so much chocolate that they can afford to throw it away.'[41] Given the sheer amount of food and petrol that was coming through to the United Kingdom, Chief Engine-Room Petty Officer De Guigain (I/N 342), predicted that, even in 1943, 'the English' could 'go on fighting for years and years.'[42] This is a particularly telling comment given his previous role in the Axis campaign to destroy Allied merchant shipping.

Several prisoners under observation also remarked on the effectiveness and superiority of British and Allied intelligence gathering, particularly in naval matters.[43] When Chief Boatswain Pontone (I/N 254) discussed the Allied landings in North Africa in November 1942 he remarked that whilst 'it's absolutely certain' that no one in Rome foresaw the amphibious attacks in

French Morocco and Algeria, 'when we make a move, they (the enemy) know about it two months beforehand.'[44] When three survivors of the submarine *Cobalto* (I/N 218, I/N 220 and I/N 235) discussed the sinking of another submarine, the *Glada*, one questioned how the British could have known it was the *Glada* they were depth charging. This drew the response, 'they know everything, they know when we started – everything!'[45] The ruthless efficiency with which the British were able to neutralise Italian submarines is also remarked upon by Ordinary Seaman Stefanni (I/N 131) who said in November 1941 that 'those bastards are knocking our submarines all to blazes. They're devils for thinking up new ways of doing you in.'[46]

As Seaman Stefanni's (I/N 131) comments have already suggested, an appreciation of British martial strength was not always synonymous with feelings of fraternity. These sources repeatedly present Britain as the principal enemy of Fascist Italy. One fighter pilot (I/A 1) recalled that 'during the Abyssinian war my father, who was 55, said if we went to war against England he would volunteer.'[47] A compelling statement, not only because it came several years before Italy's eventual declaration of war, but also because it was from someone who had lived through the period when British and Italian forces had fought side-by-side in the punishing mountain battles of the *Fronte Italiano* in the First World War. A Petty Officer (I/N 177) bluntly exclaimed 'I hope England and all her plans go up in smoke.'[48] If ever there was an agreement between Germany and the USSR, it would, in the opinion of another (I/M 3), 'only be what England deserves.'[49] One concerned Bomber-Gunner (I/A 4) lamented 'If Germany and Italy lose, there will be a regime of life in Italy worse than under the Bourbons [...] just imagine what the English will do if they win.'[50]

Much like Second Lieutenant Izzi, Artillery Lieutenant Vertua's (I/M 20) experiences left him under no illusions as to the potency of Allied air power, but his anger towards the tactics used by Western Desert Air Force ground attack aircraft is palpable. He stated that their targeting of motor tankers, and even single Bersagliere dispatch-riders, was unwavering. He also condemned British artillery batteries for shelling Italian soldiers who left their defensive positions to 'perform their natural functions.' Italian units he claimed would not have done this, they would have used a rifle instead.[51] This example underlines not only the anti-English sentiment amongst many Italians, but also suggests that the fighting in the Western Desert was not fought entirely 'without hate.' This protocol, as well as the statements from Stefanni, Petty Officer I/N 177 and Bomber-Gunner I/A 4, also contradict the analysis of soldiers' letters by Collotti and Klinkhammer which states that Italian soldiers only very rarely expressed hostility towards the enemy.[52]

On 23 December 1940 Winston Churchill made a speech to the Italian people. Here he criticised 'the criminal' Mussolini but appealed to the historic friendship with Italy to 'stop a river of blood from flowing between the British and Italian people.' The transcript of this speech was published in the *Times* on 24 December and was evidently distributed as reading material to several

68 *Friends and foes*

Italian prisoners.[53] Their discussions in the days that followed made it clear that it failed to resonate with many of them. I/N 22, the second-in-command of submarine 'C,' questioned Churchill's claims of an Anglo-Italian friendship going back to the Risorgimento. He responded that 'it's enough to make you laugh. He hasn't begun to understand the present situation,' before labelling anyone in Italy who believed Churchill as 'cracked,' as well as describing the British Prime Minister himself 'an ugly devil.'[54] Discussing the same subject in January 1941 I/N 21, a diver, stated that, 'what isn't true is what he says about the friendship between us. Where has that friendship got to? Friendship! Friendship my foot!' Churchill's oratory was, in his opinion, little more than 'a silly old woman's speech!'[55]

It was not only actions in the Second World War that were used by the CSDIC (UK) prisoners of war to attack the standing of Great Britain. Lieutenant-Colonel Ravazzoni (I/A 32) took it upon himself to educate his cellmate about atrocities committed in the name of the British Empire. For instance, the use of concentration camps against civilians during the Boer War where 'twenty, thirty, fifty thousand people' were 'massacred,' and when 'patriots defending their own country' were tied 'to the muzzles of guns.'[56] The list of British war crimes during the fighting in South Africa is extensive, particularly in the case of those who perished in the concentration camps.[57] Although it seems that Lieutenant-Colonel Ravazzoni confused the killing of prisoners by 'blowing from a gun' with events following the 1857 Indian Mutiny rather than during the Boer War.[58] Ravazzoni summarised his position when he stated that 'these English pretend to be gentlemen, but it's nothing but a word [...] They can think of nothing but their own greatness, their Empire, their domination over the whole world [...] they want to strangle every other nation in the world, but to do it with kid gloves on.'[59] Highlighting the many humiliations and insults he faced following his capture at the hands of British soldiers on Malta, he pledged to teach his son that 'you must hate the English and England.'[60]

Warrant Officer Corvisiero (I/N 211) also combed the historic record in order to attack the British, stating that 'every war there's been since 1900 has been England's fault.'[61] Petty Officer Guglielmo (I/N 89) agreed and placed 'British imperialism' at the heart of an almost 'continual state of warfare' which was blighting the peoples of Europe.[62] Corvisiero continued to state that 'we should never have come into this war if England hadn't imposed sanctions.'[63] This statement presumably referred to the sanctions imposed on Italy by the United Kingdom in the wake of the invasion of Ethiopia in 1935.[64] A number of other POWs also viewed this as a decisive moment in Anglo-Italian relations. For example, Petty Officer Pettinati (I/N 269) of the submarine *Emo*, said in December 1942 that 'before the Abyssinian business we and the English were always friends.'[65] Lieutenant-Colonel Donati (I/M 26), who had commanded a battalion of Tunisian Volunteers in North Africa, said that the British actions in 1935 generated 'hatred' amongst Italians, as it was felt 'these gentlemen invited the whole world to starve us to death.'[66] These statements add further weight to the argument that the Second Italo-Ethiopian War greatly exacerbated Anglo-Italian tensions, pushing an already tense diplomatic relationship to greater depths.[67]

In an uninterrupted diatribe that ran for two pages, Lieutenant Viani (I/N 101) passionately attacked 'the English.' He stated that 'a little hardship would do the English good. I didn't believe that such a self-satisfied people existed.' Given the 'easy lives' the British people had led for so long, 'what do they know of life or of war?' He attacked 'Democracy' as a sham, leaving 'the lower classes' without power or political agency and he branded Great Britain as a nation 'conceited and cunning,' with 'inhuman ideas born of ignorance.'[68] Similarly Petty Officer Della Pica (I/N 113) said in November 1941, 'curse the English [...]. We ought to come over here and bomb them till they're wiped out, the dirty dogs.'[69] Petty Officer Pillade (I/N 289) also labelled 'the English' as 'dirty dogs' for using their great wealth to get the Yugoslavs, Greeks and Americans to do their fighting for them.[70]

Such explicit hostility towards the British does demonstrate a crossover with official Italian propaganda, even if few go quite as far as radio journalist Mario Appelius who mocked English women as 'dames with big feet, boxers' hands, leathery skin, sharp elbows, the stride of Scottish soldiers and voices that sounded like a broken record.'[71] It was not just Mussolini who had a belligerence towards the nation of supposedly feeble umbrella carriers who thought 'only with their arses.'[72] It seems that the idea that the replacement of the 'old and selfish plutocratic democracies' with a new Fascist European order, really did reverberate extensively amongst the Italian cohort.[73] However, it is also likely that these are attitudes born of experiences on the battlefield and in captivity. If no man is a hero to his valet then he is even less likely to think fondly of his gaoler.

There are some instances within the protocols that show a sympathy of sorts *could* exist between Italian POWs and individual Britons. Having met and got to know some Britons following his capture, Boatswain Pontone (I/N 254) suggested that actual encounters could mellow intense wartime propaganda. He freely admitted that 'I knew nothing about [the English] before and listening to all that propaganda I thought they were savages. But now I've seen them, I'd never fight so willingly against them again, because I know now that they're decent people.'[74] On another occasion Pontone confessed that he much preferred the English to the Germans.[75] Likewise, a Midshipman from the submarine *Tritone* (I/N 340) said, 'if you've got to be a prisoner, then there's only one nation (which will treat you well). There's no other nation in the world so 'gentlemanly' as the English.'[76] Two days later, the same Midshipman went on to say, 'these people here – they're all right. Let them do what they like. In reality, they're good people.'[77]

There are just as many examples which show how experiences of captivity had the potential to do the very opposite. In response to I/N 340's comments on 11 April 1943 his cellmate, Midshipman Gridelli (I/N 378) was clearly frustrated with the arrogance of the English personnel he had encountered, saying 'they treat Italy as a joke. They don't pay the least attention to her. It's just as if there were no great power called Italy.'[78] In July 1942 one Petty Officer from the submarine *Calvi* (I/N 181) expressed his concern that 'when the Germans get here [in the wake of a successful German invasion], [the English] will massacre all of us prisoners.'[79] In March 1943 Lieutenant Cristini (I/N 361) recalled that during his interrogation in Algeria, there was 'a certain Captain Dixon of the Intelligence service,' who, despite initial friendliness, 'when he found out he couldn't get anything out of me said: "Very well, tomorrow morning we'll shoot you."'[80]

Overall, the attitudes towards 'the English' in the transcripts are encapsulated by a summary of the discussions recorded in transcript I/SRN 3 – 'their sentiments generally are anti-British.'[81] Both the number and intensity of anti-British outbursts is far greater than pro-British statements in the CSDIC (UK) sources. Mussolini's ramping up of public Anglophobia in 1940 may have disturbed some traditional Nationalists and 'moderate' Fascists like Balbo, Bottai and Grandi.[82] But there is little evidence that many of the CSDIC (UK) POWs objected to the vilification of the British, taking little time in joining attacks on the reputation and standing of their Great War ally.

Il Franchese

The image painted of the French in the CSDIC (UK) sources mirrors that of the British in a number of ways, reinforcing the idea that for many of those under observation, the true enemy of Fascist Italy was plutocratic and imperialistic democracy.[83] From the conversation between Second Lieutenants Rizzi (I/M 14) and Izzi (I/M 22) on 9 July 1943 it is clear there was some respect for French fighting spirit along the *Ligne Alpine* in June 1940. According to Rizzi, 'They knew that there might be a debacle at any moment, but in spite of the fact that France was on her last legs, they put up a good fight.'[84] Izzi agreed, stating that 'they gave us some nasty knocks, we never advanced at all.'[85] They both acknowledged that the Italian advance was hamstrung by superior French weaponry, poor Italian planning and an Alpine topography that favoured defence.[86] These were savvy reflections on a campaign that cost an already defeated French Army fewer than 200 killed, wounded and missing, while the Italians lost 631 killed, 2631 wounded and 616 missing, with 2151 succumbing to frostbite.[87]

There is evidence of *some* compassion for the defeated French from within the cohort. For example, both Quartermaster Franzoni (I/N 283) and Petty Officer Jarobi (I/N 348) were sympathetic of the naval losses faced by 'poor France,' even while recognising that if Italy had been knocked out of the war in 1940, the French would almost certainly have annexed a share of Italy's African colonies.[88] In a conversation that took place between senior Italian officers in August 1943, the commander of XXI Corps, General Berardi (I/M 4), suggested that war with the French should have been avoided. He said Italo-French rivalry could have been settled without war, confident that the French would have ceded Djibouti and Corsica whilst giving Italy a beneficial agreement over Tunisia and the Roia frontier zone.[89] An impression of the conflict with the French as costly, unfortunate and unnecessary, a view arguably easier to form in Italian eyes since the French – unlike the mulish British – capitulated in 1940.

These are a relatively small number of cases compared with the many more that reveal a strong mutual enmity between Italy and France. Sub-Lieutenant Mazzinghi (I/N 249) simply stated that 'My God, it's incredible the hatred the French have for us.'[90] While First Officer Guglielmo (I/N 89) accepted that the French did not hate the Italians as much as the Germans, he pointed to comments that 'we have stabbed them in the back.'[91] A diver captured in November 1940 (I/N 21) harboured resentment because 'after the last war France gave us nothing,' despite the presence of a large Italian population in French Tunisia.[92] Lieutenant Vertua (I/M 20) said on 22 June 1943 that, 'the French did nothing for us. "To hell with the lot of them," say I – but if we ever return we'll do the same and give them the hell of a time.'[93] The former commander of the submarine *Glauco* (I/N 37) attacked the pre-war French political system as 'corrupt,' before going on to say that it is only with the 'new order' imposed on them by the Germans that 'the French people are coming to life again.'[94] Rivalry with the French had been a considerable preoccupation for the *Regia Marina* during the interwar period and it is hardly surprising that this is reflected by so many of the naval personnel in the CSDIC (UK) cohort. Exploiting this was crucial in how the Italian navy secured its 'privileged position in the Fascist defence establishment,' which gave it a high level of autonomy and saw naval spending increase by 470 percent between the 1934–1935 and 1939–1940 fiscal years.[95]

Relations with the Free French were particularly tense. Second Lieutenant Rizzi (I/M 14) recalled an instance of brutality. When a German prisoner refused to get out from a cattle-truck the Lieutenant in charge of the guard 'took a rifle from one of his men and showed it to the German, and as he still didn't get out, he pulled him out by the legs, hurled him to the ground and started kicking him.'[96] Midshipman Gridelli (I/N 378) said that 'if you fell into the hands of the De Gaullists you'd come to a sticky end. We are lucky to have been captured by the English.'[97] Clashes between 'Degaullists' and officers of the Italian Armistice Commission in Algiers on the eve of the Allied invasion in 1942 were recalled by Lieutenant-Commander Bartolomei (I/N (Am) 1). The Consul at Algiers 'was beaten up by the Degaullists and badly bruised. Two officers were caught by the Degaullists as they were going to Naval H.Q. [...] they found themselves surrounded by a mob.' The pair were later rescued by the Vichy authorities but not before they had been forced 'at the point of a bayonet to attend with their hands above their heads for two hours.'[98]

That considerable tensions existed between Italian and Free French forces was a phenomenon demonstrated in several documents that made their way to the highest levels of the British political and military leadership. A minute from General 'Pug' Ismay to the Chiefs of Staff Committee refers to reports that 'the

Italians shot all the Free French prisoners they took at Tobruk.'[99] Other correspondence between the War Office and Commander-in-Chief Middle East, General Archibald Wavell, made it clear that Italian prisoners were only to be handed over to the Free French 'providing General de Gaulle undertakes to observe the Prisoners of War Convention.'[100] Both Conti and Miège have written of the suffering of the 40000 Italian prisoners who languished in French camps in Tunisia, Algeria and Morocco.[101] Oral testimonies demonstrate how Italian POWs faced summary executions, torture and widespread neglect at the hands of their Free French captors.[102] The concerns of prisoners like Midshipman Gridelli were thus not without foundation.[103]

A similar tale is told by Sub-Lieutenant Scarino (I/N 393). On 6 May 1943, the day before Allied troops entered Tunis, he and his men were arrested by Vichy French police, rounded up into lorries and driven around the city all night, 'with people beating and spitting at them.' The French civilians were 'ferocious.'[104] These are not the only instances suggesting that Italian military personnel had considerable problems with the Vichy French. A pilot captured in June 1942 (I/A 20) bemoaned the draconian decrees of the Vichy regime in Algeria. 'You couldn't go out without a policeman following you [...] there'd been demonstrations against the Italian commission [...] we couldn't even talk to a girl. Any girl who talked to us, or was friendly towards us, they put in a concentration camp.'[105]

The personnel of the Armistice Commission were caught in a challenging situation. As Lieutenant-Commander Bartolomei (I/N (Am) 1) said himself, confronted with an unending stream of requests for supplies it was a 'dilemma [because] if we gave [the Vichy French] too much, we made it possible for them to revolt against us; if we gave them too little, we risked their being overrun by the English, Americans and Degaullists.'[106] Not only this, but their staff also had to oversee the disarming of ships and defensive sites, locking up ammunition and supplies, controlling troop training and maintaining barracks.[107] Bartolomei spoke of relations with the Vichy French during the two years he was with the Commission, 'the French would never speak to us and the Italian [civilians] were afraid to be friendly towards us. The position was always very awkward, because we were hated – hated and ignored absolutely.'[108] In a separate conversation Bartolomei shared a remarkable incident where the Vichy authorities were accused of staging the beating of two senior officers – General Boselli and his assistant – to force the Italians to accept French bodyguards. With the Gendarmes stationed in front of his hotel, the assumption by Bartolomei was that rather than being there to protect the Italian officials 'they were really there to see what we were doing.'[109] Such was the Vichy French contempt for the Commission that in the autumn of 1940 the government in Rome issued official complaints about the animosity and disrespect faced in Tunisia.[110]

Rivalry between Italy and France was older even than a united Italy. It was French troops that had crushed Mazzini's Roman Republic in 1849, and French military protection of the Papal States that prevented Rome's absorption into the Italian state until 1870. In 1873 *La Riforma* wrote that 'whether it is a monarchy, a republic or an empire, France will never forgive us for being independent. Use diplomatic language, by all means, but let us keep our powder dry.'[111] But, the CSDIC (UK) POWs did not view their neighbours to the northwest in such historic terms. It was not what the French – or indeed the British – had done in the nineteenth century that so offended the POWs, but their actions in the twentieth.[112] Italy's principal geopolitical rivals, and powers who had inflicted serious reverses on the Italian military during the Second World War, there is an undeniable tension between the Italian POWs and their British and French enemies.

Although many transcripts relate to the British and French, some other nationalities were also mentioned and bear consideration. While by the start of the Second World War neither the Netherlands nor Portugal could be described as global superpowers, they nevertheless retained considerable colonial possessions. This may well explain the hostility felt towards these two 'old order' imperial powers by a Sub-Lieutenant who had served in the submarine *Glauco* (I/N 39). He felt that 'Holland could only exist because England protected her rich colonies,' and was contemptuous that 'two-thirds of Borneo, Sumatra, and Java are not exploited at all, and Holland is not even in a position to exploit them.' Portugal, he said 'will also be obliged to disgorge. She has immense colonies. She will have to hand over quite a lot whether she enters the war or not.'[113] A worldview that pitted Fascist Italy against the established imperial powers of Europe is reinforced when you consider the more positive views afforded to some of the 'lesser' European powers encountered in these sources, who, it could be argued, had similarly suffered under the dominance of the 'Great Powers.'

Italian CSDIC prisoners generally harboured positive views of the Poles. Engineer Lieutenant Cristini (I/N 361) of the submarine *Avorio* (I/N 361) may have recalled that 'I know there were several rows between my petty officers and the Poles – in fact one of my men was struck with a rifle-butt.'[114] But several others were inclined to considerable sympathy for the plight of the Poles. For example, Rear Admiral Lernardi (I/M 402) lamented their treatment at the hands of both the Nazis and the Soviets. As he said to his cellmate on 6 August 1943, the Germans have 'handed over half of Poland over to the Russians [...] the Poles, poor things –!'[115] In a 'heated discussion' that took place between a captured Bomber-Photographer (I/A 2) and a Bomber-Gunner (I/A 4), the former was broadly supportive of their German allies, while the other lambasted them 'as "cowards and scoundrels" for attacking Poland and other small countries.'[116]

This was a conviction shared with a number of high-ranking Fascist officials who in the wake of the invasion of Poland ordered the Italian embassy in Berlin to be 'generous' with entry permits for fleeing Jews and Poles.[117] On 15 May 1939 Foreign Minister Ciano wrote of his friendship with the Polish ambassador, and lamented Poland's impossible position – caught between the Nazis and the Soviets, 'whatever happens Poland will pay the price of the conflict.'[118] Another young nation with shared Catholicism and nationalist aspirations during the nineteenth century, Poland was also a relatively small international player, lacking an empire and with spheres of influence totally distinct from Italy's, Poland was not a threat to the personal or national interests of the CSDIC (UK) POWs. As a result, the Poles escape the contempt directed towards the USA, Portugal and the Netherlands, and the outright hostility aimed at Britain and France.

I russi

In contrast to the British, French, Americans, or even Poles, there is little evidence to suggest that many of the men in the CSDIC (UK) files had much direct exposure to the citizens of the Soviet Union, either on or off the battlefield. From those who did – in particular those from the *Armata Italiana in Russia* whose accounts have survived – it is clear that many viewed the war against the Soviets through a powerful and compelling 'religious dimension,' as a modern-day Crusade against the godless Bolshevik hordes.[119] Many ordinary Italians wrote to Mussolini in support of his turn against the Soviets from Operation Barbarossa onwards. On 22 June 1941 a Sicilian Capuchin Monk congratulated the *Duce* on the 'holy war' against the USSR, which was fought in 'the defence of Christian civilisation and the destruction of the Bolshevik world.'[120] Given the Church's strong anti-Communist stance, and Fascism's liquidation of Italy's domestic Marxist movements throughout the interwar period, it is in many respects hardly surprising that Mussolini's citizens could take such a view of the USSR.[121]

Nonetheless, this model of Italian public opinion sits uneasily alongside a number of those monitored by the Centre who expressed an unqualified admiration for the Soviet people, as well as for the USSR's political system, worldview, leadership and military prowess. For example, General Paolo Berardi (I/M 4), who did not ignore the 'horrors of Bolshevism,' nonetheless praised the USSR's 'universal' idea to 'improve the condition of the whole world,' in stark contrast to the vision of the British, whose position in the world sought only to 'enrich those hundred thousand oligarchs who constitute the British Empire.'[122] Signals Petty Officer Pacelli (I/N 367) could not have been clearer in his pro-Soviet stance, saying on 13 April 1943 that 'Bolshevism is not harmful. Russia is a paradise.'[123] In early January of the same year Naval Lieutenant Paladini (I/N 298) questioned 'why did we ever attack Russia?' with his cellmate, Lieutenant Badezzi (I/N 321) responding, 'I admire Russia.'[124] A lieutenant in the 10th *Flotilla MAS* (I/N 23) said 'I shall never be able not to admire the Russians. They tackled their situation with no half measures and totally without respect of persons.' His cellmate, a submarine officer (I/N 22), was clearly sceptical of the idea that 'the Russians have solved [all] their problems,' I/N 23 did acknowledge 'it will take centuries,' but nevertheless felt comfortable saying 'that they have radically tackled their problems.'[125]

The criticism directed towards France and Britain is not echoed in regard to the Soviet Union, which is extolled for its ideology, leaders, military performance and influence on the outcome of the war, even though they were an enemy power. In a conversation between two Army Lieutenants (I/M 19 and I/M 20), captured in Tunisia in May 1943 – they said that 'communism [...] is fundamentally an idealism which aims at improving the conditions of the people – after all, even Christ was a Communist in the good sense of the word.' Both officers agreed how they 'never understood why the Russians and the Italians should be enemies.' Stalin himself is lauded by the same pair as a 'capable man' for eliminating 'hypocrisy,' 'bigotry and fatalism' and killing 'all those who had to be killed,' thus forging a new and revitalised Russian people.[126] These two officers were certainly not the only ones from the CSDIC (UK) cohort to single out Stalin for praise. In October 1942 Torpedo Petty Officer Villosio (I/N 188) said, 'undoubtedly [he] is a great man, a great statesman.'[127] For all his ambivalence towards the Vichy French in North Africa, Lieutenant-Commander Bartolomei (I/N (Am) 1) said that 'although he's [Stalin] sent thousands of people to their deaths, one's bound to admit that he's rendered great services to humanity.'[128] Bartolomei's fellow prisoners agreed. Lieutenant Paladini (I/N 298) said that, 'in my opinion as far as handling masses is concerned Stalin is the greatest man there's ever been in history,' while Sub-Lieutenant Mazzinghi (I/N 249) believed 'moreover he's intelligent. Look [at] what he's done in the Caucasus, for instance. In the last war Russia's numerical strength was never used properly, but it's a bit different now.'[129] In none of these instances is Stalin's ruthless reputation ever in doubt. Instead it is often closely connected to his success as a skilled and almost selfless leader in the eyes of these prisoners. He is popular precisely for his murderous tendencies, rather than despite them.

Artillery Lieutenant Vertua (I/M 20) may have been dismissive of Russia's military record, saying 'she's lost so many wars [...] damn it all, she lost the World War. And did she win her war with Japan? And did she win the Crimean war in 1856?'[130], but it was much more common for the POWs to compliment its strength on the battlefield, and the effectiveness and influence of 'Russians' as war makers. In early September 1941, while a captured Boatswain's Mate (I/N 92) from a Motor Torpedo Boat (MTB) considered that a German victory over the Soviets was a matter of time, he nonetheless was impressed with the stand made by the Red Army in Leningrad, Odessa and Kiev. Most crucially of all, he felt that it was 'a pity the Russians didn't enter the war on the German side [...] it would have been better if we could have had the Russian Black Sea fleet working with ours in the Mediterranean.'[131] The *Regia Marina* had been reliant on Soviet oil until the early 1930s; in 1927 the Italian navy purchased 150000 tonnes of petroleum from the Soviet oilfields.[132] This suggests possible practical reasons behind such admiration for the performance of the Soviets, especially from Italian naval personnel.

76 *Friends and foes*

The Soviet Union was, according to Chief Boatswain Bergadono (I/N 343), 'going to decide this war.'[133] One unidentified prisoner bluntly said on 12 August 1941 that 'Russia has given Germany a drubbing,' while another claimed that 'it's not part of the Russian make-up to go to war and get nothing out of it.'[134] Gunners Mate Di Vito (I/N 173), a 36 year-old professional seaman, called Russia 'a great well organised nation' and said that 'if the Germans don't succeed in beating Russia, they're done for.'[135] In 1943, the Soviets were, in the opinion of Lieutenant Badezzi (I/N 321), 'too determined, too well organised and too well armed' to be struck down by a revolution as they had been in 1917.[136] Defeating them, Badezzi thought, 'is not so easy.'[137]

Midshipman Rosali (I/N 340) was confident that the Soviets would triumph in the East. 'Russia can't be pushed out. Germany hasn't succeeded in defeating her in three years while she was fresh [...] If [Germany] has not been able to knock Russia out in these three years, there's no reason why she should be able to do so now, no reason whatsoever.'[138] The performance of the Red Army at Stalingrad impressed both Rosali and Midshipman Gridelli (I/N 378),

I/N 340: [...] The Russians put up a fine show at Stalingrad, they accounted for over three hundred thousand Germans.[...]
I/N 378: The Russians were really great at Stalingrad.
I/N 340: My God they were, to an extraordinary degree![139]

Stalin and the Red Army had been left to do 'everything so far' by the Western Allies who were deliberately delaying the opening of the Second Front according to Gridelli and Lieutenant-Colonel Donati (I/M 26) in July 1943. A statement that brings together a remarkably sympathetic stance for the forces of the Soviet Union, and a strong criticism of the British and Americans. The Red Army had inflicted extensive casualties on Italian forces by this time, and yet Gridelli and his colleagues upheld considerable support for the USSR.

The existence of such pro-Soviet sentiment is further supported in the works of several prominent Italian writers of the period. In Curzio Malaparte's wartime reportage, his favourable and sympathetic portraits of the Soviet troops and civilians he encountered on the Eastern front saw him removed from the German theatre of operations, according to Malaparte, at the behest of Joseph Goebbels himself.[140] Mario Rigoni Stern – a former Sergeant Major in the Alpini Corps, and one of the lucky few to avoid death and capture during the retreat from the Don in 1943 – writes in *Sergeant in the Snow* of how often Russian civilians offered his men food, shelter and warmth in their homely *Isbas*. Stern is unable to 'hate' his enemy even in the wake of the death of his close friend Marangoni. In a bizarre turn of events, in the middle of a fierce fire-fight he stumbles across a group of Red Army soldiers who share their soup with him, a rare glimpse of a shared humanity in a theatre of war infamous for its cruelty.[141]

Others in the CSDIC documents discussed the merits of forming a 'USSR Republic of Europe' to beat the English.[142] This image of the British Empire and Commonwealth betrayed by the Soviets is cultivated with some relish in a number of other instances, on one occasion just two months after the launch of Operation Barbarossa.[143] In addition to further emphasising how much the British were viewed as the primary enemy, these statements reflect the 'deeply realistic relationship with the USSR' from a regime in Rome that signed the Italo-Soviet Pact of Friendship, Neutrality and Non-Aggression on 2 September 1933, and which only broke off diplomatic relations in 1941.[144] It was a relationship that saw Russian and Italian sailors celebrating together the anniversaries of the March on Rome and the Storming of the Winter Palace as they sailed together from Genoa to Vladivostok in 1934, the expedition itself being part of a ship building deal between the Ansaldo Company shipyards and the Soviet government.[145] The legacy of the remarkably cordial relations between these two dictatorial and totalitarian states clearly cast a longer shadow, and trickled down further through Fascist society, than a superficial reading of inflammatory wartime rhetoric and propaganda may initially suggest.

To argue that all of those under observation were uncompromisingly pro-Soviet would be disingenuous. An observer in a Cant.Z.506 seaplane (I/A 14) found it hard to believe that 'Germany would have attacked Russia,' unless 'the Russians had been planning to attack the Germans in the back, egged on perhaps by the English.'[146] The same prisoner was understanding of Russia's imperial ambitions saying that 'it is natural that a great nation like Russia should desire an outlet to the sea [...] she longs for an outlet to the Mediterranean; and quite possibly she'll now succeed in getting it.'[147] Although, I/A 14's later statement of 'let's hope that revolution will break out in Russia. That would be a solution,'[148] perhaps points to a limit to his sympathy, and the existence of a mental distinction in his mind between the Soviet Union and 'Russia.'

A similar dynamic comes across in a conversation of 20 March 1943 between Sub-Lieutenant Budini (I/N 373) and Bomber Pilot Ravazzoni (I/A 32). Budini admitted that 'I ask myself whether Socialism and Communism are really so bad as they're made out to be,' because 'Russia, which at one time held no place in either the field of medicine and the arts, now leads the world.' But, as Ravazzoni said, 'I draw a distinction between Communism and Bolshevism. If we lose the war Bolshevism will spread all over Europe.' This is a statement that Budini, for all his respect for Russian arts and medicine, agrees with, saying that 'if the Russians carry on propaganda all over Europe they'll destroy everything, because those are revolutionary ideas.'[149] It is clear that Budini and Ravazzoni were not the only prisoners greatly concerned over what may happen if the Red Army arrived in Italy. Chief Boatswain Pontone (I/N 254) confessed to his comrades that 'I'm more afraid of the Germans and the Russians than I am of the English,' as 'it appears that Churchill has promised Italy to Russia.'[150]

Chief of Staff of XX Corps (I/M 36) said in January 1944 that 'our problem is, how to keep the Russians out of Italy [...] I don't want the Russians. I don't want the Slavs. There ought not to be any Slavs on the Mediterranean because they are a people who will one day strangle us, there are too many of them, they are an incubus.'[151] For at least some of those in the CSDIC (UK) cohort then, it is clear that a pro-Russian position could be tempered with concerns about what would happen if the Soviets actually advanced into Southern Europe. However, these remain a small minority. The majority opinion suggests a surprising sympathy for the Soviets as a people and the USSR as a political entity.

I tedeschi

The historiography surrounding Italo-German relations preceding and during the Second World War has a lively history in and of itself. Goeschel's portrait of the personal relationship between Hitler and Mussolini shows its complexity – an association that was far more nuanced than one between two former corporals who shared an ideology and a penchant for militaristic trappings. During their 17 meetings between 1934 and 1944 the outward image of cooperation masked many personal and political tensions. The meetings became 'routine to keep the performance of Axis unity and friendship going.'[152] Hitler privately expressed anti-Italian racist views, Mussolini was ambivalent to early approaches from the Nazi leadership, and the vast crowds that celebrated many of the pair's meetings could be prompted as much by bribery and coercion than genuine adulation for their leaders.[153] Theirs was a 'politically constructed' and 'functional' relationship forged primarily for the 'enhancement of their own power.'[154]

Opinion was no less conflicted amongst wider Italian society. Moore, for instance, claims that the reluctance of Italian commanders swiftly to 'change sides' after the September 1943 armistice was because 'few harboured anti-German sentiments.'[155] Bosworth and Hastings on the other hand are more inclined to suggest that the majority of Italians viewed their Teutonic neighbours through a prism of fear, anger and envy.[156] Duggan shows that a variety of opinions were in evidence at this time. Plenty, especially in the Northern industrial cities of Milan and Turin, viewed a growing closeness with the Nazis with anxiety – 'if the Duce does not get off the German wagon quickly he will be forced to make Italian troops march for the triumph of Pan-Germanism in Europe.' Yet many young, radical students saw fighting alongside the Germans as an exciting next step on *la patria*'s march to martial glory and a true Fascist revolution.[157] My reading of the Italian protocols suggests that the majority of the Centre's POWs were inclined to think almost as poorly of their German allies as of their democratic enemies.

As with the Soviets and the British, the Germans are repeatedly hailed for their strength and martial qualities. Even as late as July 1942 Petty Officer Boschin (I/N 176) was 'certain that the Germans will arrive in England.'

He went on to say that 'I know the Germans. No one can offer them adequate resistance, whether they're English, French, Russians, no one at all [...] You mustn't forget that Hitler has everything at his disposal, everything.'[158] In the opinion of Ordinary Seaman Stefanni (I/N 131), the Germans were 'a people made for war.'[159] Rear-Admiral Leonardi (I/N 402) believed that 'the German nation won't give in. They are a people who would die rather than give in.'[160] To submarine officer I/N 89, the German war machine appeared unstoppable, saying 'who is able – who will be able to halt these Germans? [...] they can carry on the war for 50 years with the stuff they captured in France.'[161] A Sub-Lieutenant who had served in the submarine *Glauco* (I/N 39) was particularly impressed with the performance of Kurt Student's *Fallschirmjägers* on Crete in 1941, describing their victory as 'phenomenal.' He went on to say that 'the Germans are the only ones who fight through to the end; even if they are cut to pieces they go on until they have smashed through.'[162] These POWs echo the arguments of a generation of military historians – such as Liddell Hart, Bidwell and Barnett – who stressed the tactical excellence of the German army in the Second World War.[163]

In many other transcripts the Germans are described in much more negative terms. Paratrooper Second Lieutenant Varutti (I/M 28) described some of the Germans he had come across as 'louts' with a penchant for drunkenly molesting Sicilian women.[164] Second Lieutenant Izzi (I/M 22), who despite being of partial German heritage, saw them as exploitative leeches – 'the Germans may be said to be allies for only as long as they think they can get something out of you, and when fortunes change they push off [...] their principle is always exploiting, but never doing anything themselves.'[165] When it came to 'the German character,' General Berardi (I/M 4) believed that they were 'full of presumptuousness, but they're rather empty-headed and pretty blind too.'[166] One unidentified pilot remarked, 'they're a strange people the Germans – all of them. They make good soldiers and good sailors, but how pigheaded they are!'[167] Such was one Naval Artillery officer's (I/M 20) low opinion of the Wehrmacht forces he had served alongside, that he felt comfortable saying 'it will be lucky for us if we manage to lose the war, because if we win it we shall be under the Germans and therefore in a wretched position.'[168]

Low opinion of the conduct of German forces was not unique to those under observation. This is a point of view found well beyond the British surveillance camps. The Italian ambassador to Berlin, Dino Alfieri, wrote on 3 May 1942 that the Germans were: 'good soldiers, and strong men, [but] given more to action than to thought. Nazism has laid bare the quintessence of their race, brutally bellicose, whilst their reasoning is convoluted, subordinate and sluggish.'[169] Like I/M 20, the diplomat Luca Pietromarchi worried that an Axis victory would force all of Europe under German domination.[170] General Arturo Vacca Maggiolini (head of the Italian Armistice Commission with France), General Geloso (commander of Italian occupation forces in Greece), Blasco Lanza d'Ajeta (Ciano's cabinet chief), Amedeo Mammaldella (consul in

Dubrovnik) and General of *Carabinieri* Giuseppe Pièche all wrote in official reports of their distrust for an ally they viewed as unreliable, selfish and willing to undermine Italy's interests.[171]

Petty Officer Guglielmo (I/N 206) described how trigger-happy German sentries at Augusta regularly opened fire on, and killed, local fisherman who used the waters around the port at night time.[172] On the ground in Libya, according to one unidentified Italian officer, if Italian and German troops ever came to a disagreement, 'the Germans always used to produce their revolvers (*le rivoltelle*) – always.'[173] These would have been familiar to Air Commodore Boschi (I/A 33). He described that during the final collapse of Axis forces in Tunisia in May 1943, there had been an agreement with German commanders that stranded Italian aircrews could go to the Menzel Temime airfield where space would be found for them on German aircraft. However, on arriving at the airfield the Germans ignored the agreement and instead began to shoot at the Italians who tried to board their Junkers aircraft. In Boschi's opinion the Germans were 'barbarians [...] they lose their heads at times like those and can no longer control themselves.'[174] A German tendency to throw their Italian allies 'under the bus' in times of trouble is also remarked upon by Sadkovich, who describes how Rommel in retreat would often prioritise saving German units, while leaving tired Italian infantry formations as an exposed rear-guard.[175]

Lieutenant-Colonel Pedala (I/M 13) highlighted the absurdity of being in an alliance with a people who everyone remembered Mussolini lambasting throughout the 1920s. His personal experience of the First World War, fighting the forces of the Austro-Hungarian Empire and the German Reich on the Isonzo, made it impossible for him to see the Germans as allies.[176] That such a veteran of the Great War would be inclined to this viewpoint is hardly surprising given that the 1915–1918 Italian campaign is regarded as being one of the most 'savage' of the entire war.[177] Pedala was not alone. IAF Lieutenant-Colonel Ravazzoni (I/A 32) had also fought against the Germans in the First World War, which may go some way to explaining why he felt that they were a people that sought to 'strangle' other nations of the world.[178] Commander of the *SS Cortellazzo*, Lieutenant Paladini (I/N 298), recalled his displeasure at having Germans on board his ship as, 'I've got an old grudge against the Germans. I ran away from Trieste in the last war and fought for Italy,' and yet, 'this time I had to fight for the Germans.'[179]

A conversation that took place in March 1943 between three captured submariners (I/N 343, I/N 366 and I/N 367) serves as a reminder that there was an entire generation of Italians who had gone through the experience of being at war with the Germans. When I/N 367 pointedly remembered an acquaintance of his who said, 'how can I be expected to fight side by side with these people when they killed my father?,' I/N 343 responded that 'he isn't the only one who thinks like that,' with I/N 366 agreeing that 'the old people at home are bound to feel like that.'[180] Given how much cultural and political cachet Mussolini's regime had given to the struggle against the

Austro-Hungarians and Germans in the First World War,[181] it is hardly surprising that there were those who struggled to reframe their views of their former enemies.

Even positive remarks concerning their wartime allies could come with qualifications. A Sub-Lieutenant in the submarine service had 'the highest esteem for their military qualities' yet he certainly did not 'like' them.[182] The line between awe and jealousy is blurred in a conversation between Petty Officers regarding the production capabilities of German tank and aircraft factories.[183] Even as early as November 1940, Italian service personnel described the Germans as 'cowards and scoundrels' in their treatment of the Poles, and were themselves anxious that once the Germans had dispatched the English, it would not be long before they turned their attentions south, and began streaming through the Brenner Pass en route to Rome.[184] One of these prisoners stated that 'there is no cement in Italy now, because it is all on the Brenner'.[185] There is more than an element of truth to such hyperbole. Fascist military planners kept the programme of expanding the Brenner defences – which began in 1934 in the wake of a failed Nazi coup in Austria – in operation until 1942.[186]

A July 1942 British intelligence summary from the 10th Armoured Division reported that 'bad feeling between the German and Italian prisoners was very evident at one forward cage. Italian officers used harsh terms in speaking of the failure of the Germans to assist them and two German prisoners asked to have transport separate from the Italians.'[187] Such direct hostility is not observed on the occasions when Italian and German personnel conversed together in the CSDIC (UK) files – evidence to suggest that at least some of this anti-German sentiment existed better in the abstract than in reality. These instances may have been rare, but they demonstrate that such encounters *could* be cordial, polite and even friendly. When such good will was evident, it was regardless of the topic of conversation be it submarine numbers in the Atlantic and Mediterranean, complaining about the supply of coffee substitutes, or even exchanging lurid gossip about the sexual liaisons of Edda Mussolini.[188] While none of these discussions took place beyond the summer of 1941, and thus well before the traumatic and divisive events of 1942 and 1943, they nonetheless remind us of the fact that there was a time when German and Italian servicemen could operate in a spirit of mutual amiability.

The commander of the submarine *Glauco* (I/N 37) remembered that there was 'quite a lot of comradeship' in Bordeaux between Italian and German naval crews. From his experience, 'the Germans are very kind and polite to us.' On one occasion when his submarine was forced to wait in the Gironde estuary for a prolonged period, he was invited on board a nearby German destroyer for refreshment. As he said, 'they were all very decent and we drank and smoked all evening.'[189] Fighter Pilot Civetta (I/N (Am) 4) said that he found it 'a pleasure to work with the Germans,' praising them for their 'precision.'[190] Such was the faith that Warrant Officer Corvisiero (I/N 211) had in his allies that he simply failed to believe accounts of 'Germans running away and leaving the Italians in the lurch.'[191]

In a remarkable trend a few prisoners go even further than this, stressing the benefits of German management of Italian affairs. For example, one Fighter Pilot NCO (I/A 3) said in December 1940 that, 'what we need in Italy is German control.'[192] It would be misleading to suggest that this was anything close to a majority view amongst the CSDIC (UK) cohort, but I/A 3 was not alone in thinking this. When asked by Engineer Lieutenant Varoli (I/N 338) to imagine 'what Italy would be like under the Germans,' Lieutenant-Colonel Ravazzoni (I/A 32) responded that, 'the Germans would put the country in order [...] Under the Germans the Italians would become a great nation.'[193] Lieutenant in the 10th *Flotilla MAS* (I/N 23) said, in late 1940, that given Italy's inability to complete even the modest tasks assigned to them, at the end of hostilities 'either we shall have to beg for the honour of being admitted to the Third Reich, or else we shall have to work to make ourselves equal to the Germans. There's no other solution.'[194] However, this is rooted more in a disillusionment with the mistakes of the Italian Fascist regime, than in a particularly strong affection for the Germans, especially when you take into account Ravazzoni's hostility to the Germans seen above.

Overall, this corresponds to a trend within the CSDIC (UK) cohort by which aspects of the German wartime performance were praised, alongside a much wider wave of criticism and reproach. The Italian POWs have a lot to say about their German allies, the majority of which is negative. It is a view to a certain extent corroborated by Sullivan, who states that though Italians 'recognised the superiority of German weapons, fighting skills and generalship [...] a great many Italian soldiers [...] had come to hate and fear the German army by September 1943.'[195] Unlike Sullivan who sees this development as rooted in a reaction to German mistreatment of occupied civilians and POWs, the protocols suggest that this dislike reflected Italian anger at their own ill-treatment at German hands. An understandable, but more self-centred approach.

Conclusion

It is a challenge to find a wartime power that the Italian cohort were predominately pre-disposed towards. The Poles appear to have been the exception to this. As, paradoxically, were the Soviets, even if few POWs relished the prospect of welcoming the Red Army and Soviet-Style Communism to Italian shores. Regardless of whether they were formally ally or enemy, the protocols demonstrate there was little love lost between these Italian servicemen and the Americans, British, French, or, indeed, the Germans. Contempt for American inexperience was matched by distaste of German brutality and anger towards the arrogance of the British and French. These were opinions informed both by historical events and personal encounters. The worldview of these Italian servicemen was not defined by the fraternity and sympathy towards their fellow man as the *Italiani Brava Gente* myth would have us believe, but by a hardness and harshness towards both 'friend' and 'foe.'

Throughout the CSDIC (UK) transcripts there is plenty of evidence to support the existence of an – at best – conflicted relationship between Nazi Germany and Fascist Italy, underpinned by a lack of ideological commitment and geopolitical.[196] Many of the POWs also share an official Fascist ambivalence towards Britain and France, the plutocratic democracies which were viewed as decadent and deliberately excluding Italy from a 'place in the sun' and a hegemonic position in the Mediterranean.[197] This aggressive and un-accommodating view of the world can be seen as an expression of an 'aggrieved Italian nationalism' which had been gestating in Italy for much of the early twentieth century and given ample impetus by the policies of Fascism. Particularly the pushes towards militarism and imperialism in the 1930s which sought to 'instil a garrison-state mentality in Italians.'[198] De Felice has argued that right until the eve of Italy's entry into the Second World War, Mussolini was caught in a fraught middle ground between the Western Democracies and Nazi Germany.[199] If after the outbreak of war, the CSDIC (UK) cohort had to choose between these two sides, it would have been a decision largely defined by who they disliked the least.

Notes

1 Ken Ford, *Battleaxe Division: From Africa to Italy With the 78th Division, 1942–45* (Stroud: Sutton, 2003), 11.
2 See: Richard Lamb, *War in Italy 1943–1945: A Brutal Story* (London: J. Murray, 1993); Iris Origo, *War in the Val D'Orcia: An Italian War Diary, 1943–1944* (London: J. Cape, 1951); Eric Newby, *Love and War in the Apennines* (London: HarperCollins, 2010).
3 Notable examples include: Richard Bosworth, 'Italian Foreign Policy and its Historiography', in Richard Bosworth and Gino Rizzo, eds., *Altro Polo: Intellectuals and their Ideas in Contemporary Italy* (Sydney: University of Sydney, 1983), 65–86; Jens Petersen, *Hitler-Mussolini: Die Entstehung der Achse Berlin-Rom, 1933–1936* (Tübingen: Max Niemeyer Verlag, 1973); Denis Mack Smith, *Mussolini's Roman Empire* (London: Viking, 1976); Rosaria Quartararo, *Roma tra Londra e Berlino: Politica estera fascista dal 1930 al 1940* (Rome: Bonacci, 1980); MacGregor Knox, *Mussolini Unleashed, 1939–1941* (Cambridge: Cambridge University Press, 1982); Esmonde Robertson, *Mussolini as Empire-Builder: Europe and Africa, 1932-36* (London: Macmillan, 1977); MacGregor Knox, 'The Fascist Regime, Its Foreign Policy and Its Wars: An "Anti-Anti-Fascist" Orthodoxy?', *Contemporary European History*, 4/3 (1995), 347–365; Timothy Mason, 'Whatever Happened to 'Fascism'?', in Jane Caplan, ed., *Nazism, Fascism and the Working Class* (Cambridge: Cambridge University Press, 1995), 323–31; Wolfgang Schnieder, *Mythos Mussolini: Deutsche in Audienz beim Duce* (Munich: Oldenbourg Wissenschaftsverlag, 2013); Christian Goeschel, 'A Parallel History? Rethinking the Relationship between Italy and Germany, ca. 1860–1945', *Journal of Modern History*, 88 (2016), 610–632; Christian Goeschel, "*Italia docet?*' The Relationship between Italian Fascism and Nazism Revisited', *European History Quarterly*, 42 (2012), 480–492; Patrick Bernhard, 'Colonial Crossovers: Nazi Germany and its Entanglements with Other Empires', *Journal of Global History*, 12 (2017), 206–227.

84 *Friends and foes*

4 A May 2015 YouGov poll found that when asked 'in your opinion which one country would you say contributed most to the defeat of Germany in World War Two?', of those nations polled, the United States failed to be the most popular choice only in Norway and Britain, who selected the USSR and the UK, respectively. https://yougov.co.uk/news/2015/05/01/Britain-America-disagree-who-did-more-beat-nazis/, accessed 27 April 2016.
5 Bosworth, *Mussolini's Italy*, 470, 479.
6 I/SRM 16 – 20 June 1943, WO 208/4188, TNA; I/SRM 17 – 16 June 1943, WO 208/4188, TNA.
7 I/SRN 51 – 9 January 1941, WO 208, 4189, TNA.
8 Giorgio Rochat, *Le guerre italiane, 1935–1943: dall'impero d'Etiopia alla disfatta* (Turin: Einaudi, 2005), 305-313.
9 I/SRN 337 – 30 July 1942, WO 208/4189, TNA.
10 I/SRX 73 – 21 March 1943, WO 208/4193, TNA.
11 Alan Milward, *War, Economy and Society: 1939–1945* (Berkeley: University of California Press, 1979), 63, 71–72.
12 I/SRN 950 – 8 February 1943, WO 208/4191, TNA.
13 I/SRN 832 – 6 January 1943, WO 208/4191, TNA.
14 See: Sean Judge, *The Turn of the Tide in the Pacific War: Strategic Initiative, Intelligence, and Command: 1941–1943* (Lawrence: University Press of Kansas, 2018), 135–153.
15 Keegan, *Second*, 228–229.
16 I/SRN 331 – 29 July 1943, WO 208/4189, TNA.
17 X/SRX 1 – 29 November 1940, WO 208/4194, TNA.
18 Special Extract from SR Draft No W 327 – 2 March 1943, WO 208/4200, TNA.
19 I/SRN 337 – 30 July 1942, WO 208/4189, TNA; I/SRN 347 – 1 August 1942, WO 208/4189, TNA.
20 I/SRM 40 – 6 July 1943, WO 208/4188, TNA.
21 Bosworth, *Mussolini's Italy*, 488; Morgan, *Fall*, 42, 47, 50.
22 This occurred on 14 March 1891 in New Orleans when 11 men of Italian descent were seized from prison and murdered by an angry mob who suspected them of killing a local police chief. See: Richard Gambino, *Vendetta: The True Story of the Largest Lynching in U.S. History* (Toronto: Guernica, 1998).
23 I/SRN 44 – 3 January 1942, WO 208/4189, TNA.
24 Special Extract from SR Draft No W 327 – 2 March 1943, WO 208/4200, TNA; Extract from S.R. Draft Nos. 5891 B, 5932, 5911 B, WO 208/4200, TNA.
25 Special Extract from SR Draft No W 327 – 2 March 1943, WO 208/4200, TNA.
26 Max Hastings, *Overlord: D-Day and the Battle for Normandy* (New York: Simon & Schuster, 1985), 52. See also: Christopher Rein, 'Fredenhall's Failure: A Reexamination of the II Corps at the Battle of Kasserine Pass', *Army History*, 108 (2018), 6–21.
27 SRIG 101 – 19 June 1943, WO 208/4185, TNA.
28 SRIG 130 – 15 July 1943, WO 208/4185, TNA.
29 Denis Smyth, 'Duce diplomatico', *Historical Journal*, 21/4 (1978), 983.
30 The 'English' is a label used to encompass all the various 'British' nationalities. I have not come across any CSDIC (UK) protocols where POWs discuss 'the Welsh.' Only one example has been found to date where Italian POWs refer to 'Scots' and 'Irish' as identities distinct from being 'English.' Petty Officer Marghetta said on 27 July 1942 'they're [POW camp guards] extremely nice here. They can't be English, they must be Scots or Irish.' See: I/SRN 322 – 27 July 1942, WO 208/4189, TNA. Similarly rare are references to citizens of the 'White Dominions' – Australia, Canada, South Africa and New Zealand. See: I/SRX 32 – 2 March 1943, WO 208/4193, TNA; I/SRN 546 – 5 September 1942, WO 208/4190, TNA.

31 I/SRN 337 – 30 July 1942, WO 208/4189, TNA; I/SRN 317 – 8 August 1942, WO 208/4189, TNA; I/SRN 345 – 1 August 1942, WO 208/4189, TNA.
32 I/SRX 20 – 19 August 1941, WO 208/4193, TNA.
33 I/SRN 355 – 2 August 1942, WO 208/4189, TNA.
34 I/SRN 517 – 30 August 1942, WO 208/4190, TNA.
35 I/SRN 42 – 2 January 1941, WO 208/4189, TNA.
36 I/SRN 832 – 6 January 1943, WO 208/4191, TNA.
37 I/SRA 2 – 18 November 1940, WO 208/ 4184; I/SRA 3 – 18 November 1940, WO 208/4184.
38 I/SRA 14 – 23 November 1940, WO 208/4184, TNA. For more on RAF operations against Italian cities in 1940, see: Denis Richards, *RAF Bomber Command in the Second World War: The Hardest Victory* (London: Penguin, 2001), 53–55, 62, 90.
39 I/SRM 16 – 20 June 1943, WO 208/4188, TNA.
40 I/SRM 14 – 19 June 1943, WO 208/4188, TNA.
41 I/SRN 912 – 29 January 1943, WO 208/4191, TNA.
42 I/SRN 962 – 6 February 1943, WO 208/4191, TNA.
43 See also: Mavis Batey, 'Breaking Italian Naval Enigma', in Ralph Erskine and Michael Smith, eds., *The Bletchley Park Codebreakers* (London: Biteback, 2011), 79–92.
44 I/SRN 686 – 28 November 1942, WO 2208/4190, TNA.
45 I/SRN 548 – 5 September 1942, WO 208/4190, TNA.
46 I/SRN 178 – 19 October 1941, WO 208/4189, TNA.
47 I/SRA 15 – 10 December 1940, WO 208/4184, TNA. For more on the Ethiopian crisis and Anglo-Italian relations, see: Steven Morewood, "This Silly African Business': The Military Dimension of Britain's Response to the Abyssinian Crisis', in G. Bruce Strang, ed., *Collision of Empires: Italy's Invasion of Ethiopia and its International Impact* (London: Routledge, 2017), 73–108.
48 I/SRN 337 – 30 July 1942, WO 208/4189, TNA.
49 SRIG 196 – 3 August 1943, WO 208/4186, TNA.
50 I/SRA 16 – 11 December 1940, WO 208/4184, TNA.
51 I/SRX 86 – 23 June 1943, WO 208/4193, TNA.
52 Enzo Collotti and Lutz Klinkhammer, *Il fascism e l'Italia in Guerra* (Rome: Ediesse, 1996), 75–82.
53 'Mr Churchill Speaks to the Italian People', *The Times*, 24 December 1940, 4.
54 I/SRN 33 – 24 December 1940, WO 208/4189, TNA.
55 I/SRN 44 – 3 January 1941, WO 208/4189, TNA.
56 I/SRX 80 – 22 March 1943, WO 208/4193, TNA.
57 See: Thomas Pakenham, *The Boer War* (London: Abacus, 1992), 493–495, 501–510.
58 For more on the reprisals taken by the British authorities in the wake of the 1857 rebellion, see: Heather Streets, *Martial Races: The Military, Race and Masculinity in British Imperial Culture, 1857–1914* (Manchester: Manchester University Press, 2010), 38–41.
59 I/SRX 80 – 22 March 1943, WO 208/4193, TNA.
60 I/SRX 80 – 22 March 1943, WO 208/4193, TNA.
61 I/SRN 670 – 10 November 1942, WO 208/4190, TNA.
62 I/SRN 670 – 10 November 1942, WO 208/4190, TNA.
63 I/SRN 670 – 10 November 1942, WO 208/4190, TNA.
64 See: Gaynor Johnson, 'Philip Noel-Baker, the League of Nations and the Abyssinia Crisis, 1935–1936', in Strang, ed., *Collision*, 63–70.
65 ISRN 740 – 16 December 1942, WO 208/4190, TNA.
66 I/SRX 103 – 4 July 1943, WO 208/4193, TNA.
67 Massimiliano Fiore, *Anglo-Italian Relations in the Middle East, 1922–1940* (Farnham: Ashgate, 2010), 36, 49, 153–154, 167, 190, 192.
68 I/SRN 213 – 25 October 1941, WO 208/4189, TNA.
69 I/SRN 276 – 25 November 1941, WO W 208/4189, TNA.

86 Friends and foes

70 I/SRN 683 – 2 December 1942, WO 208/4190, TNA.
71 Bosworth, *Mussolini's Italy*, 488.
72 http://www.lrb.co.uk/v35/n03/richard-j-evans/kisses-for-the-duce, accessed 17 May 2016.
73 Christopher Duggan, *Fascist Voices: An Intimate History of Mussolini's Italy* (London: Bodley Head, 2012), xxi.
74 I/SRN 929 – 7 February 1943, WO 208/4191, TNA.
75 I/SRX 23 – 18 January 1943, WO 208/4193, TNA.
76 I/SRN 1137 – 9 April 1943, WO 208/4192, TNA.
77 I/SRN 1147 – 9 April 1943, WO 208/4192, TNA.
78 I/SRN 1147 – 9 April 1943, WO 208/4192, TNA.
79 I/SRN 328 – 27 July 1942, WO 208/4190, TNA.
80 Special Extract from SR Draft No W 327 – 2 March 1943, WO 208/4200, TNA.
81 I/SRN 3 – 30 October 1940, WO 208/4190, TNA.
82 Alan Cassels, 'Was there a Fascist Foreign policy? Tradition and Novelty', *International History Review*, 5/2 (1983), 267–268.
83 For more on Mussolini's propaganda war against the 'pluto-democracies,' see: Renzo Sereno, 'Italian War Propaganda at Home', *The Public Opinion Quarterly*, 3/3 (1939), 468–472; Arturo Marzano, 'La <<guerra delle monde>> La risposta inglese e franchese alla propaganda di Radio Bari nel mondo arabo (1938–1939)', *Contemporanea*, 1 (2012), 3–24; Manuela Williams, 'Mussolini's War of Words: Italian Propaganda and Subversion in Egypt and Palestine, 1934–1939', *Eunomia*, 1/2 (2012), 49–78.
84 I/SRM 47 – 9 July 1943, WO 208/4188, TNA.
85 I/SRM 47 – 9 July 1943, WO 208/4188, TNA.
86 I/SRM 47 – 9 July 1943, WO 208/4188, TNA.
87 Douglas Porch, *The Path to Victory: The Mediterranean Theatre in World War II* (New York: Farrar, Straus & Giroux, 2004), 43.
88 I/SRN 949 – 7 February 1943, WO 208/4191, TNA.
89 I/SRN 215 – 8 August 1943, WO 208/4186, TNA.
90 I/SRN 925 – 18 January 1943, WO 208/4191, TNA.
91 I/SRN 70 – 24 July 1941, WO 208/4189, TNA.
92 I/SRN 47 – 3 January 1941, WO 208/4189, TNA.
93 I/SRX 84 – 22 June 1943, WO 208/4193, TNA.
94 I/SRX 19 – 12 August 1941, WO 208/4193, TNA.
95 From 1360 million lire to 6393 million lire. John Gooch, *Mussolini and His Generals: The Armed Forces and Fascist Foreign Policy, 1922–1940* (Cambridge: Cambridge University Press, 2007), 121, 626.
96 I/SRM 2 – 15 June 1943, WO 208/4188, TNA.
97 I/SRN 1164 – 21 April 1943, WO 208/4192, TNA.
98 Extract from S.R. Draft No. 6017 – 16 December 1942, WO 208/4200, TNA.
99 Minute Serial No. D 142/1, General Ismay for C.O.S. Committee, 28 April 1941, PREM 3/363/1, TNA.
100 Desp. 0115 from The War Office to C.-in-C., Middle East, 27 April 1941, PREM 3/363/1, TNA.
101 Flavio Conti, *I prigionieri di guerra italiani, 1940–1945* (Bologna: Il Mulino, 1986), 363; Jean Miège, 'I prigionieri di guerra italiani in Africa del Nord' in Romain Rainero, ed., *I prigionieri militari italiani durante la Seconda Guerra Mondiale: aspetti e problemi storici* (Milan: Marzorati, 1985), 171–181.
102 Ferroni, *Italian POWs*, 92–93, 96, 114.
103 For the German experience of French captivity, see: Kurt Böhme, *Die deutschen Kriegsgefangenen in französischer Hand* (Bielefeld: E&W Gieseking, 1976); Fabien Théofilakis, *Les prisonniers de guerre allemands: France, 1944–1949* (Paris: Fayard, 2014).

104 I/SRN 1284 – 16 June 1943, WO 208/4192, TNA.
105 I/SRA 30 – 3 July 1942, WO 208/4184, TNA.
106 I/SRN 812 – 31 December 1942, WO 208/4191, TNA.
107 I/SRN 812 – 31 December 1942, WO 208/4191, TNA.
108 I/SRN 722 – 16 December 1942, WO 208/4190, TNA.
109 I/SRN 760 – 19 December 1942, WO 208/4190, TNA.
110 Paxton, *Vichy France*, 82.
111 Christopher Duggan, *Francesco Crispi, 1818–1901: From Nation to Nationalism* (Oxford: Oxford University Press, 2002), 334–336, 407–409, 610–611.
112 See: William Shorrock, *From Ally to Enemy: The Enigma of Fascist Italy in French Diplomacy, 1920–1940* (Kent: Kent State University Press, 1988).
113 I/SRN 65 – 20 July 1941, WO 208/4189, TNA.
114 Special Extract from SR Draft No. W 327 – 2 March 1943, WO 208/4200, TNA.
115 SRIG 20 – 6 August 1943, WO 208/4184, TNA;
116 I/SRA 7 – 23 November 1940, WO 208/4184, TNA.
117 Bosworth, *Mussolini's Italy*, 454
118 Galeazzo Ciano, *The War Diaries of Count Galeazzo Ciano, 1939–43* (London: Fonthill, 2015), 83.
119 Duggan, *Voices*, 317–373.
120 Christian Goeschel, *Mussolini and Hitler: The Forging of the Fascist Alliance* (New Haven: Yale University Press, 2018), 216–218.
121 For more on the ambivalence of the Italians to Soviet Russia in the 1920s and early 1930s (and vice versa), see: Giorgio Petracchi, 'Ideology and Realpolitik: Italo-Soviet Relations, 1917–33', *Journal of Italian History*, 2/3 (1979), 473–519; Giorgio Petracchi, *La Russia rivoluzionaria nella politica italiana. Le relazioni italo-sovietiche, 1917–1925* (Rome: Laterza, 1982); Rosaria Quartararo, *Italia-URSS, 1917–1941: i rapporti politici* (Naples: Ed. Scientifiche Italiane, 1997).
122 SRIG 196 – 3 August 1943, WO 208/4186, TNA.
123 I/SRN 1152 – 13 April 1943, WO 208/4192, TNA.
124 I/SRN 832 – 6 January 1943, WO 208/4191, TNA.
125 I/SRN 29 – 19 December 1940, WO 208/4189, TNA.
126 I/SRM 42 – 6 July 1943, WO 208/4188, TNA.
127 I/SRN 654 – 18 October 1942, WO 208/4190, TNA.
128 I/SRN 731 – 23 December 1942, WO 208/4190, TNA.
129 I/SRN 731 – 23 December 1942, WO 208/4190, TNA.
130 I/SRX 91 – 25 June 1943, WO 208/4192, TNA.
131 I/SRN 124 – 7 September 1941, WO 208/4189, TNA.
132 Vladimir Kostornichenko, 'The Export Vector of "Red" Oil: Soviet Oil Exports as the Main Factor Behind Industrialisation in the 1920s and 1930s in the USSR', *Oil of Russia*, 2 (2006).
133 I/SRN 950 – 8 February 1943, WO 208/4191, TNA.
134 I/SRA 22 – 12 August 1941, WO 208/4184, TNA; I/SRX 102 – 4 July 1943, WO 208/4193, TNA.
135 I/SRN 313 – 5 July 1942, WO 208/4189, TNA.
136 I/SRX 28 – 16 January 1943, WO 208/4193, TNA.
137 I/SRX 28 – 16 January 1943, WO 208/4193, TNA.
138 I/SRN 1260 – 5 May 1943, WO 208/4192, TNA.
139 I/SRN 1260 – 5 May 1943, WO 208/4192, TNA.
140 Curzio Malaparte, *The Volga Rises in Europe* (Edinburgh: Birlinn, 2000), 9. See also: Curzio Malaparte, *Kaputt* (New York: New York Review of Books, 2007).
141 Mario Rigoni Stern, *The Sergeant in the Snow* (Evanston: Northwestern University Press, 1998), 13, 23, 31, 73, 88.
142 SRIG 210 – 6 August 1943, WO 208/4186, TNA.

143 I/SRN 335 – 2 August 1942, WO 208/4189, TNA; I/SRA 22 00, 12 August 1941, WO 208/4184, TNA.
144 Bosworth, *Mussolini's Italy*, 285.
145 Joseph Clarke, *Russia and Italy against Hitler: The Bolshevik-Fascist Rapprochement of the 1930s* (New York: Greenwood Press, 1991), 154.
146 I/SRX 20 – 19 August 1941, WO 208/4193, TNA.
147 I/SRX 20 – 19 August 1941, WO 208/4193, TNA.
148 I/SRX 20 – 19 August 1941, WO 208/4193, TNA.
149 I/SRX 68 – 20 March 1943, WO 208/4193, TNA.
150 I/SRN 973 – 3 February 1943, WO 208/4191, TNA.
151 SRIG 377 – 23 January 1944, WO 208/4187, TNA.
152 Goeschel, *Alliance*, 7, 15.
153 Goeschel, *Alliance*, 293, 28, 31, 35, 11–12.
154 Goeschel, *Alliance*, 3–4. See also: Lutz Klinkhammer, Amedeo Osti Guerrazzi and Thomas Schlemmer, eds., *Die Achse im Krieg: Politik, Ideologie und Kriegführung, 1939–1945* (Paderborn: Ferdinand Schöningh, 2010), 11–48.
155 Moore, 'Enforced Diaspora', 185.
156 Max Hastings, *All Hell Let Loose: The World at War, 1939–45* (London: William Collins, 2012), 75; Bosworth, *Mussolini's*, 466.
157 Duggan, *Voices*, 327–328, 334.
158 I/SRN 325 – 27 July 1941, WO 208/4189, TNA.
159 I/SRN 169 – 18 October 1941, WO 208/4189, TNA.
160 SRIG 267 – 8 September 1943, WO 208/4187, TNA.
161 I/SRN 70 – 24 May 1941, WO 208/4189, TNA.
162 I/SRN 65 – 20 July 1941, WO 208/4189, TNA.
163 Basil Liddell Hart, *The Other Side of the Hill* (London: Cassell, 1951); Shelford Bidwell, 'The Gentleman versus the Players', *Journal of the RUSI*, 121 (1976), 82–83; Corelli Barnett, *The Desert Generals* (London: Phoenix, 1983).
164 I/SRM 59 – 22 August 1943, WO 208/4188, TNA.
165 I/SRM 19 – 20 June 1943, WO 208/4188, TNA.
166 SRIG 196 – 3 August 1943, WO 208/4186, TNA.
167 I/SRA 22 – 12 August 1941, WO 208/4184, TNA.
168 I/SRM 40 – 6 July 1943, WO 208/4188, TNA.
169 Dino Alfieri quoted in Rodogno, *Empire*, 39.
170 Luca Pietromarchi in Rodogno, *Empire*, 39.
171 Rodogno, *Empire*, 38–39.
172 I/SRN 516 – 1 September 1942, WO 208/4190, TNA.
173 The use of 'revolvers' (*le rivoltelle*), here and throughout the CSDIC (UK) protocols (see: 88, 108, 116, 181, 185 EXACT PAGE NUMBERS?) is curious given the long-standing preference in the German – and Italian – military for magazine-fed semi-automatic pistols. I/SRM 12 – 19 June 1943, WO 208/4188, TNA.
174 SRIG 41 – 27 May 1943, WO/4185, TNA.
175 Sadkovich, 'Of Myths and Men', 296–301. Other examples of this behaviour can be seen in: Michael Burleigh, *Moral Combat: A History of World War II* (London: HarperPress, 2010), 315–316.
176 I/SRM 3 – 15 June 1943, WO 208/4188, TNA.
177 Thompson, *White War*, 1.
178 I/SRX 80 – 22 March 1943, WO 208/4193, TNA.
179 I/SRN 729 – 22 December 1942, WO 208/4190, TNA.
180 I/SRN 1082 – 6 March 1943, WO 208/4191, TNA.
181 At the 'Birth of the Fascist Movement' at the Piazza San Sepolcro on 23 March 1919, Mussolini's first declaration was to 'extend [...] greetings and [...] reverent and unforgetful thoughts first of all to those sons of Italy who have given their lives for the

grandeur of the fatherland and the freedom of the world.' Benito Mussolini, 'The Birth of the Fascist Movement (Piazza San Sepolcro 9, Milan, March 23 1919),' in Charles Delzell, ed., *Mediterranean Fascism, 1919–1945* (New York: Walker & Company, 1971), 7–8.
182 I/SRN 398 – 9 August 1942, WO 208/4189, TNA.
183 I/SRN 337 – 30 July 1942, WO 208/4189, TNA.
184 I/SRA 7 – 23 November 1940, WO 208/4184, TNA.
185 I/SRA 18 – 14 November 1940, WO 208/4184, TNA.
186 J.E. Kaufmann and Robert Jurga, *Fortress Europe: European Fortifications of World War II* (Cambridge: DaCappo, 2009), 193.
187 GSI. HQ 10 Armoured Division Intelligence Summary No. 23, 20 July 1942, THF/C/5/1/1/3, KMMSC.
188 I/SRA 6 – 8 November 1940, WO 208/4184, TNA; X/SRX 2 – 28 November 1940, WO 208/4194, TNA; X/SRX 7 – 25 August 1941, WO 208/4194, TNA.
189 I/SRX 19 – 12 August 1941, WO 208/4193, TNA.
190 I/SRX 22 – 17 January 1943, WO 208/4193, TNA.
191 I/SRN 670 – 10 November 1942, WO 208/4190, TNA.
192 I/SRA 20 – 16 December 1940, WO 208/4184, TNA.
193 I/SRX 59 – 16 March 1943, WO 208/4193, TNA.
194 I/SRN 28 – 13 December 1940, WO 208/4189, TNA.
195 Brian Sullivan, 'The Italian Soldier in Combat, June 1940–September 1943: Myths, Realities and Explanations' in Paul Addison and Angus Calder, eds., *Time to Kill: The Soldier's Experience of War in the West, 1939–1945* (London: Pimlico, 1997), 204.
196 See also: Quartararo, *tra Londra*; Goeschel, *Alliance*.
197 Claudia Baldoli, 'Italian Fascism in Britain: The *Fasci all'Estero*, the Italian Communities, and Fascist Sympathisers during the Grandi Era (1932–1939)', PhD Thesis, LSE (London, 2002), 74, 92, 131–135.
198 Cassels, 'Tradition and Novelty', 257–260.
199 Renzo De Felice, *Mussolini il Duce: II, Lo Stato Totalitario, 1936–1940* (Turin: Einaudi, 1981), 332–335, 465–467, 625–793.

4 Occupation, war crimes and antisemitism

Introduction

From research on the German protocols, we know that discussion of war crimes and atrocities amongst the prisoners of war was common. The works of Neitzel and Welzer devote considerable attention to conversations between German POWs on the murder of POWs of all nationalities, the notorious 'Commissar Order' of 6 June 1941, rape and sexual violence, the summary execution of German deserters and many aspects of the Holocaust.[1] This is not surprising. The myth of the 'clean *Wehrmacht*' was greatly undermined by the work of the Hamburg Institute for Social Research with their influential exhibitions in the 1990s and 2000s. They showed without a doubt that a great number of German military personnel had knowledge of such crimes against humanity or were directly implicated in them.[2] However, the content of these transcripts remains deeply shocking even 70 years on. For example, the re-collections of Oberleutnant Wilde who described the aftermath of an SS massacre of some 35 women.[3] Or, for instance, the words of Generalmajor Walter Bruns and Generalleutnant Heinrich Kittel who detailed the murder of Jews at Riga and Dvinsk – 'they seized three-year-old children by their hair, held them and shot them with a pistol and then threw them in. I saw that for myself.'[4] The content of these protocols is disturbing. They demonstrate just how candid the German POWs could be in their discussions of atrocities. The horrors they witnessed and committed were not obscured through euphemism and allusive language but were baldly stated with a clear and unrelenting voice.

A 18 November 1942 CSDIC (UK) report on 'Enemy Atrocities' outlined that by this date the Centre had collected 105 reports containing evidence of German atrocities against Norwegians, Poles, Russians, Czechs, Yugoslavs, French, Belgians, Dutch, Jews and POWs, as well as many other instances of 'indiscriminate bombing, machine gunning, sinking etc.' Tellingly, this same report only mentions one protocol that concerns *Italian* atrocities, one 'against the Red Cross' – I/SRA 40.[5] It is likely that this refers to a July 1942 conversation that took place between Petty Officer Boschin (I/N 176) and Petty Officer Marchiol (I/N 177) where one of them confessed to stealing British Red Cross parcels: 'on January 2nd I left for Berlin to fetch the parcels for the rest of you – the English P/W's parcels.'⁶ It is clear these two were not the only Italian POWs to have discussed war crimes. Several other protocols were removed from their original files and replaced with the note 'see atrocities file in Captain Marsh's office.'⁷ With the possible exception of I/SRA 40 it has not been possible to track down these 'relocated' protocols. Nonetheless, their existence strengthens the argument that although the Italian armed forces may not have been the equals of the Wehrmacht and SS for the scale and intensity of their brutality and savagery, they *were* complicit in war crimes.

This is observed in other, unredacted, transcripts. For example, a fighter pilot captured in November 1940 (I/A 1) made it clear that Italians intervened in the fighting in France in advance of the formal declaration of war – 'we were helping Germany before we entered the war. They sent 27 a/c [aircraft] to the Fiat for repairs […] we were in the campaign in France. We were over Lyons and we machine-gunned Toulon.' On one occasion I/A 1 disobeyed orders from his commanding officer to not engage the French, as he said 'who wouldn't fight when he sees the enemy buzzing round. And then, up there I'm in command. No Major, no God almighty – I'm there alone.'⁸ Midshipman Devescovi (I/N 334) made it clear that some Italian submarines had little problem in attacking neutral shipping – 'In November 1941, off Melilla, we sank a Spanish steamer which was carrying contraband for England.' He went on to say that 'when you know that ships are carrying contraband you can't be expected not to sink them. We're not such fools as all that. We'd sink them even if they were sailing under the flag of the Vatican City.'⁹

There is some evidence to suggest an element of self-censorship on the topic of atrocities. In Osti Guerrazzi's analysis of the transcripts from high-ranking officers, there is the suggestion of a conspiracy of silence – the scant mentions of occupation policies and crimes underlining the 'total will to forget the responsibilities of the *Regio Esercito* in the ideological war fought alongside the Nazis.' For instance, General Orlando (I/M 3) makes no mention of his experiences commanding a division of Sardinian Grenadiers which fought in Ljubljana from May 1941 to September 1942. Field-Marshal Messe (I/M 2) says 'almost nothing' of his experience commanding the Italian Expeditionary Force in Russia. These convenient omissions are diagnosed as the deliberate 'cancellation of any sense of guilt and the lack of any critical rethinking' of these men's pasts.¹⁰ However, as we shall see, other Italian prisoners were far less tight-lipped.

The protocols may not contain a comprehensive record of all the crimes committed by this cohort, but the argument of Italian complicity in such crimes will be considered throughout this chapter as Italian atrocities are discussed alongside their relationship with antisemitism and the actions of Italians as occupiers in Yugoslavia, Greece and France. Atrocities committed by Italians in the protocols are by no means one of the main topics of discussion, and they often lack the detail of the German counterparts, but the transcripts do make it clear that there was a significant awareness of the 'dark side' of the Italian war effort – knowledge of war crimes was commonplace.

92 *Occupation, war crimes and antisemitism*

A distinction should be made between those CSDIC (UK) POWs who were actively involved in committing such illegal acts, and those who were aware of them – on occasion even blasé about them – but who were not actually complicit. While protocols contain examples of both the latter are far the more numerous. Individuals are responsible as much for their inactions as their actions and the terrible human cost of Italian inaction is powerfully made in the example of Croatia. Imperial expansionism was at the heart of Fascist foreign policy, and thus the record of Italian troops in their newly acquired wartime empire is an important issue. It is clear from what follows that many of the Italian forces of occupation across Southern Europe were not motivated by shared humanity with fellow Mediterranean peoples, but by far baser instincts – greed, lust, cruelty and callousness, alongside self-preservation and opportunism. The reality of life under Italian occupation from 1940 to 1943 was much darker than the *Italiani brava gente* myth would suggest.

Occupation – Greece and the Balkans

By 27 April 1941, the German invasion of Greece was almost complete. With the Swastika flying above the Acropolis, the country was carved up into occupation zones: the Germans taking the strategically important areas of Crete, Athens, Thessaloniki (Salonika), Central Macedonia and several Aegean Islands; the Bulgarians annexed East Macedonia and Thrace; the Italians took responsibility for the remainder of the country, a vast territory that amounted to two-thirds of Greece.[11] This was a region diverse in both geography and ethnicity, with the population divided into Greek, Jewish, Bulgarian, Armenian, Aromanian and Muslim Ciamuriota.[12] The Italian occupation of these regions would last for 29 months, until Italy's surrender in September 1943.[13] Italy's treatment of the local population throughout this period has been described as one 'marked by systematic violations of the laws of war and of international human rights.'[14] It bears remembering that when Italy invaded in October 1940, Greece had been a neutral power.

During the occupation, Italian armed forces were responsible for the slaughter of thousands of civilians in policies of 'organised military violence,' such as the 16 February 1943 massacre of Domenikon where at least 150 Greeks were shot to avenge the deaths of nine Italian soldiers in a partisan ambush.[15] The Italian concentration camp at Larissa was the site of extreme violence. Prisoners were regularly tortured to death and by 8 September 1943 over 1000 hostages had been sent to the firing squads at the camp.[16] Lieutenant Graff (I/M 27) of the 1st Regiment of Paratroops, may have believed that 'we treated [the Greeks] very well, woe betide anyone who raised a finger against a Greek,' but this does not sit well with the historic record.[17] In all an estimated 9000 Greeks were executed in the Italian zone of occupation.[18]

The dominant image of the Italian occupation of Greece painted by the CSDIC protocols is of a regime characterized by scandal, incompetence and corruption, even if the transcripts do not reveal horrors of camps like Larissa.[19] In the opinion of naval Captain Franchi (I/N 404), 'the one idea of our people in Greece was to have an easy time.'[20] His cellmate, Captain Bernardini (I/N 397) – the former Governor of Lampedusa – agreed enthusiastically. He recalled that 'all the officers at Italian headquarters in Greece got involved with ladies of good social position who were acting as spies.' According to Bernardini the situation provoked outrage when it became known in Rome, and the subsequent inquiry showed 'that they had all behaved like fools,' prioritising the 'amorous affections' of their mistresses above basic security concerns.[21]

This was not idle gossip, a June 1943 investigation undertaken by former navy chief Admiral Cavagnari records in detail the rampant financial, disciplinary and sexual improprieties committed by senior Italian officers in Greece. These allegations led to the dismissal of dozens from the Italian headquarters, including its Commander-in-Chief, General Carlo Geloso.[22] In Bernardini's opinion this situation easily explained the German successes in Greece following Operation *Achse* – the neutralising of the Italian military in the wake of the 8 September 1943 surrender. The commanders of the Italian forces of occupation were supposedly little more than 'stupid old idiotic fossils who had failed even in the elementary duty of setting an example.'[23] As is shown here – and will be demonstrated in greater length in the discussion of the Italian presence in Bordeaux – sexual relations between occupied and occupier were more than just a pastime. It was an integral aspect of the occupation power dynamic.

If a conversation between Sub-Lieutenant Budini (I/N 373) and Engineer Lieutenant Francesali (I/N 377) is to be believed, lurid sex scandals were matched by rampant profiteering. Francesali told of a relative, a lowly private soldier, who was able to make 100000 lira exploiting a loophole in the exchange rate between the lira and Greek drachma. Budini confirmed that almost everyone was profiting from this scheme, even the Governor of Greece. He also claimed that Count Ciano had bought islands in the Ionian from the funds he generated from this. The situation got so bad that the Bank of Italy 'protested, because there was a danger of inflation.'[24] Despite Budini's naval rank he had been attached to the Italian Air Force. This may explain his awareness of a smuggling ring that brought high-end black market goods into Greece. With the full cooperation of airfield commanders in Italy and Greece, planes would be sent to Taranto for unnecessary 'overhauling' so that they could return with valuable cargoes, such as furs, with values that could run into the millions of drachmas.[25] In another instance that evokes the surreal cynicism of *Catch-22*,[26] Budini told the tale of a naval officer who stole so much public and private property during his time in Greece that he chartered a transport ship to take all of his ill-gotten gains back to Italy. Unfortunately for the officer in question, his plan was discovered, an inquiry was instigated and the goods seized. Instead of the goods being returned to their rightful owners however, the President of the Court of Inquiry took it for himself.[27]

The impact of the economic misconduct inflicted on the Greek people by Italian forces should not be understated. The transgressions of the Italian occupation were more than torture and massacres. Both Germany and Italy strong-armed the Bank of Greece into paying huge occupation expenses. Between April 1941 and October 1942 these amounted to 32 billion drachma to the Italians and 92 billion to the Germans. The payments for the year 1941–2 amounted to more than 113 percent of Greece's annual national product, effectively bankrupting the country.[28] In the Ionian Islands, the devaluation of Greek currency and the accompanying hyperinflation destroyed the financial position of many so that by 1943 hunger was rampant.[29] The famine that ravaged the country during the war years was entirely a construct of the Axis occupation.[30] It has been calculated that by the end of the war the Greek population was 280000 to 300000 lower because of the starvation and malnourishment that were a direct result of Italian and German economic mismanagement.[31]

Greece was not the only country in the Eastern Mediterranean to face the trials and tribulations of Italian occupation. After the 6 April 1941 invasion of Yugoslavia, Italy occupied large parts of Croatia, Slovenia, Montenegro and coastal Dalmatia. Many key figures in the military and political administration of these territories such as the Governor of Dalmatia, Giuseppe Bastianini, the Governor of Montenegro, General Alessandro Pirzio Biroli, the commander of 11th Army Corps in Slovenia, General Mario Robotti and the commander of the 2nd Army in Yugoslavia, General Mario Roatta have been described as 'pioneers of repression.'[32] Approximately 90000 Yugoslavs were imprisoned in appalling conditions in Italian-run concentration camps where thousands would die.[33] On 1 March 1942 General Roatta published pamphlet '3C,' detailing the methods his commanders should use to repress the Yugoslavs, including summary executions, reprisals, hostage taking and the burning of settlements. This decree stood in direct violation of both the 1899 and 1907 Hague Conventions and was written to undermine the idea of the Italian occupier as a 'buono Italiano.'[34] For all that the Italian authorities in the Balkans did prevent Jewish communities from being handed over to the Germans before 1943, the fact remains that the Italians in Yugoslavia could match their ally in their wretched treatment of the occupied Slavs.[35]

The discussion of the events in the Balkans in the protocols underline the extent of Italian brutality in the region. Lieutenant Paladini (I/N 298) believed that 'we've turned everybody in Yugoslavia against us, thanks to our army of occupation.'[36] Chief Boatswain Bergadono (I/N 343) said, 'we're paying dearly for our occupation of Yugoslavia now [...] for the last two years they've been massacring our soldiers. If you go there, you see everything burnt up with flame-throwers.'[37] A Sergeant-Major in the 1st Regiment of Paratroops (I/M 29) described his experiences in Montenegro. Although safe inside their fortified positions, his unit faced fierce attacks whenever they left. Whole units could find themselves surrounded and totally destroyed – 'in one place where the Alpini went [the partisans] did a whole battalion of them, they cut them to pieces [...] they burnt a lot of Alpini alive by pouring petroleum over them, then they quartered them, and some were buried up to their necks [...] they died like that.'[38] On another occasion he came across, 'people with their hands cut off, people who had been quartered and hanged on trees, or with their hearts stuck in their mouths.' His unit came across Italian remains in pigsties – 'they even fed their pigs on us.'[39] It was not that this soldier was without compassion, but rather that it was reserved for Italians – his comrades. There was no sensitivity to his account of heavy-handed Italian anti-partisan tactics, 'we followed on behind them and did the final mopping up with hand-grenades and set fire to the place. In fact we destroyed entire villages.' All-in-all this soldier remained totally disillusioned with what he had been a part of, 'it's no use denying, we couldn't possibly make a success out of it in Montenegro.'[40]

Lacking much contextual detail, it is a challenge to assess the reliability of these specific accounts. But, that they were not disputed by anyone who heard them suggests that they reflected an experience of violent occupation that the CSDIC (UK) cohort were familiar with. Furthermore, there is ample evidence to support the argument that the occupied Balkans was a place of pitiless and cruel warfare where Italian units committed atrocities as a matter of policy. Roatta's March 1942 '3C' pamphlet was a 'manifesto for repression' rooted in earlier Italian policies of colonial repression and Fascist racism towards the Slavs.[41] Between July and August 1942 Robotti's troops in Slovenia summarily executed 1236 suspected partisans, alongside 1053 killed in combat and 1381 captured, for the loss of 139 wounded and 43 dead Italians.[42] Robotti was the sort of commander to complain that his officers were 'not slaughtering enough people.'[43] On 5 November 1942, the 11th Army Corps boasted of causing 7000 enemy casualties. Its statistics however did not distinguish civilian from combatant deaths or civilian hostages executed in reprisal for partisan actions.[44]

The brutality of Italian occupation policy is made clear by a Sub-Lieutenant from the submarine *Asteria* (I/N 376) in April 1943. He described how a gunman disguised as a priest shot and killed the 'Parish Priest of Lubiana' and his nephew, before escaping. In reprisal, the Italian authorities shot 25 communist prisoners in batches of five each day, every time demanding that the shooter give himself up – a clear example of the cold, calculated yet ultimately counter-productive anti-Partisan tactics enacted by the Italians throughout occupied Slovenia.[45] Both the Sub-Lieutenant and his cellmate (I/N 377) agreed that the blame for these deaths remained squarely with the resistance and not the Italian authorities.[46] Revealingly I/N 376 went on to vilify Yugoslavs as a 'vile people' who 'make national instinct, of which they have none, an excuse to give vent to their bestial instincts, that's the truth. There may be genuine patriots amongst them, but the majority are nothing but brigands.'[47] Derogatory language was also used by high-ranking Italian

Generals to describe a number of the ethnic groups in the region. The Croats were labelled as 'scoundrels' while another said the Serbs had 'a certain primitive naiveté [sic.] despite all their barbarity.'[48] These outbursts confirm how in the 'Fascist environment of hate,' Italian military leaders had been heavily influenced by a long-standing racist narrative that presented the people of the Balkans as 'a dark and foreboding spectre,' lawless, immoral, primitive and uncivilised.[49]

The protocols reject the arguments of those in the immediate post-war era who were keen to present ordinary Italian soldiers and their 'honourable' commanders as incapable of atrocities. In 1947 Luigi Longo claimed, 'it never could have been the Italian infantrymen, alpinists, or bersaglieri to obey the orders to burn a village or shoot women and children: these were actions only the Germans and fascists could have carried out.'[50] While in 1946 Roatta himself defended Italian conduct: 'Italians war criminals? At most one can admit to soldiers stealing a few chickens (or pigs) during battle without the knowledge of their superiors [...].'[51] In reality Italian personnel at all levels were perfectly capable of racism, cruelty and murderousness in the Balkans. There is no great disconnect between the content of these transcripts and the beliefs of those like Ciano, that dissenting Albanian intellectuals must be sent to concentration camps – 'there must not be the least sign of weakness.' Or the Italian general who said to his troops as they arrived in the Balkans, 'I have heard that you are good family men. That's very well at home, but not here. Here, you will never go too far in being thieves, murderers and rapists.'[52] War crimes were not just committed by Blackshirts and Germans, even if so many of those like Roatta avoided facing justice at the end of the war.[53]

The Independent State of Croatia (*Nezavisna Država Hrvatska*, or *NDH*), founded on 10 April 1941 and governed by the ultra-nationalist Ustaše regime of Ante Pavelić, has a well-earned reputation for bloodshed. With a political ideology that 'postulated a demonized concept of the Serb,' Pavelić directed a merciless campaign to engineer a 'final solution' for the two million Orthodox Serbs who lived in the NDH.[54] The United States Holocaust Memorial Museum has calculated that Croat authorities were directly responsible for the deaths of between 12000 and 20000 Jews, 25000 Roma and over 320000 ethnic Serbs.[55] The Jasenovac concentration camp, described as 'the Yugoslav Auschwitz,' was the site of some of the worst of these atrocities.[56] The Jasenovac Memorial Site has painstakingly compiled a list of 83145 named victims, of whom 20101 were children under the age of 14.[57]

Knowledge of such persecution is demonstrated in a conversation between three Italian generals. General of Artillery Belletti (I/M 6) recalled that 'when they founded the Kingdom of Croatia in April [1941], they started off with the idea of suppressing two million adherents of the Orthodox Church, and they killed 350,000.'[58] A remarkably accurate calculation. Belletti went on, 'do you know they went around with orders to see who could kill the most, including women and children, without distinction.'[59] Commander of XX Corps General Orlando (I/M 3) confirmed this, mentioning a story he had been told 'about a woman whose stomach they opened, and how a live child came out.'[60] The officers in question agreed that these atrocities took place while the government in Rome was 'shutting an eye to it.'[61] What is particularly important here is that these senior officers *were* aware of the depraved politics of the Pavelić regime. In this way they do confirm a model of Italian military opinion outlined by Trifković that suggests Italian officers were deeply shocked at what the saw in Croatia. Which may go some way to explain why in the summer of 1941 the Ustaše were 'pushed out of the zone under Italian control' in a move that provided greater security to Serbian communities.[62]

Just because some senior Army officers were appalled by what was happening in Croatia does not mean that Italian forces can be absolved of complicity in the crimes of the Ustaše regime. While it can be argued that the Italian position in Croatia was eventually eclipsed by the Germans,[63] the NDH was a formal Protectorate of the Kingdom of Italy between 1941 and 1943. Furthermore, the killing of thousands of Serbs, Jews, Roma and others did not stop after Pavelić's officials were removed from the Italian zone in 1941. Until the 1943 surrender, Italy maintained a formidable presence in Croatia and it is hard to argue that they did all they could to halt the bloodshed. The Italian military had a clear responsibility for what happened in their sphere of influence. This gets to the core of Italy's position as an occupying power across this region. It is important that Mussolini's troops shoulder responsibility for their inactions as much as their actions, and for all that they might not have been the most sadistic or brutal, the charges of atrocity that can be levelled against them *are* extensive. The legacy of the Italian occupation of the Balkans can be put into wider historical significance when one considers just how much the inter-ethnic bloodshed of the 1990s Yugoslav Wars was underpinned by the 'shattering memory of the Second World War' in the region.[64]

On Jews and antisemitism

On 29 November 1940, a conversation took place between a captured German fighter pilot (A 633) and an Italian submarine officer (I/N 22). Amid discussions of convoy escort duties and Cretan coastal defences, the Italian officer remarked that 'there is only one people that must be exterminated: the Jews, who have wronged the whole world.'[65] Seven decades later this comment remains shocking, not least of all for the violence of its language. This sentiment also casts a light on the continuing debate about Italian complicity in the extermination of European Jews. This Italian officer was not the only one in the CSDIC (UK) cohort to harbour antisemitic views. In January 1941 a *Tenente di Vascello* in the 10th *Flotilla MAS* (I/N 23) said, 'all the Jews are mobilised against us, and the Jews are in possession of 80 percent of the wealth of the world.'[66] The language of I/N 23's antisemitism overlooks the biological racism of the 14 July 1938 *Manifesto della Razza* and the subsequent *Leggi Razziali* which the Fascist regime had sought to instill in Italian minds through widely distributed publications like *La Difesa della Razza*.[67] I/N 23 preferred the longstanding – and enduring – an antisemitic canard that Jews form a threatening global financial cabal.[68] While calls to outright violence towards Jewish people were rare amongst the transcripts there is a vein of antisemitism that runs through many of the POWs' discussions of Jewish people. Just because I/N 22 was the only one to outwardly support a Jewish genocide does not mean that this group was above antisemitism.

In January 1943 Midshipman Devescovi (I/N 334) said that he could 'never understand' the anti-Jewish campaign that Mussolini undertook from 1938.[69] This was a campaign that turned against a group that had played a key role in the early years of Italian Fascism. About 230 Jews were officially present in March on Rome, and in 1930 one in four Italian adult Jews were PNF members, in contrast to 10 percent of the rest of the population.[70] The persecution of Italian Jews between 1938 and 1943 saw them stripped of their civil rights, especially those relating to education, employment and property. While they were not at risk of outright murder by the government at this time, the lists of Italian Jews created to help enforce the Racial Laws proved invaluable to the Nazis as they sought to round up all Jews in the Italian Social Republic between 1943 and 1945. Thousands would subsequently be killed in the German camps.[71]

Previously stationed in Poland, Petty Officer Marchiol (I/N 177) was unimpressed with the restrictions put in place by the Germans on the movement of Poles and Jews.[72] On 12 June 1943, Lieutenant Colacicchi (I/M 5), Aide-de-Camp to Field-Marshal Messe, described the German programme of forcible sterilisation of Jews as 'wrong from the beginning.'[73] In his opinion the Jews had not 'bothered' Italy as they had the Reich.[74] Colacicchi believed the majority of Jews in Italy were 'true Italians,' and most of them who had fled abroad were 'Italians first and Jews second.'[75] Colacicchi's comments reveal a number of antisemitic underpinnings. Just because they were not in Italy, Jews are nonetheless 'bothersome' elsewhere. Additionally, you can question the extent to which Colacicchi would have retained his sympathies for Italian Jews had he considered their allegiances to have been principal to their Jewish identity rather than to the Italian nation. This points to a longstanding antisemitic mistrust of Jewish identity as a threat to traditional ideas of patriotism.[76]

Sympathy for Jewish people amongst the CSDIC (UK) cohort could be both conditional on their patriotism and underpinned by unflattering stereotypes. This can be seen in a conversation that took place between four naval personnel in April 1943. Sub-Lieutenant Budini (I/N 373) was clear that 'it was really disgusting to prohibit Jewish boys from attending schools.' He went on to say that,

> They are all very capable people, I don't know what it is, but they always get on. And as they are becoming assimilated and are becoming Italians, why not leave them alone? Because they are in touch with international

financial circles and have great power. By doing this we have made enemies for ourselves at home and especially in America, where they are behind everything. [...] they are powerful not only in industry and commerce but also in politics.[77]

According to this perspective, the reason why the Fascist state should not have persecuted this minority was not because doing so was cruel or immoral, but because it made an enemy of a powerful global Jewish community. An argument that is rooted in an antisemitic view of the supposedly pernicious influence of Jews in global politics, economics and commerce. Budini evidently had a level of sympathy and admiration for Italian Jews. He viewed them as hard-working, successful and prepared to 'become' Italian. However, this was a process by which they would have become 'less' Jewish. This hardly reflects a progressive view of Jewish identity. Their value in Budini's eyes was conditional on their contribution to *la patria* as opposed to their inherent worth as human beings.

A Sub-Lieutenant in the submarine *Asteria* (I/N 376) was similarly unhappy that a Jewish sailor in the submarine *Ametista* had been forcibly demobilised. He said, 'in the *Ametista* there was a Jewish sailor from Leghorn and an order came from the higher command to send him to the depot to be demobilized. The lad wept. I am sure that an Italian Jew is an Italian, and not (first and foremost) a Jew.'[78] This officer was clearly unhappy as many Jews had 'fought in the last war as officers, some were decorated for bravery, some of them behaved very well, they lived industrious lives, they were doctors, engineers, professional men, and then they say: "This man is a Jew." But damn it, does all a man has done count for nothing? Has it no value?'[79] Like Colacicchi, Budini and others, this officer was without a doubt sympathetic to Jews who faced oppression under the Fascist regime. But the transcripts do give a sense that this sympathy had its limits and could be conditional on social position, military service and patriotic sentiment.

The protocols do not tell us much about how the Italian armed forces 'protected' Jewish people in their zones of occupation.[80] But they do corroborate much of what Steinberg says about the ethos that underpinned the acts of 'national resistance' by which many Jews were not given up to the Nazis. These acts,

> Took place in the face of a great evil and was carried out by people who were [...] often precisely the same people who interned and tortured innocent Slovene and Croatian civilians. They were no angels nor were many of them free of the guilt of crimes committed in the name of Fascism or Italian imperialism. Many of them disliked Jews. Others were indifferent. They agreed out of a mixture of horror, humanity, prestige, sense of honour, military necessity and self-interest that there was a border beyond which they could not and would not go.[81]

The majority views expressed in the transcripts are neither those of unprejudiced *Italiani brava gente* nor of *Einsatzgruppen* in Italian uniform. They are those of a middle ground, presenting a culture of severe antisemitism, even if it ignored much of the racial rhetoric expounded by the regime and even if it lacked the murderous intent of Nazism. None of this however should obscure the very real suffering faced by Jews at Italian hands from 1938 to 1943. It would take until January 1944 before the antisemitic legislation of Fascism was revoked by Prime Minister Badoglio.[82]

Occupation – Bordeaux

The Italian occupation of France lasted from June 1940 to September 1943 and grew to incorporate the eight south-western French *departments*.[83] Part of the German zone of occupation, Bordeaux was nonetheless home to 3000 Italian submariners, *San Marco* marines, *Carabinieri*, technicians and senior commanders of the *11° Gruppo di Sommergibili*.[84] Fighting alongside the German 12 U-Boat Flotilla, which arrived on 15 October 1942, this garrison formed the BETASOM submarine base from which several dozen Italian submarines would go on to sink or seriously damage 112 Allied ships between September 1940 and September 1943. These were victories that cost the *Regia Marina* 15 submarines of their own and the lives of 751 Italian seamen.[85] The operational history of BETASOM has been well-charted.[86] However, historians have overlooked the interactions of Italian service personnel with the population of Bordeaux. They are not considered in the research of Robène, Bodin, Héas, Langeo and Soo, and receive only a fleeting mention by Bécamps.[87] This conforms to a wider historiographic trend identified by Varley whereby relations with Italy and the presence of Italians are overlooked in histories of the occupation.[88]

Given the over-representation of naval personnel within the CSDIC (UK) Italian cohort it is of little surprise that there are dozens of protocols that include discussion of life in the Bordeaux naval base. This concentration of transcripts covers a variety of issues, from the massive increase in the price of champagne, wine and cognac under occupation to the graphic aftermath of RAF bombing raids.[89] However, this sub-chapter will be primarily used as an extended case study to consider how Italian servicemen acted in their role as occupiers in France, as well as the complexity of Italo-German relations in Bordeaux. The experience of the submarine crews as they sailed down the Gironde estuary and into the Atlantic will be dealt with in Chapter Five.

The presence of these thousands of Italian naval personnel had a major impact on the lives of the *Bordelais* they encountered. This sub-chapter explores these relationships through the words of Italian submariners. The private conversations within the transcripts – which amount to very early oral testimony of the Italian forces in Bordeaux – reveal a tendency to present their experiences as characterised by violence and exploitation of the occupied French population. This is a view of the Italian man in uniform that undermines the myth of the *Italiani brava gente*. It also provides a new perspective on the wartime history of the city and those who occupied it and is representative of wider issues concerning the experience of Italian occupation and the attitudes of Italians as soldiers in this period.

It is important to note at the outset that the *San Marco* marines in particular were within the standards of the Italian military an 'elite' force – especially when compared to the under-trained and poorly equipped massed ranks of the conscript army.[90] Significantly for the tales of violence and brutishness recounted below, the proximity to similarly 'elite' German U-Boat personnel appears to have radicalised many Italians. Many BETASOM veterans – particularly the marines – would fight for the Italian Social Republic (RSI) between 1943 and 1945.[91] In all, some 3200 *San Marco* marines remained fighting for the Axis after 1943, but this was not universal. For instance, only around 100 of the thousand strong 'Caorle' marine battalion would follow suit in September 1943. Even amongst the much vaunted, *Decima Flottiglia MAS* commandos, only half of those stationed at their La Spezia headquarters chose to join the Germans at that time.[92] By highlighting the radicalism amongst Italian personnel in Bordeaux in particular, this expands on and develops the research of Capra Casadio, who has charted the strains of 'radicalisation' and 'fascistisation' that ran through many of the naval special units in the years preceding the 1943 armistice.[93]

Bordeaux: Encounters with the French

As the previous chapter made clear the Centre transcripts give a strong sense of the antipathy between Italians and French during the Second World War. The accounts given by several prisoners suggest that the relationship between Italian occupiers and French men in Bordeaux were no different – mutual hostility and violence were common. Petty Officer Marchiol (I/N 177) described an incident during which an inebriated Frenchman aggressively insulted him as a 'sale macaroni!'[94] Clearly not satisfied with mere verbal aggression: 'then he raised his hand to strike me. I gave him a shove and he tripped over the curb and finished up on the steps of the bar. He drew a knife and went for me.'[95] The assailant was soon restrained, arrested and beaten by the *Carabinieri*. According to Marchiol, when questioned the attacker confessed he was motivated primarily by hatred for the Italians. He was given a commuted death sentence and served three months in prison. Marchiol himself was given 'a maximum sentence of field punishment,' presumably for brawling with the Frenchman in the street.[96] The account of the attack, which did not suggest any great personal valor on the part of Marchiol, grants it an air of authenticity.

A February 1943 conversation between three naval Petty Officers (I/N 294, I/N 336 and I/N 350) shows the dangers faced by submarine crews based in Bordeaux, an almost constant climate of tension. As Petty Officer Pullio (I/N 336) said, in the wake of numerous lethal attacks against them, naval crews took up the habit of carrying sidearms as they moved through the city.[97] Ordinary Seaman Stefanni (I/N 131) confirmed this practice amongst BETASOM personnel. He said that, 'there's a lot of disorder at the Atlantic base [Bordeaux]. The sergeants and officers went about armed with revolvers (*le rivoltelle*) after there had been some cases of attacks made on one or two of them who were alone.' He went on to say, 'even the biggest fool carried a revolver down there, or a dagger or something.'[98] It reached a point where orders were issued from the commanders of BETASOM 'for everybody to be armed.'[99] Stefanni stated that when the 'civil population' initially began turning away from Italians on the street, even spitting on the ground as they passed, 'several of [the civilians] got beaten up – we didn't stand for that sort of treatment […] We were ordered to hit back. The commander said: "The first man who appears here in this base with a black eye will be sent back to Italy (in disgrace)".'[100] Street fights 'were just everyday routine.'[101] When it came to 'proper' conduct in an occupied territory, maintaining peace with the civil population was subordinated to upholding national honour by means of rough justice. Insults from the despised French against the Fascist ideal of the 'Italian warrior' were countered with direct violence. The Italians were expected to demonstrate their martial masculinity in such clashes.

While Bordeaux lacks a strong reputation for acts of resistance, the city was by no means a haven for Axis personnel. In August 1940 alone, a German sailor was killed, shots were fired at a German patrol and three people were arrested for subversive activity. In September, the telephone cable between La Rochelle and Royan was cut. All this took place before the establishment of an organised resistance framework.[102] The first successful SOE operation in occupied France – 'Josephine B' – took place in June 1941 in the Bordeaux suburb of Pessac, causing substantial damage to a power station and hampering BETASOM operations for weeks.[103] On 20 October 1941 the resistance killed a German *Feldkommandantur* officer with 98 French hostages shot in reprisal. On 21 October 1942, there was another killing of Axis personnel in Bordeaux.[104] Spanish Republican exiles working for the Organisation Todt were particularly prone to acts of violent resistance, acting as accessories to the shooting of the *Feldkommandantur* officer and mortally wounding another German officer with a sharpened key in 1941. They would go on to commit further attacks on the occupying forces in December 1942 and January 1943.[105]

Violence between Italian sailors and French civilians were issues of public order in a city that thronged with young men and women on the hunt for alcohol-soaked escapism. The Loire ports of Nantes and St. Nazaire have been described as 'a drinking and partying mecca,' where the 'freewheeling atmosphere could easily slip into drunken brawls.'[106] When in September 1941 two German soldiers were injured in such an altercation in Nantes, the investigating French police commissioner wrote: 'incidents often happen in these places because of the mingling of males and females and the abuse of alcohol.'[107] As the accounts of the CSDIC (UK) POWs demonstrate,

Bordeaux was no different. Whether the violence came from idealistic *résistants* or an inebriated Frenchmen riled by an Italian marine chatting up his girlfriend, Bordeaux – and many French cities like it – was a hive of danger to the Axis service personnel stationed there. This is a view of Italian occupation at odds with the rosy image of *Captain Corelli's Mandolin* or *Mediterraneo*.

Petty Officer Marchiol (I/N 177) 'loathed' the French and Spanish workmen he came across in Bordeaux. He said, 'they stood about doing nothing. If it was a question of smuggling, then they were ready enough [...] but for honest work they were useless.'[108] From a story that Chief Boatswain Pontone (I/N 254) told in January 1943, it is clear that tensions between the French population of Bordeaux and Italian naval personnel worsened in the aftermath of air raids by the RAF. As Italian sailors passed through the town in their uniforms, 'the French pelted us with tomatoes and rotten eggs and spat at us [...] the first evening the sailors just let things happen but on the second evening they jumped off the trams and there was a free fight.'[109] Sartre and Knapp have written of the anger amongst French civilians in the wake of Allied bombing raids.[110] Often this was directed at the bombers themselves, but it does make sense that it could also be aimed at the presence of the occupying forces who were, after all, the raid's primary target.

When one considers why this level of aggression developed there are several possible political explanations. In addition to simply being an occupying force, the Italians' belated entry into the war and their poor military performance along the *Ligne Alpine* in June 1940 resulted in a French tendency to deny Italy's legitimacy as conqueror. The Germans had at least comprehensively defeated the forces of the Third Republic on the battlefield. This bred a contempt towards the Italian presence, compounded by Italian smugness at finally being in control of long-desired French territory.[111] From the Italian perspective, the Fascist Government and its propaganda had identified France as one of Italy's foremost rivals during the interwar era.[112] Count Galeazzo Ciano's famous *Diario* abounds with references to efforts to stoke Francophobia amongst the Italian populace.[113]

Such Fascist propaganda rested on a long-standing historical foundation. Antagonism between Italy and France pre-dated even the unification of Italy, with French interventions throughout the nineteenth century repeatedly blocking *Risorgimento* efforts to wrest control of Rome from the Papacy.[114] In the mid-1930s, French political and public opinion was outraged by the Italian invasion of Abyssinia and intervention in the Spanish Civil War. From November 1936 to October 1938, France had even withdrawn its Ambassador from Rome in protest.[115] While it is unlikely that many French civilians would have pulled a knife on an Italian sailor exclusively to right the wrongs of the Second Italo-Abyssinian War, or that Italian submariners would go on violent benders as revenge for the injustices of the *Risorgimento* era, it seems probable that mutual antipathy between Italians and French men was underpinned both by personal tensions, sexual jealousies and political factors that pre-dated the outbreak of hostilities in the summer of 1940.

The shame of the 1940 defeat and subsequent occupations precipitated a crisis in French masculinity and virility that would go on to influence post-Liberation French society through the 'massive demonstration of sexual violence' against women accused of collaboration who had their heads publicly shaved as punishment.[116] The idea of the violence directed towards the Italian forces in Bordeaux also being based in a crisis in French masculinity is convincing especially given the fact that according to the protocols, sexual relations between French women and Italian sailors was very common. As the commander of the *Glauco* said, 'at Bordeaux all my crew managed to find girlfriends. They got on well with the French girls.'[117] This highly sexualised environment is reflected in the great many sexually explicit cartoons and jokes found amongst the pages of the *Vedetta Atlantica*, the BETASOM base newspaper made by submariners for submariners.[118]

Ordinary Seaman Stefanni (I/N 131) said that 'every Italian in Bordeaux had a mistress, from the ordinary seaman to the admiral.'[119] A radio-telegraphy Warrant Officer (I/N 65) described the dynamic, 'with all the husbands P/W in Germany and all the men missing, there are plenty of women in Bordeaux ready for a bit of fun.' His own mistress was the wife of a captured French pilot.[120] So numerous were these relationships that the military authorities established a dedicated office to destroy the effects of missing submariners. This was because, according to Sub-Lieutenant Villa (I/N 174), 'married men, especially, may have compromising letters and photographs.'[121] The military, in this case, placed the protection of these men's marital betrayal over transparency for families in Italy.[122]

There was genuine affection and even a level of innocence in some of these relationships. As Torpedo Rating Diddi (I/N 191) described, relations between Italian men and French women were not exclusively sexual. He spoke of an evening shared with some comrades and French women in a 'lock-in' at a Bordeaux restaurant, called *Giuliella's*. 'We made [the proprietor] shut the doors at eleven o'clock. We had brought a kilogram of Gorgonzola cheese with us [...]. We spent the whole night eating [...] we had a wonderful time.'[123] Petty Officer Paoli (I/N 175) said that some of the women 'got genuinely fond of us,' and that 'one or two of the older men lost their heads' when it came to French women. For example, he knew of one man who had refused to go back to his wife and family in Italy on leave because he wished to spend it with his mistress instead.[124] For all of the complications of occupation it is not a surprise that some individuals would seek company in this way as an escape from the drudgery and trauma of the war.

A similar phenomenon is observed between German prisoners of war and American women during the Second World War where 'the authorities had trouble keeping local girls away from the prisoners,' and searches of POW bunks would often uncover stashes of contraceptives.[125] Another example from this time were the forbidden sexual relationships between German women and the 1.5 million French POWs used as labourers throughout the Reich.[126] Whilst sexual fraternization with the occupiers could be motivated by a range of factors – financial, political, self-preservation – many French women did so for comparatively innocent reasons. As Madame Sandrine from Toulouse remembered,

> We had lived through a dismal period: women wanted to enjoy themselves, to push away all this dreariness, all the problems, especially in the towns. Who had the money to have a good time? The Occupying forces, the black-market racketeers, those who were making the big money.[127]

The Italian sailors stationed in Bordeaux, after all, found themselves in a country which had been abruptly stripped of some 1.5 million young Frenchmen.[128]

To argue that *all* such relations discussed in the transcripts were defined by affection would be misleading. There was a sinister side to many such encounters. As Petty Officer Paoli (I/N 175) mentioned, Italian sailors could exploit the genuine feelings felt towards them to borrow money from their admirers.[129] Petty Officer Marghetta (I/N 179) said, 'there's not a decent woman in Bordeaux – they're all prostitutes.'[130] That the level of sexual exploitation could descend to the grooming and rape of underaged girls is made clear by Ordinary Seaman Stefanni (I/N 131). He recalled that there reached a point when the Italians became 'fed up with going with women, so they [began] to run after young girls.'[131] Shortages of luxuries, money and even food in Bordeaux meant that all it could take to attract such girls were gifts of make-up or perfume.[132]

> Some girls they were, I can tell you! Bit by bit, they all went the same way! There was a shortage of food you see; they had no money, and stuff like a bottle of scent, for which they used to pay next to nothing, now costs a heap of money. [...] I bought six or seven litres and made a lot of little friends! [...] So I got to know a girl, and the second day I used to bring her a lip-stick or a little bottle of scented water; then to win her over completely you went to the cinema, and when you went in you made a sign to the proprietor, and he at once gave you a dark box [...] The girl would ask "why in here?" but she didn't go away. Then the fun began.[133]

Evidence of this dark side to Franco-Italian sexual relations gives valuable context as to why 'feelings against Italians were particularly strong after the Liberation.'[134] Stefanni's example of evident sexual exploitation involved the cooperation and collusion of French and Italian men. French women in this context were caught between foreign occupation and wider patriarchal oppression. They stood to be liberated from more than just Axis subjugation at the end of the war.[135]

For other Italian sailors, sex was directly purchased and prostitution became a booming industry in Bordeaux. One prisoner recalled speaking to one sex worker who had amassed savings of 40000 francs.[136] But it was evidently not without its risks. Petty Officer Villosio (I/N 188) reported that the availability of opiates in some Bordeaux brothels could turn their customers 'half crazy.'[137] Contracting sexually transmitted diseases was of course, another risk and it is clear from the protocols that they were rife amongst Italian personnel in Bordeaux. Seaman Stefanni (I/N 131) estimated that 'seventy percent of the Italians at Bordeaux had some form of venereal disease, and I can't tell you how many have been sent home suffering from syphilis.'[138] Sub-Lieutenant Villa (I/N 174) reported that, 'there were two hundred cases of syphilis amongst officers and petty officers in Bordeaux […] and as for gonorrhoea! It's got to the point that a man who hasn't caught gonorrhoea is looked upon as a fool.'[139] This was a state of affairs bluntly corroborated by Petty Officer Di Cesare (I/N 187) who claimed that, 'at Bordeaux everybody has gonorrhoea.'[140] Petty Officer Della Barbera was nostalgic for the days when one did not have to worry about such things. He blamed the Germans for the rise in sexually transmitted infections, saying 'there wasn't nearly so much venereal disease before they arrived in the port.'[141]

Prostitution was a recurring concern for the authorities in occupied France and given what is told in the Centre reports this seems only prudent. There was a well-developed system of regulated prostitution across the occupied zone, including Bordeaux. Yet so called 'covert' – unregulated – prostitution remained common and the target of many official clampdowns. For instance, a French police sweep in Angers uncovered 41 covert sex workers of whom 12 were infected with a sexually transmitted disease.[142] Outside of France, Italian health reports from Greece also expressed concern over high rates of venereal diseases amongst Italian garrisons, particularly in urban areas.[143]

Seaman Grosso (I/N 179) of the submarine *Glauco* – a vessel which operated across the Mediterranean and Atlantic – said that 'we all paid visits to the brothels before leaving' on a submarine patrol.[144] But as the following excerpts make clear the submarine crews that operated out of Bordeaux were far from the only units in the Italian Navy to make a habit of frequenting brothels. Nor were they the only Italian servicemen to pay a physical cost for doing so. Midshipman Gianni (I/N 250) described the situation at Cagliari where there was 'a lot of gonorrhoea. […] a friend of mine caught it and I went with the same girl a few days later.' He suffered from a similar fate in La Spezia where he said, 'once I went to a brothel with two friends and we all three got gonorrhoea.'[145] Gianni's candid admission underlines the absolute normality of venereal disease amongst Italian naval personnel, a cause neither of surprise nor of shame.

As Midshipman Manisco (I/N 297) of the 10th *Flotilla MAS* makes clear, it was a trend that could have an impact on the operational effectiveness of Italian vessels. He described how a submarine carrying Italian 'SLC' or *Maiale* human torpedoes was compromised when one of the torpedo's crew realised he had contracted gonorrhoea while ashore. This put him out of action and meant that a reserve crew had to be used for his SLC.[146] The Italian military were not alone in facing manpower problems as a result of hospitalization due to VD in the Second World War. In France in 1939 then General Montgomery issued a memorandum to his 3rd Division on the 'Prevention of Venereal Disease' following 44 cases admitted to the divisional Field Ambulances in just one month.[147] Amongst the US Army in Italy in April 1944 the 'VD rate' was approximately 163 per 1000 men, a rate five times the 'acceptable standard' calculated by the War Department and a level SHAEF medical officers thought could compromise Allied success.[148] This demonstrates a grubbier side to both the experience of the Allied 'good war' and the idea of the *Italiani brava gente* which conveniently overlook the contracting of and passing on of sexually transmitted diseases to the sexual partners of Italian servicemen.

Germans in Bordeaux

As the regional occupying power, and with the presence of the 12th U-Boat Flotilla, encounters with the Germans were common for the Italians stationed in Bordeaux. There is a case to be made that there was *some* level of camaraderie between German and Italian submariners in Bordeaux, perhaps a fraternity due to the shared extreme nature of their service. Seaman Stefanni (I/N 131) described the pomp and ceremony when his submarine returned to port. A band greeted them at the dock playing both the Italian national anthem and the 'Hitler march.' There was excitement, bread, wine, letters from home and even a crowd of enthusiastic Germans. 'They'd stick you, with your long beard, in the middle of forty Germans and take a photograph of you – it's a riot.'[149]

On another occasion Stefanni described how Germans and Italians would drink and talk together when they were on shore leave. The *Kriegsmarine* personnel could be very friendly to their counterparts, although Stefanni does admit that the Italians could become bored if the Germans spoke for too long. Nonetheless, he felt that this friendliness dried up after early Italian defeats in Africa. After that point, they apparently 'would no longer look at us.'[150] A dynamic in many ways mirrored at the highest level of Italo-German relations. By 1941, Hitler's one-time admiration of Mussolini as a forceful and dynamic man of action had been almost entirely undermined by Italy's growing string of military defeats, Mussolini's declining health and the corruption of the Italian fascist party. Amongst his generals at the Wolf's Lair, Hitler openly pitied Mussolini for his inability to bring the Italian monarchy to bear.[151]

Petty Officer Paoli (I/N 175) described how the Germans and Italians, 'kept aloof from one another,' as in Bordeaux 'the Germans are interested in drinking and nothing else.'[152] Paoli was captured along with all the other survivors of the submarine *Calvi* on 14 July 1942. This goes some way to support Stefanni's claim that by 1941–1942 a very real frostiness had developed between the personnel of the two allies. Others go even further in their descriptions of Italo-German antagonism. Chief Boatswain Pontone (I/N 254) recalled that Italians could be barred from entering the sophisticated air raid shelters built by the Germans around Bordeaux. Before one RAF raid four Italian sailors who had been quarantined with scabies were denied shelter by the Germans. All four of them were killed by British bombs as a result.[153] These accounts are reminiscent of the hostile relations between Italians and Germans already encountered in Chapter Three.

The brutality of German reprisals following acts of resistance is remarked upon by several Italians under observation. The Italians in Bordeaux appear divided in their reactions, with some disconcerted with the level of German violence. Pontone (I/N 254) commented on German brutishness when he recalled an incident when a tram refused to stop for him and a waiting German. In response, 'the German pulled out a revolver (*una rivoltella*) and started firing at the tram; he broke all the windows and wounded two people.' When the tram stopped, the German climbed on board, 'pointed [his pistol] at the driver and ordered all the passengers to get out [...] The German told me to get in [...] All the other passengers were left standing in the street.'[154] Petty Officer Grupposo (I/N 292) described how even minor infractions by the civil population could be punished by withholding meat for two weeks. More seriously, he reported that 11 Frenchmen were publicly executed by firing squad following accusations that they had been signaling to Allied bombers.[155] While both seem to be uncomfortable witnesses, neither Pontone nor Grupposo condemned these actions.

Petty Officer Spinelli (I/N 151) cited an even bloodier response to the shooting of a German Major in the city, whereby 50 people were shot and a substantial fine levied.[156] Yet there is evidence that Italian troops could join in with such violent – and illegal – occupation policies. Seaman Stefanni (I/N 131) reported that, 'when the air raid sirens went, both German and Italian pickets would go round firing at lighted windows.' This was done without warning and with no consideration of who was sheltering inside.[157] The men of the San Marco battalion – Italian marines – apparently 'used to set off in parties of six or seven in the evening as if they were going on a binge.'[158] Even accounting for the fact that the *San Marco* battalion was a particularly 'radical' unit, the trigger-happy nature of Italian marines in Bordeaux and the readiness of some to condone German repressive measures, is remarkable. German troops – especially those returning from service on the Eastern Front – had a well-documented habit of shooting up the French towns were they where billeted if 'provoked' by closed-up cafes and brothels, catching bystanders in the cross-fire.[159] It is a serious undermining of the *Brava Gente* myth that Italian marines indulged in the same trigger-happiness in Bordeaux.

Conclusion

As in Greece, corruption can be added to the burgeoning list of Italian vices in Bordeaux. A September 1942 conversation that took place between Warrant Officer Corvisiero (I/N 211) and Petty Officer Marchiol (I/N 177) revealed how luxuries sent from home for fighting units were pilfered by unscrupulous profiteers at the naval base. Just one instance of this was how an entire lorry load of panettone sent by the Motta organisation for submarine crews was taken instead by the Quartermaster at Bordeaux and sold in his stores for 40 francs apiece.[160] The site of widespread corruption, exploitation and violence, Bordeaux – as in Greece and Yugoslavia – suffered under the Italian presence between 1940 and 1943. Even though the words of the occupiers themselves – the very perpetrators of repression – this perspective has not obscured the grimness and brutishness of the Italian presence in the city.

Frequent bloody clashes with local men meant that personal protection was ensured by carrying sidearms and daggers. Perceived slights to Italian honour were met with officially sanctioned brute force and many Italian marines demonstrated little reluctance in joining their German colleagues in terrorising the local populace. Meanwhile, Bordeaux's women faced sexual exploitation on an almost systematic scale. The high rates of sexually transmitted infections and references to violent drug use make it clear that such encounters could be incredibly risky. That some Italian personnel pursued young girls removes any gloss provided by those French women and Italian men who were genuinely fond of each other. While lacking the concentration camps, massacres and wanton reprisals of Italian occupation policy in the Balkans, there is nonetheless a distinct grubbiness and bloodiness to the Italian military presence in Bordeaux, much of which had support from official channels. The transcripts reveal a side to the Italian experience of the Second World War that fundamentally contradicts the image of the *Italiani brava gente*.[161]

Notes

1. Neitzel, *Tapping*, 53–56, 167–236; Neitzel and Welzer, *Soldaten*, 74–119.
2. 'Crimes of the German Wehrmacht: Dimensions of a War of Annihilation, 1941–1944 – An Outline of the Exhibition', The Hamburg Institute for Social Research (Hamburg, 2004).
3. Special Extract from S.R. Draft No. 9116 – 25 September 1944, WO 208/4200, TNA.
4. Neitzel, *Tapping*, 202–210, 226–228.
5. CSDIC (UK), 'Enemy Atrocities', 18 November 1942, WO 208/4198, TNA.
6. Extract from S.R. Draft 2128, CSDIC (UK), 26 July 1942, WO 208/4198, TNA.
7. See: I/SRX 1, WO 208/4193, TNA; I/SRA 40, WO 208/4184, TNA; I/SRN 360, WO 208/4189, TNA; I/SRN 219, WO 208/4189, TNA; I/SRN 150, WO 208/4189, TNA.
8. I/SRX 6 – 3 December 1940, WO 208/4193, TNA.
9. I/SRN 925 – 18 January 1943, WO 208/4191, TNA.
10. Osti Guerrazzi, *odiare*, 7, 10–13, 238–279.
11. Violetta Hionidou, *Famine and Death in Occupied Greece, 1941–1944* (Cambridge: Cambridge University Press, 2006), 13.
12. Rodogno, *Empire*, 103–108.
13. See: Marco Clementi, *Camicie nere sull'Acropoli: l'occupazione italiana in Grecia (1941–1943)* (Rome: DeriveApprodi, 2013); Francesco Casati, *Soldati, generali e gerarchi nella Campagna di Grecia. Aspetti e tematiche di una guerra vista da prospettive differenti*

110 *Occupation, war crimes and antisemitism*

(Rome: Prospettiva, 2008). Fabio Verardo, *La campagna di Grecia di Guerrino Bragato alpino della Julia* (Udine: Aviani & Aviani, 2011) outlines the experience of a single Alpini unit during the Greek campaign.

14 Lidia Santarelli, 'Muted violence: Italian war crimes in occupied Greece', *Journal of Modern Italian Studies*, 9/3 (2004), 281.
15 Santarelli, 'Muted violence', 293.
16 Santarelli, 'Muted violence', 290–291.
17 I/SRM 53 – 7 August 1943, WO 208/4188, TNA.
18 Guido Knopp, *Die Wehrmacht - Eine Bilanz* (Munich: Goldmann, 2009), 193.
19 It is possible that files related to Larissa are amongst those which cannot be located. For more on Larissa and Italian-run concentration camps, see: Geoffrery Megargee, Joseph White and Mel Hecker, eds., *The United States Holocaust Memorial Museum Encyclopedia of Camps and Ghettos, 1933–1945: Vol III: Camps and Ghettos under European Regimes Aligned with Nazi Germany* (Bloomington: Indiana University Press, 2018), 389–558.
20 SRIG 293 – 13 September 1943, WO 208/4187, TNA.
21 SRIG 293 – 13 September 1943, WO 208/4187, TNA.
22 Report from Admiral Domenico Cavagnari to the Comando Supremo and Undersecretary of War, 16 June 1943, Binder H5 r. 34, Archivio dell'Ufficio Storico dello SME.
23 SRIG 293 – 13 September 1943, WO 208/4187, TNA.
24 I/SRN 1249 – 2 March 1943, WO 208/4192, TNA.
25 I/SRN 1249 – 2 March 1943, WO 208/4192, TNA.
26 Joseph Heller, *Catch-22* (London: Vintage, 2004).
27 I/SRN 1249 – 2 May 1943, WO 208/4192, TNA.
28 Rodogno, *Empire*, 233–234, 438.
29 Santarelli, 'Muted Violence', 289.
30 Santarelli, 'Muted Violence', 286.
31 Polymeris Voglis, 'Surviving Hunger: Life in the Cities and the Countryside during the Occupation', in Robert Gildea, Olivier Wievorka and Anette Warring, eds., *Surviving Hitler and Mussolini: Daily Life in Occupied Europe* (Oxford: Berg, 2006), 23.
32 James Burgwyn, 'General Roatta's war against the partisans in Yugoslavia, 1942', *Journal of Modern Italian Studies*, 9/3 (2004), 319. See also: Tobias Hof, 'Extreme Violence and Military Identity – The Italians on the Balkans (1941–1943)', *Zeitschrift für Genozidforschung. Strukturen, Folgen, Gegenwart kollektiver Gewalt*, 16/1 (2018), 57–84.
33 Burgwyn, 'Yugoslavia, 1942', 322.
34 Burgwyn, 'Yugoslavia, 1942', 314, 316, 319.
35 Burgwyn, 'Yugoslavia, 1942', 326.
36 I/SRN 731 – 23 December 1942, WO 208/4190, TNA.
37 I/SRN 962 – 6 February 1943, WO 208/4191, TNA.
38 I/SRX 107 – 7 July 1943, WO 208/4193, TNA.
39 I/SRX 107 – 7 July 1943, WO 208/4193, TNA.
40 I/SRX 107 – 7 July 1943, WO 208/4193, TNA.
41 Rodogno, *Empire*, 332–334.
42 Rodogno, *Empire*, 339.
43 Quoted in Morgan, *Fall*, 56.
44 Rodogno, *Empire*, 339.
45 Amedeo Osti Guerrazzi, *The Italian Army in Slovenia* (London: Palgrave and Macmillan, 2013).
46 I/SRN 1223 – 25 Apr, WO 208/4192, TNA.
47 I/N 376 echoes the language of the so-called 'Brigand Wars' of the 1860s, which were re-used to also describe Libyan and East African resistance. I/SRN 1223 – 25 Apr, WO 208/4192, TNA.

Occupation, war crimes and antisemitism   111

48 SRIG 54 – 2 June 1943, WO 208/4190, TNA; SRIG 56 – 3 June 1943, WO 208/4190, TNA.
49 Burgwyn, 'Yugoslavia, 1942', 324.
50 Luigi Longo, *Un popola alla macchia* (Milan: Mondadori, 1947), 66.
51 Mario Roatta, *Otto milioni di baionette* (Milan: Mondadori, 1946), 178–179.
52 Ciano, *War Diaries*, 82, 264.
53 Filippo Focardi and Lutz Klinkhammer, 'The Question of Fascist Italy's War Crimes: The Construction of a Self-Acquitting Myth (1943–1948)', *Journal of Modern Italian Studies*, 9/3 (2004), 332–336, 343–344.
54 Srdjan Trifković, 'Rivalry between Germany and Italy in Croatia, 1942–1943', *The Historical Journal*, 36/4 (1993), 879–904.
55 https://www.ushmm.org/wlc/en/article.php?ModuleId=10005456, accessed 19 October 2017.
56 See: Vladimir Dedijer, *The Yugoslav Auschwitz and the Vatican: The Croatian Massacre of the Serbs During World War II* (Buffalo: Prometheus Books, 1992) and Jovan Byford, "When I say 'The Holocaust,' I mean 'Jasenovac': Remembrance of the Holocaust in contemporary Serbia', *East European Jewish Affairs*. 37/1 (2007), 51–74.
57 http://www.jusp-jasenovac.hr/Default.aspx?sid=6711, accessed 19 October 2017.
58 SRIG 38 – 26 May 1943, WO 208/4185, TNA.
59 SRIG 38 – 26 May 1943, WO 208/4185, TNA.
60 SRIG 38 – 26 May 1943, WO 208/4185, TNA.
61 SRIG 38 – 26 May 1943, WO 208/4185, TNA.
62 Trifković, 'Rivalry', 881.
63 Trifković, 'Rivalry', 880.
64 Misha Glenny, *The Fall of Yugoslavia: The Third Balkan War* (London: Penguin, 1996), 27, 81–82, 89–90, 140, 205–206, 283; Lenard Cohen, *Broken Bonds: The Disintegration of Yugoslavia* (Boulder: Westview Press, 1995); Catherine Baker, *The Yugoslav Wars of the 1990s* (London: Palgrave, 2015), 17–19.
65 X/SRX 1 – 29 November 1940, WO 208/4194, TNA.
66 I/SRN 51 – 9 January 1941, WO 208/4189, TNA.
67 Sandro Servi, 'Building a Racial State: Images of the Jew in the Illustrated Fascist Magazine, *La Difesa della Razza*, 1938–1943', in Joshua Zimmerman, ed., *Jews in Italy under Fascist and Nazi Rule, 1922–1945* (Cambridge: Cambridge University Press, 2005), 114–157.
68 Derek Penslar, *Shylock's Children: Economics and Jewish Identity in Modern Europe* (Berkeley: University of California Press, 2001), 5.
69 I/SRN 940 – 28 January 1943, WO 208/4191, TNA.
70 Bosworth, *Mussolini's Italy*, 414–421.
71 See: Robert Gordon, *The Holocaust in Italian Culture: 1944–2010* (Stanford: Stanford University Press, 2012); Michele Sarfatti, *Gli ebrei nell'Italia fascista: Vicende, identità, persecuzione* (Turin: Einaudi, 2000); Renzo De Felice, *Storia degli ebrei italiani sotto il fascismo* (Turin: Einaudi, 1988).
72 I/SRN 455 – 16 August 1942, WO 208/4190, TNA.
73 It is probable that Colacicchi found out about these secretive Nazi Eugenics policies through his relationship with Field Marshal Messe. Messe had commanded Italian forces on the Eastern Front 1941–1942, where he would have worked closely with high-ranking German military and political personnel who could have informed him of these practices.
74 SRIG 76 – 12 June 1943, WO 208/4185, TNA.
75 SRIG 166 – 26 July 1943, WO 208/4186, TNA.
76 An argument famously put forward in Mark Twain, 'Concerning the Jews', *Harper's Magazine*, September 1899, 527–535. See also: David Aberbach, *The European Jews,*

Patriotism and the Liberal State, 1789–1939: A Study of Literature and Social Psychology (London: Routledge, 2013), 90.

77 I/SRN 1231 – 27 April 1943, WO 208/4192, TNA.

78 I/SRN 1231 – 27 April 1943, WO 208/4192, TNA. The bracketed '(first and foremost)' is as it appears in the Anglophone version of this transcript. The Italian transcript reads: 'Io sono sicuro che l'ebreo italiano era un italiano e non era un ebreo.'

79 I/SRN 1231 – 27 April 1943, WO 208/4192, TNA.

80 Examples of sources that do include: Ivo Herzer, ed., *The Italian Refuge: Rescue of Jews during the Holocaust* (Washington DC: Catholic University of America Press, 1989); Leon Poliakoff and Jacques Sabille, *Jews Under the Italian Occupation* (New York: Howard Fertig, 1983).

81 Jonathan Steinberg, *All or Nothing: The Axis and the Holocaust, 1941–43* (London: Routledge, 1991), 133.

82 Meir Michaelis, *Mussolini and the Jews: German-Italian Relations and the Jewish Question in Italy, 1922–1945* (Oxford: Clarendon Press, 1978), 342.

83 Ousby, *Occupation*, 103; Emmanuele Sica, *Mussolini's Army in the French Riviera* (Chicago: University of Illinois Press, 2016).

84 Mathieu Marsan, 'Bordeaux-Bacalan: Des Bassins à Flot à la Base Sous-Marine', *Aquitaine Historique*, 120 (2013), 3.

85 BETASOM was the Italian military acronym of 'Beta' ('B' for Bordeaux) and 'Som' ('*Sommergibile*' – submarine). See: http://www.regiamarina.net/detail_text.asp?nid=90&lid=1. Accessed 30 December 2019; Francesco Mattesini, *BETASOM: La guerra negli oceani (1940–1943)* (Rome: USMM), 8–9; Dominique Lormier, *Bordeaux sous l'Occupation* (La Crèche: Geste, 2015), 38–56; Walter Ghetti, *Storia della Marina Italiana nella Seconda Guerra Mondiale: Vol. II* (Rome: De Vecchi, 2001), 26; Janusz Piekalkiewicz, *Sea War: 1939–1945* (London: Blandford Press, 1987), 106.

86 Mattesini, BETASOM, 27–484; Jean-Pierre Gillet, *Les Sous-marins Italiens en France: Grandeur et Servitude Italienne Atlantique et Océan Indien, 1940–1943* (Le Vigen: Les Editions Lela Presse, 2002); Juan Benítez, 'The Italian War in the Mid-Atlantic: Blockade Runners and Submarines in the Canary Islands (1940–1943)', *The Mariner's Mirror*, 100/2 (2014), 186–197; Marco Mascellani, ed., *Vedetta Atlantica: Storie di vita nella base dei sommergibili Italiani a Bordeaux, nelle pagine della rivista di Betasom* (Sarasota: Bianchi Gianni, 2011), 10–49, 382–404.

87 Luc Robène, Dominique Bodin and Stéphane Héas, 'Bordeaux et les Politiques d'Équipement Sportif Durant l'Occupation (1940–1944): Des Enjeux Idéologiques aux Contingences Locales', *Modern & Contemporary France*, 13/2 (2005), 175–192; Erwan Langeo, *Bordeaux 1940–1944: Les Bases de Sous-Marins* (Bordeaux: Association Bunker Atlantique Patrimonie Archéologie, 2017); Scott Soo, 'Ambiguities at Work: Spanish Republican Exiles and the Organisation Todt in Occupied Bordeaux', *Modern & Contemporary France*, 15/4 (2007), 457–477; Pierre Bécamps, *Bordeaux sous l'Occupation* (Rennes: Ouest France, 1983), 47, 64, 77, 80, 87.

88 Karine Varley, 'Between Vichy France and Fascist Italy: Redefining Identity and the Enemy in Corsica During the Second World War', *Journal of Contemporary History*, 47/3 (2012), 506; Karine Varley, 'Vichy and the Complexities of Collaborating with Fascist Italy: French policy and Perceptions Between June 1940 and March 1942', *Modern and Contemporary France*, 21 (2013), 318. See also: Romain Rainero, *Mussolini e Pétain Storia dei Rapporti tra l'Italia e la Francia di Vichy (10 giugno 1940 – 8 settembre 1943)* (Rome: USSME, 1992).

89 I/SRN 334 – 30 July 1942, WO 208/4189, TNA; I/SRN 223 – 28 October 1941, WO 208/4189, TNA; I/SRN 279 – 24 November 1942, WO 208/4189, TNA.

90 Sullivan, 'Italian Soldier in Combat', 177–205. Though selective and specialised, even these forces were hugely impacted by poor high command planning and a lack of resources for equipment and training. Piero Crociani and Pier Paolo Battistelli, *Italian*

Navy and Air Force Elite Units and Special Forces, 1940–45 (Oxford: Osprey, 2013), 4, 61–62.
91 Crociani and Battistelli, *Navy and Air Force*, 44.
92 Crociani and Battistelli, *Navy and Air Force*, 42–44.
93 Fabio De Ninno, *I sommergibili del fascismo. Politica navale, strategia e uomini tra le due guerre mondiali* (Milan: Unicopli, 2014); Luigi Fulvi, Giuliano Manzari, Tullio Marcon, Ottorini Ottone Miozzi, *Le fanterie di marina Italiane* (Rome: Ufficio Storico della Marina Militare, 1998); Massimiliano Capra Casadio, *Storia della Xa Mas 1943–1945* (Milan: Mursia, 2016).
94 Translation: 'dirty macaroni.' 'Macaroni' is a French anti-Italian ethnic slur similar to 'wop.'
95 I/SRN 465 – 18 August 1942, WO 208/4190, TNA.
96 I/SRN 465 – 18 August 1942, WO 208/4190, TNA.
97 I/SRN 1034 – 12 February 1943, WO 208/4191, TNA.
98 I/SRN 165 – 17 October 1941, WO 208/4189, TNA.
99 I/SRN 165 – 17 October 1941, WO 208/4189, TNA.
100 I/SRN 166 – 17 October 1941, WO 208/4189, TNA.
101 I/SRN 165 – 17 October 1941, WO 208/4189, TNA.
102 Julian Jackson, *France: The Dark Years, 1940–1944* (Oxford: Oxford University Press, 2003), 286–287.
103 Foot, *SOE*, 243; Michael Foot, *SOE in France: An Account of the Work of the British Special Operations Executive in France, 1940–1944* (Abingdon: Routledge, 2006), 157–159.
104 Jackson, *Dark Years*, 182, 423.
105 Soo, 'Ambiguities at Work', 470–471.
106 Nicholas Stargardt, *The German War: A Nation Under Arms, 1939–1945* (London: Vintage, 2015), 127–128.
107 Stargardt, *German*, 127.
108 I/SRN 351 – 2 August 1942, WO 208/4189, TNA.
109 I/SRN 865 – 6 January 1943, WO 208/4191, TNA.
110 Jean-Paul Sartre, 'Paris Under Occupation', *Sartre Studies International*, 4/2 (1998), 9–10; Andrew Knapp, 'The Destruction and Liberation of Le Havre in Modern Memory', *War In History*, 14/4 (2007), 489.
111 Paxton, *Vichy France*, 82; Burrin, *Collaboration*, 166; Varley, 'Complexities', 319–321; Varley, 'Redefining Identity', 507.
112 Knox, 'Anti-Anti-Fascist', 347–365; Marzano, 'La <<guerra delle monde>>', 3–24.
113 Ciano, *War Diaries*, 37, 38, 40, 51.
114 Duggan, *Crispi*, 334–336, 407–409, 610–611. See also: Michael Broers, 'Cultural Imperialism in a European Context? Political Culture and Cultural Politics in Napoleonic Italy', *Past and Present*, 170 (2001), 152–180.
115 Jackson, *The Fall of France*, pp. 65, 70–71.
116 Fabrice Virgili, *Shorn Women: Gender and Punishment in Liberation France* (Oxford: Berg, 2002), 240.
117 I/SRN 83 – 15 August 1941, WO 208/4189, TNA.
118 Like a more reverent *Wipers Times*, *Vedetta Atlantica* was published in 37 editions between 6 November 1941 and 1 December 1942. See: Mascellani, *Vedetta Atlantica*, 53–380.
119 I/SRN 231 – 28 October 1941, WO 208/4189, TNA.
120 I/SRN 94 – 22 August 1941, WO 208/4189, TNA.
121 I/SRN 557 – 11 September 1942, WO 208/4190, TNA.
122 For more on the masculinity of Italian soldiery and relationships with families at home, see: 150–157.
123 I/SRN 464 B – 18 August 1942, WO 208/4191, TNA.

124 I/SRN 571 – 12 September 1942, WO 208/4190, TNA.
125 Matthias Reiss, 'Bronzed Bodies behind Barbed Wire: Masculinity and the Treatment of German Prisoners of War in the United States during World War II', *The Journal of Military History*, 69/2 (2005), 492–497.
126 Raffael Scheck, 'Collaboration of the Heart: The Forbidden Love Affairs of French Prisoners of War and German Women in Nazi Germany', *The Journal of Modern History*, 90/2 (2018), 351–382.
127 Hanna Diamond, *Women and the Second World War in France, 1939–1948: Choices and Constraints* (Harlow: Longman, 1999), 71, 84.
128 Stargardt, *German*, pp. 127–128.
129 I/SRN 571 – 12 September 1942, WO 208/4190, TNA.
130 I/SRN 334 – 30 July 1942, WO 208/4189, TNA.
131 I/SRN 149 – 15 October 1941, WO 208/4189, TNA. Other instances of Italian soldiers sexually harassing French children can be found in Sica, *French Riviera*, pp. 103–104.
132 For more on economic shortages in the city, see: Lormier, *Bordeaux*, pp. 80–83. TNA WO 208/4189, I/SRN 334 – 30 July 1942 and TNA WO 208/4189, I/SRN 223 – 28 October 1941, both describe the massive increases in the cost of consumer goods during the occupation period.
133 I/SRN 149 – 15 October 1941, WO 208/4189, TNA.
134 Virgili, *Shorn*, 14–15.
135 Diamond, *Women*, 204.
136 I/SRN 166 – 17 October 1941, WO 208/4189, TNA.
137 I/SRN 434 – 14 August 1942, WO 208/4190, TNA.
138 I/SRN 247 – 16 November 1941, WO 208/4189, TNA.
139 I/SRN 588 – 11 September 1942, WO 208/4190, TNA.
140 I/SRN 330 – 29 July 1942, WO 208/4189, TNA.
141 I/SRN 322 – 27 July 1942, WO 208/4190, TNA. Similar charges would be levelled the Allies in Southern Italy. See: Julie Le Gac, '"*Le mal napolitain*": les alliés et la prostitution à Naples (1943–1944)', *Genre et Histoire*, 15 (2014/2015).
142 Robert Gildea, *Marianne in Chains: Daily Life in the Heart of France during the German Occupation* (London: Pan, 2003), 76–77.
143 Paolo Fonzi, 'The Italian Occupation of Crete during the Second World War', in Emanuele Sica and Richard Carrier, eds., *Italy and the Second World War: Alternative Perspectives* (Leiden: Brill, 2018), 69.
144 I/SRN 84 – 14 August 1941, WO 208/4189, TNA.
145 I/SRN 768 – 21 December 1942, WO 208/4190, TNA.
146 I/SRN 802 – 30 December 1942, WO 208/4191, TNA.
147 Hugh Sebag-Montefiore, *Dunkirk: Fight to the Last Man* (London: Penguin, 2007), lxiii.
148 Mary Roberts, *What Soldiers Do: Sex and the American GI in World War II France* (Chicago: University of Chicago, 2013), 163. For further comparison, see: Mary Roberts, 'The Price of Discretion: Prostitution, Venereal Disease, and the American Military in France, 1944–1946', *The American Historical Review*, 115/4 (2010), 1002–1030; Le Gac, '"*napolitain*"'.
149 I/SRN 155 – 16 October 1941, WO 208/4189, TNA.
150 I/SRN 231 – 28 October 1941, WO 208/4189, TNA. For more on antagonisms between the Axis in Africa, see: Fabio Degli Esposti and Alessandro Massignani, 'Nuovi documenti sulla Guerra nel Mediterraneo nel 1942: La Logistica dell'Asse', *Italia Contemporanea*, 203 (1996), 305–331.
151 Goeschel, *Alliance*, 226–229, 243
152 I/SRN 562 – 1 September 1942, WO 208/4190, TNA.
153 I/SRN 865 – 6 January 1943, WO 208/4191, TNA.

154 I/SRN 956 – 8 February 1943, WO 208/4191, TNA.
155 I/SRN 1105 – 14 February 1943, WO 208/4192, TNA.
156 I/SRN 280 – 26 November 1941, WO 208/4189, TNA. This is possibly a reference to the reprisals taken in the wake of the lethal shooting of a German soldier on 20 October 1941 in Bordeaux. See above.
157 I/SRN 180 – 19 October 1941, WO 208/4189, TNA.
158 I/SRN 180 – 19 October 1941, WO 208/4189, TNA.
159 Gildea, *Marianne*, 78.
160 I/SRN 628 – 27 September 1943, WO 208/4190, TNA.
161 See also: Alex Henry, 'Everybody to be Armed': Italian Naval Personnel and the Axis Occupation of Bordeaux, 1940–1943', *The British Journal of Military History*, 6/3 (2020), 23–41.

5 Warriors of land, sea and air

Introduction

One of the most striking aspects of the protocols' treatment of the experiences of frontline service during the Second World War, is the sheer range of topics addressed – from the threats of violence needed to motivate one company to attack during the Greek Campaign, to black-market activity just behind the front line in Tobruk.[1] From prolonged discussions on the merits of infantry versus paratrooper defensive tactics, to admiring comments on the beards sported by the crew of a German commerce raider.[2] The more you read of these transcripts, the more you are struck by how far they support the two central arguments of this book as a whole: first that it is necessary to jettison the myths of *Italiani brava gente*, *furberia* and *arrangiarsi*, and the second that we must recognise the extent to which the war fought between Fascist Italy and the Western Allies between 1940 and 1943 was tough and hard. These points will be underlined through examining what is said about experiences of combat, opinions on equipment and supplies, thoughts on leadership, the status of prisoners, motivations to fight and the Italian home front. In short, this chapter seeks to better understand the outlook of this group of Italian servicemen as fighting men.

Italy fought a remarkably diverse war between 1940 and 1943. In the space of less than a year, the Army invaded France (June 1940), Greece (October 1940) and Yugoslavia (April 1941). Major campaigns were mounted across East and North Africa. A large Italian expeditionary force – which became the Italian 8th Army – fought in the Soviet Union. By the summer of 1943, the *Regio Esercito* also had to mount a defence of the *patria* in Sicily and Southern Italy.[3] The *Regia Marina* operated submarines out of Bordeaux, the Red Sea Flotilla from Massawa, fast attack craft on the Black Sea and Lake Ladoga and even a naval presence in the Pacific at the Italian concession of Tientsin. The Navy's main base of operations, however, was the Mediterranean, fighting several surface fleet actions including those at Taranto (11–12 November 1940), Cape Matapan (27–29 March 1941) and Cape Bon (13 December 1941). Considerable effort was expended in the Mediterranean on defending supply convoys to Libya, submarine and light vessel attacks on Allied shipping and raids by frogmen and naval commandos. The 11 December 1942 raid on Algiers is a prominent example of such an assault.[4] Lacking any aircraft carriers and with only a small fleet air arm, the Navy depended on the air support of the *Regia Aeronautica* for most of the war. Indeed, the Italian Air Force's *Stormi* were present in all the above Navy and Army campaigns. Dedicated bombing campaigns were also mounted against Malta, Gibraltar, England and Palestine.[5]

Combat on land and in the air

Reflecting the numerical dominance of naval personnel in the cohort, accounts of fighting at sea far outnumber those of fighting on land or in the air, and as a result they assume a central position in my analysis. Regardless of the service branch of those being taped, what many of these protocols show is that for the servicemen in question, their war was a hard-fought and pitiless experience. Although the wartime record of Mussolini's armed forces has been consistently denigrated, these sources reinforce the idea that there were many Italians who fought with determination and resilience against their enemies and who paid a heavy price for doing so. In this way, they give a voice to a group of fighting men that has often been overlooked.

One of the few instances where land combat was discussed in any meaningful detail was that relating to the 1943 Sicilian Campaign. Paratrooper Second Lieutenant Rizzo (I/M 45) of the '10th Regiment Arditi' was captured on 15 June 1943 in North Africa and, therefore, had not experienced combat in Sicily first-hand. Nevertheless, his views on the fighting reveal a view that Italian forces on the island should have fought to the last in defence of *la patria*,

> How can a town like Palermo be taken just like that? A town can be defended for months and months like the Russians did at Stalingrad. In the defence of our own country we ought to have fought to the last man, without caring a damn about the towns; as they were able to fall into enemy hands anyway, it would have been better if we had destroyed them ourselves. [...] I would rather destroy my house than let others come into it. I would rather kill my wife than let her fall into someone else's hands and be raped, don't you agree? [...] They ought to have defended Sicily to the last man [...] I would have shot all those who retreated in Sicily, because every square yard lost in Sicily is a square yard of Italian soil which falls into enemy hands.[6]

These are intense remarks, evoking the feminization of *la patria* and drawing parallels between the invasion of his homeland and the sexual violation of his wife.[7] It is possible that Rizzo's comments were rooted in a desire to hide his own insecurity at becoming a prisoner of the British instead of fighting to the last himself. It is also fair to say that it was comparatively easy for Rizzo to say all this when he was safely out of the firing line and when he had not participated in the fighting in Sicily himself.

Rizzo came from an elite unit. The *X Reggimento Arditi* was formed in April 1942 as a direct response to attacks by British Commandos, SAS and Long Range Desert Group. By May 1943 they had grown to a strength of four battalions, divided between companies of *Arditi Paracadutisti* (paratroopers), *Arditi Camionettisti* (truck-mounted) and *Arditi Nuotatori* (swimmers).[8] This was a unit that selected only the 'best of the best' from Army volunteers, chosen for their mental and physical resolve, fighting experience and combat decorations. Even if they were not totally isolated from the problems of supply and inter-service coordination that thwarted the Italian armed services between 1940 and 1943 the 10th Regiment remained comparatively well equipped, highly trained and motivated. Their missions were extremely risky and it was not unheard of for these units to fight to the bitter end, as demonstrated by the *Camionettisti* of the 103a *Compagnia* at Enfidaville in March-May 1943.[9] Whilst Rizzo's 'elite' background may not have been common in the Italian Army, it is significant that he aired his views so openly around his fellow prisoners, and that none of his cellmates – including Flying Officer Alvisi (I/A 35), who had been captured in Sicily – appears to have challenged or disputed them.[10] Rizzo's views remain sentiments that do challenge many ideas of the kindly and non-martial *Italiani Brava Gente*.

A number of those from the CSDIC (UK) cohort who *did* experience the fighting in Sicily gave the impression that, notwithstanding the weaknesses in the Italian defences, the fighting was extremely serious. Colonel Ingargiola (I/M (Am) 1), commander of the 206th Coastal Division, did not reject the impression of Rizzo that the stand made by Italian units during the invasion could have been stronger. But instead of saw the defeat as a product of the defenders' want of resolve, he blamed the huge gulf between the firepower of his troops and those of the enemy. According to the Colonel, the Italian defence was compromised by a lack of armour, ammunition, aircraft and naval units. Furthermore, his artillery batteries were poorly-sited, which meant that their full weight of fire could not be brought to bear on the Allied armada pouring forces onto the island.[11] His men were totally overwhelmed by the Allied assault,

> In Sicily on the morning of the 10th [July], ships everywhere! [...] they dropped dozens of parachutists who surrounded all the batteries so that the gunners had to defend their batteries. They fired, but they ought to have fired much more. [...] [Allied] Aircraft came over and plastered them, they had a lot of men killed. No sooner had they fired a few rounds than swarms of aircraft came in from the sea, and that was the end of it.[12]

In fairness to the Colonel and his men, his division found itself at the very centre of Operation Husky, defending 90 of the 100 miles of coastline that was assaulted by Allied forces. To confront the majority of the 80 battalions of infantry, 400 tanks and 1800 heavy guns that made up the invasion force, Ingargiola had just 7500 men, 56 pieces of artillery, 34 mortars, 700 machine guns and very limited motor transport.[13] It seems likely that the Colonel would have agreed with the description of the fighting on Sicily by an unidentified senior Italian officer as a 'damned bad business.'[14] Even if the Sicilian campaign was far from the most costly in human lives of the Second World War,[15] Ingargiola's recollections nevertheless show that for many Italian units at the 'sharp end' it was a hard-fought experience in which the odds were heavily stacked against them.

Lieutenant-Colonel Pedala's (I/M 13) description of the defences on Sicily supports Ingargiola's statements – 'Those little popguns of ours can't fire more than seven or eight kilometres from the coast at the most [...] and do you know where they put them? Four or five kilometres from the coast, inland, so that they couldn't fire more than two kilometres out to sea.'[16] Making it impossible for the defending troops to counter sustained Allied bombardment which could come from vessels stationed 15 or 20 km from the coast. This greatly reduced Italian fighting spirit – '"To hell with this. Why should I risk my skin? I'm not such a fool as that,"' was an attitude Pedala believed many of the defenders of Sicily shared.[17] He summed up the whole situation in Sicily when he said, 'it isn't that our soldiers don't want to fight; on the contrary, they do want to fight, but they haven't got the equipment to fight against these people.'[18] Pedala's image of Sicily is one of unrealized potential. He was frustrated, not with the war-shy attitude of the Italian defenders but with structural weaknesses in the Sicilian defences that undermined the resolve of the defenders.

As with accounts of the fighting on land, prolonged discussion of aerial combat in the transcripts is rare. Nevertheless, the few accounts that exist cast light on these experiences. For example, Lieutenant-Colonel Ravazzoni (I/A 32) gave a detailed account of how his unit of Savoia-Marchetti 84 bombers was attacked by RAF night fighters over Malta in August 1942. He dropped his bombs on ships at Valletta, but despite taking evasive manoeuvres, his plane was tracked down by a Bristol Beaufighter. Ravazzoni described how, 'at that very moment – errrammmmm! The damned fellow was right behind us [...] He fired with his 20mm cannon. My aircraft became a flaming torch [...] the flames were all around me.'[19] Ravazzoni was able to bail out of the aircraft into the sea. But this was just the start of his ordeal. The pilot officer hit the water with such force that he broke his arm and leg. Having been dragged for some distance across the sea surface as wind hit his parachute, he was left to orient himself in the cold water with serious burns on his face that caused his eyesight to fail. He battled low temperatures and even 'ferocious' attacks by jellyfish for 17 hours before he was picked up by fishermen and rushed to hospital in Gozo.[20] There, he no doubt faced a hostile reception – after months of heavy bombardment the mood in Malta had hardened. It was not uncommon for stranded Axis aircrews to be shot at and strafed, and one captured German airman was decapitated by a civilian mob.[21] The terrifying nature of Ravazzoni's ordeal can help to explain his strongly anti-English views already outlined in Chapter Three. Given all that he suffered, his hostility towards the British is understandable.

The human cost of aerial attacks is also made clear in protocols that report on the effects of Allied bombing. The Allied Desert Air Force (DAF) was undeniably one of the most significant 'architects of British victory' in the Western Desert and Mediterranean, giving the Allies a massive tactical advantage and pushing German and Italian units to breaking point.[22] Artillery Lieutenant Vertua (I/M 20) described the aftermath of an air raid on Sousse, 'then I saw a man half in and half out of the window, dead [...] then a girl about eighteen years old, quite pretty, fair-haired, who had her arm completely torn off.' One sheltering Italian sailor was caught in a bomb blast that 'blew both his buttocks off.' He had to run to the local hospital, 'with his backside in his hands.'[23] The suffering inflicted by such bombing was also psychological. Flying Officer Alvisi (I/A 35) reported how a comrade of his had a total nervous breakdown and went 'mad' because of heavy Allied bombing.[24] Paratroop Second Lieutenant Rizzo (I/M 45) explained how, 'at Tobruk several Army officers went mad [...] For instance I saw an officer of my division who was taken to hospital, he was struck dumb with fear!'[25] The experience of fighting for these Italian servicemen was a serious one, fraught with terror and inclined to foster a desire for vengeance towards their Allied enemies.

The war at sea

It is tempting to think of the war at sea as fought at a distance, where combat took place through periscopes and radar, technology eerily devoid of the immediacy of violence. Numerous protocols, however, make it clear that submarine personnel were subject to the naked brutality of war first-hand. For example, Gunner De Seta (I/N 165) told of how when a gas explosion on the *Ferraris* killed two of his comrades, their remains had to be stored in empty torpedo tubes.[26] Seaman Stefanni (I/N 131) recalled that the *Baracca* often came across corpses floating in the water and, on one occasion, even 'an entire ship's bridge.' It was all that remained of a convoy devastated by aerial attack.[27] These are reminders that,

> Most of those who perished at sea lost their lives in the grimmest circumstances. The fortunate ones died swiftly, blown up by torpedoes or, in the case of the U-Boat crews, by depth-charges or machine-gun fire. Others were trapped in sinking hulls or asphyxiated by toxic fumes. Some died from their wounds in vessels which lacked anaesthetics or surgeons, or, very often, both; some drowned because lifeboats had been smashed into flotsam or because, after days or weeks adrift without food and water, they succumbed to insanity and threw themselves overboard.[28]

The experience of salvaging the wreck of the destroyer *Lampo* off the coast of North Africa brought others face-to-face with the bodies of former comrades. The *Lampo* had run aground near Sfax, Tunisia, as a result of the Battle of the

Tarigo Convoy on 16 April 1941.[29] By the time Italian salvaging teams arrived local Arabs had ransacked the wrecked ship and the only way of identifying many of the dead was by examining the remnants of their uniforms.[30] Petty Officer Diver Guglielmo (I/N 206) was tasked with investigating the ship. He told his cellmate in August 1942, 'you ought to have seen all the dead men [...] their heads were skeletons, but their stomachs were still swollen. They were lying on top of the other like sacks of flour.'[31]

Similarly, Lieutenant Varoli (I/N 338) told of an instance in which sailors had to recover bodies from an Italian submarine that had become stranded on a reef and subject to RAF strafing. By the time the recovery team had arrived, the dead had been left for almost two weeks and were in an advanced stage of decomposition. There were few volunteers willing to help collect the dead and it was left to one man from Turin to do alone. He reported that the bodies left on the deck, 'which had been exposed to the sun, were in a better state.' But, 'those below [the deck] were all half-decomposed.' When he tried to move them, the bodies would simply fall apart in his hands.'[32] Such horrors did not obstruct practical concerns. After the bodies had been cleared, fresh air was circulated around the submarine and it was towed back to port for repairs.

Even before they reached the frontlines, the life of Italian naval divers was riddled with danger.[33] Petty Officer Diver Guglielmo (I/N 206) recalled how his superiors 'used to experiment on us without telling us anything about it. They used to give us lime, to see whether it made us liable to fainting attacks.'[34] On one occasion when three men fainted underwater repairing the Mole at Spezia they were almost impossible to locate because there were no search lights. Luckily for the men in question they did eventually 'come to' and surfaced.[35] Others had clearly not been so lucky. As Guglielmo said, 'it's a dangerous business you know. If a man's unconscious when he gets to the surface nobody can save him, neither a doctor nor anybody else.'[36] He described how after a prolonged period underwater, 'the pressure gets inside your costume [...] it even gets into your flesh. The movement you make while walking takes your skin right off, from your testicles and the end of your penis.'[37] Nor was Guglielmo the only one to have suffered serious physical injury as a result of such exercises. Midshipman Manisco (I/N 297) of the 10th Flotilla MAS, said 'I nearly killed myself with work,' complaining that he now had a 'palpitating heart,' which greatly limited what he could do underwater.[38]

Italian divers were not alone in facing intense hardships, the risks of submarine warfare were also incredibly high. Engineer Lieutenant Varoli (I/N 338) recalled in March 1943 that 'nobody was saved from the *Granito*,' nor from the *Alabastro*, the *Veniero*, the *Marconi*, the *Malaspina* and the *Marcello*.[39] Across all of Italy's naval theatres of operations, the submarine service lost 98 vessels, two-thirds of its total strength.[40] In total 3144 Italian submariners perished.[41] Regardless of nationality, German and Italian submariners faced the same dangers in their war at sea, and both inflicted significant losses on Allied shipping. The Italian submarine force operating from Bordeaux was able to sink 582719 tonnes of shipping for the loss of 16 vessels of their own, while during the same period the Germans destroyed 11440310 tonnes for the loss of 282 U-Boats.[42] Liddell Hart's dismissive suggestion that the contribution of the Italian navy in the Battle of the Atlantic was 'negligible' and amounting to 'virtually nothing' ignores both the losses and determination of the Italian submarine service.[43]

In July 1942, Petty Officer Lazzari (I/N 182) could not believe all 'the submarines we have lost from our Atlantic base!'[44] Lieutenant Badezzi (I/N 321) articulated the disastrous position facing the Italians when he bluntly exclaimed, 'my God! What a lot of submarines we've lost!'[45] It is not without good reason that Seaman di Fario (I/N 203) described Italian submarines as 'coffins.'[46] On the eve of war the *Regia Marina* possessed a massive numerical superiority in submarines over the Royal Navy in the Mediterranean, 115 Italian to 12 British. But exploiting technological and tactical shortcomings allowed the British to sink ten Italian submarines in the first 20 days of the war alone.[47] Sullivan echoes di Fario's words when he said Italy's 'vaunted submarines represented little more than steel coffins for their crews.'[48]

The experience of being depth-charged left a lasting impression on many submariners. Seaman Stefanni (I/N 131) recounted the physical and mental effects of a sustained attack. Surfacing after 80 depth-charges had exploded around them, the crew of the submarine *Baracca* was completely overwhelmed: 'some of us had been crying all day and came up half dead. Others could be heard praying to the Madonna [...] nobody had a clear head, some were laughing, some crying [...] a couple of us kept on eating.'[49] A Sub-Lieutenant in the submarine *Glauco* (I/N 40) said of being depth-charged, 'there is nothing you can compare with it in civil life – the danger I mean – when you hear it getting nearer, so slowly, calmly and accurately.'[50] Petty Officer Pettinati's account of the return of the *Argo* to Cagliari show the dangers from depth-charges could linger well after Italian submarines had escaped the Allied destroyers and corvettes. He described how the *Argo*'s decks were littered with unexploded depth-charges, any one of which could have slipped off the hull and detonated beneath them, killing all those on board.[51]

The fate of the crew of the *Medusa* is identified by several CSDIC POWs as particularly terrible. It had been conducting technical trials at slow speeds on the sea surface when it was hit by a British torpedo fired from HMS *Thorn* on 30 January 1942, not far from Pula, Croatia. This caused a violent explosion that devastated the side of the ship and it sunk in less than ten minutes.[52] Most of the 58 crew were killed immediately, but some 14 sailors were left trapped 30 metres below the waves. They were able to communicate with surface vessels with a telephone buoy, but very little else. There were attempts to pump fresh air down to the men and efforts to use a 'huge pontoon' to raise the stricken submarine, but, as the weather turned, the rescuers were forced to abandon their efforts. After the pontoon's hawsers snapped, Sub-Lieutenant Bersani (I/N 247) recalled that the rescuers, 'gave it up. Those men were left to die [...] as if nobody cared a damn.'[53] Sub-Lieutenant Villa (I/N 174) and Lieutenant Amicarelli (I/N 207) also described the incident. For all the high-ranking officials that rushed to the scene, the crew – predominantly made up of 'cadets of sixteen or seventeen' – were nonetheless destined to perish. It was a fate that both officers agreed to be 'very terrible' and 'horrible,' far worse than being 'killed in action.'[54]

The harsh nature of the war at sea goes a long way to explain the hardened attitudes of many CSDIC submarine POWs towards 'the enemy.' Thus, Lieutenant Varoli (I/N 338) delighted in news of the sinking of Allied troopships. He said, 'that's good news – five thousand men who'll never get here to fight. My God, I'm glad. My God, what a coup! How pleased they must have felt when they saw all that offal drowning!'[55] A Midshipman in the submarine *Tritone* (I/N 340) lacked Varoli's hatred, but nonetheless voiced in detail his pleasure at sinking enemy shipping. He said, 'when you are at sea, you say: "Hell, it must be grand to sink something" [...] How rotten we felt when we fired at two destroyers and saw the torpedoes go, and then miss [...] Gosh, how rotten we felt.'[56] Similarly Sub-Lieutenant Ferucci (I/N 204) recalled with pride how his submarine, the *Calvi*, sank '48,000 tons of shipping in nine days,' including one steamer that 'blew up and vanished completely' leaving no survivors.[57] Leading Electrical Rating Fallini (I/N 222) and the rest of the crew of the *Cobalto* may have had less luck hunting down enemy ships but he still harboured the same desire for success on the high seas, a longing for glory and fame measured in the number of Allied lives taken. 'The greatest satisfaction we could have had would have been to sink something and go into port' to receive accolades from their commanders and the Italian press.[58] All these men were highly motivated in their struggle against the Allies, an enemy they had come to genuinely despise. These comments reveal a capacity to dehumanise their enemies, which fits uneasily with the myth of the humane and sympathetic Italian servicemen.[59]

The brutality of the war at sea becomes clear from the conversations of several prisoners as they discussed often callous responses to stranded enemy crews. Sub-Lieutenant Villa (I/N 174) made it clear that in his experience there was very little mercy for Allied sailors. He described the idea of Italian submarines' rescuing people as 'nonsense [...] When we sink anything, we push off!'[60] Seaman Stefanni (I/N 131) also confirmed this view, asking the rhetorical question, 'who's going to bother about [picking up] survivors?'[61] On an earlier occasion he stated that, 'submarines never pick up anybody.' He maintained that orders had been issued prohibiting the practice.[62] This was possibly a policy primarily dictated by practical concerns. Submarines were cramped, vulnerable and dangerous spaces at the best of times with little capacity to hold large numbers of enemy prisoners. Yet, there is evidence that this was an attitude rooted in something darker. For example, Petty Officer Guglielmo (I/N 206) recalled an instance where, 'the *Toti* sunk a submarine and then left the crew in the water, though she could have saved some of them.'[63]

124 *Warriors of land, sea and air*

As a result of attacks by American aircraft on German and Italian submarines attempting to rescue survivors of the RMS *Laconia* in September 1942, Grand Admiral Karl Dönitz issued the 'Laconia Order' which stated:

> All attempts to rescue the crews of sunken ships will cease forthwith. This prohibition applies equally to the picking up of men in the water and putting them aboard a lifeboat, to the righting of capsized lifeboats and to the supply of food and water. Such activities are a contradiction of the primary object of war, namely the destruction of enemy ships and their crews.[64]

In March 1944 the U-Boat U-852 commanded by Hanz-Wilhelm Eck used machine guns and grenades to kill the survivors of the Greek merchant vessel *Peleus* in the South Atlantic.[65] However, both the Laconia order and Eck's actions should be taken as exceptions to an 'overall pattern' in the German navy between 1939 and 1943 of looking 'benevolently' on enemy ship-wrecked survivors.[66] This stands in contrast to the excerpts from Italian sailors in the Centre transcripts which suggest an attitude far more in line with the Laconia order. It would be incorrect to deduce from this that Villa, Stefanni and Guglielmo are on a par with Eck, but their words offer a clear example where Italian views of the war could be more severe than their German allies.

The harshness of the war at sea is evident in the accounts from several POWs recalling the sinking of their submarines. Such narratives are a common theme of conversation. You may be forgiven for thinking that once a submarine had been damaged to the degree that it had to surface its battle was over. Their threat now neutralised and in the presence of enemy ships, were Italian submarine crews not relatively safe? For example, in the case of the submarine *Ferraris* it was a situation that allowed the commander calmly to explain to his men that 'it's no good shedding blood. There are aircraft over us and two destroyers. What can we do? It's useless to put up a fight!'[67] Indeed, when the *Ferraris* was sunk the majority of the crew did survive with only 11 casualties out of a crew of 55.[68] The expectation must have been that once a submarine had been knocked out, the fighting would stop and convention would dictate that survivors were rapidly rescued. Other protocols, however, suggest that the fate of the crew of the *Ferraris* was unusual: Allied seamen did not rush to the aid of stricken Italians, just as Italian servicemen made scant effort to rescue their Allied counterparts. Moreover, the experience of most Italian sailors and submariners was that combat and its consequences were fraught with panic, danger and death.

One example is the case of the submarine *Millo*, which was sunk off the coast of Calabria on 14 March 1942 with only 15 survivors.[69] One of those on board – Petty Officer Balasco (I/N 213) – recalled that, once the depth charges had done their work, the ship began to list. This provoked 'general pandemonium' as the surviving crew rushed to escape. After the *Millo* had surfaced the crew of the destroyer hunting it mistakenly believed that the Italian submariners now rushing around the deck were trying to man their guns; the British crew opened fire on the submariners, cutting many of them down.[70] As Sub-Lieutenant Bersani (I/N 247) made clear, those men who escaped faced considerable peril in the water. He estimated that some 30 men made it out of the *Millo* alive but half of these 'disappeared at once,' including the commanding officer. He suggested that at least some of the blame for this rested on defective life jackets, which failed to prevent these men from drowning.[71]

In the case of the submarine *Pietro Calvi* – sunk south of the Azores by HMS *Lulworth* on 15 July 1942 – there are also reports of panic on board as the vessel went down.[72] Suffering serious depth-charge damage the *Calvi* was forced to the surface where it engaged with Allied vessels. As with the *Millo*, some of the crew were struck down by bullets and shells as they left the ship including one Boatswain Bertorelli who 'was hit in the face with a machine gun bullet.'[73] One of the most significant events in the sinking was the death of the Captain, Primo Longobardo. Some of the survivors argued that he had mishandled evading their pursuers, but Torpedo Rating Crozzi (I/N 196) felt that 'when the C.O. was killed we were like children who had lost their father; we felt overwhelmed.'[74] Such was the panic on board that Sub-Lieutenant Ferucci (I/N 204) claimed he heard revolver shots from those trapped inside the ship, saying that 'it may be that one or two of the men actually shot themselves.'[75] It is almost impossible to verify this, but that Ferucci could even contemplate this as a possibility is emblematic of the stark choices many Italian servicemen faced during their war at sea.[76]

The accounts of the survivors of the submarine *Emo* are remarkable in the detail they give of the human cost of Italian naval warfare. In the view of Petty Officer De Blasio (I/N 255) the panicking of some officers on board was infectious and precipitated a slide into chaos.[77] Midshipman Gianni (I/N 250) remembered the terror of a number of his comrades, 'I had to hit some of the men who came rushing into the control room, trampling upon each other.'[78] On reaching the deck of the *Emo*, Gianni and others went to man the deck guns and managed to fire some shots at the pursuing Royal Navy ship. This elicited a ferocious response. Petty Officer Cioni (I/N 272) described how, 'bullets were hitting the deck and splinters were flying in all directions.' One man jumped in the water to escape the hail of metal but he tripped on some loose wires, hit his head on the side of the boat as he fell and sunk unconscious into the water below.[79] The carnage on deck was confirmed by De Blasio who described the 'pile' of bodies he saw by the galley hatch. They had been 'mowed down' by British machine gun fire as they attempted to escape the stricken vessel.[80]

For all the hardships endured by Cioni, Ferucci, Bersani and Balasco, they were the lucky ones. Ultimately, they survived the sinking of their vessels, the downing of their aircraft and the assaults on their positions. They were fortunate enough to be safely captured. As we have seen, many of their comrades suffered far worse fates. It is important not to forget that a great many Italian service personnel did perish at sea, in the air and on land between 1940 and 1943.[81] Aside from what had been left behind in written letters or diaries, their memories of their experiences died with them. For those that did survive and were chosen to be a part of the Centre's programme, what they articulated about combat and fighting clearly demonstrated that the Italian experience of the Second World War could be as hard, brutal and unpleasant as that of the Allies or other Axis powers. Just because these men were Italians fighting in Western Europe and North Africa, did not mean they were insulated from the perils and the horrors of war.

On equipment and supplies

The Second World War is a conflict visually defined by some of the iconic equipment and weaponry used: the German Tiger tank, the British Spitfire fighter, the American B-17 Flying Fortress, the Soviet T-34 tank and the Japanese A6M 'Zero' fighter. The closest that Italy comes to contributing to this list is with the SLC *'Maiale'* manned torpedos.[82] They were truly innovative weapons, but for all their advanced technology their use was incredibly dangerous and they still depended on the individual bravery and heroism of their operators. They stand as a metaphor for Italy's armed forces in the Second World War. Whatever the weaknesses, there were in the Italian war effort, these did not primarily lie in the attitudes and outlooks of Italian service personnel who often had to over-compensate for such shortcomings with their own ingenuity and bravery. The reputation of Italian military equipment in the Second World War is not formidable. Examples of laughably poor-quality supplies are easy to find. For instance, crews training with the Italian MR35 tank could only do so in the cool of the morning to prevent the engine from overheating. It had, however, been developed specifically for use in the scorching North African desert.[83] Italo Balbo commented on the fighting in North Africa that, 'our light tanks, already old and armed only with machine guns, are completely out-classed. The machine guns of the British armoured cars pepper them with bullets which easily pierce their armour.'[84]

The poor quality of much Italian weaponry or materiel did not preclude extensive discussion of equipment and supplies, which remained a common talking point within the protocols. It was a subject of interest to personnel of all ranks and all service branches. In many respects this is hardly surprising. For self-evident reasons, military personnel have always been concerned with the quality of their kit. These were also comparably neutral and unifying topics of conversation, unlikely to provoke emotive differences of opinion. What becomes clear in these exchanges is that while individual items of Italian equipment could be popular, there were much wider structural problems in Italian military procurement. Something about which these men were well-aware. They cared about the war and wanted to fight as effectively as possible. However, they were let down not because of any want of fighting-spirit determined by national character but by political, economic and military systems, which failed to supply them with weaponry and equipment of sufficient quantity and quality.

The Beretta Model 38 submachine gun (or MAB 38) has been described as one of the best weapons of its type in the Second World War, proving popular with Italian, German and Allied forces.[85] Its popularity with Italian troops is certainly made clear in an August 1943 conversation between several Army and Air Force junior officers. Whilst the Breda 30 light machinegun was accused of being 'clumsy' and heavy, the MAB 38, or 'Mitra,' is described by Second Lieutenant Rizzo (I/M 45) as 'worth its weight in gold.' Whenever he was armed with the weapon he felt, 'like a ruddy lion.' The only criticism he had was that he could never get his hands on enough of them. Such was the reputation of the MAB 38 that even his Flying Officer cellmate (I/A 35) – who presumably had far less service experience with the weapon – believed it was a superb firearm.[86]

The MAB 38 was not the only weapon popular amongst the CSDIC (UK) cohort. In July 1942 two pilots (I/A 19 and I/A 20) discussed at length the impressive handling characteristics of a number of Italian aircraft.[87] Similarly, three captured members of the 1st Regiment of Paratroops (I/M 30, I/M 32 and I/M 33) had supreme confidence in the new armaments for Macchi fighters which would make them the terror of the skies. One was prepared to predict that 'the Flying Fortresses will run away from these [...] more than that, they'll never get near them.'[88] In a conversation with a German *Luftwaffe* gunner (A 881), one MTB Boatswain (I/N 92) described Italian E-Boats as 'very good [...] very fast, very beautiful,' capable of high speeds on the water thanks to their well-designed engines.[89] What these exchanges demonstrate is a clear pride and faith in elements of the Italian arsenal amongst the cohort. There are few grounds to doubt that these positive sentiments were genuinely held, but a great many other transcripts reveal outrageous deficiencies in Italian military manufacturing and supply.

It is clear from the testimony of many that Italian troops frequently lacked even the most basic of equipment. When discussing a want of anti-aircraft machine-guns on military trains, Sub-Lieutenant Scarino (I/N 393) pointed out that, 'if they haven't enough of them to send to the front, how do you suppose they could put them on trains.'[90] In regards to the fighting in Tunisia, Midshipman Devescovi (I/N 334) reported that, notwithstanding the numbers of elite troops sent to North Africa, their presence was futile as they lacked sufficient munitions to put up a serious fight:'but what's the good of it all? They send them into the frontline without even providing them with four magazines of ammunition.'[91] Even soap was an unobtainable luxury at times in occupied France according to Sub-Lieutenant Ferucci (I/N 204). Quite simply, 'there wasn't any.' Instead they were issued with a 'so-called substitute made of sand, which you couldn't wash with at all.'[92] During a parade in Rome, Petty Officer Guglielmo (I/N 206) reported that all the submarine men were issued with brand new uniforms and boots. But as soon as the event ended, they were made to hand all their new equipment back.[93] It was all for show, a Potemkin-esque exercise for the cameras.[94]

In contrast, Engine-Room Warrant Officer Corvisiero (I/N 211) was deeply impressed with the periscope fitted to his submarine. As he said,

> At Muggiano one day one of our electricians was cleaning the periscope and pointed it towards the hill below Pitelli, which is a thousand metres away from Muggiano. There was a peasant woman there relieving nature – out in the fields, she was a peasant woman – and you could actually see the steam rising from her excrement. That shows you what a clear image the lens gives you!

But, crucially, it was a German-made periscope. As Lieutenant Vertua (I/M 20) made clear, Italian-made equipment could be disappointing in the extreme. He recalled that the protective metal shields of artillery pieces he saw at Stampalla on the Aegean were more rust and paint than metal. They were so weak that he was able to snap one of them by just standing on it.[95] Lieutenant-Colonel Donato (I/M 26) spent two years of his career putting together highly detailed maps of the enemy defences present on the Slovenian border. Every fort, tank trap, artillery battery and ditch of the frontier defences was painstaking logged by Donato and his team. But, when war was declared his maps were not distributed to the divisions entrusted with seizing Ljubljana. Even when the Italian war machine had the resources it needed, there was no guarantee that it could use them effectively. It was a frustration felt personally by Donato: 'ought we not to have got hold of the people responsible and put them up against a wall? [...] How could such a thing be possible?'[96]

These excerpts all point to an essential reality of the Italian war effort between 1940 and 1943. Individual pieces of Italian equipment could be very good, but overall weaknesses in Italian industry and supply infrastructure meant that not nearly enough equipment was made, and what was produced was not always made available to those who needed it. Such fundamental economic weaknesses were not lost on one *Tenente di Vascello MAS* (I/N 23) who, even in January 1941, was aware that Italy could not make sufficient motor transport, had no coal, no iron, no rubber and insufficient gold reserves and even clothing to fight a modern war against formidable adversaries. Italy's extensive agricultural output – 'oranges, onions and green stuff' – was quite simply 'not enough.'[97] Mussolini's 'Battle for Grain' could only do so much.[98] Two submarine Lieutenants (I/N 361 and I/N 375) ridiculed Mussolini's famous statement that Italy's success on the battlefield was assured with her fighting force of 'eight million bayonets.' I/N 361 lamented that 'if only we had them! Where are these eight million bayonets?' I/N 375 responded that they *only* had the bayonets, when what Italy really needed was a potent way of responding to Allied tanks, planes and warships.[99] It was left to the men in the fighting zone to compensate for these deficiencies in industrial production and supply. As Artillery Lieutenant Vertua (I/M 20) remarked, it was a situation in which Italian infantrymen were forced to fight with 'old-fashioned Molotov cocktails and tommy-guns against tanks.'[100]

At best, the system of Italian military supplies was inconsistent. Whilst the design of Italian water bottles was popular with both Italian and Allied soldiers in the East Africa,[101] the same cannot be said for their artillery ordnance in the same campaign. During the battle for the Marda Pass one British officer estimated that 40 percent of the shells fired at his men were defective.[102] Certainly, these were shortcomings that had a history outside of Fascism. The glacial pace of reform through the bureaucracy of the Italian Army is witnessed by the 14 years it took for the army to procure from abroad – not even develop domestically – a new 75mm artillery piece. The new weapon only reached Italian units in 1916.[103] The military and political leaders of the Fascist era bear ultimate responsibility for the extent to which Italian troops were hampered in their conduct of the war by inadequate quantity and quality of weaponry, transport, uniforms and food. As Mack Smith has argued, 'if military provision was insufficient, the reason must be sought in politics.'[104] Likewise Sullivan has commented that, 'by lying to themselves and to Mussolini about their readiness for war in 1940 and by their failures to prepare for that war over the previous twenty years, the Italian military leadership betrayed their country.'[105] This was a failure on many levels: a failure of planning; a failure to introduce modernised manufacturing methods; a failure to sustain design innovation; a failure to manage industrial interests; a fiscal failure; a failure to secure raw materials; a failure of both quality and quantity; and, most strikingly, a failure of leadership.

On leadership at the front

Several exchanges in the CSDIC protocols stress the gulf between the lives of officers and enlisted men in the *Regia Marina*, a cause of real grievance. For instance, when an unnamed Chief Petty Officer (I/N 6) noted that, 'it appears the Italian Government have only considered [a POW allowance] for officers here, the gentlemen officers,' his complaint is clear.[106] His cellmate, diver I/N 21, was even more direct in his criticism. He responded, 'yes, we're just sons of servants, lousy blighters, ragamuffins to be cast aside as soon as we have served their purpose. By God! It makes one become revolutionary [...] my blood is boiling.'[107] Petty Officer Della Barbera (I/N 185) would have agreed. He felt that, 'in Italy they pay too little attention to the other ranks and too much to the officers. There's too big a gulf between them.' He admired the German *Kriegsmarine* for, in his opinion, narrowing this gap and where the 'officers don't have so much luxury.'[108] The privilege with which some senior Italian officers conducted themselves is made clear by Engineer Lieutenant Cristini (I/N 361). He recalled how he was once sent to Rome from Cagliari on a 'secret' and 'special' mission to deliver a parcel to Admiral Legnani – commander of the Italian submarine fleet 1941–1943. After a long and frustrating journey, he was successful in his task only for the Admiral to exclaim, 'at last that silly fool has remembered to send me those lobsters.'[109]

The experiences of these sailors are not the only evidence to suggest the existence of an unjust gulf between how Italian men and officers were treated in the Italian armed forces. Sullivan highlights a long-standing military culture within the *Regio Esercito* that enforced, 'rigid distinctions among conscripts, NCOs, and junior and senior officers.'[110] Enlisted men stationed in North Africa experienced dreadful conditions and lacked even basic levels of water and firewood. Illness and disease were predictably common, as was resentment that conditions for staff officers were far superior.[111] This considerably diminished the Army's ability to fight a mentally and tactically flexible war as enlisted men struggled with mutual understanding, trust and communication.[112] As the protocols demonstrate, a similar tale can be told in regard to the Italian navy.

From several transcripts it is clear that the submarine service was a fairly hard-drinking arm of the Italian armed forces. Sub-Lieutenant Ferucci (I/N 204) reported that the *Calvi* carried some 2700 bottles of wine, enough for an average daily consumption of 30 bottles for a 90-day period.[113] Ordinary Seaman Battaglini (I/N 171) claimed that one of the Lieutenants on board his submarine personally bought 3000 francs worth of alcohol for a single patrol.[114] Quite bluntly, Petty Officer Villosio (I/N 188) believed that most naval officers – and especially those in the submarines – drank 'like hogs.'[115] Some reported how excessive consumption of alcohol while on duty could compromise the leadership of some naval officers. A Gunner Petty Officer in the *Baracca* remembered how his commander – Commandante Bertorelli – once got so drunk on a cruise that he was unable to comprehend incoming W/T communications. The situation got so bad that his second-in-command had to forcibly assume command.[116]

Nor is this the only example of leadership incompetence at sea to be found in the protocols. During a prolonged outburst Petty Officer Boschin (I/N 176) made it clear he had little faith in the ability of the officers on board the *Calvi*. He described them as careless, inexperienced and unconcerned for the well-being of their men. Quite simply they made him 'sick,' making 'mistakes at every turn.'[117] The example set by a number of officers on the *Calvi* during its sinking was poor according to one Seaman (I/N 202) and Gunner Pittei (I/N 199). In their opinion, the officers were primarily to blame for the chaos that unfolded. They failed to maintain discipline and were too preoccupied with their own safety to effectively coordinate the submarine's defence and evacuation.[118]

10th *Flotilla MAS* Lieutenant Badezzi (I/N 321) recalled a 'pretty big mistake' made by a torpedo boat (MTB) officer he knew from the Naval Academy. According to Badezzi, 'he approached a steamer, circled round it and waved his hand to the captain. He thought he had got to Sicily and that it was an Italian steamer. Then he went towards the coast and all of a sudden the steamer and the coastal batteries opened fire on him.' The officer in question had brought his vessel to the coast of Malta.[119] As a member of the absolute elite of the Italian navy, it is not surprising to see Badezzi mocking the incompetence of others. However, such criticisms of leadership are not isolated to *Decima MAS* personnel. Lieutenant Cristini (I/N 361) scathingly remembered how officers he encountered on shore were more preoccupied with completing crosswords than with supporting submarine crews.[120] Similarly, one Sub-Lieutenant in the Naval Reserve (I/N 35) was frustrated with the 'great negligence' the Navy displayed when allotting crews for vessels. According to him, 'fishermen from Ischia were turned down' while they took on medical students.[121]

In an anecdote that exposed corruption and inefficiency in the naval shock units Petty Officer Botti (I/N 318) recalled three incompetent instructors at a training base who did not know how to swim. In his frustration he exclaimed, 'even in our lot things are going to the dogs now! Very, very slowly decay is setting in, even in the shock units.'[122] In his criticisms of the 10th *Flotilla MAS* Sub-Lieutenant Morello (I/N 329) was scathing: 'Damn the 10th Flotilla! They're a pack of scoundrels, a flotilla with no organisation at all [...] Just wait until I tell you afterwards about the disorganisation there, it was enough to make you want to shoot yourself, hell's bells!'[123] A fellow veteran of the 10th Flotilla, Midshipman Manisco (I/N 297) recalled the uninspiring leadership of one officer called 'Spaccarelli.' Manisco recalled that, '[he] was a man who thought that he was inspired, that he was destined to be the saviour of Italy. [...] He used to read books on Italian history and make long speeches and generally get everybody's backs up [...] because he never really understood anything, but just repeated what he had read.'[124] Mansico is possibly reflecting frustrations with programmes of training in the Italian armed forces that prioritised book-based classroom instruction. Even in 1940 the navy lacked sufficient experienced officers and petty officers, as well as technological equipment like radar and searchlights, to offer a high standard of practical training to their seamen.[125]

This is not to say that no one in the CSDIC (UK) cohort had anything positive to say about their officers, some men spoke with respect and affection. Both Sub-Lieutenant Mazzinghi (I/N 249) and Lieutenant Paladini (I/N 298) viewed the Commander-in-Chief of BETASOM Romolo Polacchini as a 'very intelligent man' and a 'nice fellow.'[126] Mazzinghi also respected submarine Commandante Grossi for engaging with an RAF Short Sunderland patrol plane. Instead of submerging and trying to escape, Grossi took the fight directly to the aircraft, managing to shoot it down with his deck-mounted machine guns.[127] Likewise Boatswain Borghetti (I/N 280) viewed his commander, Lieutenant Franco (I/N 248), as a 'damned fine CO,' praising the occasion 'he went into the middle of a[n enemy] formation, launched four torpedoes and hit a tanker and sank a cruiser.'[128]

Such positive sentiments are comparatively rare and could be tempered with qualifications. A Torpedo Petty Officer of the submarine *Avorio* (I/N 366) accepted that, in his experience, in the naval shock units there was a good sense of comradeship between officers and enlisted men. But he did go on to say that this was not the case in the submarine service. He said that 'before the war there was good feeling between the officers and ourselves, but now we've got the new generation who had no respect for anything.'[129] All-in-all the picture painted in the protocols of Italian military leadership at sea is largely negative. But there is a clear sense that many did wish that it was otherwise. These POWs wanted to be led by motivated and aggressive officers. When officers displayed bravery and put themselves at risk they won their men's respect. What lost that respect was a lack of drive, incompetence and ineptitude. None of these CSDIC (UK) POWs suggest that Italian servicemen wanted their officers to be *furbi*; Italian sailors, soldiers and airmen here valued broadly traditional martial virtues in their leaders.

Case Study in leadership: captain salvatore todaro

Capitano di Corvetta Salvatore Todaro (1908-1942), offers a case study of a well-known and popular commander amongst several of the CSDIC (UK) POWs. Born in Messina, he was a career naval officer who served on submarines during the Spanish Civil War and operated out of Bordeaux on the *Manara* and the *Cappellini* from June 1940. He served with the *4th Flottiglia MAS* on the Black Sea from November 1941 before being recalled to the Mediterranean in 1942, where he was killed in action on 13 December.[130] He was a highly decorated officer winning a Bronze Medal, three Silver Medals and a posthumous Gold Medal for Military Valor. The citation for the last of these describes him as a 'superior officer of high military and civil virtues. Very capable, strong-willed, tenacious, aggressive, very daring [...] a very bright example of calm, intelligent courage and absolute dedication.'[131] It is difficult to verify the truth of any of the tales told of Todaro in the transcripts. Next to nothing about Todaro has been written in English and it seems that a number of these stories are being told at least second-hand.[132] But it is telling how rarely Todaro's exploits were viewed with cynicism or scepticism. In this way, they give a valuable insight into which leadership qualities were most prized by Italian submariners. The most prominent being bravery in the face of danger, initiative and a willingness to stand up to the Germans and his own High Command.

A Leading Seaman in the submarine *Baracca* (I/N 123) was extensive in his praise for the Captain. He said, 'Todaro is an extraordinary chap [...] He attacks with gunfire anything and everything – cruisers, destroyers, no matter what it is.' I/N 123 also respected how Todaro treated his crew, looking after them, working hard to defend their interests and even standing them drinks when they were on leave.[133] This same source did admit that 'the Staff and the Admiral can't stand him,' but you do not get a sense this is a problem as far as I/N 123 was concerned. Rather, when you consider the hostility many other CSDIC (UK) POWs had towards their military 'senior management,' this may have added to Todaro's standing.[134] In the same conversation, Seaman

Stefanni (I/N 131) confirmed this view of Todaro, labelling him a 'splendid worker' and a 'fine sailor.'[135] Both his dauntlessness under fire and his sense of duty to his men were highlighted when Stefanni recalled how, on one patrol, Todaro 'engaged an auxiliary cruiser carrying troops, and a destroyer. First he shelled them with his guns, some of his crew being killed during the fight; then he torpedoed them. It was just off the coast; he took the dead and wounded to Spain afterwards.'[136]

Todaro's insouciant disregard for his own safety is made clear in an incident told by Sub-Lieutenant Mazzinghi (I/N 249). He said that, on one occasion when spotted by an enemy aircraft on patrol, Todaro wirelessed the plane directly and reported back to the pilot how his bombs were falling. Despite fruitlessly using up its payload the plane continued to follow the submarine which irked the Captain. At which point he wirelessed, 'my course is so-and-so, speed so-and-so many knots; go away and leave me alone.' Todaro's outburst worked and the plane moved on, replying, 'thank you, Bon Voyage.'[137] Such a devil-may-care attitude may very well have endangered the lives of his men, but it was something that Mazzinghi admired and he was not the only crew member won over by Todaro's bravery.

Torpedo Petty Officer Villosio (I/N 188) noted with respect the way in which Todaro made a point of attacking enemy ships on the surface with his deck guns.[138] Villosio also recalled how Todaro – on his own initiative – had planned to hide men from the *San Marco* battalion in his submarine. Arming them to the teeth, he intended to land them in England, causing chaos and taking prisoners. Once his commanders got wind of this scheme he was forced to abandon it as 'they were sure he would lose the boat.' One of the most remarkable aspects of the story is that all of the *San Marco* marines involved were willing volunteers.[139] Such a plan is reminiscent of the operations of the British No. 62 Commando, also known as the Small Scale Raiding Force (SSRF), who mounted highly dangerous raids along the Atlantic Wall between 1940 and 1943.[140] The Italian navy was not without commanders who could motivate their men and who were keen to take the fight to the enemy, like the British Commandos. Todaro's exploits here undermine the idea that Italian servicemen were always reluctant warriors, unwilling to go above and beyond their regular duties.

Petty Officer Paoli (I/N 175) admired Todaro's ethos at sea, that 'when a ship's at sea, I'm in command,' and lauded him for the initiative to move beyond the narrow scope of his orders when opportunities presented themselves.[141] For all of Todaro's martial spirit, Quartermaster Franzoni (I/N 283) nevertheless described him as a man of honour who went out of his way to rescue prisoners from the sea.[142] Sub-Lieutenant Bersani (I/N 247) corroborated the existence of Todaro's plan to put armed sailors ashore in England in order to cause destruction and chaos in the enemy's homeland. He said that, 'he planned to put them ashore at some point on the English coast, smash up an aerodrome and then go home.' He even went as far as having a stock of 'hunting knives and axes' on board for this very purpose.[143] Bersani was clearly a little wary of some of Todaro's eccentricities, saying 'they say he's one of those men who talk in such a way that you've never quite certain whether he's joking or in earnest.' An apparent 'devotee of the occult,' he had apparently learned at a séance that he would survive the war, inspiring his bravery.[144] Todaro conforms to a longstanding Italian tradition of enigmatic figures leading small groups to pull off extraordinary feats of bravery. For example, the 13 knights of the *Disfida di Barletta* in 1503, Garibaldi's Thousand Red Shirts in 1860 or the pilots of D'Annunzio's 87th Fighter Squadron as they flew over Vienna in August 1918.[145]

Sub-Lieutenant Mazzinghi (I/N 249) told of an incident where Todaro was willing to stand up to the Germans. Having kept quiet at a dinner with senior German and Italian officers, 'Todaro asked a German admiral whether he would mind giving him a list of steamers which had been sunk by German submarines. This was because he didn't want to sink a steamer which had already been sunk by [German] submarines.' This impudent questioning of the *Kriegmarine's* record earned Todaro a 'kick under the table' from the BETASOM Commander, and an awkward silence from the German officer.[146] Midshipman Devescovi (I/N 334) confirmed Todaro's at best strained relationship with the Germans, describing an incident where he clashed with none other than Admiral Karl Dönitz, accusing him of failing properly to support his Italian comrades in the supply of charts of British waters.[147] Todaro was tapping into a groundswell of Italian antagonism towards their German allies already demonstrated in the CSDIC (UK) protocols in Chapter Three. In these cases, he was saying what so many others are thinking, but not able to say themselves.

There were at least some POWs who lamented that there was only one Salvatore Todaro. For example, Sub-Lieutenant Morello (I/N 329) of the 10th *Flotilla MAS* who longed for 'three men like Todaro' to take over central command of the Italian shock units. Morello wanted officers with 'brains' and not posturing 'blockheads.' It is clear that he considered Todaro to be one of the former.[148] Another veteran of the 10th *Flotilla MAS*, Engineer Lieutenant Arena (I/N 319) wished that his 'rotten' commander could be replaced with Todaro as he was a 'smart man' who ensured his men were properly supplied.[149] As demonstrated above, this could not be taken for granted for many Italian servicemen during the Second World War. Given Todaro's unconventional leadership style, it is hardly surprising that virtually all those who hail him in the protocols are low-ranking enlisted men and junior officers. The reports give the sense that Todaro was an effective leader of men but an awkward subordinate. But to those he commanded he was clearly immensely popular. In these sources, he is repeatedly respected for his bravery in the field and praised for standing his ground against truculent senior Italian and German commanders. Todaro's case cuts to the heart of several issues that defined the experience of war for many Italians.

The home front

In discussions of the 'home front' two issues dominate – shortages of essential foodstuffs and the impact of Allied bombing on Italian towns and cities. The reader of such conversations is left with little doubt that both phenomena seriously affected everyday life for the inhabitants of the Italian peninsula. In doing so it reinforces the idea that the suffering of the Italian people was intense well before the fierce fighting of the 1943–45 Italian Campaign. The war fought between Italy and the Western Allies from 1940–43 caused hardship and suffering for a huge number of Italian civilians as well as service personnel. This fact was not lost on those under CSDIC (UK) surveillance. The regularity with which these matters are discussed indicates how very important these issues were to captured Italian servicemen and helps cast light on their outlook and values.

When it came to the availability of food, the situation in wartime Italy was dire. Speaking in July 1942, Torpedo Rating Diddi (I/N 191) admitted that, 'the last time I was on leave – at Genoa – I was struck by the sight of the women queuing up outside the shops.'[150] As early as August 1941 one MTB Boatswain's mate (I/N 92) described shortages of cheese, tea, coffee and coffee substitute in Italy.[151] Given this, it is scarcely surprising that Ordinary Seaman Serena (I/N 286) remarked that 'rationing is badly managed in Italy.'[152] In July 1943 Lieutenant-Colonel Donato (I/M 26) pronounced that, 'if you don't want your family to starve to death, you've got to go back [to Italy] and get a soft job.'[153] Donato's message that you needed influence in order to procure additional food supplies confirms the popular joke that the acronym of the Italian Fascist Party – PNF – really stood for *Per Necessità Familiari*.[154]

Poor government planning and a lack of state control over opportunist food producers meant that for many Italian civilians – especially women – the war was a time of hunger, and endless queuing for poor quality foodstuffs like the infamous wartime 'black bread' – rationed and made with adulterated flours.[155] Though hardly a man of the people, even Ciano repeatedly wrote of his concerns about food shortages from the Autumn of 1941 onwards. On 11 October he wrote in his diary that Italians were 'pulling in their belts to the last hole: the one that the Italians call the "foro Mussolini" – "the Mussolini hole".'[156] The system of Italian rationing hit hard a society that struggled to feed itself even in peacetime.[157] Sugar rationing began in February 1940, three months before Italy entered the conflict, and meat was initially not rationed because so few in the country could afford it anyway. The small quantities of food available meant that by 1943 the official ration in some areas only amounted to 1000 calories a day.[158] It is striking the extent to which Italian war literature highlights an obsession with food even before the summer of 1943. One good example is the opening chapters of Moravia's *La Ciociara* which offers an image of the hardship of surviving in wartime Rome.[159]

Given the problems with regulated food supplies, many Italians used the black market for their staple foodstuffs. As Flying Officer Alvisi (I/A 35) made clear, 'the food situation in Italy was such that one couldn't live without having recourse to the black market.'[160] So desperate were some people for food that they, 'contrived to get themselves called to the colours in order to get enough to eat.'[161] The authorities were aware of such activity and did try to stem the tide. As Petty Officer Boschin (I/N 176) recalled, during one week the stationmaster at Padua, 'confiscated 450kg of [black market] olive oil, and in addition to that salami, meat, butter; there was even some coffee; there was everything, there was flour.'[162]

The pressures on the Italian food supply system led to a huge increase in prices. In Central and Southern Italy by 1943 prices for food had risen to over five times their 1938 levels, while incomes had only risen by less than two times.[163] Signalman Sauro (I/N 198) remembered that, 'in my village black market bread costs 4 lire a kilo. Black market flour costs 12 lire a kilo.'[164] Petty Officer Boatswain Losi (I/N 239) recalled that, 'the last time I was at home [...] eggs cost three lire each and a flask of olive oil cost fifty lire.'[165] These prices were undoubtedly a struggle for many on low incomes, as leading Engine-Room Rating Feleppa (I/N 160) made clear, 'people who earn 8 lire a day can't pay the fantastic prices the stuff costs.'[166] Petty Officer Di Fiori (I/N 221) simply said, 'I pity the poor devils who have to live on their ration-cards.'[167] As Grampp has argued, the black market, 'touched everybody in Italian society [...] because the amount of food distributed through the rationing system was wholly insufficient.'[168]

The responses to such tales of the black market were overwhelmingly negative and met with hostility. Second Lieutenant Rizzo (I/M 45) lambasted all those who had used the war to enrich themselves – 'there are people who have made fortunes, people who have made millions out of Italian blood, out of the blood of the fallen.'[169] Concerns were naturally heightened when the shortages at home adversely affected friends and family. In December 1942 Lieutenant Paladini (I/N 298) reported that, 'my wife, who weighed 65 kg last year, has lost 12 kg and this year it will be worse.'[170] Likewise, Petty Officer Spinelli (I/N 151) was concerned that, 'my mother manages to keep going for the present, but when winter comes it will be terrible. And there are certain things which I couldn't help seeing during that month's leave – two or three times even men who were crying.'[171] Whether this was from hunger itself or the frustration of being unable to provide for their families is not clear. But what is obvious is that the dire situation on the Italian Home Front was having severe effects on the health and welfare of civilians and this was filtering down to affect the morale of those in the fighting services.

It is worth considering how much this position is determined by the situation in which these men found themselves. Isolated from and unable to directly help their families, the prisoners adopted a principled line of criticism of black marketers. They reject the model of *furberia* and *l'arte di arrangiarsi*. Had they been able to get home, to operate networks, to take advantage of connections to look after their families themselves, they may have thought very differently about the 'spivs' selling over-priced goods. But emasculated and stuck in a prisoner of war camp, they believed that the black marketeers were exploitative, and hoped that someone would step in.

The discussion of Allied bombing raids on Italian urban areas also reinforces many points about the starkness of Italy's war from 1940 to 1943. This began just one day after Italy joined the war, with an RAF raid on the Turin Fiat plant on 11/12 June 1940. With UK-based Bomber Command raiding the north and Mediterranean Allied Air Forces marauding throughout the south, Italians were victim to a rolling campaign of bombing. Between September 1940 and December 1941 alone Bomber Command flew 300 sorties against Italian targets, growing to 1646 sorties between 22 October 1942 and 12 December 1942.[172] The cities of Turin, La Spezia, Genoa and Milan bore the brunt of these attacks and suffered considerable damage as a result. On one raid on 14/15 February 1943, 142 Lancaster bombers destroyed 27 Milanese factories for the loss of just 2 aircraft (a loss rate of 1.4 percent). This was at a time when average RAF losses for Berlin raids were 5.6 percent.[173] As a precursor to the invasion of the island in 1943, Sicilian cities were ruthlessly targeted. Trapani was hit 41 times; Augusta 43; Messina 58; Palermo 69; and Catania 87. On 19 July 1943, the Mediterranean Allied Strategic Air Force sent over 500 aircraft to bomb Rome's railway marshalling yards. The tracks were hit 45 times, the rolling stock was devastated, and 700 Italians were killed. It was the largest daylight raid yet mounted in the war, and a very deliberate expression of Allied strength in the air.[174]

The impact of such bombing is noted in many conversations. Sub-Lieutenant Budini (I/N 373) described Turin devastated by Allied bombing raids – 'a disaster – almost everything was destroyed. The public services have almost stopped working and nearly everybody has left the town.'[175] A Sub-Lieutenant (I/N 39) described the aftermath of a bombing raid on Cagliari – 'a steamer was burning [...] trams overturned and smashed, and in the town [...] on the ground were found the entrails of one of the port sentries. Poor fellow, that's all they found of him.'[176] The human cost of the bombing war fought in Italy was considerable. Recent scholarship has estimated that 80000 were killed in Italian cities during the Second World War.[177] While this figure includes fatalities from the period 1943–1945 – thus also those killed by the *Luftwaffe* – other statistics show that deaths before 1943 numbered in the high thousands. For example, in 1943 alone 6097 were killed in Naples.[178]

There were numerous prisoners who blamed the senior Fascist leadership for such devastation and human suffering. For Midshipman Gridelli (I/N 378) it was clear who was at fault: 'of course, they bomb our towns, but I know what was our undoing – the fact that Mussolini requested the honour of bombing London.' Gridelli felt that once this became known to the British, they bombed Italian cities as acts of retaliation.[179] Naval Rating Allegre (I/N 356) spoke of the response of the people of Genoa to aerial and naval bombardment,

> If you go to Genoa it makes you sit up a bit! And Turin – my word! [...] the places which have got it worst are Genoa and Turin. And Genoa has had a naval bombardment too [...] At Corrigliano near Genoa they wrote on the walls: 'Duce, if you come to Genoa, we'll see you never leave it again.' (Laughs).

It seems Gridelli was supportive of these Genoese sentiments. The city was bombed six times in October and November 1942, raids which directly killed 500 and destroyed thousands of homes.[180] In October, panicked crushes and suffocation killed 694 more in Genoa's inadequate tunnel shelters.[181] The Royal Naval bombardment in February 1941 damaged or sunk 20 *Regia Marina* vessels but caused 386 civilian casualties and decimated the residential and industrial areas by the docks.[182] In the Genoese *comune* of Recco – targeted for its viaduct – bombing raids killed 127 and destroyed 90 percent of its buildings.[183] Whatever British motives for bombing key cities, the fate of Genoa showed how devastating the consequences could be. While losses were considerably smaller when compared to Dresden or Hamburg,[184] the Genoese experience of Allied bombing raids remained one of terror and destruction.

The anger directed at Italy's leaders makes sense when you consider the poor state of Italian aerial defences during the Second World War. Despite Mussolini's public claims to impenetrable defences, there were enormous shortages of anti-aircraft weaponry and air-raid shelters. The organisation tasked with coordinating air-raid defence – the National Union for Anti-Aircraft Protection (UNPA) – had little funding, and by May 1939 Italy's shelters could only accommodate 300000 people. Many of these offered little protection from large explosions and if overcrowded could suffocate their occupants.[185] No resources had been used to update Italy's system of aircraft detection and AA weaponry before 1940, meaning that most anti-aircraft batteries were of a First World War vintage. While the British had pioneered the use of state-of-the-art radar, the Italian military was forced to rely on 'aerophones' – listening devices often operated by the blind, because it was believed they had better hearing.[186]

The poor preparations were repeatedly described by several CSDIC (UK) POWs. For instance, Lieutenant Padesso (I/N 392) stated. 'I saw the batteries firing at Flying Fortresses [American B-17 bombers] over Naples; they were pitiable.'[187] The commander of the submarine *Asteria*, Lieutenant Morone (I/N 375) vented his frustrations,

> For God's sake, with all these damned raids – anyone could forsee how it would end. Without any AA defence, without a shelter in the vital points, for instance at ports. If they come over those are the chief objectives on which they drop bombs. These wretched people have to be as brave as lions standing out in the open watching the bombs falling on their heads. Where in hell is there a proper shelter?[188]

Engineer Lieutenant Cristini (I/N 361) outlined how essential command centres in Rome were protected by just 20 cm of concrete, which could be cracked open by just one 50 kg bomb.[189] While the majority of Second World War air raid shelters would have struggled to survive a direct hit of any kind, given that even an early war British bomber like the Handley Page Hampden could be loaded with eight 500 lb. bombs (227 kg each) the quality of defences insufficient, especially for such vital locations.[190]

These conversations also gave an outlet for strong anti-British sentiment, reinforcing the analysis in Chapter Three. Chief Boatswain Bergadono (I/N 343) remembered how, 'in Piedmont I saw all the families on the move, all looking for new homes. There's hatred for the English there.'[191] A similar tale dominated an exchange between Chief Boatswain Luciani (I/N 325) and Petty Officer Diver Varini (I/N 294) in January 1943,

I/N 325: The English have made a great mistake – I can tell you that. If they hadn't bombed Milan, Turin and Genoa, there would be no resistance on the part of the people to an English landing.

I/N 294: True. For instance, before the bombing attacks on Genoa, the Genovese always used to say: 'The English aren't really so bad; they've always been friends of Italy.' But it's different now. Now they hate them – they hate them with a mortal hatred.[192]

Proud son of Genoa, Midshipman Franchini (I/N 379), confirmed this in his description of damage done to the many historic and cultural sites of Genoa, he said,

> But this is the work of those filthy, dirty accursed pigs [the RAF] [...] When I went on leave and saw all of this [...] I wept. All the dearest and most beautiful things we had in Genoa, the most precious things [...] admired by everybody, even by these pigs when they used to come to Italy, all in ruins.[193]

Many other Italians were angered by the destruction of their country's cultural sites. Milanese Grazia Alfieri Tarentino wrote of her bitterness towards the RAF as she saw La Scala theatre engulfed in flames, it was: 'all that had remained of the heart of the city.'[194] Franchini's sentiments are both completely understandable in the circumstances, and can be seen as part of a wider picture of anti-British sentiment already outlined in Chapter Three.

In late June 1943 Lieutenant-Colonel Pedala (I/M 13) spoke of the mindset of his men, and his own concerns about the Italian home front,

> War-weary men, worried about their families [...] there are many men who are worried about their families, the air raids, the food. The men worry terribly about those things. [...] Look at me, for example, I am worried to death; my father and my brother are at Palermo, and I don't

know where my other son is. My wife is in Rome, but I don't know what the hell is happening to her, whether she is getting enough to eat or not [...] I am more concerned about them than I am about myself.[195]

Pedala encapsulates the image of the Italian home front as a place of considerable hardship which itself caused much anxiety amongst the CSDIC (UK) cohort. The dual pressures of hunger and bombing created a febrile atmosphere in Italy, a collapse in morale whereby dissent shifted from the private to the public sphere. In the industrial north, the winter of 1942–1943 was a period of considerable unrest, protests and absenteeism – which amounted to some 20 percent of Fiat workers.[196] In spring 1943 Piedmont and Lombardy were rocked by a wave of industrial strikes launched in an effort to convince the RAF to halt the bombing,[197] a testament to how the misery of the Italian experience of war had led many Italians to outright defeatism.

Conclusion

For Torpedo Petty Officer I/N 84, his family was his primary concern, regardless of the result of the war. He said, 'I want to get back to Italy, no matter who wins. It's all very fine fighting for one's country, but one has got to think of one's family as well.'[198] The primacy of getting home above all else was a sentiment echoed by an unnamed member of the *Regia Aeronautica* (I/A 2 or I/A 4). He said, 'I want to know when we shall be liberated. Victors or vanquished, I don't mind, I want to go home.'[199] However, others amongst the CSDIC (UK) cohort could be far more patriotic and determined to fight. During a conversation with his cellmate (I/N 373), Lieutenant Colonel Ravazzoni (I/A 32) stated, 'whatever happens I shall fight for my country and I won't fight for [the Allies]. You'll never see me fire a single shot side-by-side with an English or American soldier [...] After all, whoever you may be, blood is blood – one mustn't forget that.'[200]

At least one part of Petty Officer Guglielmo's (I/N 206) drive to keep fighting was a desire to avenge fallen comrades. He said how he wanted to 'avenge Giobbe and Moccagatta,' two comrades who had been killed during a raid on Malta.[201] Similarly Sub-Lieutenant Mazzinghi (I/N 249) described at length why he decided to quit a comparatively safe job ashore,

> Do you know that I could have had a shore job since last year? Because when I left my ship I was in such a state that I could hardly stand up. I applied for another job afloat as soon as I had read the conditions for joining submarines, but it wasn't in order to fight for this filthy abominable regime, but because I felt myself humiliated and insignificant in comparison with all my friends who have died, and all the men I know who have sacrificed their lives. That was the reason. I did it for their sake![202]

Mazzinghi's words, like those of Ravazzoni, Guglielmo and I/N 84, point towards the risks of 'essentialising' a specifically 'Italian' experience of the Second World War. While concern over family and personal aggrandisement are often seen as particularly 'Italian' they are not exclusively so. The views expressed here – as in this chapter as a whole – are diverse and can challenge many of our pre-conceived ideas about the 'Italian' experience of the Second World War.

Mussolini's Italy was in an almost continuous state of war from 1935 to 1945,[203] during which the military suffered a long list of set-backs and defeats – Guadalajara, Sidi Barrani, Keren and Taranto are to name just a few. While it may be tempting to blame these defeats on weaknesses in the Italian 'character,' this is simply not the case. As this chapter has repeatedly shown the notion of the *Italiani Brava Gente* is a myth, and to brand Italian service personnel as disinterested, cynical and unmotivated, is lazy and disinguous. It is also important to reframe many of our ideas about the 1940-1943 'Italian War.' When seen through the eyes of the Italians who experienced it, it was not a sideshow. While Italian servicemen experienced the many traumas of combat on land, sea and air, Italian civilians had to endure the privations of rationing and the horrors of Allied bombing. The CSDIC (UK) prisoners of war also took a considerable professional interest in their equipment, even if wider structural problems in the Italian military supply chain meant there were serious deficiencies in their quality and quantity. The Italian soldiers, sailors and airmen observed in these transcripts also admired courageous and determined leaders, but the cohort remained ever ready to criticise the corrupt, the lazy and the weak, a position which will become ever more apparent in the following chapter as attitudes to Italian political leadership are considered.

Notes

1. I/SRN 207 – 24 October 1941 – WO 208/4189, TNA; I/SRM 26 – 24 June 1943, WO 208/4188, TNA.
2. Ordinary Seaman Stefanni (I/N 131): 'You ought to have seen some of the beards on board that ship. Some of the young chaps had beards, and of course six months' beard is getting on for a fine growth. It was a sight!,' I/SRN 169 – 18 October 1941, WO 208/4189. For discussion of tactics, see: I/SRX 129 – 7 August 1943, WO 208/ 4193, TNA.
3. The *L'Ufficio Storico dello Stato Maggiore* (Historical Office of the Italian General Staff) has produced a considerable number of official histories of the conflict. These include: Mario Montanari, *Le Operazioni in Africa Settentrionale, Vol. I: Sidi el Barrani (Giugno 1940 – Settembre 1941)* (Rome: USSME, 2000); Marco Cuzzi, *'L'Occupazione Italiana della Slovenia (1941–1943)* (Rome: USSME, 1998); Luigi Longo, *Immagini della Seconda Guerra Mondiale la Campagna in Tunisia (1942–1943)* (Rome: USSME, 2007).
4. Official histories include: Giorgio Fioravazo, *Le Azioni Navali in Mediterraneo dal 1 Aprile 1941 all'8 Settembre 1943* (Rome: USMM, 2001); Pier Lupinacci, *Attivita in Mar Nero e Lago Ladoga* (Rome: USMM 2003); Mori Ubaldini, *I Sommergibili Negli Oceani* (Rome: USMM, 2002); Carlo De Riso, *I Mezzi D'Assalto Nella Seconda Guerra Mondiale* (Rome: USMM, 2013).

5 Official histories include: Ferdinando Pedriali, *L'Italia nella Guerra Aerea da El Alamein alle Spiagge della Sicilia (4 Novembre 1942 – 9 Luglio 1943)* (Rome: USAM, 2010); Ferdinando Pedriali, *L'Italia nella Guerra Aerea dalla Difesa della Sicilia all'8 Settembre* (Rome: USAM, 2014); Cesare Gori, *Il Savoia Marchetti S.M. 79 nel Secondo Conflitto Mondiale* (Rome: USAM, 2004).
6 I/SRX 130 – 7 August 1943, WO 208/4193, TNA.
7 The idea of Italy as a woman whose honour and virtue must be defended is dealt with at length in several works by Alberto Mario Banti. See: Alberto Banti, *La nazione del Risorgimento. Parentela, santità ed onore alle origini dell'Italia unita* (Turin: Einaudi, 2000); Alberto Banti, *L'onore della nazione. Identità sessuale e violenza nel nazionalismo europeo dal XVIII secolo alla grande guerra* (Turin: Einaudi, 2005); Alberto Banti, *Sublime madre nostra. La nazione italiana dal Risorgimento al fascismo* (Rome: Laterza, 2011).
8 Piero Crociani and Pier Battistelli, *Italian Army Elite Units and Special Forces, 1940-43* (Oxford: Osprey, 2011), 44–45.
9 Crociani and Battistelli, *Army Elite Units*, 44–52.
10 I/SRX 130 – 7 August 1943, WO 208/4193, TNA.
11 I/SRX 139 – 22 August 1943, WO 208/4188, TNA.
12 I/SRX 139 – 22 August 1943, WO 208/4188, TNA.
13 Eric Morris, *Circles of Hell: The War in Italy, 1943–1945* (New York: Crown, 1993), 42, 45.
14 SRIG 115 – 10 July 1943, WO 208/4185, TNA.
15 Italian losses during the Sicilian Campaign (9 July–17 August 1943) have been calculated as 4678 killed, 32500 wounded and 152933 missing and captured. See: Alberto Santoni, *Le operazioni in Sicilia e in Calabria (luglio – settembre 1943)* (Rome: USSME, 1993), 400–401.
16 I/SRX 104 – 10 July 1943, WO 208/4193, TNA. Holland has argued this stemmed from Italian high command's desire to keep the batteries protected and out of range of naval gunfire. James Holland, *Sicily '43: The First Assault on Fortress Europe* (London: Bantam Press, 2020), 108.
17 I/SRX 104 – 10 July 1943, WO 208/4193, TNA.
18 I/SRX 104 – 10 July 1943, WO 208/4193, TNA.
19 I/SRX 31 – 2 March 1943, WO 208/4193, TNA.
20 I/SRX 31 – 2 March 1943, WO 208/4193, TNA.
21 Bungay, *Alamein*, 54.
22 Holland, *Together*, 242, 284, 349, 384, 670, 695, 700, 707.
23 I/SRX 85 – 22 June 1943, WO 208/4193, TNA.
24 I/SRX 26 – 4 August 1943, WO 208/4193, TNA.
25 I/SRX 26 – 4 August 1943, WO 208/4193, TNA.
26 I/SRN 284 – 26 November 1941, WO 208/4189, TNA.
27 I/SRN 151 – 15 October 1941, WO 208/4189, TNA.
28 Jonathan Dimbleby, *The Battle of the Atlantic: How the Allies Won the War* (London: Penguin, 2016), xxi.
29 Michael Whitley, *Destroyers of World War Two: An International Encyclopedia* (Annapolis: Naval Institute Press, 1988), 166.
30 I/SRN 475 – 18 August 1942, WO 208/4190, TNA.
31 I/SRN 488 – 24 August 1942, WO 208/4190, TNA.
32 I/SRX 55 – 8 March 1943, WO 208/4193, TNA.
33 For more on the Italian naval divers, see: Valerio Borghese, *Sea Devils: Italian Navy Commandos in World War II* (Annapolis: Naval Institute Press, 2009); Jack Greene and Alessandro Massignani, *The Black Prince and the Sea Devils: The Story of Valerio Borghese and the Elite Unites of the Decima MAS* (Cambridge: Da Capo, 2004); Lazzero Ricciotti, *La decima Mas* (Milan: Rizzoli, 1984).
34 I/SRN 646 – 10 October 1942, WO 208/4190, TNA.

35 I/SRN 646 – 10 October 1942, WO 208/4190, TNA.
36 I/SRN 644 – 8 October 1942, WO 208/4190, TNA.
37 I/SRN 651 – 17 October 1942, WO 208/4190, TNA.
38 I/SRN 767 – 21 December 1942, WO 208/4190, TNA.
39 I/SRX 42 – 5 March 1943, WO 208/4193, TNA. Respectively these vessels were sunk on 14 September 1942 (Mediterranean); 7 June 1942 (Mediterranean); 28 October 1941 (Atlantic); 10 September 1941 (Atlantic); 22 February 1941 (Atlantic). See: Kevin Moeller, 'The Italian Submarine Force in the Battle of the Atlantic: Left in the Dark', Masters Thesis, US Army Command and General Staff College (Fort Leavenworth, 2014), 78–82.
40 Moeller, 'Dark', 60.
41 http://www.regiamarina.net/sub_casualties.asp?nid=196&lid=1, accessed 17 April 2018. These remain proportionally in line with *Kriegsmarine* U-boat losses in the Second World War. Of the 1167 U-boats commissioned by the *Kriegsmarine* between 1935 and 1945, 757 were lost giving a loss-rate of 65 percent. Over 30000 German naval personnel were killed as a result of this. See: Axel Niestle, *German U-Boat Losses During World War II: Details of Destruction* (London: Frontline, 2014), 11; Timothy Mulligan, *Neither Sharks Nor Wolves: The Men of Nazi Germany's U-Boat Arm, 1939–1945* (Annapolis: Naval Institute Press, 1999), pp. 251–256.
42 Sadkovich, *The Italian Navy*, 51.
43 See: Liddell Hart, *History*, 447.
44 I/SRN 331 – 29 July 1942, WO 208/4189, TNA.
45 I/SRN 863 – 6 January 1943, WO 208/4191, TNA.
46 I/SRN 424 – 11 August 1942, WO 208/4190, TNA.
47 Brian Sullivan, 'A Fleet in Being: The Rise and Fall of Italian Sea Power, 1861–1943', *The International History Review*, 10/1 (1988), 121.
48 Sullivan, 'Fleet in Being', 121.
49 I/SRN 146 – 15 October 1941, WO 208/4189, TNA.
50 I/SRN 76 – 29 July 1941, WO 208/4189, TNA.
51 I/SRN 785 – 18 December 1942, WO 208/4191, TNA.
52 There were only two survivors, one of whom later died of his wounds. http://www.regiamarina.net/detail_text_with_list.asp?nid=84&lid=1&cid=28, accessed 17 April 2018.
53 I/SRN 528 – 30 August 1942, WO 208/4190, TNA.
54 I/SRN 616 – 13 September 1942, WO 208/4190, TNA.
55 I/SRX 57 – 16 March 1943, WO 208/4193, TNA.
56 I/SRN 1159 – 13 April 1943, WO 208/4192, TNA.
57 I/SRN 609 – 16 September 1942, WO 208/4190, TNA.
58 I/SRN 549 – 7 September 1942, WO 208/4190, TNA.
59 Yet, it is a phenomenon that is all too familiar in literature on the armed forces of Nazi Germany and Imperial Japan. For examples of the extremes this can lead to, see: Christopher Browning, *Ordinary Men: Reserve Police Battalion 101 and the Final Solution in Poland* (New York: HarperCollins, 2017); Iris Chang, *The Rape of Nanking: The Forgotten Holocaust of World War II* (New York: Basic Books, 1997).
60 I/SRN 353 – 2 August 1942, WO 208/4189, TNA.
61 I/SRN 169 – 18 October 1941, WO 208/4189, TNA.
62 I/SRN 148 – 15 October 1941, WO 208/4189, TNA.
63 I/SRN 635 – 29 September 1942, WO 208/4190, TNA.
64 Karl Dönitz, *Memoirs: Ten Years and Twenty Days* (Barnsley: Frontline, 2012), 263.
65 G. H. Bennett, 'The 1942 Laconia Order: The Murder of Shipwrecked Survivors and the Allied Pursuit of Justice, 1945–46', *Law, Crime and History*, 1 (2011), 23.
66 Bennett, 'Laconia', 22.
67 I/SRN 241 – 12 November 1941, WO 208/4198, TNA.
68 https://www.wrecksite.eu/wreck.aspx?142179, accessed 9 November 2017.

69 http://www.regiamarina.net/detail_text_with_list.asp?nid=84&lid=1&cid=30, accessed 9 November 2017
70 I/SRN 560 – 11 September 1942, WO 208/4190, TNA.
71 I/SRN 559 – 7 September 1942, WO 208/4190, TNA.
72 I/SRN 353 – 2 August 1943, WO 208/4189, TNA; I/SRN 348 – 1 August 1943, WO 208/4189, TNA.
73 I/SRN 353 – 2 August 1943, WO 208/4189, TNA.
74 I/SRN 434 – 14 August 1942, WO 208/4190, TNA. For criticisms of Longobardo, see: I/SRN 338 – 30 July 1942, WO 208/4189, TNA and I/SRN 403 – 9 August 1942, WO 208/4190, TNA.
75 I/SRN 340 – 31 July 1942, WO 208/4189, TNA.
76 To compare with the experience of *Kriegsmarine* submariners and Royal Navy sailors, see: Hans Goebeler, *Steel Boat, Iron Hearts: A U-boat Crewman's Life Aboard U-505* (El Dorado Hills: Savas Beatie, 2013); Patrick Mahoney, *The Sinking of the Prince of Wales and Repulse* (Barnsley: Pen & Sword, 2014).
77 I/SRN 690 – 28 November 1942, WO 208/4190, TNA.
78 I/SRN 688 – 30 November 1942, WO 208/4190, TNA.
79 I/SRN 710 – 5 December 1942, WO 208/4190, TNA.
80 I/SRN 682 – 28 November 1942, WO 208/4190, TNA.
81 The *Istituto Centrale di Statistica* calculated in 1957 that Italy suffered 86370 military deaths between 1940 and the armistice on 8 September 1943. See: Dana Glei and Silvia Bruzzone, 'Effects of War Losses on Mortality Estimates for Italy: A First Attempt', *Demographic Research*, 13 (2005), 379.
82 The manned torpedos are discussed on several occasions in the CSDIC (UK) transcripts, including by Petty Officer Botti (I/N 318) who suggests that the nickname *Maiale* (pig) comes from the grunting noise made by water pumping out of the exhausts. I/SRN 853 – 9 January 1943, WO 208/4191, TNA. See also: I/SRN 381 – 6 August 1942, WO 208/4189, TNA; I/SRN 878 – 8 January 1943, WO 208/4191, TNA.
83 Lucio Ceva and Andrea Curami, *Le Meccanizzazione Dell'Esercito Fino Al 1943: Vol. 1 & Vol. 2* (Rome: USSME, 1989), 453.
84 Eddy Bauer, *The History of World War II* (London: Silverdale, 2000), 95. For more on the Italian armed forces in North Africa, see: USSME, *La preparazione del conflitto – l'avanzata su sidi el Barrani (ottobre 1935 – settembre 1940)* (Rome: USSME, 1955); USSME, *La prima controffensiva italo-tedesca in Africa Settentrionale (15 febbraio – 18 novembre 1941)* (Rome: USSME, 1974); USSME, *Terza offensive Britannica in Africa settentrionale – la battaglia di El Alamein e il ripigamento in Tunisia (6 settembre 1942 – 4 febbraio 1943)* (Rome: USSME, 1961).
85 Roy Dunlap, *Ordnance Went Up Front* (Plantersville: SATPC, 1948), 58; Philip Jowett, *The Italian Army: 1940–45 (1), Europe 1940–43* (Oxford: Osprey, 2000), 48.
86 I/SRX 136 – 15 August 1943, WO 208/4193, TNA.
87 I/SRA 44 – 11 July 1942, WO 208/4184, TNA.
88 I/SRM 22 – 23 June 1943, WO 208/4188, TNA.
89 X/SRX 4 – 20 August 1941, WO 208/4194, TNA.
90 I/SRX 95 – 29 June 1943, WO 208/4193, TNA.
91 I/SRN 840 – 4 January 1943, WO 208/4191, TNA. Other accounts have claimed that Italian paratrooper units were sent to Tunisia in January 1943 without event steel helmets. Crociani and Battistelli, *Navy and Air Force*, 40.
92 I/SRN 579 – 17 September 1942, WO 208/4190, TNA.
93 I/SRN 554 – 9 September 1942, WO 208/4190, TNA.
94 For a similar example of Potemkinism during Hitler's 1938 visit to Rome, see: Goeschel, *Alliance*, 97.
95 I/SRX 87 – 23 June 1943, WO 208/4193, TNA.

96 I/SRX 109 – 7 July 1943, WO 208/4193, TNA.
97 I/SRN 58 – 17 January 1941, WO 208/4189, TNA.
98 Alexander Nützenadel, *Landwirtschaft, Staat und Autarkie: Agarpolitik im Faschistischen Italien (1922–1943)* (Tübingen: De Gruyter, 1997); Jons Cohen, 'Fascism and Agriculture in Italy: Policies and Consequences', *The Economic History Review*, 32/1 (1979), 70–87.
99 I/SRN 1150 – 10 April 1943, WO 208/4192, TNA.
100 I/SRX 88 – 22 Jun 1943, WO 208/4193, TNA.
101 Stewart, *First Victory*, 122–123.
102 Stewart, *First Victory*, 141.
103 John Macdonald and Željko Cimprić, *Caporetto and the Isonzo Campaign: The Italian Front, 1915–1918* (Barnsley: Pen & Sword, 2011), 25.
104 Mack Smith, *Roman Empire*, 176.
105 Brian Sullivan, 'The Italian Armed Forces, 1918–1940', in Allan Millet and Williamson Murray, eds., *Military Effectiveness, Volume 2: The Interwar Period* (Boston: Allen & Unwin, 1988), 205.
106 I/SRN 43 – 3 January 1941, WO 208/4189, TNA.
107 I/SRN 43 – 3 January 1941, WO 208/4189, TNA.
108 I/SRN 463 – 19 August 1943, WO 208/4190, TNA.
109 I/SRX 35 – 2 March 1943, WO 208/4193, TNA. Fresh seafood was an unimaginable luxury to frontline troops who had to make do with hardtack and cold canned food. The Army had mobile field kitchens, but they relied on wood – a resource hard to find in the sparsely wooded Western Desert and the Russian Steppe. Knox, *Italian Allies*, 155.
110 Sullivan, '1918–1940', 200.
111 Sullivan, 'Italian Soldier', 182.
112 Sullivan, '1918–1940', 200.
113 I/SRN 581 – 20 September 1942, WO 208/4190, TNA.
114 I/SRN 247 – 16 November 1941, WO 208/4189, TNA.
115 I/SRN 450 – 16 August 1942, WO 208/4190, TNA.
116 I/SRN 228 – 29 October 1941, WO 208/4189, TNA.
117 I/SRN 429 – 9 August 1942, WO 208/4190, TNA.
118 I/SRN 366 – 2 August 1942, WO 208/4189, TNA.
119 I/SRN 868 – 17 January 1943, WO 208/4191, TNA.
120 I/SRN 1151 – 10 April 1943, WO 208/4192, TNA.
121 I/SRN 61 – 4 June 1941, WO 208/4189, TNA.
122 I/SRN 895 – 14 January 1943, WO 208/4191, TNA.
123 I/SRN 874 – 12 January 1943, WO 208/4191, TNA.
124 I/SRN 904 – 13 January 1943, WO 208/4191, TNA.
125 Sullivan, '1918–1940', pp. 202–203.
126 I/SRN 773 – 24 December 1942, WO 208/4191, TNA.
127 I/SRN 726 – 17 December 1942, W0 208/4190, TNA.
128 I/SRN 708 – 7 December 1942, WO 208/4190, TNA.
129 I/SRN 1048 – 2 March 1943, WO 208/4191, TNA.
130 http://www.marina.difesa.it/storiacultura/storia/medaglie/Pagine/TodaroSalvatore. aspx, accessed 17 July 2018. See also: Armando Anzoletti, *Il Comandante Salvatore Todaro* (Rome: Giovanni Volpe, 1970).
131 http://www.quirinale.it/onorificenze/insigniti/12675, accessed 17 July 2018.
132 For example: I/SRN 542 – 3 September 1942, WO 208/4190, TNA. His sinking of the Belgian steamship Kabalo is briefly mentioned in James Duffy, *The Sinking of the Laconia and the U-Boat War: Disaster in the Mid-Atlantic* (Lincoln: University of Nebraska Press, 2013), 28.
133 I/SRN 134 – 12 October 1941, WO 208/4189, TNA.

134 I/SRN 134 – 12 October 1941, WO 208/4189, TNA.
135 I/SRN 134 – 12 October 1941, WO 208/4189, TNA.
136 I/SRN 134 – 12 October 1941, WO 208/4189, TNA.
137 I/SRN 797 – 25 December 1942, WO 208/4191, TNA.
138 I/SRN 442 – 16 August 1942, WO 208/4190, TNA.
139 I/SRN 442 – 16 August 1942, WO 208/4190, TNA.
140 Foot, *SOE in France*, 167–168. See also: Brian Lett, *The Small Scale Raiding Force* (Barnsley: Pen & Sword, 2013).
141 I/SRN 484 – 25 August 1942, WO 208/4190, TNA.
142 I/SRN 817 – 30 December 1942, W0 208/4191, TNA.
143 I/SRN 542 – 3 September 1942, WO 208/4190, TNA.
144 I/SRN 542 – 3 September 1942, WO 208/4190, TNA.
145 Giuliano Procacci, *La disfida di Barletta: Tra storia e romanzo* (Milan: Mondadori, 2001); Lucy Riall, *Garibaldi: Invention of a Hero* (New Haven: Yale University Press, 2008), 207–225; Lucy Hughes-Hallett, *The Pike: Gabriele D'Annunzio, Poet, Seducer and Preacher of War* (London: Fourth Estate, 2013), 441–443.
146 I/SRN 773 – 24 December 1942, WO 208/4191, TNA.
147 I/SRN 908 – 18 January 1943, WO 208/4191, TNA.
148 I/SRN 911 – 13 January 1943, WO 208/4191, TNA.
149 I/SRN 878 – 8 January 1943, WO 208/4191, TNA.
150 I/SRN 332 – 27 July 1942, WO 208/4189, TNA.
151 X/SRX 7 – 25 August 1941, WO 208/4194, TNA.
152 I/SRN 674 – 26 November 1942, WO 208/4190, TNA.
153 I/SRM 38 – 4 July 1943, WO 208/4188, TNA.
154 Translated as: 'For the need of the family.' See: Francesca Tacchi, *Storia Illustrata del Fascismo* (Florence: Giunti, 2000), 104.
155 Miriam Mafai, *Pane Nero: Donne e vita quotidiana nella seconda guerra mondiale* (Milan: Mondadori, 1987), 123.
156 Ciano, *War Diaries*, 265, 270, 271, 281, 304, 315.
157 Indeed, Helstosky has argued that the Italian diet was shaped above all by varying degrees of scarcity during the nineteenth and twentieth centuries. See: Carol Helstosky, *Garlic and Oil: Food and Politics in Italy* (Oxford: Berg, 2004).
158 Perry Wilson, *Women in Twentieth-Century Italy* (London: Palgrave Macmillan, 2009), 100. See also: Aurelio Lepre, *Le illusioni, la paura, la rabbia: Il fronte Italiano, 1940–1943* (Naples: Edizioni Scientifiche Italiane, 1989), 83–91.
159 Alberto Moravia, *La Ciociara* (Milan: Tascabili Bompiani, 1957).
160 I/SRX 124 – 6 August 1943, WO 208/4193, TNA.
161 I/SRX 124 – 6 August 1943, WO 208/4193, TNA.
162 I/SRN 418 – 12 August 1942, WO 208/4190, TNA.
163 Williani Grampp, 'The Italian Lira, 1938–45', *Journal of Political Economy*, 54/4 (1946), 309–310.
164 I/SRN 393 – 7 August 1943, WO 208/4189, TNA.
165 I/SRN 519 – 3 September 1942, WO 208/4190, TNA.
166 I/SRN 300 – 30 November 1941, WO 208/4189, TNA.
167 I/SRN 519 – 3 September 1942, WO 208/4190, TNA.
168 Grampp, 'Italian Lira', 315.
169 I/SRM 59 – 22 August 1943, WO 208/4188, TNA.
170 I/SRN 784 – 28 December 1942, WO 208/4191, TNA.
171 I/SRN 300 – 30 November 1941, WO 208/4189, TNA.
172 Richards, *Hardest*, 53–55, 90.
173 Richards, *Hardest*, 62, 152–153, 164–165, 171, 195–197, 299.
174 Holland, *Sicily*, 124, 380–382.
175 I/SRX 60 – 20 March 1943, WO 208/4193, TNA.

176 I/SRN 69 – 24 July 1941, WO 208/4189, TNA. For further discussion of RAF bombing raids, see: I/SRX 33 – 2 March 1943, WO 208/4193, TNA; I/SRN 312 – 6 December 1941, WO 208/4189, TNA.
177 Marco Gioannini and Giulio Massobrio, *Bombardate l'Italia: Storia della Guerra di distruzione aerea, 1940–1945* (Milan: Rizzoli, 2007), 492.
178 Gabriella Gribaudi, *Guerra Totale. Tra bombe alleate e violenze naziste: Napoli e il front meridionale, 1940–1944* (Turin: Bollati Boringhieri, 2005), 161.
179 I/SRN 1125 – 8 April 1943, WO 208/4191, TNA.
180 Marta Nezzo, 'The Defence of Works of Art from Bombing in Italy during the Second World War', in Claudia Baldoli, Andrew Knapp and Richard Overy, eds., *Bombing, States and Peoples in Western Europe, 1940–1945* (London: Continuum, 2011), 109
181 Claudia Baldoli and Andrew Knapp, *Forgotten Blitzes. France and Italy under allied air attack, 1940–1945* (London: Continuum, 2012), 155, 189, 228.
182 Baldoli and Knapp, *Forgotten*, 123.
183 Baldoli and Knapp, *Forgotten*, 236.
184 The bombing of Hamburg in Operation Gomorrah in July 1943 killed 42600 civilians. Those against Dresden between 13 and 15 February 1945 killed between 22700 and 25000. See: Noble Frankland and Charles Webster, *The Strategic Air Offensive Against Germany, 1939–1945, Volume II: Endeavour, Part 4* (London: HMSO, 1961), 260–261; Rolf-Dieter Müller, Nicole Schönherr, Thomas Widera, eds., *Die Zerstörung Dresdens: 13. bis 15. Februar 1945. Gutachten und Ergebnisse der Dresdner Historikerkommission zur Ermittlung der Opferzahlen.* (Göttingen: V&R, 2010), 48.
185 Wilson, *Women*, 99.
186 Baldoli and Knapp, *Forgotten*, 86.
187 I/SRN 1295 – 19 June 1943, WO 208/4192, TNA.
188 I/SRN 1150 – 10 April 1943, WO 208/4192, TNA.
189 I/SRX 36 – 2 March 1943, WO 208/4193, TNA.
190 Harry King, 'The "O/400" Tradition with the Hampden Bombers', *The War in the Air: 1939–45*, 12 (1990), 25–30. (Originally published in Flight on 16 May 1940).
191 I/SRN 950 – 8 February 1943, WO 208/4191, TNA.
192 I/SRN 905 – 27 January 1943, WO 208/4191, TNA.
193 I/SRN 1268 – 9 May 1943, WO 208/4192, TNA.
194 Grazia Tarentino, *La festa di Muncalè: Storia minore della gente di Milano che qualcuno vorrebbe mettere nella zona grigia senza averne conosciuta la vera natura* (Genoa: Erga, 2005), 117.
195 I/SRM 24 – 25 June 1943, WO 208/4188, TNA.
196 Baldoli and Knapp, *Forgotten*, 227–228.
197 Marco Fincardi, 'Anglo-American Air Attacks and the Rebirth of Public Opinion in Fascist Italy', in Baldoli et al, *Bombing, States and Peoples*, 244–250.
198 I/SRN 63 – 19 July 1941, WO 208/4189, TNA.
199 I/SRA 5 – 20 November 1940, WO 208/4184, TNA.
200 I/SRX 81 – 22 March 1943, WO 208/4193, TNA.
201 I/SRN 481 – 24 August 1942, WO 208/4190, TNA.
202 I/SRN 903 – 18 January 1943, WO 208/4191, TNA.
203 See: Wolfgang Schieder, *Faschistische Diktaturen: Studien zu Italien und Deutschland* (Göttingen: Wallstein, 2008); Rochat, *Le guerre italiane*.

6 Attitudes towards Italian political leadership

Introduction

In June 1943, Artillery Lieutenant Vertua (I/M 20) and Engineer Second Lieutenant I/M 21 voiced their opinions on the war's most prominent political leaders,

I/M 20: It's all the fault of the men at the head of affairs. I should like to get hold of Mussolini, Hitler, Stalin and Churchill, tie them to a stake all together and drop bombs on them.
I/M 21: Yes, but not hit them at once. Leave them there for ten days on end, dropping bombs on them all the time, so that they first lose an eye, then an arm, then a leg and so on.
I/M 20: Yes, they deserve it after the crimes they've committed.[1]

These officers longed for a painful death even for their own leader, a powerful reflection of their low regard for Italy's political leadership. This was not an uncommon sentiment amongst the protocols. Highly critical statements can be found directed at almost every part of the Fascist political spectrum be it members of the Blackshirt militias, lowly Party functionaries, the ideology of Fascism itself and high-ranking individuals like Count Galeazzo Ciano and Benito Mussolini. The transcripts reveal a lack of ideological commitment to Fascism and a profound disillusionment with a self-serving and incompetent regime. It is the anger directed at corruption and ineptitude which is key to the disillusionment with the Party, Fascism and Italy's political leaders.

Here, we observe the failure of Fascist leadership. Forsaking Machiavelli, Mussolini was neither feared nor loved and without a cadre of respected and effective lieutenants, his own shortcomings could not be outweighed in the eyes of a clear majority of the prisoners.[2] The Italian service personnel here do not appear to long for an infallible superhuman to lead them. They accept the Roman aphorism: *nemo sine vitio est* (no-one is without fault).[3] As demonstrated in Chapter Five, the CSDIC (UK) cohort was not inherently averse to danger, but they wanted political leaders who shared some of those risks. The sense you get in these sources is that many wanted something worth fighting for: an aim, a leader, an ideology to follow and to make the sacrifice worthwhile. It is evident that Fascism and its leaders did not provide this.

Historiography – Popular support for Fascism

The past decade has seen considerable historiographical interest in popular opinion in Fascist Italy. Primarily through the use of letters and several hundred diaries from the *Archivio Diaristico Nazionale di Pieve Santo*, Duggan has written an 'intimate history of Italy under fascism,' which documents 'the feelings that ordinary people articulated in Mussolini's Italy and what these feelings might tell us otherwise about the regime.'[4] Duggan argues that for most of its history Mussolini's regime was highly effective at mobilising public support for Fascism. Co-opting the spirit of religion, 'the regime was able to draw itself into realms of belief and feeling that frequently went beyond the trappings of mere public display and penetrated intimate mental recesses.'[5] The cult of personality built around Mussolini was particularly strong. The image of him as a potent, generous and omniscient father to the nation was a crucial part of his public image, and one taken up eagerly by an idolising Italian public.[6] While faith in the Fascist Party itself was eventually eviscerated – descending into 'terminal decline' by the late 1930s – Mussolini's reputation stood 'uncontaminated' even in the face of the massive military defeats of 1940-43.[7]

Corner offers a rather different picture of Fascist Italy and Italian mentalities in his analysis of the failure of the Fascist Party in its pursuit of public support. The professed aim of the *Partito Nazionale Fascista* (PNF) had been to develop, 'a sense of common collective purpose amongst Italians: the generation of a "community of believers".'[8] Corner goes on to argue that, 'the picture [...] is that of a Fascist Party increasingly unable to come to terms with widespread popular discontent and, in many situations, itself one of the prime causes of that discontent [...] In its task of generating 'totalitarian' support for the regime [...] the PNF was a failure.'[9] In Corner's view the decline set in well before the outbreak of war in 1940: 'the wheels were falling off the fascist movement before the outbreak of the Second World War [...] the crisis of the regime was not provoked by the disastrous course of the war for Italy but by a dramatic collapse of popular identification with fascism in the second half of the 1930s.'[10] Some historians – notably Emilio Gentile – disagree with Corner's explanation for why this occurred.[11] However, even Gentile does not dispute either 'the disastrous condition of the PNF at the end of the 1930s' or 'the levels of corruption and abuse of power among Fascist officials that had produced that disastrous condition.'[12] This is a crucial point: there is consensus that at the outbreak of war the party was deeply unpopular. This is demonstrated repeatedly in the CSDIC (UK) protocols, as is the fact that, in contrast to Duggan's view, there are very few who supported Mussolini, especially by 1942-1943.

There is considerable overlap between the trends found in the protocols and those identified in *confinati* records by Bosworth.[13] He argues that, 'at minimum, the words of the defeatists demonstrate that fascism did not exert totalitarian control over all Italian minds [...] although the Fascists may have preached a new civic religion and sought to sacralise politics, many of their conversions were only skin deep.'[14] According to Bosworth, Fascism's encroachment into everyday Italian life was uneven. It was an 'inescapable part of being Italian' between 1922 and 1945, but it did not prevent Italians from drawing 'their identities from, and craft their behavior around, other strands of their lives.'[15] Echoing much of the sentiment in the transcripts, Italian Fascism may have been socially omnipresent, but it was not omniscient and omnipotent. A substantial portion of the Italian populace maintained hostility towards their German allies, were disillusioned with expansionist war, unenthusiastic for empire and distrusted the Party.[16] One of the few areas, but significant, of disagreement is that unlike the *confinati*, few CSDIC (UK) POWs 'nourished an admiration for rich and powerful Anglo-Saxons,'[17] even if the CSDIC (UK) cohort did acknowledge British and American economic clout. This was a situation that made Mussolini frequently 'work towards Italians', adapting his position to reflect or accommodate widely-held views.[18] There is repeated evidence from the protocols to support the position that, 'the Fascist control over its subjects' mental world was always partial.'[19]

The CSDIC sources are clear. Amongst this group, the PNF was deeply unpopular and the sheer variety of opinion on political matters points to the failure of Fascism's plans to mould a monoculture of the mind. The reason for this failure may have been the lack of a rigid Fascist ideology. This was a point Mussolini did not shy away from, that Italian Fascism did not need a long and detailed definition was one he made repeatedly. As he told General Franco in October 1936 the basis of 'universal fascism' was having a regime that was 'authoritarian,' 'social' and 'popular.'[20] Fascism was such a broad church that it tolerated quite high degrees of internal disagreement. This allowed people to carry on making their own judgements, including those that were negative about the regime. The transcripts show that Mussolini's reputation did not remain 'uncontaminated' during the war. There is an anti-authoritarian streak running through many of the debates about politics and leadership in the protocols, reflective perhaps of the experience of participating in a war effort defined by weaknesses in military leadership.[21]

The Fascists

Created by the Fascist Grand Council on 15 December 1922, the *Milizia Volontaria Sicurezza Nazionale* (MVSN) was the 'military expression of Fascism.'[22] Also known as the *Camicie Nere*, or 'Blackshirt' militias, they were initially founded to maintain public order and to exert control over independently-minded radical *Squadre d'Azione*.[23] From 1 August 1924 they were reorganized to be part of the Italian armed forces and, from 29 March 1930, the Fascist Grand Council decreed that two MVSN battalions should be attached to every regular Army infantry division.[24] From this point, Blackshirt units were involved in all of Mussolini's military campaigns: Ethiopia, Spain and in every theatre of Italy's Second World War.[25] In June 1940 the MVSN had a strength of 312000 men and, by January 1943, it was able to field 110 battalions. Of these 33 were in Yugoslavia, 22 in Italy, 14 in Greece, 11 on the Eastern Front, 10 in Corsica, 8 in Montenegro, 6 in Albania, 4 in the Aegean and 2 in Libya.[26] Even though the majority of Blackshirts fulfilled rear-echelon roles as anti-Partisan and garrison troops, they paid a heavy price for their involvement in the Second World War. From 10 June 1940 to 31 August 1943 they suffered 14900 casualties, of which 2560 were fatalities. On the Eastern Front alone, total losses by February 1943 had reached 4012 MVSN personnel.[27]

There are some transcripts which contain positive views of the Fascist Militias. In early July 1943, Lieutenant-Colonel Donato (I/M 26) was clear he had, 'seen some very fine "M" [MVSN] Battalions, well-disciplined and efficient.'[28] After the invasion of Sicily and the successful overthrow of Mussolini on the 25 July 1943, General Berardi (I/M 4) – former commander of XXI Corps, 1st Italian Army – was concerned for the status of the Blackshirt militias in the uncertain times to come: 'what will become of the Fascist Militia?' After all, they supposedly came from 'the good side of Fascism [...] those who went out and [fought] whilst the others were sleeping with pretty girls in Rome.' Both Berardi and his cellmate General Orlando (I/M 3) remembered the close attachment they had had with the militia units they had commanded.[29]

Both men retained a loyalty to the Fascist units under their own commands which serves as a reminder that not all in the Italian Army were hostile to the Blackshirts as a matter of principle. However, the way their thoughts were phrased does suggest another perspective. For all that 'their' Militiamen demonstrated a good side of Fascism, by extension there must have been a 'bad side,' whether this was demonstrated by shirkers in Rome or other Militia units who were less disciplined and lacked efficiency. The praise of these senior officers clearly had its limits. The sense is that they were sympathetic almost despite their Fascist credentials, because they had served alongside them. They were 'brothers in arms' and so it was possible to look beyond their ties to the Fascist party. It is also worth highlighting that the 'M' Battalions to which Lieutenant-Colonel Donato referred were crack fighting units, the elite of the MVSN. Named for Mussolini himself, they were given longer training at dedicated camps, received better supplies and were instilled with an 'elite' ethos. In total 22 'M' battalions were created of which 11 were sent to the Eastern Front, six to Yugoslavia, one to Tunisia and the other four becoming specially trained *da sbarco* amphibious landing battalions.[30] The units which Donato admired only ever formed a minority of MVSN battalions.

Many other CSDIC (UK) personnel were far more direct in their critiques of the Blackshirts. Lieutenant-Colonel Pedala (I/M 3) exclaimed, 'those damned Militia people! Talk about the Germans being offensive, they were worse than the Germans! Revolting, ignorant lumps of filth! That's the Militia, the English ought to send them to the stake every day.'[31] He recalled the words of an artillery Major who had served alongside Pedala in North Africa, 'I simply won't have anything to do with those Militia people, I'd like to spit in their face, I can't bear the sight of them.'[32] On another occasion Pedala said that he could not 'understand why there should be these Blackshirts who are almost like irregulars; it is a thing which causes friction amongst the troops themselves. There are so many squabbles going on already.'[33] In this way, Pedala highlights that the policy by which two MVSN battalions were integrated into each regular Army division was met with resentment and hostility from Army officers.[34]

'Squabbles' considerably understate the friction between Militiamen and other services described by Chief Boatswain Bergadono (I/N 343). He believed that the existence of much higher Blackshirt rates of pay was a, 'dirty business' that bred discontent and anger. On one occasion in Piedmont, 'the Militia were confined to barracks for a whole week. If they'd gone outside they'd have been murdered. There were some fine scraps.'[35] In this instance Bergadono was operating under something of a misconception. For all that the MVSN did provide valuable incentives to their volunteers, such as holidays, insurances and pensions, Blackshirts in the Second World War were paid regular army wages.[36] It is possible that Bergadono is confusing the rates of pay for those who signed up for the *Corpo Truppe Volontarie* (CTV) who fought in Spain. Recruiting heavily from the ranks of the MVSN, the financial benefits for joining this were considerable. On top of a baseline 20 lire per day – topped up with between two and five pesetas a day by the Spanish Nationalist Government – CTV volunteers were given a 20000 lire life insurance policy and were initially offered a 3000 lire bonus for signing up.[37] What is striking here is that, while Bergadono was clearly mistaken, he was profoundly resentful of the Militia – it was not just officers who disliked the MVSN.

All the above criticisms come from the spring or summer of 1943, a point when the Allied invasion of metropolitan Italy demonstrated the bankruptcy of Fascism's war effort. But the Militia had its opponents long before the Allied invasion. Criticism of the MVSN was not dependent on the progress of the war. The following exchange between the Second-in-Command of the submarine 'C' (I/N 22) and a *Tenente di Vascello* of the 10th *Flotilla MAS* (I/N 23) took place in January 1941,

I/N 23: All those who are good for nothing else get into the Fascist Militia, a lot of wasters. At least in the Navy the officers are chosen from many candidates and there is three years preparation at the Academy (Navy School).
I/N 22: Ah yes! A good-for-nothing can always become an N.C.O. in the Fascist Militia.
I/N 23: Returning to Leghorn on Sunday's I used to see many of them in the train. They were disgusting. Torn braid, open tunics, unbuttoned trousers, a dirty lot, quite loathsome.[38]

The 1930s had seen a fair degree of tension between other branches of the Italian armed services and the MVSN. Clashes between off-duty

Militiamen and *Carabinieri* officers appear not uncommon at pre-war football matches. This included on one occasion in Lecce in 1937 when a crowd – including uniformed MVSN members – turned ugly after the attempted arrest of a man, 'standing on the bottom step of the terracing who had exposed his genitals and taken them in his hands, showing them to the Stabia [away] goalkeeper and repeatedly shouting, "eat this!".'[39] There was evidently a rich vein of hostility towards the Blackshirt Militias from within the CSDIC (UK) cohort, which could be rooted in encounters well before the war. It is curious that the points of friction here stem from physical rather than ideological or political differences between regular and Militia service personnel. Divergences in rates of pay, discipline and attitudes to personal appearance lay at the root of the tensions articulated in these protocols.

The organisation and structure of MVSN units may also explain such rancor. Mobilised for the short-term during times of conflict they were structured as semi-permanent light infantry units and depended on army service units for everything other than the most basic unit support: artillery, communications, medical care, sappers and Staff work all had to be supplied by regular units.[40] This created a fundamental tension between MVSN units and the Army as a whole. They also cultivated an ethos which emphasised their differences. Unlike the rest of the Army, Blackshirt battalions were made up entirely of volunteers. They had their own adapted uniforms and peculiar mannerisms, such as using the Roman salute, and raising daggers on parade. The Blackshirts deliberately created a cult of themselves which created distance from the regular Army. Within Fascism's consciously militarised society, and within the Italian armed forces, long-riven by a culture of inter-service rivalry,[41] the conduct *and* the structure of the MVSN was guaranteed to cause resentment and antipathy. However, within the protocols, there are not comparable levels of dislike between, the Army, Navy or Air Force. This is a hostility reserved for the militia because they are viewed as corrupt and slovenly soldiers.

This is echoed in discussions of the Fascist Party in the transcripts. Engine-Room Petty Officer Galliott (I/N 154) made his frustration with Party officials clear when he recalled an incident with a local Fascist Party representative whilst on leave. He was summoned to the 'Fascio' were he was reprimanded for not being a Party member,

> Then he talked a lot of rot about thinking of the poor soldiers at the front etc., and a lot of fine things like that. So I said: 'Just let me say something. You're winning the war at your desk here and thinking of the poor soldiers at the front, while I'm just amusing myself etc.' Then I pulled out my naval identity card and showed it to him. 'Look at that,' I said. 'I'm fighting and I've been away from Italy for a year in the submarine *Ferraris*' [...] I said: 'You're spending the war in this room, while we're risking our lives out there.'[42]

A dislike of party officials was combined with a dislike of men with safe jobs on the home front, if Galliott even distinguished between the two.

According to Sub-Lieutenant Budini (I/N 373) by March 1943 he had, 'no faith in [Party officials], they're traitors, they don't care a damn – a lot of fine words, but they've never done anything [...] they're quite capable of betraying Italy to the Germans, of knocking everybody on the head who doesn't agree with them.'[43] In the words of Sub-Lieutenant Mazzinghi (I/N 249), the 'greatest humiliation I've ever had to suffer,' was being awarded his War Cross by an unspecified Fascist Party leader. At the ceremony itself Mazzinghi jokingly told a friend that he would shoot himself out of shame.[44] Like many of the young Italian men in uniform, Chief Boatswain Pontone (I/N 254) had little memory of life in Italy before the Fascists took over, 'when the [...] revolution took place I was only a child. I don't remember anything about it.'[45] That did not mean he was unaware of the opinions of those old enough to make the comparison with pre-Fascist Italy. His appraisal was not favourable to Mussolini's regime, claiming that, 'all the people over forty now realised how Italy has been ruined. They've seen the changes. There are such a lot of men in the Party and in the Government who are real scoundrels.'[46] Criticism of the PNF could take many forms and it was cast variously as a refuge for those who wanted safe desk jobs – the classic *Per Necessità Familiare* – or a group of people who were ideologically-convinced and, therefore, ultimately to blame for a war that brought so much suffering.

Even instances of support could be unenthusiastic. As Petty Officer Villosio (I/N 188) made clear, Fascism like, 'every political party has its good points, but there's a reverse to every medal.'[47] After 20 years of rule this was not a strong endorsement of Fascism's record in power. That many prisoners of war were deeply critical of the Fascist political experiment is clear. Their distaste for the Fascists was rooted in the régime's brutality, corruption, greed and ineptitude. It does not appear to come down to inherent political differences with Fascism as a political ideology however. This indicates a pragmatic political outlook amongst these men where leaders were judged primarily on outcomes more than rhetoric.

A similar pattern of opinion can be seen regarding the Foreign Minister Count Galeazzo Ciano. There were some CSDIC (UK) POWs with positive things to say about Mussolini's son-in-law, but even these had serious qualifications. For example, Petty Officer Electrician Boschin (I/N 176) said of Ciano, 'even he, with all his faults, has some good qualities.' For all his many 'stupid mistakes,' Boschin believed that 'at heart he's Italian, he's in good faith.'[48] There were, however, other prisoners who would have objected to even this limited approval. Naval Lieutenant Melosi (I/N 209) believed that, 'Ciano does nothing except ape Mussolini, that just shows he's got no initiative, no intelligence, because nobody would behave in that ridiculous way.'[49] *Tenente di Vascello* I/N 23 said in January 1941 that Ciano had, 'never been popular with anybody in Italy.' His cellmate (I/N 22) agreed, 'yes, that was the greatest mistake, the case of Ciano. He thinks he's God Almighty just because he's Mussolini's son-in-law. And the people saw there was nepotism even in Fascism; that was a grave psychological blunder.'[50] Disappointment with corruption was keenly felt given how much it contradicted Fascist 'preaching about the discipline and vigour of the Fascist new man.'[51]

Disillusionment with Ciano's corruption also comes from the Captain of the SS *Polinnia* (I/N 88), 'if you take a trip round [Italy] you see, "Ciano estate", "Ciano Reserve" etc. All the party bosses have amassed vast fortunes. We must avoid dishonesty.'[52] As the surviving records of the *Segretaria Paricolare del Duce* – Mussolini's private office – show, many leading Fascists were denounced for their nefarious activities.[53] Corruption had not been introduced to Italy by Fascism,[54] but the gulf between the regime's professed aims and its actions was clearly problematic for many Italians and I/N 22 was no exception to this.

In November 1940 Petty Officer Marghetta (I/N 179) believed, 'the invasion of Greece was a mistake on the part of that half-wit Ciano.'[55] Many others in Italian society shared Marghetta's view. By December 1940 Italian police reported considerable bitterness towards Ciano because of his role in the invasion of Greece.[56] Ciano had played a leading role in orchestrating the attack on Greece and, as such, these are fair criticisms. It was Ciano who in August 1940 had ordered the Viceroy of Albania, General Francesco Jacomoni, to prepare for new Italian operations along the Greek frontier.[57] Ciano had even written the ultimatum that Emmanuele Grazzi, the Italian Envoy to Athens, presented to the Greek Prime Minister Ionnis Metaxas on 28 October 1940. As he said, it was a 'document that allows no way out for Greece. Either she accepts occupation, or she will be attacked.'[58]

Ciano's 'open' marriage to Edda Mussolini was also used to critique him, as an exchange between Ordinary Seaman Stefanni (I/N 131), Petty Officer I/N 91 and a Medical Petty Officer (I/N 118) shows,

I/N 118: Edda Mussolini's a slut (*una bagascia*). Anyone can sleep with her.
I/N 131: Yes. She's a beautiful woman, you know – a very charming lady.
I/N 91: She's intelligent. She's the only one who takes after her father.
I/N 131: They say 'Ciano's a fool.'
I/N 118: He's just a mate for that slut. He's no good.
I/N 91: I've nothing against him. After all, he married the Duce's daughter.
I/N 131: Why should he be made Foreign Minister just because he married the daughter?[59]

Similarly, one Bomber Pilot (I/A 5) thought, 'Ciano is not a great politician, but Edda plays a great role in politics. At the same time she is very feminine – too much of a woman […] she is extremely sensual. My friend slept with her since she married Ciano.'[60] These statements confirm that the Cianos' difficult marriage was common knowledge.[61] Whatever the sexism of such remarks, they support an image of Ciano as an embarrassment to his country, corrupt, and prone to costly mistakes. The notion of labelling Ciano a *cornuto* or cuckold is significant, as it remains one of the most potent insults that can be levelled at an Italian man.[62] The anger directed against Ciano can be positioned amongst a much broader attack on Fascism within the transcripts.

In the protocols, Italy's leaders were presented as out of touch and isolated from the challenges of life on the front lines. Engine-Room Petty Officer Montinaro (I/N 91) is typical – 'I can just imagine those dear political leaders of ours sunning themselves on the beaches in Italy or playing about with the wives of the poor devils at the Front. They're good when it's a matter of bragging, but they see to it that they get safe jobs.'[63] There was especial disillusionment with those in the capital. Second Lieutenant Izzi (I/M 22) believed that, 'those gentlemen in Rome don't understand what it means, because they've never experienced being bombed.'[64] Lieutenant Cristini (I/N 361), Lieutenant Varoli (I/N 338) and Lieutenant-Colonel Ravazzoni (I/A 32) took these sentiments one step further, actually willing the Allies to bomb the capital – 'if they'd only bomb Rome [...] those people are our worst enemies.'[65] Even Field Marshal Messe (I/M 2) said that,

> In Rome they never understood. They wasted their time chattering and making fine speeches, and drawing maps of the 'Impero' when their knowledge of it was limited to the 'Via dell'Impero' in Rome (laughter). My God! You wage war with battleships, aircraft and tanks. Nothing else matters. They have so sense of reality in Italy.[66]

These officers inadvertently echo a secret police report from Milan that recorded how many Milanese were 'decidedly pleased' that Rome had been bombed on 13 July 1943.[67] Romans had been supposedly sheltered from the hardships of war for too long and now it was their turn to suffer. As the capital of Mussolini's new Roman Empire and the seat of all major government branches it is easy to place such opinion within this wider trend of disillusionment with the Fascist regime.

On Fascism

In May 1943 Army Lieutenant Colacicchi (I/M 5) told a joke to a room of senior army commanders – General Orlando (I/M 3), General Berardi (I/M 4) and Field Marshal Messe (I/M 2). It went as follows,

> Mussolini once went into a factory and asked how many Socialists were amongst the workers. The manager answered: 'There may be twenty percent.' 'And Communists?' 'They must be fifty to sixty percent.' 'And Fascists?' 'Oh. They are all Fascists!'[68]

That this junior officer felt comfortable telling such a seditious joke to such a senior audience is remarkable. It adds further weight to the image of disillusionment with Fascist figures and officials already encountered. It is also reminiscent of another popular pre-war joke,

> Mussolini visits an insane asylum. All of the patients have been instructed, with the help of sedatives and straightjackets, to shout 'DUCE! DUCE!' when the leader arrives.
> One man is silent.
> 'And why don't you shout, "Viva Il Duce!"?' Mussolini asks.
> 'I'm not a mental patient. I'm a doctor.'[69]

Colacicchi's joke encapsulates a trend found in the CSDIC (UK) protocols and parts of wider Italian society, that allegiance to Fascism as an ideology was weak and superficial.

One who retained some level of faith in the Fascist project is Diver I/N 21. For all his disenchantment with the leadership, he believed: 'The principle of Fascism is good, although there may be rascals at the top. The principle is good: the individual doesn't count, what counts is the country.'[70] Chaplain to G.H.Q., 1st Italian Army, Captain Salza (I/M 52), is another of the very few prisoners who retained a strong allegiance to Fascism. G.H.Q. Liaison Officer, Major Nani (I/M 50) described how Salza had acted as Chaplain in American POW camps following his capture in North Africa. After several 'moving' sermons Salza stated, '"Now, I'm going to talk about politics",' and from then on, 'when he preached a sermon, he used to be 100% pro-Mussolini.' The situation was serious enough that when word of this got back to the camp authorities he was 'removed' as an 'isolation measure.'[71] In his own words, Salza wanted revenge on those who told the Allies of his pro-Fascist speeches in the POW camps,

> They've [Allied authorities] got a letter describing me as a very clever and incorrigible Fascist propagandist. A 'maggiore' and a 'tenente' gave me away. But I'll find those fellows again, because one of them lives in Rome and the other in Bologna, I've got their addresses and if I lose the addresses, I'll find them through the Ministry of War.[72]

Salza does not refute the accusations made against him, even his label as an 'incorrigible Fascist propagandist' which is discussed repeatedly.[73] In October 1943 he defended Mussolini as 'an able man' and remained 'convinced that Germany will win.'[74] Salza's belief in Fascism and the Axis cause was unyielding. In early November 1943 he defended his continued use of the 'Roman salute' which every other prisoner had stopped using. This was done along the grounds that, 'this is the Roman salute, with which the Christians used to salute each other.'[75] Salza conveniently overlooked how the 'Roman salute' had been a prominent and deliberate part of Fascist public pageantry since the mid-1920s.[76] It is nonetheless interesting that he felt the need to openly disassociate himself from this connection in his defence of the 'Roman salute.'

The devoted Captain Salza would have been disheartened to hear Ordinary Seaman Stefanni's (I/N 131) analysis that, 'I should say that in Italy ten percent are convinced, ardent Fascists, the remainder belong to the party for what they can get out of it.'[77] The instinct towards self-preservation and opportunism was significant in Stefanni's view. The desire to join the Party also came from those who has been persecuted by the *squadristi* during the early years of Fascism, who nevertheless later wore 'the badge, maybe, but only on his jacket.'[78] This 'paper tiger' aspect to Party membership is reinforced by one bomber-gunner's (I/A 4) claim that, 'I bet amongst all the volunteers and those prisoners here, there is not one convinced Fascist.'[79] By the late 1930s membership of the PNF was essential to all those seeking a public sector career. The Party's 1938 constitution affirmed that anyone 'who ceases to be a member of the *Partito Nazionale Fascista* is to be relieved of all positions and responsibilities he may perform.'[80] The pressure on public servants and those in the armed forces to join has been used to explain the dramatic rise in PNF membership from approximately 300000 in 1921 to 5000000 in 1943.[81] There were many motivating factors beyond political idealism to join the Party.[82]

Others were direct in voicing their disillusionment. In January 1943 Lieutenant Badezzi (I/N 321) bluntly stated that, 'I don't care a damn about the Party.' Lieutenant Paladini (I/N 298) replied, 'I've torn up my membership card.'[83] Leading Torpedo Rating I/N 162 believed that, 'Italy was getting along all right before Fascism. We've got to thank Fascism for this war.'[84] Lieutenant-Colonel Pedala (I/M 13) spoke of a 'disgusting [and] typical Fascist arrogance.'[85] Petty Officer Boatswain Losi (I/N 239) recalled that, 'my father is always praying to the Madonna that the English may land in Italy. When he's drunk he goes out into the street and shouts: "Down with Fascism!"'[86] Petty Officer Losi's father's desire to see the English in Italy may have been rare, but the anti-Fascism that underpinned it was not. Nor indeed was the combination of inebriation and dissent. Police files record that Achille Clerici (born 1896, Novara) yelled when drunk that the war was hopeless for Italy because, 'the English eat four times a day whereas we can't even manage half a time.' Fellow dipsomaniac Virgilio Stucchi (born 1894, Naples) longed for an Allied victory so that Mussolini and his coterie 'could be boiled in oil.'[87]

Lieutenant-Colonel Pedala (I/M 13) lived in his native Sicily before commanding a coastal defence battalion and then joining the Adjutant General's Department in Tunisia. He believed in July 1943 that,

> In Sicily every single man would have gladly let himself be killed in the defence of his country if it hadn't been for Fascism. They would have defended it inch by inch, even with their finger-nails, even the women, if it hadn't been for Fascism. But as it is they won't do a thing, and provided they can get rid of Fascism they'll welcome the English, the Turks, the Normans, the Saracens or the Arabs – they'll say: 'Come on!' to anybody, provided they don't have to listen to 'Giovinezza' anymore.[88]

According to Pedala, by this point in the war anything was preferable to Fascism. Even the many invading armies of the past, recognisng Sicily's long history as a conquered island. Fascism had not only failed to motivate the Sicilians to defend their island from invasion but was so unpopular that they favoured Italy's defeat in the campaign. He also highlighted that the strongest resentment amongst Sicilians was directed against mainland Italians – Bourbons and House of Savoy – rather than towards the foreign invader.

That loyalty to Fascism could be completely distinct from feelings of patriotism is seen with Quartermaster Franzoni (I/N 283) who stated, 'I'm an Italian first – not a Fascist.'[89] Such sentiments can also be observed in the case of Lieutenant-Colonel Ravazzoni (I/A 32). As we have already seen, the Great War veteran was a self-confessed patriot, a critic of both the Soviets and the British, and a determined warrior. Yet even he said,

> I'm an anti-Fascist now after all the things I've seen in Italy. I used to be an active member (squadrista). With four men I founded the Genoa 'Fascio' [...] [But] when I saw which way Fascism was beginning to tend, I said to myself: 'No, I've fought for the liberty and honour of Italy, but now I realize that the political side of it is far removed from what our idealism imagined it to be, so I'm going to retire from the Party.'[90]

He even symbolically relinquished his Party membership card.[91] With a few notable exceptions amongst the prisoners the allure of Fascism was dulled. They may have been patriotic, but they were uncommitted to the Fascist project and what it had become.

Propaganda

If there was severe disillusionment with Fascism generally, then a distrust of the regime's propaganda was particularly acute. This hollowness is made clear in a conversation between Ravazzoni and Sub-Lieutenant Budini (I/N 373). Budini recalled that to impress Hitler when he visited Taranto for a naval review the *Regia Marina*'s submarine fleet was artificially enlarged by Potemkin vessels built from barges.[92] In response, Ravazzoni told how he had written a report stating that 75 percent of Italy's bomber manufacturing materials were imported while only 25 percent were produced domestically. When the findings were presented in the Senate Chamber these figures were reversed at Mussolini's insistence.[93] These anecdotes reveal dishonesty at the highest levels of Italy's political leadership. Both these officers were aware of the damage that such deception caused and were clearly unhappy with limited press freedoms in Italy which obstructed the truth.[94] Budini believed that, 'the press ought to be a critic of the Government,' while Ravazzoni stated, 'if I were to become head of the Government tomorrow, the first law I would promulgate would be one granting freedom of the press and freedom of thought [...] anyone can write what he likes provided he can prove it is in accordance with fact.'[95]

Academic research has begun to reject to image of the Italian press as a monolithic ally to the Fascist regime, being able to maneuver around the direct and indirect pressures to become outlets for strictly Fascist journalism,[96] but these are not nuances identified by these CSDIC (UK) prisoners. Budini and Ravazzoni were not the only ones in the CSDIC (UK) cohort to harbour strong views about the press. I/A 3, a fighter pilot captured on 11 November 1940 felt that the Italian press was worthless saying, 'if I were a dictator, I would abolish the Press completely.'[97] Similarly, an unspecified survivor from the submarine *Calvi* felt that, 'our news bulletins don't tell you anything. They won't say that the *Calvi* has been sunk. They never said anything about the *Bianchi* though she never came back.'[98] A general distrust of Italian print media is clear. A MAS *Tenente di Vascello* (I/N 23) believed that, 'the only really decent, really excellent newspaper is the *Regime Fascista*.'[99] This title was certainly part of the Fascist propaganda machine, founded in Cremona in 1926 by then PNF head Roberto Farinacci. Pro-Nazi, anti-Clerical and a proponent of the *Leggi Razziali*, it had a strong national following amongst Fascist diehards.[100] But, it remains telling of a wider disenchantment that it is the *only* paper to be lauded – ignoring other hardline Fascist and regime-controlled publications like, *Il Popolo d'Italia*, *Il Tevere*, *Il Giornale d'Italia* and *Critica Fascista*. Seaman Montaldo (I/N 207) harboured a strong skepticism of what he heard over Italian airwaves. He recalled that, 'we used to listen to the wireless at home. They said: "Fifty-two enemy aircraft were shot down and two failed to return." But that means fifty-two of ours and two of the English.'[101]

Although Montaldo now found himself exposed to the Allied press in the CSDIC camp, it did not mean he was ready to believe the output of British propaganda. He said, 'the London wireless never has anything good to say about Italy when it talks about the war [...] the London wireless abuses everybody.'[102] Montaldo had a kindred spirit in Torpedo-Rating Ancona (I/N 190), a 22-year-old civilian mechanic from Apulia. He believed that, 'everything you hear on the wireless is propaganda. I often used to listen to their [Allied] news, but I didn't believe it. I'm through with propaganda, Italian or English.'[103] These statements are telling given the effort expended by *Radio Londra* – the BBC European Service in Italy – in deliberately distancing themselves from the official Fascist broadcasts of the EIAR (*Ente Italiano per le Audizioni Radiofoniche*) through a distinct style, tone and commitment to verifiable facts.[104] This suggests that Montaldo and Ancona's cynicism was not exclusively anti-Fascist. It points to a weary skepticism of both friend *and* foe. In this way it links into the existence of a deeper cynicism towards authority amongst the CSDIC (UK) cohort.

The monarchy

If faith in the Fascists was severely limited, the remarks of Field Marshal Messe (I/M 2) show that there was another option for leadership in Italy, the Royal Family. In early March 1943 he said:

All that's necessary is for the King to make some gesture! We're a nation which doesn't need parties, because the party spirit is alien to the Italian people. As far as I'm concerned I'm attached to our royal family, just as the English are to theirs. If they once try to touch the royal family, there'll be trouble.[105]

As this statement demonstrates, Mussolini's interwar campaign to win over the hearts of minds of the Army leadership was only ever a partial success. There was always a distinct 'Monarchist-conservative' block that looked to the King above the *Duce* and wove together opposition to the his growing power with obstruction of the reforms proposed by the 'Fascist-innovator' block.[106] As Knox has written, 'the levers of ultimate power nevertheless remained in the hands of the king and of the senior generals of the *Regio Esercito*' who supported him.[107]

Osti Guerrazzi has written of the loyalty to the monarchy of the senior Italian army officers held at Wilton Park,[108] and there were others in the CSDIC (UK) cohort that had some level of faith in the leadership of the King. But they frequently remained frustrated at the monarch's inaction and his inability to seize back political leadership from Mussolini and the Fascists. Midshipman Devescovi (I/N 334) lamented, 'my God, if King Vittorio had only said something to the Italian people to reject Fascism.' He was certain that if the King gave the word, the Italian nation would, 'rise up to a man.'[109] Sub-Lieutenant Mazzinghi (I/N 249) was sure that, 'the Italians would have let themselves be cut to pieces for little Victor.'[110] That being said, by January 1943 this had failed to happen. The King had not turned against the Fascists in this way. This helps to explain Mazzinghi's obvious disgust that all the military power had been passed to Mussolini and why he referred to the head of state as an 'old rascal' (*altro filibustiero*).[111]

Second Lieutenant Rizzi (I/M 14) would have agreed. Showing clear contempt when he said, 'the King showed himself to be as meek as a lamb when he sanctioned those Fascist laws as he did. Our King is asleep; he has been asleep for the last twenty years; he can't expect Italy to acknowledge him.'[112] Respect for the monarch was also lacking in the words of Leading Engine-Room Rating Allegre (I/N 356), 'England hasn't lost anything to us, she's beaten us – she's seized our Empire. All they've left us is Albania. And yet they go on calling him the King-Emperor (Laughter).'[113]

The descent into outright criticism of the monarchy is felt keenly in remarks concerning Victor Emmanuel's heir, Prince Umberto. Whilst disappointment in the inaction of the King could be tempered a little, his son faced an unremitting barrage of hostility from the CSDIC (UK) prisoners. In the opinion of Sub-Lieutenant Mazzinghi (I/N 249), Umberto was a 'vile swine' and a 'damned fool' who 'never did a damned thing except let himself be awarded decorations.' 'The only people who love him,' said Mazzinghi, 'are the prostitutes.'[114] Engine-Room Petty Officer Desiderio (I/N 290) also considered him, 'a damned fool.'[115] Second Lieutenant Rizzi (I/M 14) said, 'the

Prince is a blockhead [*una testa di cazzo*] [...] and they make him a Field Marshal and put him in command of an Army,'[116] an opinion that reflected both hostility towards the Prince, as well as the military and political leadership that surrounded him. On an earlier occasion Lieutenant-Colonel Pedala (I/M 13) had confided to Rizzi that, 'the Prince is a mental defective, he's an idiot.'[117]

These excerpts demonstrate that Italian military opinion regarding the Royal Family could be more nuanced – and much more hostile – than is suggested by the traditional image of the monarchist 'Royal' Italian Armed Forces. This points to a wider disillusionment with traditional authority figures and gives valuable context to the post-war shift to Republicanism that had its roots well before the devastating public relations effects of the 'Flight of the Damned' of the King and government from Rome in September 1943, fearing reprisals for their role in overthrowing Mussolini in June.[118]

Benito Mussolini

On 3 September 1943 in Reggio, Italy, Sergeant J.A. West of the No. 2 Film and Photographic Unit took a photograph of two British Eighth Army soldiers strolling past a sign on a wall which read, '*Viva il Duce.*' However, the '*Duce*' had now been crossed through.[119] It is unclear whether this act of vandalism was made by the newly arrived invaders or recently 'liberated' locals. Nonetheless, it is a deeply symbolic image. A sign which once stood as a constant reminder of the omnipresence and purported omnipotence of Benito Mussolini was now a focal point of Allied derision as thousands of enemy troops continued their conquest of *la patria*. The transcripts also stand as an example of how Mussolini's position in Italian society had changed beyond all recognition by 1943. They demonstrate that he was not immune to the distrust, disillusionment and dislike of Italy's political leadership already observed in this chapter, but rather served as the ultimate embodiment of these critiques. Very few CSDIC (UK) POWs came out in support of the man whose image and words had once adorned postcards, murals, stamps, calendars, bars of soap and even women's bathing suits.[120]

Positivo e Negativo

Given the hostility directed against almost every other element of Fascism, it is not surprising that many CSDIC POWs were similarly negative about Mussolini. All the more so given how much the *Duce* had centralised power around him. Except for a break between 1929 and 1933, he had been minister for all three armed forces since 1922. In 1940, he had even wrested the position of commander-in-chief from the king. Politically Mussolini had left himself nowhere to hide.[121] But titles were not synonymous with power, and his domestic weakness was highlighted by Lieutenant-Colonel Ravazzoni (I/A 32) who said in March 1943, 'even Mussolini can't impose his will everywhere, he's never succeeded in imposing it on the industrialists. [...] It's the industrialists who dictate to the government.'[122] For all of Fascism's early anti-Capitalist rhetoric, once in power Mussolini worked with the existing financial elites to further his economic aspirations. Ideas like 'Corporatism' and 'Productivism' may have sounded 'leftist' but very much suited the interests of business owners and industrialists and by 1935 Mussolini had discarded most of the economic radicals in the Party leadership.[123] The desire to appease the industrialists impeded the development of Italy's armed forces. For example, in 1938-1939 the *Regia Aeronautica*'s attempts to find a new fighter were delayed and complicated by a culture of developing great numbers of 'prototypes.' This was a policy designed to keep aviation firms in business as opposed to making significant numbers of the best planes. As a result, only 12 models of the superior Re. 2000 were ordered while 200 obsolete CR. 42s, 182 unreliable MC. 200s and even a handful of Ca. 165s and G. 50s were bought.[124]

Midshipman Gridelli (I/N 378) pulled few punches in April 1943, 'in Venice I knew a girl whom I liked very much. In fact, I love her as much as I now hate the Duce.'[125] Torpedo Rating Crozzi (I/N 196) was critical of Mussolini's fortune. 'Think of the amount of money he must have put aside. And where did he get it all from? He got it from the people, from you and me.'[126] Bosworth has written that 'hypocrisy and corruption [...] were a structure of Fascist Italian life' and Mussolini was not above this. Some 334 of his relatives are known to have 'extracted funds from the Fascist government.' As early as 1927 the *podestà* – the authoritarian mayor – of Bologna wrote to the council of Mussolini's hometown of Predappio saying, 'the *Duce* is literally besieged by his relatives with requests for subsidies. The matter has become annoying and even indecent.' Nonetheless, he still sent on 60000 lire in cash to be distributed amongst the beseeching wider family.[127]

Mussolini's modest background is used as a stick beat to him by General Orlando (I/M 3). That Mussolini was prepared to take the wife of an Air Force officer as his mistress demonstrated 'his lack of breeding.'[128] *Il Duce*'s affairs are also remarked upon by Rear-Admiral Leonardi (I/N 402) who believed, 'it was a sort of sign of decay the way he allowed his lady friends to get the upper hand over him.' Leonardi felt that, 'the Duce has been going to pieces for the last five or six years, ever since the Abyssinian war.'[129] As Ollas has written, 'sex [...] was at the centre of the myth of Mussolini [...] His image as a man or power [...] drew directly on the idea of his sexual potency.'[130] Some estimates of the number of Mussolini's sexual conquests range into the thousands, and are never less that several dozen. Even Mussolini's wife Rachele gave the comparatively conservative figure of 'about twenty.'[131]

Having a succession of mistresses and extra-marital affairs became something of a 'standard practice' amongst the Fascist leadership: Italo Balbo and Filippo Marinetti are prominent examples.[132] Beyond the long history of powerful men abusing their position for their own sexual gratification and sexual conquest as a statement of power, this practice may have been heightened by Fascism's chauvinistic obsession with male dominance.[133] However, it is curious that Leonardi subverts Mussolini's sex life in this context, using it as an avenue of criticism, not praise. Others had also sought to use Mussolini's sexual appetite against him. In March 1939, American Diplomat Joseph Kennedy suggested that the best way to control the *Duce* diplomatically would be to send 'six American chorus girls' to Rome.[134]

Criticism of Mussolini was not limited to his upbringing and sex life but also his inadequacies as a leader. Leonardi was not the only one in the protocols to use Fascism's earlier wars to criticise Mussolini. In January 1943, Midshipman Devescovi (I/N 334) showed himself uncompromising in his opposition to *il Duce*. Italian intervention in Abyssinia and Spain were, in his view, costly ways of hoodwinking the Italian people into making money for the powerful. In doing this he was a 'silly blockhead! Betraying his own country!'[135] This was not the only occasion Devescovi had spoken at length of his disdain for Mussolini. A few days earlier, he expressed the following to Lieutenant Badezzi (I/N 321),

> It's Mussolini who has ruined Italy. [...] He's a traitor. Because you don't send people out to fight in that way. [...] I tell you that if I could go back to Italy now, the first thing I'd do would be to go to Palazzo Venezia and put a revolver (*rivoltella*) through his head. Because that man's a criminal! [...] Even Abyssinia had declared war on us! Damnation! Even the Republic of Panama and Guatemala have declared war on us. There's no getting away from it, Fascism has been the ruin of Italy.[136]

Ethiopia had indeed declared war on Germany, Japan and Italy on 14 December 1942. This news would still have been fresh in Devescovi's mind, as would have been the capture of Tripoli by the British Eighth Army on 23 January 1943. Devescovi's abhorrence of Mussolini had reached such an extreme that he was prepared to murder him. *Il Duce* had crossed the line from making costly mistakes to a fundamental betrayal of his people, particularly those who had been sent to war. He had become the ruin of *la Patria*.

Leading Engine-Room Petty Officer Allegre (I/N 356) could not support Petty Officer Desiderio's (I/N 290) claim that Mussolini's foreign policy had only aimed to 'make Italy greater.' In Allegre's view, Mussolini's ambition was reckless and unnecessary, 'he wanted this war. The Italian people didn't want war. They were quite happy. [...] Greater my foot! Live and let live! He'd conquered Abyssinia and he'd got Libya. Why the hell couldn't he be satisfied with that?'[137] Even as early as December 1940, the words of one IAF bomber-gunner (I/A 4) betray a weariness with Mussolini's sabre-rattling. He said, 'they always used to say that the Duce wouldn't die without giving his name to a war, and now he's already caused three wars. We could have avoided this one too.'[138] I/A 4 is clear that given all of Mussolini's own appointments, 'if we lose the war tomorrow, the responsibility will fall on his shoulders.'[139] These foot soldiers of Mussolini no longer subscribed to his grandiose plans for a resurgent and vast Roman Empire: in so-doing they demonstrated a keener awareness of Italy's actual capabilities than their leader.

As these protocols demonstrate, the Spanish and Abyssinian Campaigns used up the mental appetite for war of these men. What connects so many of these criticisms is a serious disaffection with greed: a lust for money, power and territory with which, by 1943, the CSDIC (UK) cohort had overwhelmingly lost patience. I/N 6, a submarine Chief Petty Officer, was sure that Mussolini could have had the best of both worlds had he remained neutral. In January 1941 he said, 'he has thrust us into every calamity which has come along. What do we care about an Empire? [...] We ought to be sending our ships on the sea not under it [...] all this could have been done had we remained neutral.'[140] His diver cellmate I/N 21 agreed. He said, 'Mussolini has shoved us into every kind of trouble that has come along. Abyssinia, Spain and now this. It is always war for us fools.'[141] The military ventures in East Africa and Spain had been hugely costly to Italy in men and materiel. Between 1935 and 1940, 19555 Italian troops were killed in Ethiopia with a further 188000 sick and wounded.[142] A total of 4157 Italians who had fought with the Nationalists were buried in Spain.[143] Involvement in the Spanish Civil War also cost Italy 759 aircraft, 157 tanks, 6791 trucks, 3486 machine guns and an estimated 8.5 billion lire.[144]

While it is important not to ignore those who felt differently about Mussolini, the reality is that the majority of CSDIC POWs were hostile to the *Duce*. Nevertheless, on the question of war guilt a Sub-Lieutenant who had captained a tanker (I/N 35) was certain that, 'it wasn't he who began the war. Mussolini did everything he could to prevent it [...] you must never say that he started (the war) because it isn't true. He did all he could to keep England's friendship [...] they threatened us and so we were forced to defend ourselves.'[145] This Sub-Lieutenant's view has much in common with the arguments of Quartararo and De Felice who play down the *Duce's* ideological kinship with the Nazis and emphasise his eagerness to balance Berlin and London in the hope of amassing concessions from the Western Allies.[146] Similarly positive towards Mussolini is one *Tenente di Vascello* (I/N 23) who believed, 'in the past five or six years [he] has become, not the political leader of Italy, but the political leader of the world [...] the Duce is a man on a really higher plane [...] the Duce besides being a first-rate man, is, I believe, an honest man.'[147] Another *Tenente* (I/N 1) said in October 1940, 'tell the others to cheer up and trust the Duce. They must be patient.'[148] There is no doubt that some retained a faith in Mussolini but even at the start of the war there were many 'others' who needed much more by way of convincing.

Finito Mussolini: The fall of the Duce

By late 1942 the level of hostility towards Mussolini became ever more intense in the protocols. As the cohort began to hope for the fall of the *Duce*. In early

April 1943, Torpedo Rating Colombo (I/N 358) fully supported the Allied bombing of Rome because he believed it was done in the hope of killing the Fascist leader.[149] Colombo blamed all the troubles unleashed by the war on 'that wretch who sits in Rome.'[150] Another example of this view comes from General Orlando (I/M 3) who said in July 1943, 'let him die. If he were to die it wouldn't mean anything. Let's have another man who has not compromised himself like Mussolini has [...] we can't let the country go to the dogs for the whim of a man [i.e. Mussolini] who has gone mad.'[151] This is a woeful reflection of Mussolini's reputation.

Other Centre prisoners went even further than this and numerous protocols contain long discussions about assassinating Mussolini. In these discussions the CSDIC (UK) POWs had the precedents of several attempts to kill him in the 1920s: on 4 November 1925 by the Socialist Tito Zaniboni with a sniper rifle; on 7 April 1926 by the Anglo-Irish aristocrat Violet Gibson who managed to wound his nose with her revolver; on 11 September 1926 by the Anarchist Gino Lucetti who threw a bomb; and on 31 October 1926 by the teenager Anteo Zamboni, who was lynched after trying to shoot him.[152] Of course, given their capture these POWs were in no position to act on what they said. Unlike Zaniboni, Gibson, Lucetti and Zamboni, their discussions remained theoretical. Yet it is an incredible reflection of how low Mussolini's reputation had sunk amongst these men that these exchanges took place at all.

By late 1942 Midshipman Gianni (I/N 250) was profoundly disillusioned as 'for the last few years it's been impossible to make Mussolini understand how things really are. He's got a swollen head.'[153] He discussed the leader further with his cellmate Sub-Lieutenant Mazzinghi (I/N 249),

I/N 250: If he doesn't shoot himself, somebody else will do it for him.
I/N 249: He'll certainly never shoot himself. Even if they say he's done it, I shall refuse to believe it. I should be perfectly certain that he'd never have the courage – though he might get somebody to do it for him.
I/N 250: When people see the final collapse, the end, somebody is sure to have a shot at him. They've tried so often without bringing it off –
I/N 249: I'm fed up with those swine for not making an attempt on his life. After all you risk your life, but you risk it for something worthwhile.[154]

As their conversation developed, both men discussed specific details of a potential assassination plan,

I/N 249: If you fired a revolver (*rivoltella*) shot at him at ten metre's range it would shatter the coat of mail. Or why not a bullet through his head!
I/N 250: It's not so easy to shoot him through the head. You need a man with the pluck to go right up close to him and fire, and he'd have to be a good shot.
I/N 249: Damn it all, if he isn't a good shot it's no good his trying it.

I/N 250: The trouble is that if somebody draws a revolver to shoot him, there's always somebody else who'll pull him down.[155]

For Gianni and Mazzinghi this was a prolonged and multi-faceted discussion. According to them, it was a matter of when, not if, someone would make another attempt on Mussolini's life.

In April 1943 Midshipman Rosali (I/N 340) and Midshipman Gridelli (I/N 378) were two more CSDIC (UK) POWs who openly discussed the specific challenges an attempt against Mussolini's life would need to overcome,

I/N 340: Do you know that the Duce always wears a steel thing underneath?
I/N 378: A steel vest.
I/N 340: He always wears one.
I/N 378: But against what bullets will it protect him? Calibre nine. You know a twenty-millimetre bullet will penetrate a twenty-millimetre armour-plate.[156]

Gridelli was confident that if a defeated Mussolini fled to a neutral country, 'someone will do him in. [...] One fine day, he'll show his nose outside the door and somebody will do him in, that's obvious. [...] If he goes to a neutral country some Italian will do him in. He won't be able to get away with it.'[157] That the British intelligence services would be so interested in recording conversations of this nature is given an added dimension when you consider their own plots to kill Mussolini. There is surviving – if fragmentary – documentary evidence proving the Special Operations Executive in Cairo conceived of just such a plot in 1942. Unlike SOE's conspiracy to kill Adolf Hitler in Operation Foxley, the plan to kill the *Duce* received the 'green light,' only for it to be scrapped because of the indiscretions of the would-be assassin, a Sicilian ex-artilleryman Giovanni di Guinta.[158]

That such a plot against Mussolini could be politically – and legally – legitimate in the eyes of CSDIC (UK) prisoners of war is corroborated by a March 1943 conversation between Sub-Lieutenant Morello (I/N 329) and Sub-Lieutenant Budini (I/N 373),

I/N 329: All the same, if I went and assassinated Mussolini, I should be committing murder, it would be the same as if I killed any other Italian – that's the trouble.
I/N 373: But you would also be helping Italy. Political assassination isn't murder. Why do we kill criminals? Because they're a danger to society. And isn't Mussolini an enemy of Society?[159]

Morello may have been more cautious – if not morally opposed to such action – but Budini was clear. Mussolini had become an existential threat to Italian society and as a result his assassination could not be condemned as common murder. There is an irony here that he could fall foul of a culture of political violence that he had done so much to cultivate during the interwar period. By 25 July 1943 the *Duce* had fallen yet he remained alive until his execution by partisans on 28 April 1945. For all that his 1943 overthrow was a bitter humiliation,[160] as these transcripts demonstrate, by the summer of 1943 there were several Italians who were at the very least speculating on how best to assassinate him.

As the first Axis leader to be toppled, the overthrow of Benito Mussolini in 1943 was a defining moment of the Second World War. Fascism's 'first serious political defeat in twenty years' outraged leading Nazis like Hitler and Goebbels as much as it inspired a glimmer of hope in the hearts of anti-Fascists.[161] In the meeting of the Fascist Grand Council on 24 July, Dino Grandi had fiercely criticised his rule. His motion put to the Council that Mussolini's leadership had risked the 'the unity, independence and liberty of the motherland [...] and the life and future of the Italian people.'[162] According to the former Education Minister Giuseppe Bottai, Grandi had sarcastically asked of Mussolini, 'It is the dictatorship that has lost the war [...] in the seventeen years in which you have held the three armed forces ministries, what have you done?'[163] These were sentiments with which many of those in the Italian cohort would have agreed. As a group, the POWs strongly suggest that by the summer of 1943 Mussolini and the Fascists were widely detested.

Once news of Mussolini's fall reached the high-ranking military officers in captivity, for Field Marshal Messe (I/M 2), it became the topic of considerable and varied discussion. He reminded those around him, 'I should like to say that I foresaw this. I foresaw that the proper moment the King would do this [i.e. intervene in the resignation of Mussolini]. [...] Our hope must be: "God save the King".'[164] Messe here seems to have forgotten a conversation he had a month earlier with his *aide-de-camp*, Lieutenant Colacicchi (I/M 5), in which he said, 'but I myself would never advise the monarchy to do that [conspire to end the Fascism regime] because it wouldn't take much to plunge the country into civil war.'[165] Unfortunately, this is exactly what did happen. Between 8 September 1943 and 2 May 1945 a vicious civil war was fought in Italy between the forces of the *Reppublica Sociale Italiana* (RSI) and the *Comitato di Liberazione Nazionale* (CLN), facilitated by the Germans and the Allies.[166]

The commander of the Spezia Division, *Generale di Brigata* Seattini (I/M 18) was suspicious of the reports of Mussolini's fall, 'one must look behind the screen of words to try and see what happened. [...] Undoubtedly there must be something going on behind the scene.'[167] Seattini was also unhappy with the coverage of Mussolini's resignation in the English press which made 'no mention of the positive side [of his achievements]! After all he did abolish trade unions, you can't deny that he has done something.'[168] Lieutenant Colacicchi (I/M 5) and Captain Colombo (I/M 12) were at odds about what Mussolini's resignation meant for the future of Fascism in Italy. Colacicchi appealed to Colombo, 'yes, but Fascism is done with in Italy, you must realise what has happened.' Colombo was having none of it. He responded, '(Ironically) Fascism done with! The war over! That's all twaddle.' Colacicchi was left to end the conversation saying, 'as we have got to this point, don't let's argue about it anymore.'[169]

On 29 July, Field Marshal Messe (I/M 2) assembled all the senior officers and their Aide-de-Camps. It is not clear exactly why, but a note on the relevant protocol suggests that it may have been done in response to quarrelling that had taken place on the previous day. In a strict parade, Messe addressed them all at 9 am, 'speaking under the stress of great emotion,'[170] he said,

> [...] the midst of the crisis we are passing through, it cannot be necessary for me to give you any instructions, as each one of you will be acutely and deeply conscious of his own responsibility at such a moment [...] we must be very prudent and very reserved and sparing of our words in judging the events of really historic importance which are now taking place in Italy and throughout the world. [...] What is certain is that an epoch has come to an end. It is not for us to sit in judgement upon it, we lack the necessary details to enable us to form a judgement [...] like the good soldiers we are, accustomed to obey and to do our duty as soldiers, we must accept everything that is happening in Italy, and accept it calmly. One thing is certain, and that is that the star of Italy has not set, it is still well above the horizon [...] Italy has risen again so many times in the course of the centuries, and she cannot die. Nevertheless, her destiny will be accomplished through trials and through further sacrifices, through blood and pain [...] We must be prudent and reserved, we must be proud, but not boastful, and each of us must probe his conscience and ask himself whether he has done his duty [...] whether his thoughts are always turned towards his chief, the King (audience rises to its feet). The people here are certain to say that Italy has changed the colour of her coat. [...] The rule, the watchword among the English is to ignore Italy and Italian courage. [...] [But Italy has] held the forces of the British Empire in check for two and a half years [...] I remind these people here that all nations had their difficult periods and moments – I reminded them of Dunkirk, Singapore, Hong Kong, Tobruk – in short, every nation has its disasters. [...] The best solution is to say very little, then you are all right, if you do that it is difficult to go wrong. [...][171]

That Italy faced a period of crisis and deep uncertainty was without question. Messe's speech was given to a group of men finding their feet in the wake of dramatic events that signaled the defeat and fall of the Fascist regime. His watchwords were duty, obedience, prudence, pride, sacrifice and courage.

As a group these men remained – publicly at least – loyal to the King, their 'chief.' Mussolini was barely mentioned at all, only to say that the idea that the British were conducting a 'crusade against Mussolini and against Fascism' was a convenient excuse for them to wage war on Italy.[172] For all Mussolini's attempts to win the favour of the leadership of the Italian armed forces, this group of senior officers did not mourn his passing. Messe's call for calm was unimaginative but given the circumstances of captivity a prudent one. Cut off from sources of information, Messe could not know for sure how Italy's German allies would react, or how Italian forces still in the field were reacting to this news. Mussolini had been arrested, but he was still alive. As events would later show, following his dramatic rescue by German commandos on 12 September, he still had a role to play in Italian politics. Messe may have had concerns about what would happen to *il Duce* in the long term. Or he might not have found it easy to suddenly imagine an Italy without Mussolini at its head.

Conclusion

In August 1943, Second Lieutenant Izzi (I/M 22) and Midshipman Gridelli (I/N 378) discussed the heady days of early summer 1942 where Axis advances threatened the entire position of British and Commonwealth forces in North Africa. Victory appeared tantalizingly close,

I/M 22: You ought to have seen what it was like in Rome when we reached El Alamein. Everybody wanted to go to Libya, trainloads of people who were going to take part in the triumphant entry into Alexandria. It was really laughable. Everybody was going.
I/N 378: Gosh, everything went wrong for Mussolini. He wasn't able to make a triumphal entry anywhere.
I/M 22: He went down with his white horse. They sent the white horse down. He came back and left the horse behind.
I/N 378: It has probably fallen into the hands of the British, or else it has been eaten by the Italians.[173]

Once again, the hubris of Mussolini and his party is skewered by the CSDIC (UK) POWs. Theirs was a hostility towards *il Duce* that swung from frustration at his political powerlessness, through disillusionment with his ambitious foreign policy, to unbridled hatred and fantasies of assassination. Such ill-will towards Mussolini was not universal, but it was dominant.

The resentment was not, however, restricted to Mussolini. Almost every element of the Italian political infrastructure encountered in the protocols comes in for similarly forceful criticism: undisciplined Blackshirt militiamen, foolish Fascist Party officials, the corrupt Count Ciano, the wanton Edda Mussolini, the idiotic Prince Umberto or even the pusillanimous King Victor Emmanuel III. Ineffective, distant and self-serving, this is a model of political leadership that inspires little confidence. Nor is there an abundance of faith to be found in the ideology of Fascism itself. An unbending allegiance is rare indeed, only to be found in a handful of prisoners. For many others Fascism was something subscribed to for pragmatic reasons, making it easy to criticise when no longer compelled to toe the party line. It took three years of war to bring these weaknesses to breaking point, leaving many ordinary Italians to reflect on the years of Fascist rule. It seems likely that many would have agreed with Lieutenant Vertua (I/M 20) who coolly reflected that, 'it has been such a disappointment.'[174]

Notes

1. I/SRM 12 – 19 June 1943, WO 208/4188, TNA.
2. Keith Grint, *Leadership: A Very Short Introduction* (Oxford: Oxford University Press, 2010), 40, 105.
3. Grint, *Leadership*, 99.
4. Duggan, *Voices*, xii–xiii.
5. Duggan, *Voices*, 210–211.
6. Duggan, *Voices*, 221–230.
7. Duggan, *Voices*, xx; Christopher Duggan in Emilio Gentile, Paul Corner and Christopher Duggan, 'Two New Books on Fascism: A Review, the Authors' Responses and the Reviewer's Comments', *Journal of Modern Italian Studies*, 19/5 (2014), 676.
8. Paul Corner, *The Fascist Party and Popular Opinion in Mussolini's Italy* (Oxford: Oxford University Press, 2011), 3.
9. Corner, *Opinion*, 274.
10. Corner, *Opinion*, 8.
11. For detail of Gentile's criticisms of Corner's work, see: Gentile et al, 'Two New Books', 665–683.
12. Gentile et al, 'Two New Books', 674.
13. *Confinati* being those subject to *confino*, a punishment of internal exile to remote Italian villages for political dissidents.
14. Richard Bosworth, 'War, Totalitarianism and "Deep Belief"' in Fascist Italy', *European History Quarterly*, 34/4 (2004), 475–305.
15. Bosworth, *Mussolini's Italy*, 561–562.
16. Bosworth, 'Totalitarianism', 488–497.
17. Bosworth, 'Totalitarianism', 491.
18. Bosworth, 'Totalitarianism', 497.
19. Bosworth, 'Totalitarianism', 498.
20. Bosworth, *Mussolini's Italy*, 564.
21. Sullivan, 'Italian Soldier', 177. See also: Charles O'Reilly, *Forgotten Battles: Italy's War of Liberation, 1943–1945* (Lanham: Lexington Books, 2001).
22. Piero Crociani and Pier Battistelli, *Italian Blackshirt, 1935-45* (Oxford: Osprey, 2010), 19.
23. 'Decree Establishing the Fascist Militia (MVSN)', 14 January 1923, in Delzell, *Mediterranean Fascism*, 52–53.
24. Crociani and Battistelli, *Blackshirt*, 8.
25. Crociani and Battistelli, *Blackshirt*, 5–17.
26. Crociani and Battistelli, *Blackshirt*, 9, 17.
27. Crociani and Battistelli, *Blackshirt*, 18, 40. See also: Andrea Rossi, *Le guerre delle camicie nere: la milizia fascista dalla guerra mondiale alla guerra civile* (Pisa: BFS, 2004); Lucio Ceva, *Storia delle forze armate in Italia* (Turin: UTET, 1999).
28. I/SRM 41 – 6 July 1943, WO 208/4188, TNA.
29. SRIG 191 – 30 July 1943, WO 208/4186, TNA.
30. Crociani and Battistelli, *Army Elite Units*, 56–60; Crociani and Battistelli, *Blackshirt*, 18, 38, 48.
31. I/SRM 13 – 19 June 1943, WO 208/4188, TNA.
32. I/SRM 13 – 19 June 1943, WO 208/4188, TNA.

33 I/SRM 41 – 6 July 1943, WO 208/4188, TNA.
34 Jowett, *The Italian Army*, 4.
35 I/SRN 1082 – 6 March 1943, WO 208/4191, TNA.
36 Crociani and Battistelli, *Blackshirt*, 42.
37 Christopher Othen, *Franco's International Brigades: Adventurers, Fascists, and Christian Crusaders in the Spanish Civil War* (London: Hurst, 2013), 145–146; John Coverdale, 'The Battle of Guadalajara, 8–22 March 1937', *Journal of Contemporary History*, 9/1 (1974), 74.
38 I/SRN 58 – 17 January 1941, WO 208/4189, TNA.
39 Excerpt from a Police report in David Gould, 'Sport and Fascism: A Beautiful Friendship? – A Study of Relations between the State and Elite Sport in Mussolini's Italy', PhD Thesis, the University of Reading (Reading, 2002), 123–126.
40 Crociani and Battistelli, *Blackshirt*, 19.
41 Gooch, *Mussolini and His Generals*, 188.
42 I/SRN 298 – 1 December 1941, WO 208/4189, TNA.
43 I/SRX 72 – 21 March 1943, WO 208/4193, TNA.
44 I/SRN 828 – 28 December 1942, WO 208/4191, TNA.
45 I/SRN 912 – 29 January 1943, WO 208/4191, TNA.
46 I/SRN 912 – 29 January 1943, WO 208/4191, TNA.
47 I/SRN 472 – 22 August 1942, WO 208/4190, TNA.
48 I/SRN 453 – 16 August 1942, WO 208/4190, TNA.
49 I/SRN 543 – 3 September 1942, WO 208/4190, TNA.
50 'Si, questo un grandissimo errore, questo caso di Ciano. Crede che è il Padre Eterno semplicemente perché è genero di Mussolini. È il popolo ha visto che c'è il nepotismo anche nel fascismo: questo era un grande errore psicologico.' I/SRN 57 – 18 January 1941, WO 208/4189, TNA.
51 Bosworth, *'Per necessità famigliare'*, 368.
52 I/SRN 66 – 23 July 1941, WO 208/4189, TNA.
53 Bosworth, *'Per necessità famigliare'*, 358–359.
54 See: Franco Cazzola, *Della Corruzione: Fisiologia e Patologia di un Sistema Politico* (Bologna: Il Mulino, 1988).
55 I/SRN 347 – 1 August 1940, WO 208/4189, TNA.
56 James Sadkovich, 'The Italo-Greek War in Context: Italian Priorities and Axis Diplomacy', *Journal of Contemporary History*, 28/3 (1993), 447.
57 Jerzy Borejsza, 'Greece and the Balkan policy of Fascist Italy, 1936–1940', *Journal of the Hellenic Diaspora*, 13/1-2 (1986), 57.
58 '22 October 1940' in Ciano, *War Diaries*, 218.
59 I/N 118's use of *bagascia* – a word associated with Neapolitan and Sicilian dialects – suggests he may have come from the South of Italy. I/SRN 214 – 27 October 1941, WO 208/4189, TNA.
60 I/SRA 6 – 8 November 1940, WO 208/4184, TNA.
61 Howard McGaw Smyth, 'The Ciano Papers: Rose Garden', 13/2 (1969), Studies Archives Indexes, Center for the Study of Intelligence, CIA.
62 Tobias Jones, *The Dark Heart of Italy* (London: Faber & Faber, 2005), 143–144.
63 I/SRN 124 – 7 September 1941, WO 208/4189, TNA.
64 I/SRM 16 – 20 June 1943, WO 208/4188, TNA.
65 I/SRX 58 – 8 March 1943, WO 208/4193, TNA.
66 SRIG 50 – 2 June 1943, WO 208/4185, TNA.
67 Bosworth, *Mussolini's Italy*, 483.
68 SRIG 23 – 22 May 1943, WO 208/4185, TNA.
69 Alexander Stille, *Benevolence and Betrayal: Five Italian Jewish Families under Fascism* (New York: Picador, 1991), 112.
70 I/SRN 56 – 13 January 1941, WO 208/4189, TNA.

71 SRIG 357 – 24 November 1943, WO 208/4187, TNA.
72 SRIG 353 – 17 November 1943, WO 208/4187, TNA.
73 SRIG 325 – 15 October 1943, WO 208/4187, TNA.
74 SRIG 325 – 15 October 1943, WO 208/4187, TNA.
75 SRIG 343 – 4 November 1943, WO 208/4187, TNA.
76 So closely tied to Fascism was this symbolic act that the traditional handshake was officially castigated as 'degenerate' and 'bourgeois.' See: Falasca-Zamponi, *Spectacle*, 110–113.
77 I/SRN 174 – 19 October 1941, WO 208/4189, TNA.
78 I/SRN 174 – 19 October 1941, WO 208/4189, TNA.
79 I/SRA 16 – 11 December 1940, WO 208/4184, TNA.
80 Adrian Lyttelton, *Liberal and Fascist Italy, 1900–1945* (Oxford: Oxford University Press, 2002), 161, 165–166.
81 John Pollard, *The Fascist Experience in Italy* (London: Routledge, 2005), 62.
82 See also: Francesco Ferrari, *Il Regime Fascista Italiano* (Rome: ESL, 1983), 277; Corner, *Opinion*, 64; Duggan, *Voices*, 164.
83 I/SRN 832 – 6 January 1943, WO 208/4191, TNA.
84 I/SRN 279 – 24 November 1941, WO 208/4189, TNA.
85 I/SRM 17 – 16 June 1943, WO 208/4188, TNA.
86 I/SRN 517 – 30 August 1942, WO 208/4190, TNA.
87 Bosworth, 'Totalitarianism', 494, 499.
88 I/SRX 104 – 10 July 1943, WO 208/4193, TNA.
89 I/SRN 1030 – 22 February 1943, WO 208/4191, TNA.
90 I/SRX 74 – 22 March 1943, WO 208/4193, TNA.
91 I/SRX 38 – 6 March 1943, WO 208/4193, TNA.
92 I/SRX 79 – 22 March 1943, WO 208/4193, TNA.
93 I/SRX 79 – 22 March 1943, WO 208/4193, TNA.
94 See: George Talbot, *Censorship in Fascist Italy, 1922-43* (Basingstoke: Palgrave Macmillan, 2007). For Fascism's censorship of literature, see: Guido Bonsaver, *Censorship and Literature in Fascist Italy* (Toronto: University of Toronto Press, 2007).
95 I/SRX 74 – 22 March 1943, WO 208/4193, TNA.
96 Mauro Forno, *La stampa del ventennio: strutture e trasformazioni nello stato totalitario* (Catanzaro: Rubbettino, 2005). For more on the nature of the press before the fascist period, and changes in the early stages of the Fascist regime, see: Valerio Castronovo, *La stampa italiana dall'Unità al Fascismo* (Rome: Laterza, 1984).
97 I/SRX 7 – 6 December 1940, WO 208/4193, TNA.
98 I/SRN 330 – 29 July 1942, WO 208/4189, TNA.
99 I/SRN 57 – 18 January 1941, WO 208/4189, TNA.
100 Luigi Petrella, *Staging the Fascist War: The Ministry of Popular Culture and Italian Propaganda on the Home Front, 1938–1943* (Oxford: Peter Lang, 2016), 224.
101 I/SRN 383 – 6 August 1942, WO 208/4189, TNA.
102 I/SRN 383 – 6 August 1942, WO 208/4189, TNA.
103 I/SRN 332 – 27 July 1942, WO 208/4189, TNA.
104 Ester Lo Biundo, *London Calling Italy: La Propaganda di Radio Londra nel 1943* (Milan: Unicopli, 2014), 39–40. See also: Maura Caprioli, ed., *Radio Londra 1940–1945: inventario delle trasmissioni per l'Italia* (Rome: MBCA, 1976).
105 I/SRN 1082 – 6 March 1943, WO 208/4191, TNA
106 Sullivan, '1918–1940', 169.
107 MacGregor Knox, 'The Italian Armed Forces, 1940-4', in Allan Millett and Williamson Murray, eds., *Military Effectiveness, Volume 3: The Second World War* (Cambridge: Cambridge University Press, 2010), 137.
108 Osti Guerrazzi, *odiare*, 112–130.
109 I/SRN 902 – 18 January 1943, WO 208/4191, TNA.

174 *Attitudes towards Italian leadership*

110 I/SRN 902 – 18 January 1943, WO 208/4191, TNA.
111 I/SRN 902 – 18 January 1943, WO 208/4191, TNA. '*Altro filibustiero*' could also be translated as 'another freebooter/buccaneer/shyster.' A change of tone, but it remains a strong insult. The use of 'another' could also be interpreted as lumping the King in with the 'freebooters' in the PNF.
112 I/SRM 32 – 1 July 1943, WO 208/4188, TNA.
113 I/SRN 1107 – 10 February 1943, WO 208/4191, TNA.
114 I/SRN 902 – 18 January 1943, WO 208/4191, TNA.
115 I/SRN 1017 – 10 February 1943, WO 208/4191, TNA.
116 I/SRM 46 – 9 July 1943, WO 208/4188, TNA.
117 I/SRM 6 – 16 June 1943, WO 208/4188, TNA.
118 Robert Katz, *The Fall of the House of Savoy* (New York: Macmillan, 1971), 353–364; George Botjer, *Sideshow War: The Italian Campaign, 1943–1945* (College Station: A&M University Press, 1996), 50; Richard Bosworth, 'Nations Examining Their Past: A Comparative Analysis of the Historiography of the 'Long' Second World War', *The History Teacher*, 29/4 (1996), 506.
119 J. West, 'British Soldiers smile at a Viva il Duce slogan on a wall in Reggio, Italy, September 1943', NA 6230, IWM. Another example of post-liberation defacement of Mussolini's image can be found here: 'A Badly Defaced Portrait of Mussolini', US Embassy Second World War Photography Library, NYF 9892, IWM.
120 Falasca-Zamponi, *Spectacle*, 65–88.
121 Morgan, *Fall*, 13.
122 I/SRX 61 – 10 March 1943, WO 208/4193, TNA.
123 David Baker, 'The Political Economy of Fascism: Myth or Reality, or Myth and Reality?', *New Political Economy*, 11/2 (2006), 231–232, 250.
124 James Sadkovich, 'The Development of the Italian Air Force Prior to World War II', *Military Affairs*, 51/3 (1987), 130, 133.
125 I/SRN 1164 – 21 April 1943, WO 208/4192, TNA.
126 I/SRN 462 – 18 August 1943, WO 208/4190, TNA.
127 Bosworth, '*Per necessità famigliare*', 367–368.
128 SRIG 133 – 13 July 1943, WO 208/4186, TNA.
129 SRIG 209 – 6 August 1943, WO 208/4186, TNA.
130 Roberto Ollas, *Il Duce and His Women: Mussolini's Rise to Power* (Richmond: Alma Books, 2011), 3.
131 Richard Bosworth, *Claretta: Mussolini's Last Lover* (New Haven: Yale University Press, 2017), 29, 256.
132 Bosworth, *Claretta*, 33–34.
133 See: Victoria De Grazia, *How Fascism Ruled Women: Italy, 1922–1945* (Berkeley: University of California Press, 1992).
134 Bosworth, *Claretta*, 4.
135 The original Italian reads as 'Che testa di cazzo!' Alternative translations to 'blockhead' may be 'dickhead', 'asshole' or 'shithead.' See: I/SRN 940 – 28 January 1943, WO 208/4191, TNA.
136 I/SRN 927 – 23 January 1941, WO 208/4191, TNA.
137 I/SRN 1019 – 10 February 1943, WO 208/4191, TNA.
138 I/SRA 17 – 13 December 1940, WO 208/4184, TNA.
139 I/SRA 17 – 13 December 1940, WO 208/4184, TNA.
140 I/SRN 43 – 3 January 1941, WO 208/4189, TNA.
141 I/SRN 43 – 3 January 1941, WO 208/4189, TNA.
142 Alberto Sbacchi, 'The Price of Empire: Towards an Enumeration of Italian Casualties in Ethiopia, 1935–1940', *Ethiopianist Notes*, 2/2 (1978), 35–46.
143 Brian Sullivan, 'Fascist Italy's Military Involvement in the Spanish Civil War', *The Journal of Military History*, 59/4 (1995), 713.

144 Bosworth, *Mussolini's Italy*, 402.
145 I/SRN 60 – 26 April 1941, WO 208/4189, TNA.
146 Quartararo, *tra Londra*, 519–22, 624–5; De Felice, *Lo Stato Totalitario, 1936–1940*, 332–335, 465–467.
147 I/SRN 57 – 18 November 1941, WO 208/4189, TNA.
148 I/SRN 2 – 31 October 1940, WO 208/4189, TNA.
149 I/SRN 1113 – 7 April 1943, WO 208/4191, TNA.
150 I/SRN 1113 – 7 April 1943, WO 208/4191, TNA.
151 SRIG 131 – 10 July 1943, WO 208/4186, TNA.
152 David Williamson, *The Age of the Dictators: A Study of the European Dictatorships, 1918-53* (London: Routledge, 2007), 107–108. For more on the Honourable Violet Gibson, see: Frances Saunders, *The Woman Who Shot Mussolini* (London: Faber, 2010).
153 Original Italian: 'Gli è andato un po'alla testa.' I/SRN 694 – 4 December 1942, WO 208/4190, TNA.
154 I/SRN 694 – 4 December 1942, WO 208/4190, TNA.
155 I/SRN 694 – 4 December 1942, WO 208/4190, TNA.
156 I/SRN 1235 – 29 April 1943, WO 208/4192, TNA.
157 I/SRN 1235 – 29 April 1943, WO 208/4192, TNA.
158 It is worth stressing however that this operation suffered greatly from a lack of planning and resources. Head of SOE from 1943 onwards, Colin Gubbins, called it 'rather a scatter-brained project [that] revealed a poverty of operational conceptions.' See: Bailey, *Target Italy*, 156–174.
159 I/SRN 1107 – 24 March 1943, WO 208/4191, TNA.
160 It was a turn of events that precipitated a further decline in Mussolini's physical and mental health. He wrote to his sister soon afterwards that he was now, 'defunct', 'a heap of skin and bones in process of organic decomposition.' Richard Bosworth, *Mussolini* (London: Bloomsbury, 2002), 403.
161 Morgan, *Fall*, 31–33.
162 'Dino Grandi's Resolution at the Fascist Grand Council', Palazzo Venezia, Rome, 24–25 July 1943, in Delzell, *Mediterranean Fascism*, 222.
163 Morgan, *Fall*, 14.
164 SRIG 155 – 26 July 1943, WO 208/4186, TNA.
165 SRIG 109 – 27 June 1943, WO 208/4185, TNA.
166 See: Claudio Pavone, *A Civil War: A History of the Italian Resistance* (London: Verso, 2013); Roberto Battiglia, *Storia della Resistenza Italiana* (Turin: Einaudi, 1970); Guido Quazza, *Resistenza e Storia d'Italia* (Milan: Feltrinelli, 1976).
167 SRIG 157 – 26 June 1943, WO 208/4186, TNA.
168 SRIG 157 – 26 June 1943, WO 208/4186, TNA.
169 SRIG 156 – 26 June 1943, WO 208/4186, TNA.
170 SRIG 165 – 29 July 1943, WO 208/4186, TNA.
171 SRIG 165 – 29 July 1943, WO 208/4186, TNA.
172 SRIG 165 – 29 July 1943, WO 208/4186, TNA.
173 I/SRX 133 – 17 August 1943, WO 208/4193, TNA.
174 I/SRM 42 – 6 July 1943, WO 208/4188, TNA.

7 Winning and losing the war

Introduction

This chapter traces the linked trajectories of diminishing belief in victory and mounting defeatism amongst the Italian CSDIC (UK) cohort. While the period 1940–1941 was one where most prisoners remained confident in an Axis victory, by 1943 most had become much more negative. A few clung onto their faith in an Italian victory, but for many more, by the fourth year of Italy's involvement in the Second World War anger at individual failures had slid into a total collapse of faith in the Axis cause. The crucial period of transition is from the summer and autumn of 1942 onwards, where mounting pressure on the Axis in all theatres of the war fatally undermined the POWs' confidence. However, in some cases, this is a nuanced shift. Confidence did not always skip abruptly to outright pessimism, but could go through stages of optimism saturated with underlying desperation; the idea that Italy simply *had* to win after all the years of bloodshed and suffering.

Victory

In January 1943 Chief Boatswain Pontone (I/N 254) and Medical Petty Officer Botti (I/N 318) reflected on the heady days of 1940,

I/N 318: If Hitler had made peace proposals after defeating France, do you think it would all have been over.
I/N 254: Yes. England would have accepted.[1]

However close the British government actually came to capitulation after the defeats in France, it is evident that a significant number of CSDIC (UK) POWs were confident of victory.[2] Speaking in November 1940, submarine officer I/N 22 was clear,

> A war is never won by defensive measures [...] since the English cannot take the offensive, they have lost the war. The most important thing is to drive all the English out of the Mediterranean [...] we'll drive the English out. [...] It is impossible for us to lose, even if the Americans join the English.[3]

Bomber-Photographer I/A 2 was convinced, 'we shall always be successful, thanks to our German friends. The Germans won't lose the war.'[4] In late October 1940, *Sottotenente di Vascello* I/N 2 and *Guardiamarina* I/N 3 had also discussed how long the war would last. According to the summary of their conversation: 'P/Ws agreed that it might be over by the spring, but would more probably last another two years. They were confident of Germany eventually occupying England and of Italy's ability to hold out in the Mediterranean.'[5]

For these POWs, victory was certain, but I/N 3 and I/A 2 were clear that Italy's contribution to it would be secondary. It was Germany that would shoulder most of the burden. This situation is reflected in several predictions for the invasion of Great Britain. Petty Officer I/N 6 anticipated that, 'the "Stukas" will soon reduce the [British] coastal batteries to silence [...] They [the *Wehrmacht*] could meet much resistance in the interior, of course, but I'll give them a month to occupy everything once they have set foot on the coast.'[6] Such was the anticipated ferocity of the German assault on London and the South-East that I/N 6 hoped to move to the relative safety of a Scottish prisoner of war camp by then.[7] MAS *Tenente di Vascello* I/N 23 described at length his vision for the invasion:

> By the end of January they (the Germans) will have 12–13,000 a/c. Let's say they drop 200 tons of bombs on some place. [...] 20,000 mines in the Channel. Then on the appointed night would come 2,000 a/c with 100 men in each at least, and 200 stukas. Their (the British) air defence will be powerless. [...] The British forces will be compelled to withdraw. [...] The moment the British fleet appears on the spot, they start a submarine barrage. [...] At daybreak they land. It'll be a fine show, no mistake.[8]

In late 1940 MAS *Tenente di Vascello* (I/N 23) was genuinely impressed with the achievement of his allies, saying in December: 'I'll tell you something. Few human achievements could equal the Battle of France, in conception and in destructive effect. Ah! Those chaps have got thirteen times as much guts as other men.'[9] In these transcripts, it is the Germans who lead the way in the British defeat.

This could be perceived as an Italian inferiority complex,[10] or an example of the Italian capacity to internalise the widespread prejudices about their martial prowess, especially those held by their German allies.[11] However, it also reflects a pragmatic assessment of German and Italian achievements and unit concentrations. By the beginning of 1941, the Germans had defeated Poland, Denmark, Norway, Belgium, the Netherlands, Luxembourg and France, with their armed forces poised to strike along the Channel coast. Meanwhile, the Italians had managed to mount a costly assault on the *Ligne Alpine*, had suffered the losses of the *Corpo Aereo Italiano* in the Battle of Britain and had been forced into retreat by the British at Sidi Barrani and by the Greeks on the Albanian frontier. Admittedly, there had been some successes in East Africa, with advances into Sudan, Kenya and British Somaliland. Achieved entirely without German support, nonetheless, these victories could not conceal the reality that the Duke of Aosta's army was isolated and vulnerable to counter-attack.[12] On this balance sheet, the Italians compared unfavourably with their Axis allies.

Regardless of who would be the primary agents of success, many prisoners retained confidence in Axis victory that endured into 1942. I/N 23 remarked in January 1941, 'in England they're boasting about victory. They don't know that in four months we shall finish them off.'[13] I/N 23's vision of the post-war world was rosy, with Italian control over the *Mare Nostrum*: 'After the war we shall have our naval bases at Taranto, Alexandria, Trapani and Bizerta. We shan't need Malta. It will be used for supplies, but not as a base.'[14] The extension of the war to the Soviet Union in the summer of 1941 did nothing to dull the confidence of IAF observer I/A 14. In August he said: 'It'll all be over in Russia in another month [...] then it will be England's turn.'[15] With the Empire of Japan now joining the Axis in war, Sub-Lieutenant Villa (I/N 174) looked to the future: 'Once Russia has been defeated and the Middle East cleared, with India threatened by a Japanese invasion, I think we can really start thinking about peace.'[16]

In August 1942, self-confessed optimist Petty Officer Boschin (I/N 176) believed, 'at the very most a year more and the war will be over. I've complete confidence that we'll win.'[17] That month the Eighth Army in Africa had been pushed back to El Alamein and was demoralised after the fall of Tobruk in June and April 1942; this followed on from the disasters in the Far East and the Japanese advances in the Pacific. On 25 June a motion was put to the House of Commons to the effect that the House, 'had no confidence in the central direction of the war.' In the wake of the humiliating Singapore surrender, the Sydney *Bulletin* would describe the British government as 'the greatest calamity that Britain has had in the line of governments' since that which had lost the American War of Independence.[18]

In April 1943 Torpedo Petty Officer Costanzo (I/N 385) was contemptuous of Allied assurances of victory: 'they want to persuade me that they're going to win the war, but I believe that we shall win it.'[19] In March, a discussion between Chief Boatswain Pontone (I/N 254), Engine-Room Petty Officer De Guigan (I/N 342) and Petty Officer Boatswain Pati (I/N 369) made it clear that others also held on to the prospect of victory when discussing 'general mobilisation' in Italy,

I/N 369: Mobilisation is a sign of weakness.

I/N 254: They mobilised everybody after Caporetto. And how long did that last? Only a few months.

I/N 342: But after Caporetto things were going badly for us, whereas now they're, going well. [...] there is no fighting in Italy.

I/N 254: We've got to knock out Russia, then we shall be all right. Even if they have taken Libya! Once we knock out Russia, they'll be ready enough to make friends. Libya doesn't matter a damn! [...]

I've no fear of the war being brought to Italy. If we can knock out Russia, that will be the first step. Then these fine gentlemen over here will see that they're up to their necks in it and they'll be ready to start negotiations. If they don't make up their minds to do so, then with all the forces at our disposal we can launch an attack anywhere we like.[20]

De Guigan makes an interesting point. The losses sustained by the Italian armed forces in the Second World War were dwarfed by those losses at Caporetto.[21] Having suffered the humiliation of these losses in 1917 the Italian Army was still capable of regrouping and mounting the decisive counter-attack of Vittorio Veneto in October 1918 which completely broke Austro-Hungarian resistance on the Italian front.[22] This was a link made by Diver I/N 2. When discussing losses in Libya in 1941, he remarked, 'well after Caporetto came Vittorio Veneto. I see it like that.'[23] It remained helpful to these men to have an example of such resurgence from recent Italian military history.

The 1st Italian Army was the last Axis unit to surrender to the Allies in North Africa, entering captivity on 12 May 1943 as part of the 250000 Italian and German service personnel who surrendered in Tunisia.[24] As a result of this Axis defeat, the prospect of Allied landings across occupied Europe became an imminent reality. Even in the face of this, some belief in the Axis cause remained. Both Lieutenant Molinari (I/M 19) and Second Lieutenant Izzi (I/M 22) were sceptical of Allied success in such amphibious operations. Molinari believed that, 'if the [Allied] landing is a failure, they won't even try again [...] if things go badly, my dear chap, they'll lose everything.' In a separate protocol Izzi expanded further: 'no matter where they land in Europe [...] they will stick there [...] once they set foot on land, each one of us is worth a hundred of them.'[25] Izzi felt, 'I have the impression that if our Air Force is doing nothing, it's because we're saving it up' to be unleashed on Allied beachheads.[26] Izzi's comments here are reminiscent of the German propaganda of the *Wunderwaffe* or 'miracle weapons' which was used by the Nazis to maintain German morale as the war situation worsened for the Reich.[27]

The confidence of Molinari and Izzi that Allied landings would be repelled was not mere bluster. The Allied record of offensive amphibious operations was chequered at best. The St. Nazaire Raid (28 March 1942) was a success in that it achieved all its objectives – destroying the *Normandie* dry dock and causing considerable damage to the surrounding port facilities. But, at a high human cost. Of the 621 British Navy and Commando personnel that took part in the raid, only 218 made it back to Britain.[28] The Dieppe Raid (19 August) was similarly sanguinary for Allied forces, whilst failing to meet almost any of its aims.[29] In this operation the Canadian Army had more of its men taken prisoner – 1946 – than in the entirety of the 1944-45 North-West Europe Campaign.[30]

Tactical and strategic amphibious successes in 1942 need to be contextualised. Operation Torch (8–16 November 1942) *was* an overall Allied victory. It put Algeria and French Morocco under Anglo-American occupation for the 'rather modest cost' of 1469 Allied casualties, just 1.2 percent of the 125000 Allied personnel involved in the operation.[31] It was a considerable achievement, particularly for the American armed forces who at this stage had had little experience of conducting substantial amphibious operations.[32] Nevertheless, it is worth noting that the Vichy French forces that opposed them had been deliberately weakened by the terms of the 1940 armistice with Germany. There admittedly were several hundred well-piloted planes and a nominal 120000 men across North Africa, but they had no medium or heavy artillery, only small numbers of obsolete armoured vehicles and only three regiments of anti-aircraft artillery.[33] The Vichy French forces thus lacked the maneuverability and potency to mount decisive counter-attacks and they were not the most testing of opponents.

Defeat

Within the CSDIC (UK) cohort faith in an Axis victory was far from universal. From the second half of 1942 onwards, there was a growing trend towards defeatism in the protocols. The timing here is significant. On 23 October the start of the Second Battle of El Alamein precipitated an Allied advance that would push the Axis out of Egypt – and then North Africa – for good. Beyond the Western Desert, the groundwork for the victories at Guadalcanal and Stalingrad was also in an advanced stage. The bombing of mainland Italy also intensified from this period. In order to support the fighting in Egypt, new heavy British bombers like the Avro Lancaster were joined by American B-17s and B-24s to allow for around-the-clock raiding of Italian targets.[34] As Winston Churchill wrote in his history of the war, 'it may almost be said, "Before Alamein we never had a victory. After Alamein we never had a defeat."'[35] This classically Churchillian flourish ignored successes such as those in East Africa in 1941, but it did encapsulate an essential truth about the war: years of hard fighting followed, but from this point onwards the Axis was in decline on all fronts. That CSDIC (UK) POWs were discussing the Allied invasion of 'fortress Europe' at all was telling of how far the fortunes of war had changed. The shifting progress of the war is well encapsulated in the statement of Midshipman Gridelli (I/N 378) in April 1943: 'there's little to be said. Three years ago there was talk of a landing in England, now people are talking about a landing on the Continent.'[36]

It was not that victories completely eluded Italy from the autumn of 1942. For example, on 11 December, manned torpedoes and elite frogmen of the *Decima Flottiglia MAS* successfully raided Allied shipping in Algiers harbour.[37] On land, the Italian 131st *Centauro* Armoured Division played an 'instrumental role' in the Axis victory at the Kasserine Pass in February 1943.[38] But these were individual tactical victories that could not overturn the strategic direction of the war which now favoured the Allies. As time went on, it is only reasonable that the CSDIC (UK) cohort would have become more aware of this. They had grounds to be sceptical of Allied amphibious successes, but once the landings in North Africa had taken place there was a clear sense of shock.

Chief Boatswain Pontone (I/N 254) said, 'nobody foresaw that (the landings in North Africa). It's absolutely certain that nobody knew anything about it.'[39]

In September 1942 Sub-Lieutenant Bersani (I/N 247) was concerned with the direction of the war,

> I am afraid this war is going to last for several years. It will be some time before Russia is beaten and then Germany will have to invade England. That will be difficult, but it isn't impossible. They'll have to surround England with all the submarines the Axis has at its disposal. Germany won't take the risk of attacking England before she's forced Russia to lay down her arms.[40]

Superficially, Bersani retained some faith in an eventual Axis victory. But this would only be after several more years of hard fighting. Even after the long campaign against the Soviets had come to an end, victory over the English would still only be 'not impossible,' suggesting that Bersani entertained doubts despite his belief in victory. When placed alongside the wider context of other transcripts, Bersani's comments are part of the trend towards pessimism.

That events in North Africa shaped the outlook of CSDIC (UK) POWs is beyond question. In December 1942 Sub-Lieutenant Mazzinghi (I/N 249) said: 'What a lot the war in Libya has cost us! And what a lot more it's going to cost us! And after all that, we shall get the worst of it. If the war isn't over by Easter, we're done for, in my opinion.'[41] On 12 December, Rommel's forces had retreated to the Mareth Line in Tunisia, the last defensive position before Tripoli. When the port fell to the Allies on 23 January 1943 Petty Officer I/N 316 was clear that all was lost: 'So Tripoli has fallen! Well, let's hope that now the war will end as quickly as possible. There's nothing more we can do.'[42] Even in November 1942, Petty Officer Guglielmo (I/N 206) believed that this would be a decisive moment: 'It seems to me that this means the final defeat of the Italian and German forces (in Libya). This time the English will get to Tripoli.'[43]

This was a sentiment echoed within the British Eighth Army. In a 12 January 1943 personal message to his troops, General Bernard Montgomery said: 'Tripoli is the only town in the Italian Empire overseas still remaining in their possession. Therefore, we will take it from them; they will then have no overseas Empire.'[44] In that moment Mussolini's 'new Roman Empire' would have ceased to exist. When Montgomery himself entered Tripoli, the *Tripoli Times* reported that 'the [Italian] crowd below [...] looked up and saw [the Union Fag] flying over a statue of Romulus and Remus being suckled by the wolf, it meant the end of an epoch.'[45] The fall of Tripoli was a crucial moment in the war fought between Italy and Great Britain. The impact on both British and Italian morale should not be underestimated.

In the transcripts themselves, the language of the Italian POWs shifts throughout 1942. Categorical guarantees of an Axis victory make way for more limited hopes. In December 1942 the following exchange took place between Petty Officer Villosio (I/N 188) and Petty Officer Pettinati (I/N 269),

182 *Winning and losing the war*

I/N 269: It would be worth being a P/W for twenty years if we can only win the war.
I/N 188: Ah, if we can win it! But England hasn't done so badly in this war, both with her navy and with her Army.[46]

Likewise, in August 1942 Able Seaman Vincenzi (I/N 197), Signalman Sauro (I/N 198) and Seaman Montaldo (I/N 208) had also discussed the prospect of an Axis victory,

I/N 198: It's certain that we shall stay here until the end of this year.
I/N 197: The English can hold out until October, but not longer.
I/N 198: That's what I hope too.
I/N 208: How do you expect the war to finish by October?[47]

Able Seaman I/N 194 said in late July 1942, 'if we can finish off Russia before the winter, England will lose the war. But I think this cursed war will last another two years.'[48] These conversations are notable for their qualified belief in victory – 'I hope,' 'if we can only win the war,' the use of the subjunctive – which implies a degree of uncertainty ('che finisca in ottobre') – as well as direct challenges to their more confident utterances.

Genuine optimism recedes and desperation grows from the autumn of 1942. Petty Officer Paoli (I/N 175) said in September 1942, 'Italy has simply got to win – we just can't afford to lose.'[49] For Paoli, victory had acquired its own inherent momentum, powered by a dread of the alternative more than an actual appreciation of the strategic landscape facing Italy's armed forces. In August 1943 General Orlando (I/M 3) stated: 'we've got to attempt some sort of solution. […] Italy is still alive and perhaps stronger than before, and she will continue to resist. We've got to tackle the military problem and not worry about the nonsense spread by propaganda.'[50] While Orlando remained firm in his deluded belief in Axis victory despite the Allied seizure of Sicily, he was in no doubt about the serious 'problems' faced by Italy that required an immediate resolution. His belief that Italy is 'perhaps stronger than before' is guarded.

1942–1943 was a transition period in the outlook of the CSDIC (UK) cohort. By June 1943, Lieutenant-Colonel Pedala (I/M 13) had little faith in an Italian victory and demonstrated a clear contempt for the regime's propaganda when he discussed news of Italian bombing raids: 'Despite the fact that everybody realises the situation. […] We're all pretending to be idiots and saying: "Oh yes, we're going to win."'[51] At the same time, Second Lieutenant Rizzi (I/M 14) believed that after Italian losses in Russia, Tunisia and Libya, 'in Italy there's nothing left […] and now these people here [the British] have got so many prisoners they don't know where the devil to put them. They've captured half the population of Italy! And what are they going to do in Italy now?'[52] In total, some 397916 Italian POWs found their way into British hands, at camps throughout the British Isles, Africa, India, the Middle East, the Mediterranean, the Caribbean, North America and Australia.[53]

If thoughts of Axis victory in 1940 had rested with German success, thoughts of defeat in 1942 and 1943 rested on German failure. Gunner Petty Officer Marchiol (I/N 177) also gave a pessimistic overview of the overstretched manpower situation facing their allies in August 1942,

> The Germans have lost a mass of men on the Russian front. Then there's occupied France, occupied Holland, Austria, Czechoslovakia; they have troops in Yugoslavia, Greece and Africa and the whole of the Russian front. Whereas England hasn't yet begun to fight seriously. They've masses of men, in Australia, India, Africa, and they can send the Americans to Africa. Supposing Germany defeats Russia, even so she'll be weakened.[54]

In late January 1943, Naval Lieutenant Franco (I/N 248) spoke at length of the weakening position of the Axis,

> America can send ten million men to fight in Europe or against Japan. The English are now in a position to throw us out of Africa. The Allied Nations have a population four times as great as that of the Axis countries, because Russia is so enormous. So what can we do? We have an immensely long coastline to defend, including Spain and the Balkans and everything. The Balkans are really against us and in addition to that we've got to be on our guard against an internal revolution and at the same time prepare to meet an invasion. If we have to fight through another winter, then it's definitely all up with us. It's difficult to know exactly what's happening now, but one thing is certain, and that is that the Germans are losing thousands of men every day in Russia.[55]

To which Engineer Lieutenant Ziccardi (I/N 295) responded: 'I think sooner or later Germany will be exhausted.'[56]

By June 1943 the power of the Allied air forces had worn down General Berardi's (I/M 4) resolve: 'I have no longer any faith: after all, with the number of aircraft they can put in – on any stretch of beach they can establish a bridgehead where they can land.'[57] The dominance of Allied airpower was a key element of Lieutenant Paladini's (I/N 298) thoughts on the war in December 1942,

> It's no longer a question of whether we're going to lose the war, but when! In Italy we have no defences; I repeat no defences [...] if the English go on bombing our cities, the populace will say: 'We've had enough of this: let's put an end to the war.' [...] I don't know whether we've got more than thirty merchantmen left. We're done for! I repeat, we are done for![58]

184 *Winning and losing the war*

As demonstrated in Chapter Five, the impact of Allied bombing on undermining Italian civilian morale was critical. This was complimented by the tactical effectiveness of the Allied Air Forces to support military operations in the Mediterranean. Erwin Rommel often described the intensity of 'non-stop' RAF attacks on his units during the latter months of the North African campaign, particularly regarding the September 1942 failure of the German advance at Alam el Halfa. The defeat was blamed on the, 'non-stop and very heavy air attacks by the RAF, whose command of the air had been virtually complete, had pinned my army to the ground.'[59] While Operation Flax – the April 1943 Allied effort to sever the air supply lines to Axis troops in Tunisia – destroyed 432 German and Italian planes, 35 Allied planes were lost.[60]

In September 1942 Petty Officers Villosio (I/N 188) and Losi (I/N 239) did not doubt that Italy would lose the war. Nonetheless, they were determined that the *Patria* should go down fighting,

I/N 188: Mark my words, the shock units will bring off another coup or two. But next time it won't be down there at Malta, it will be up here (in England). We're not going to lose the war without showing what we can do first.
I/N 239: So that we can at least say that we lost it, but we lost it –
I/N 188: Fighting. Like the Greeks.[61]

Petty Officer De Pasquale (I/N 212) lacked the desire to see Italy fighting to the last, but also felt totally disillusioned with the progress of the war. When asked in October 1942, 'who's going to win,' he responded: 'I don't care a damn. It's enough for me if the war ends and we go home. […] [The war has] been going badly for us ever since it started.'[62] In September 1942 De Pasquale stated, 'the fact remains that among our lot [presumably meaning submarine crews] there's no enthusiasm for the war.'[63] Speaking in January 1943, Lieutenant Badezzi (I/N 321) said, 'what a lot of men have got to lose their lives in this cursed war. Let's hope that this is the last war Christmas.'[64]

Not all the POWs who predicted Italy's defeat were so pessimistic. In July 1942 Reconnaissance Pilot I/A 19 believed: 'our only hope is, the officer will come in one morning and say: "I've got good news for you. Italy has asked for an armistice and wants friendship with England." That's our last hope!' To which his cellmate, Pilot I/A 20, replied: 'yes, and we'll go to London and have a proper night out.'[65] On the eve of the invasion of Sicily in July 1943 Artillery Lieutenant Vertua (I/M 20) said: 'it will be lucky for us if we manage to lose the war, because if we win it we shall be under the Germans and therefore in a wretched position.'[66] Midshipman Gridelli (I/N 378) felt in April 1943 that: 'all the same, it would really be better if we lost the war, if you think of all the advantages it would bring to us […] The important thing is to lose it quickly.'[67] Whether pessimists or optimists, many CSDIC (UK) POWs shared a belief that Italy would be defeated by 1943.

The totality of the collapse in Axis resistance in North Africa in May 1943 was described by Artillery Lieutenant Vertua (I/M 20),

> There were some regiments which surrendered en bloc without firing a shot. [...] It was a madhouse. [...] It was a complete collapse. Everybody surrendered. They resisted just a little bit at Cape Bon, because they were cut off, you know, nobody knew what they should do. [...] There were units which abandoned their batteries and assembled in civilian houses, where they just waited for the English to arrive. [...] To give you an idea of what the collapse was like, they captured everybody including Messe, not a soul succeeded in escaping. Not a boat, not even a pin could get through. They captured everything.[68]

Allied units became victims of their own success in Tunisia in May 1943 when they found 'enemy troops surrendering in such large numbers that they clogged the roads, impeding further advance.'[69] The Australian war correspondent and iconic chronicler of the North African war Alan Moorehead painted a similar picture to that of Lieutenant Vertua,

> Weeks were going to elapse before a final count revealed the total at over a quarter of a million prisoners, the biggest single haul made by the Allies since the war had begun. In all, the Axis had lost close on a million men in Africa. Now they had nothing, absolutely nothing to show for it. [...] No Axis aircraft has been able to take off into a sky filled with British and American aircraft, no Axis ship of any size had been able to put to sea. All the Axis generals, with only one notable exception, had now been taken. [...] All Africa was ours.[70]

It was a tremendous achievement for the Western Allies, one of the great victories of the Second World War. It is evident that each Centre prisoner of war rationalized defeat – and victory – in their own way but, a great many CSDIC (UK) POWs had been mentally preparing for defeat well before 1943. By the autumn of 1942, optimism had given way to desperation and despondency for many of the Italian cohort. Italy's war was far from over in May 1943, but faith in an Italian victory had almost completely evaporated. Defeatism had developed its own self-sustaining momentum.

Sicily – The nail in the coffin

If faith in victory had been seriously undermined by May 1943, Allied successes in the Sicilian campaign finally eviscerated the hopes of the few who still retained some faith in Italy's ability to hold out. According to some transcripts, there was degree of confidence in the fighting quality of the Italian forces on the island before the invasion began. On 10 July 1943 – the first day of the invasion – Midshipman Gridelli (I/N 378) was taken aback by the news now reaching him: 'My word, I never thought they'd land in Sicily, because it's one of the strongest points of our coastline.'[71] In April, Torpedo Rating Colombo (I/N 358) and Petty Officer Schiselli (I/N 389) had discussed Sicily's formidable defences; from the gun batteries ringing Messina to the sheer number of men stationed there. Schiselli concluded: 'I wonder how many millions (Sic.) of men we've got there. And the way it's fortified! The airfields, my word!'[72] In the same month, Chief Boatswain Pontone (I/N 254) and Chief Petty Officer Boatswain Stefanelli (I/N 387) were skeptical of supposed British expectations that they could 'occupy the whole of Sicily in two days.' Stefanelli was resolute: 'Never. There are more troops there than they even dream of.'[73]

General Berardi (I/M 4) believed that those defending the Sicilian coast to be 'stout fellows,'[74] while Field Marshal Messe (I/M 2) considered Italian forces to be in a good position on the island. This time it was the Allies fighting with their backs to the sea. The Italians would supposedly also be inspired because they were 'defending the soil of the fatherland,' Messe concluded that 'there is no doubt that all the requisites (for putting up a good defence) are there.'[75] One statement from Brigadier Mancinelli (I/M 9) on 19 July 1943 makes it clear that at least one senior CSDIC (UK) POW doubted the ability of Italian commanders on Sicily: 'Our Generals in Sicily have no idea of modern warfare. Guzzoni has been in Albania, but fighting the Albanians is a very different matter. […] these are bad hours, bad days.'[76] As Lieutenant-Colonel Donato (I/M 26) said, whatever the state of Italian defences on Sicily the stakes were very high as the campaign began: 'If our people put up a good show, it means there must still be some spirit left in them! If, on the other hand, the English should occupy Sicily, that will be the end of us. It will mean the end of Italy.'[77] However, even optimists like Messe and Berardi stopped short of predicting a complete military redemption for Italy in Sicily. Making a decent stand and totally reversing the growing impetus of an Allied victory were not synonymous.

Allied planners for the invasion – Operation Husky – were themselves apprehensive, and very aware that Sicily could present a serious challenge. In a letter to the Chief of the Imperial General Staff, General Brooke on 5 April 1943, the commander of 18th Army Group, General Sir Harold Alexander, considered that although, 'I think we are on a good wicket […] the margin between success and failure is small.' On the eve of the invasion Alex's boss, General Eisenhower, felt like his stomach was 'a clenched fist.' Ike's naval aide Harry Butcher considered, 'it is no small event to be sending 150,000 men on a highly dangerous landing on an enemy coast highly fortified with mines in the water and on land, shore batteries, U-Boats and worst of all, close air bases for havoc-wreaking fighter bombers.' Dogged Italian resistance in the closing stages of the Tunisian campaign did not help settle nerves. In April, 8th Army commander General Montgomery wrote to Alex, 'planning so far has been based on the assumption that the opposition will be slight and that Sicily will be captured relatively easily. Never was there a greater error. The Germans and also the Italians are fighting desperately now in Tunisia and will do so in Sicily.'[78]

Axis forces on Sicily were sizeable. The commander of the Italian 6th Army, General Alfredo Guzzoni, could call on 200000 Italian and 62000 German personnel. He was also supported by 434 German and 145 Italian aircraft on the island itself.[79] But in reality, Guzzoni's force was weak. His Italian units were demoralized, poorly equipped, badly trained and inexperienced. The Aosta, Assietta and Napoli divisions, as well as the coastal defence units, had never been in combat. There were also major deficiencies in heavy weapons and transport, crucial for counter-attacking Allied beachheads.[80] The German divisions were in a better shape, but not without problems. Whilst the Herman Göring Panzer division lacked infantry support, over half of the German contingent in Sicily were *Luftwaffe* groundsmen, not trained Army personnel. Even the beaches themselves lacked mines and obstacles. One Intelligence Officer of the British 51st Highland Division found more female bathers than anti-landing obstacles on aerial reconnaissance photos of his assault beaches.[81] One Italian engineer officer tasked with preparing defences around Gela resorted to constructing 'fake' bunkers out of cardboard given the chronic shortages of cement, and in order to fool the Allies into thinking Italian positions were more formidable than they were.[82]

The heightened expectations of the Italian defence made the successful Allied invasion even more shocking. Chief Boatswain Pontone (I/N 254) and another unidentified prisoner of war were appalled,

> I/N 254: Heavy fighting! What the hell, heavy fighting! What the devil are they doing? How many men have they landed? About a thousand men?
> ?: What a defeat for Italy, damn it! I didn't think that Sicily – it was all right as long as it was Tunisia, but I never thought they'd succeed in landing! But seeing that they have landed, I think, that the war will soon be over. I think that a revolution will break out at once in Italy[83]

The spectre of defeat on the shores of the *Patria* was understandably a pivotal moment. It was one defeat too many, and one whose impact could not be assuaged by distance from the homeland.

Flying Officer Alvisi (I/A 35) had been captured on Sicily on 19 July 1943. He drew a direct link between the collapse of Axis forces on the island and a total loss of faith in the continuation of the war when he spoke with Infantry Captain Pesce (I/M 44) and Paratrooper Second Lieutenant Rizzo (I/M 45),

> I/M 44: But with what we had at our disposal we might at least have shown ourselves to be men of honour.
> [...]

I/A 35: Defeat will be a bad thing for Italy. I am convinced of that.
I/M 44: I never thought it possible [...] because we imagined, after all, that we should at least defend our own territory [...]
[...]
I/A 35: This morning I was saying that I still had a faint hope, that I still had faith in something, but now –
I/M 45: I have lost faith.[84]

The cost of the defeat in Sicily was far higher than the thousands of Italians killed, wounded and taken prisoner.[85] As D'Este makes clear, the defeat in Sicily 'led directly to the fall of Mussolini and the dissolution of Fascism in Italy.'[86] Amongst the prisoners it was the moment where the final flickers of hope of avoiding defeat where snuffed out.

Conclusion

The invasion of Sicily in 1943 was the last chapter in a debate amongst the CSDIC (UK) about victory and defeat that had been ongoing since Italy's formal entry into the Second World War. In 1940 it seemed impossible that the Axis could lose. By the summer of 1943, the strategic balance had reversed, and Italy faced its greatest military and political disaster since unification. The momentum that the Allies had generated in the Mediterranean since the previous summer had become unstoppable. Confronted by massive Allied forces, it was impossible to end the war on Italy's terms. Throughout their discussions about the progress of the war, it is curious how the cohort struggled to shift ideas about Italian military inferiority. Even in the heady days of 1940, 'victory' was framed around the achievements of the Germans. It is also curious how many of the prisoners also wove into these discussions the context of previous conflicts and the fully global scope of the Second World War. In doing so they demonstrated an outlook that went far beyond the traditional Italian spheres of interest in the Mediterranean and Africa.

Notes

1 I/SRN 916 – 18 January 1943, WO 208/4191, TNA.
2 For more on the debates amongst the British War Cabinet in May 1940, see: John Lukacs, *Five Days in London, May 1940* (New Haven: Yale University Press, 2001), and Martin Gilbert, *Churchill: A Life* (London: Pimlico, 2000), 645–678.
3 X/SRX 1 – 29 November 1940, WO 208/4194, TNA.
4 I/SRX 4 – 28 November 1940, WO 208/4193, TNA.
5 I/SRN 1 – 30 October 1940, WO 208/4189, TNA.
6 I/SRN 40 – 29 December 1940, WO 208/4189, TNA.
7 I/SRN 37 – 26 December 1940, WO 208/4189, TNA.
8 I/SRN 35 – 27 December 1940, WO 208/4189, TNA.
9 I/SRN 35 – 27 December 1940, WO 208/4189, TNA.

Winning and losing the war   189

10 Rodogno writes of the inferiority complex, or *Minderwertigkeitsgefühl*, of Italians during the 'parallel war' they fought alongside that of the Germans in the occupied territories. Rodogno, *Empire*, 37.
11 Patriarca, *Vices*, 108–132. For German attitudes towards Italians, see: Neitzel and Welzer, *Soldaten*, 236, 242, 252, 266–268.
12 For more on the East African campaign, see: Stewart, *First Victory*.
13 I/SRN 48 – 6 January 1941, WO 208/4189, TNA.
14 I/SRN 52 – 9 January 1941, WO 208/4189, TNA.
15 I/SRX 18 – 14 August 1941, WO 208/4193, TNA.
16 I/SRN 441 – 14 August 1942, WO 208/4190, TNA.
17 I/SRN 411 – 10 August 1942, WO 208/4190, TNA.
18 Bungay, *Alamein*, 115–116.
19 I/SRN 1135 – 9 April 1943, WO 208/4192, TNA.
20 I/SRN 1067 – 3 March 1943, WO 208/4191, TNA.
21 In the Caporetto offensive (Twelfth Battle of Isonzo) the Italian Army lost an estimated 670000 soldiers killed, wounded, taken prisoner, deserted and 'missing.' In comparison during the Second World War the Italians lost 89000 men in Russia, 19000 men at El Alamein and 200000 in Tunisia. See: Mario Morselli, *Caporetto 1917: Victory or Defeat?* (London: Routledge, 2007), p. 130; and Macdonald and Cimprić, *Caporetto*, 172.
22 Thompson says that 'the Battle of Vittorio Veneto meant something to Italians that cannot be found in a summary of operations. It brought the balm of victory and the promise of peace.' From 30 October to 2 November, the British 48th Division on the Piave alone took more than 20000 Austro-Hungarian prisoners while only suffering 145 casualties. See: Thompson, *The White War*, 356–351, 364.
23 I/SRN 47 – 3 January 1941, WO 208/4189, TNA.
24 Walker, *Iron Hulls*, 193, 199.
25 I/SRM 40 – 30 June 1943, WO 208/4188, TNA.
26 I/SRM 29 – 20 June 1943, WO 208/4188, TNA.
27 Adam Tooze, *The Wages of Destruction: The Making and Breaking of the Nazi Economy* (London: Penguin, 2007), 611–618 and Ian Kershaw, *The End: Germany, 1944–45* (London: Penguin, 2011), 15, 20.
28 Charles Forbes, 'The Attack on St. Nazaire, 1942', *Supplement to the London Gazette*, 2 October 1947, 4633–4640.
29 John Hughes-Hallett, 'The Dieppe Raid', *Supplement to the London Gazette*, 14 August 1947, 3823–3828.
30 Charles Stacey, *The Official History of the Canadian Army in the Second World War, Volume I: Six Years of War: The Army in Canada, Britain and the Pacific* (Ottawa: DND, 1955), 387.
31 Charles Anderson, 'Algeria – French Morocco: 8 November 1942 – 11 November 1942', *The US Army Campaigns of World War II* (Washington: USACMH, 1993), 27.
32 Anderson, 'Algeria – French Morocco', 27.
33 George Howe, *North West Africa: Seizing the Initiative in the West* (Washington: USACMH, 1993), 21.
34 Fincardi, 'Anglo-American Air Attacks', in Baldoli et al, *Bombing, States and Peoples*, 244.
35 Winston Churchill, *The Second World War, Volume IV: The Hinge of Fate* (London: Penguin, 2005), 541.
36 I/SRN 1164 – 21 April 1943, WO 208/4192, TNA.
37 William Schofield and P.J. Carisella, *Frogmen: First Battles* (Wellesley: Branden, 2014), 166–170. The Algiers raid is also discussed at length in several CSDIC (UK) protocols: I/SRN 813 – 8 January 1943, WO 208/4191, TNA; I/SRN 822 – 8 January 1943, WO 208/4191, TNA; I/SRN 827 – 4 January 1943, WO 208/4191, TNA; I/SRN 831 – 8 January 1943, WO 208/4191, TNA; I/SRN 835 – 5 January 1943, WO 208/

190 *Winning and losing the war*

    4191, TNA; I/SRN 864 – 6 January 1943, WO 208/4191, TNA; I/SRN 880 – 7 January 1943, WO 208/4191, TNA; I/SRN 899 – 12 January 1943, WO 208/4191, TNA; I/SRN 901 – 12 January 1943, WO 208/4191, TNA; I/SRN 944 – 1 February 1943, WO 208/4191, TNA.
38. Walker, *Iron Hulls*, 184–188.
39. Brackets are as they appear in the protocol. See: I/SRN 686 – 28 November 1942, WO 208/4190, TNA.
40. I/SRN 518 – 1 September 1942, WO 208/4190, TNA.
41. I/SRN 714 – 17 December 1942, WO 208/4190, TNA.
42. I/SRN 885 – 24 January 1943, WO 208/4191, TNA.
43. I/SRN 669 – 9 November 1942, WO 208/4190, TNA.
44. Eighth Army Personal Message from the Army Commander (General B.L. Montgomery), 12 January 1943, THF/C/5/1/3/9, KMMSC.
45. The *Tripoli Times* took over the offices of the *Corriere di Tripoli* following the British occupation of the city on 23 January 1943. Staffed by military journalists from the *Crusader* and *Eighth Army News*, it was 'the first newspaper to appear after the British occupation'. *Tripoli Times*, Vol. 1 – No. 1, 25 January 1943, THF/C/5/4/7, KMMSC.
46. I/SRN 775 – 19 December 1942, WO 208/4191, TNA.
47. I/SRN 397 – 8 August 1942, WO 208/4189, TNA.
48. I/SRN 332 – 27 July 1942, WO 208/4189, TNA.
49. I/SRN 562 – 1 September 1942, WO 208/4190, TNA.
50. SRIG 196 – 3 August 1943, WO 208/4186, TNA.
51. I/SRM 3 – 15 June 1943, WO 208/4188, TNA.
52. I/SRM 4 – 15 June 1943, WO 208/4188, TNA.
53. There were also 124251 in American-run camps and 37500 in French hands. See: Moore, 'Enforced Diaspora', 182.
54. I/SRN 464 B – 18 August 1942, WO 208/4190, TNA.
55. I/SRN 917 – 22 January 1943, WO 208/4191, TNA.
56. I/SRN 917 – 22 January 1943, WO 208/4191, TNA.
57. SRIG 83 – 11 June 1943, WO 208/4185, TNA.
58. I/SRN 771 – 22 December 1942, WO 208/4190, TNA.
59. Erwin Rommel in Basil Liddell Hart, ed., *The Rommel Papers* (New York: Harcourt, Brace & Company, 1953), 283, 306, 307.
60. Alan Levine, *The War Against Rommel's Supply Lines, 1942–1943* (Westport: Praegar, 1999), 166; Bungay, *Alamein*, 197–198.
61. I/SRN 627 – 29 September 1942, WO 208/4190, TNA.
62. I/SRN 649 – 12 October 1942, WO 208/4190, TNA.
63. I/SRN 572 – 11 September 1942, WO 208/4190, TNA.
64. I/SRN 832 – 6 January 1943, WO 208/4191, TNA.
65. I/SRA 30 – 3 July 1942, WO 208/4184, TNA.
66. I/SRM 40 – 6 July 1943, WO 208/4188, TNA.
67. I/SRN 1147 – 11 April 1943, WO 208/4192, TNA.
68. I/SRX 86 – 23 June 1943, WO 208/4193, TNA; I/SRX 87 – 23 June 1943, WO 208/4193, TNA.
69. Charles Anderson, 'Tunisia: 17 November 1942 – 13 May 1943', *The US Army Campaigns of World War II* (Washington: USACMH, 1993), 26.
70. Alan Moorehead, *African Trilogy* (London: Landsborough, 1944), 579–580.
71. I/SRX 99 – 10 July 1943, WO 208/4193, TNA.
72. I/SRN 1116 – 7 April 1943, WO 208/4191, TNA.
73. I/SRN 1171 – 13 April 1943, WO 208/4192, TNA.
74. SRIG 116 – 11 July 1943, WO 208/4185, TNA.
75. Brackets are as they appear in the original protocol. SRIG 116 – 11 July 1943, WO 208/4185, TNA.

76 SRIG 117 – 13 July 1943, WO 208/4185, TNA.
77 I/SRM 39 – 10 July 1943, WO 208/4188, TNA.
78 All quoted in Holland, *Sicily*, 47, 50–51, 158.
79 This was divided between General Mario Arisio's 12th Corps (Aosta Division; Assietta Division; 202nd, 207th 208th Coastal Divisions; Three 'Mobile Groups'; Four 'Tactical Groups; two-thirds of the 15th Panzer Grenadier Division) and General Carlo Rossi's 16th Corps (Napoli Division; Livorno Division; 206th, 213th Coastal Divisions; 18th and 19th Coastal Brigades; Five 'Mobile Groups'; Four 'Tactical Groups'; the Herman Göring Panzer Division; one-third 15th Panzer Grenadier Division). C.J.C. Molony, *The Mediterranean and Middle East: Volume V: The Campaign in Sicily 1943 and the Campaign in Italy 3rd September 1943 to 31st March 1944* (London: HMSO, 1973), 40–48. See also: Johannes Steinhoff, *The Straits of Messina* (London: Deutsch, 1971).
80 Molony, *Volume V*, 40–48.
81 Molony, *Volume V*, 40–48.
82 Holland, *Sicily*, 105–106.
83 I/SRN 1302 – 11 July 1943, WO 208/4192, TNA.
84 I/SRX 123 – 4 August 1943, WO 208/4193, TNA.
85 D'Este estimates Italian losses of approximately 2000 killed, 5000 wounded and 137000 taken prisoner. Holland has calculated the Sicilian Campaign cost 4678 German lives and 4325 Italian. A remarkably similar figure. See: Carlo D'Este, *Bitter Victory: the Battle for Sicily, 1943* (London: HarperCollins, 2008), 609; Holland, *Sicily*, 493.
86 D'Este, *Bitter*, 554.

Conclusion: A hopeful future?

By 1943, Italy's future was deeply uncertain. On 10 July Allied troops invaded Sicily, taking the island by mid-August, despite the escape of many Axis troops to continental Italy. On 19 July, hundreds of Allied planes bombed Rome: 1168 tonnes of explosives were dropped on the Eternal City inflicting thousands of civilian casualties. By 25 July, the Grand Council of Fascism had stripped Mussolini of his powers and the next day a new government led by the King and General Badoglio had taken control. Secret negotiations with the Allies led to the signing of an armistice on 3 September, as the Allies landed on mainland Italy which became public on the eighth.[1] What immediately followed was a period of confused fighting as German units rushed to take over critical defensive positions and Italian commanders struggled to keep control of events. Only in Sardinia, Corsica, Apulia and Calabria did Italian forces hold out long enough to be relieved by the Allies; the remainder were overwhelmed by German forces and as in the case of the *Acqui* Division in Cephalonia, ruthlessly liquidated.[2]

Confusion was rife, for instance when German guided bombs sunk the Italian battleship *Roma* off the coast of Sardinia on 9 September, the Italian Naval Command publicly blamed the British.[3] Matters were further complicated when German paratroopers dramatically freed Mussolini on 12 September 1943. Having released him from his imprisonment at Campo Imperatore the German occupiers installed him at the head of the puppet Italian Social Republic (RSI).[4] The Italian Campaign that followed continued until 2 May 1945 with the unconditional surrender of the *Wehrmacht's* Army Group C. It was a campaign of bitter infantry fighting as the combined forces of the Western Allies advanced North.[5] Partisan activity and the splitting of the Italian military between those loyal to the RSI and those who joined the Allied Co-Belligerent Army created deep fissures within the nation. Some of the divides were ideological, some opportunist and some simply the consequence of chance and geography – reflecting where an individual happened to be within the peninsular at a particular moment. The legacy of historians such as Pavone and the debates he triggered about a civil war in Italy have highlighted the incredibly complex position in which Italians found themselves in between 1943 and 1945.[6]

Conclusion: A hopeful future? 193

The defeat, marginalization and occupation of Italy forced Italian prisoners of war to reflect on their position more radically. As war came to their homeland several CSDIC (UK) POWs looked to the future and the possibility of revolution in Italy.[7] Such sentiments were easy to detect even before Operation Husky was launched. Lieutenant Paulo Monechi (I/M 337) was clearly concerned: 'we've got to be on our guard against an internal revolution.'[8] In March 1943, Petty Officer Pacelli (I/N 367) and Petty Officer I/N 366 predicted that Italy in the 1940s would face a situation akin to Spain in the 1930s,

I/N 366:   In Italy whether we win or lose –
I/N 367:   There's bound to be a revolution.
I/N 366:   Then things will go as they did in Spain.[9]

Bloodshed and violence were forecast by Petty Officer De Guigan (I/N 342) who would look after himself by any means necessary: 'There'll be a revolution in Italy. Once the war is over, I shall grab hold of the first machine-gun and defend myself.'[10] There were those who saw revolution as an opportunity to start again. Artillery Lieutenant Vertua (I/M 20) believed: 'Italy has become a cesspool, in fact we need a revolution.'[11] The April 1943 conversation between Midshipman Rosali (I/N 340) and Midshipman Gridelli (I/N 378) articulated their desire to participate in revolutionary violence,

I/N 340:   If they land in Sicily revolution will break out at once. I shall try and get myself sent to Italy immediately. There would at least be the moral satisfaction of causing a schomozzle in Italy.
I/N 378:   Rifles and tommy-guns, by jingo, tat-tat-tat! Hell, how …… I'd like to do it, hand-grenades, armed to the teeth.[12]

These fears were not unfounded and the years 1943–1945 would, indeed, see the Italian peninsula consumed by occupation, invasion and civil war.[13]

Yet there were some voices in the CSDIC (UK) cohort who viewed the future with hope, looking to make a 'new Italy.' In March 1943 Lieutenant-Colonel Ravazzoni (I/A 32) spoke to Sub-Lieutenant Budini (I/N 373) of the future,

I/A 32:   At the end of the war we shall have a lot to say and certain things which we shall insist on. We've done our duty to the full, and we have a right to build a new Italy.
I/N 373:   There's certainly a lot that needs doing.[14]

Budini envisioned a new Italy that was independent, progressive and democratic,

> When the war is over we must chase out everybody, and above all the Germans. We'll put up a good Government, but not a Nationalist one, for goodness sake. One something like the English one. I rather like a

194 Conclusion: A hopeful future?

Republic, in which everybody can say what he thinks. [...] and let's do away with the Vatican, away with it![15]

A sustainable peace was also a priority for this optimistic Naval Officer who said: 'The very thing we've got to try and get rid of after the war is the hatred generated by war. We've got to co-operate. If we can't do that, we shall go on having wars all the time.'[16] It is striking how, despite over 20 years of Fascist propaganda, Italians were thinking and arguing freely.

Amongst many predictions to be found within the Italian transcripts Budini's are amongst the more accurate. In the post-war world a 'new Italy' did emerge, even if Italian politics remained periodically chaotic and violent. From the late 1940s into the 1950s, there were fears of a continuation of the civil war, an upsurge in *Mafiosi* activity in Sicily, a campaign of vigilante justice against former Fascists, Communist militancy across rural and urban areas and even acts of terrorism by neo-Fascist groups.[17] However, the state-sanctioned repression and terror of the Fascist era had gone. Italy became a Republic on 2 June 1946 as the result of a referendum, a revolution fought at the ballot box. Its colonial possessions were lost forever, but Italy carved out a more co-operative role in global politics by joining NATO in 1949 and becoming a founding member of the European Economic Community (EEC) in 1957. Although, the post-war dominance of the Christian Democrats in the Italian Government may have frustrated Budini's desire to reduce the power of the Catholic Church in Italian society.[18]

For CSDIC (UK), the autumn and winter of 1943 marked the end of their Italian operations. As Table III and V demonstrate there is an abrupt cut-off after 1943 whereby no more Italian prisoners were handled. Even after September 1943 there is a tapering off the number of protocols made. We are left with just a small number from October, November and December and a mere handful from January and February 1944.[19] No explanation is given for this in the official histories of MI19 and the Centre. Presumably, this was a decision made because Italian forces no longer posed a strategic threat to the Allies and, therefore, did not fulfil CSDIC (UK)'s professed aim to provide 'long-term strategic and technical examination of selected Ps/W.'[20] Any captured personnel of the RSI would then have been better served by the theatre-level CSDICs.

CSDIC (UK)'s records tell us nothing of the individual fates of the Italian prisoners. However, some details of the post-war careers of the Senior Italian officers held at Wilton Park's 'White House' are known. Giovanni Messe, returning to Italy soon after the armistice, was made Chief of the General Staff of the Italian 'Co-Belligerent' Army. He retired from the military in 1947 and found success in politics, being elected to the Italian Senate in 1953. He died in Rome in 1968. Taddeo Orlando and Paolo Berardi returned to Allied-controlled Italy with Messe and served the Badoglio government. Orlando was appointed Minister of War on 11 February 1944 and later commanded the *Carabinieri* Corps. Berardi served as Army Chief of Staff between 18 November 1943 and 10 February 1945, after which he led the *Comando Militare della Sicilia* (Palermo) until 1946. Giuseppe Mancinelli served as Chief of the Italian Defence Staff (1954–1959) and was Chairman of the NATO Military Committee (1956–1957). Messe's former ADC, Paolo Colacicchi, became a post-war journalist, writer and translator, living in London for many years until his death in 1975.[21] From these prominent positions and in their popular post-war writing, Messe, Orlando, Berardi and Mancinelli in particular, would become influential architects of the *brava gente* myth and shirking any personal responsibility for Italy's crimes and the violence that had been unleashed on their homeland.[22]

Wilton Park itself, the CSDIC (UK) facility most focused on Italian matters, would be repurposed at the end of the war as a re-education centre for German POWs, becoming a model for political re-education camps that would be used by the British in Greece and Malaya.[23] It also served as the headquarters of Eastern Command 1954-1972 and was the location of the Defence School of Languages for many years, although the 'White House' was demolished in 1968. Latimer House became the home of the National Defence College in 1953 and is now run as a luxury hotel, branded as 'De Vere Latimer Estate.'[24] After the war, Trent Park was used as a college of education by the Ministry of Education, the University of London, and Middlesex University. Though purchased by building firm Berkeley Homes in 2015, there has been a successful – and ongoing – campaign to establish a museum at the site commemorating the work of 'the secret listeners.' Though yet to open, it will be a long-overdue tribute to this often overlooked but significant intelligence programme.[25]

For all their occasional messiness, the protocols remain a fascinating resource offering a unique insight into the experiences and thoughts of hundreds of Italian service personnel during the most catastrophic conflict in world history. The individual conversations may offer just a snapshot of the experiences of these men, but they are nonetheless snapshots rich in colour and detail. No other sources bring us as close to the actual conversations of Italian servicemen during the war. These protocols are devoid of the distortions of post-war memory found in oral histories and memoirs, and the performative languages of letters. In the same set of sources, the perspectives of influential commanders are found alongside those of humbler rank, on a range of topics of enduring historical importance.

While there has been some historiographical attention on the German protocols and those from senior Italian officers in the works of Osti Guerrazzi, Neitzel and Welzer,[26] this study is the first to examine the Italian sources in much broader terms, so that the views of lower ranking soldiers, as well as naval and air force personnel, are also included. This project fills a gap in the historiography for a wider exploration of the Italian transcripts that provides their all-important context, as well as providing a rare opportunity for Anglophone audiences to hear authentic voices of the Italian experience of the Second World War. This is of particular significance in a national context where this conflict is still culturally, politically and socially very important and yet wider understanding of the 'Italian war' remains limited.

The transcripts allow a significant reshaping of numerous debates about the Italian experience of the Second World War. They reject many stereotypes of the Italians at war and the 'Italian War.' The CSDIC (UK) cohort are not the *brava gente* of post-war myth, nor are they *furbi* uncompromisingly adhering to the art of *arrangiarsi*. The Italian cohort may have lacked the genocidal racial hatred generally associated with the Nazi state, but they were capable of intense antisemitism and racism. Confirming the arguments of researchers like Rodogno and Schlemmer,[27] the protocols show how the Italians had few qualms about subjecting the occupied peoples of the Balkans and France to economic corruption, casual violence, sexual exploitation and administrative incompetence. If a community in the occupied zones dared oppose its Italian occupiers, it would suffer from policies of reprisal little different from those used by the German military machine. Within the Centre transcripts, discussions of the future were as varied and complicated as those regarding the experience of fighting, other nationalities, war crimes, Italy's political leadership, victory and defeat.

The Italian POWs may have been largely – and perhaps surprisingly – positive in their judgement of the Soviets and sympathetic towards the Poles, but they were deeply critical of most of the other wartime powers. Criticism was most intense in relation to the violent and uncooperative French and the arrogant and hypocritical British, but they also saw the Americans as decadent and foolish and their German allies as brutish and untrustworthy. Above all, from this bottom-up view of Fascist foreign policy it is clear that most Italian servicemen saw their principal enemy as the old elites of the plutocratic, imperial democracies. As a group, the Italian POWs whose conversations were recorded by CSDIC (UK) had little compunction about waging war and destroying their enemies. Indeed, many of their complaints about the Italian military system focused on how shortages of equipment and poor leadership had hindered the unleashing of destruction.

As the protocols have repeatedly shown, the 'Italian War' was similarly brutal and tough. The fighting faced by the POWS of the CSDIC (UK) was hard, forcing them to exist under immense physical and psychological pressures. Whether fighting against the British and American armies on Sicily, against determined partisans in the Balkans, against Allied shipping in the Atlantic, or combatting the RAF aircraft in the skies above Malta, or sheltering Italy's industrial cities from heavy bombers, the Italian experience of the conflict from 1940 to 1943 was traumatic and unromantic. The POWs spent so much time discussing these experiences because these brushes with death had had a huge impact on them psychologically and emotionally, but also in terms of their wider political and moral world view.

The experience of war hardened these men's beliefs, and, while they took different lessons from their experiences, they left them cynical and highly critical of Italy's political leadership: the POWs felt it was legitimate to attack those in authority and to criticise everyone from the King downwards.

However, it was the *Duce* and the Fascists who became particular objects of hatred. Even allowing for a tendency to privilege the transcription of conversations that showed a distaste for Italy's political status quo, it is striking how so many POWs expressed such fierce anger and contempt for Fascist Italy's ruling élites on account of their privilege, ineptitude and cowardice, especially when the cohort internalized other aspects of the Fascist message, such as hatred of the British and French 'pluto-democracies.' Yet, despite being prisoners and despite the disapproval and resentment they manifest for the *Duce* and his party, many Italian servicemen did believe in an Axis victory through 1940, 1941 and early 1942. Only in the summer and autumn of 1942 did Allied victories on all fronts fatally undermine these hopes. By 1943, with the start of Allied amphibious operations against metropolitan Italy, it was only a tiny minority who held out any hope that Italy could escape defeat. It is these themes, as well as the hostility of the CSDIC (UK) Italian prisoners of war to the British and French, their antisemitism, their poor record as occupiers and the toughness of their combat experiences that are the most striking elements within the protocols.

The words of men like Ordinary Seaman Stefanni (I/N 131), Lieutenant-Colonel Ravazzoni (I/A 32) and Second Lieutenant Rizzi (I/M 14) are preserved as they were spoken between 1940 and 1943. While what they said was, of course, determined by the fact that they were speaking to an audience of their fellow prisoners, these conversations nonetheless avoid the distorting effects of time and hindsight which can so muddy the waters of memory. The conversations preserved as CSDIC transcripts are just a snapshot of the conversations these men had during their war service and captivity. The protocols offer only a glimpse of the attitudes and frames of reference of these service personnel, but it is a very detailed glimpse, vibrant and full of historic interest. These sources offer a perspective on the experience of the Second World War that cannot be found elsewhere. They are especially important in relation to the overlooked and misunderstood Italian experience of the conflict where both Anglophone and Italian historiography has often cast Italian soldiers as cartoonish *brava gente* and the wider 'Italian War' as an inconsequential sideshow. As this study has demonstrated, there is scant support in the transcripts for either of these positions: the Italian War was a brutal war fought in large part by soldiers, airmen and sailors who were themselves quite capable of brutality.

Notes

1. Luisa Quartermaine, *Mussolini's Last Republic: Propaganda and Politics in the Italian Social Republic* (Exeter: Elm Bank, 2000), 9–12.
2. O'Reilly, *Forgotten Battles*, 87–106.
3. Vincent O'Hara and Enrico Cernuschi, *Dark Navy: The Regia Marina and the Armistice of 8 September 1943* (Ann Arbor: Nimble, 2009), 46–47.
4. See: Greg Annussek, *Hitlers Raid to Save Mussolini* (Cambridge: Da Capo, 2005); Óscar López, *Freeing Mussolini: Dismantling the Skorzeny Myth in the Gran Sasso Raid* (Barnsley: Pen & Sword, 2018).

198 *Conclusion: A hopeful future?*

5 See: Brian Holden-Reid, 'The Italian Campaign, 1943–45' in John Gooch, ed., *The Decisive Campaigns of the Second World War* (London: Cass, 1990), 129–161; Peter Caddick-Adams, *Monte Cassino: Ten Armies in Hell* (London: Arrow, 2013).
6 Pavone, *A Civil War*; Philip Cooke, *The Legacy of the Italian Resistance* (New York: Palgrave Macmillan, 2011).
7 Aside from it being bloody and violent, it is not clear precisely what sort of revolution these servicemen were predicting. There were a variety of options. For instance, an overthrow of the Fascist state, a communist seizure of power, a military coup, the dissolution of the monarchy or some of sort revolutionary rising that was Fascist but nevertheless purged the corrupt regime that had been in power since the 1920s.
8 I/SRN 954 – 8 Februay 1943, WO 208/4191, TNA.
9 I/SRN 1082 – 6 March 1943, WO 208/4191, TNA.
10 I/SRN 950 – 8 February 1943, WO 208/4191, TNA.
11 I/SRX 87 – 23 June 1943, WO 208/4193, TNA.
12 I/SRN 1191 – 17 April 1943, WO 208/4192, TNA.
13 Roger Absalom, 'Hiding history: The Allies, the Resistance and the Others in Occupied Italy 1943–1945', *The Historical Journal*, 38/1 (1995), 111–131; Ada Gobetti, *Partisan diary: A Woman's Life in the Italian Resistance* (Oxford: Oxford University Press, 2014); Italo Calvino, *The Path to the Spiders' Nest* (London: Penguin, 2009).
14 I/SRX 68 – 20 March 1943, WO 208/4193, TNA.
15 I/SRN 1217 – 27 April 1943, WO 208/4192, TNA.
16 I/SRX 80 – 22 March 1943, WO 208/4193, TNA.
17 Christopher Duggan, *The Force of Destiny: A History of Italy since 1796* (London: Penguin, 2008), 534, 539, 542–544.
18 See: Paul Ginsborg, *A History of Contemporary Italy: Society and Politics, 1943–1988* (London: Penguin, 1990); Tony Judt, *Postwar: A History of Europe since 1945* (London: Vintage, 2010), 80–81, 217–218, 258–259, 361–362.
19 See: SRIG 322 – 13 October 1943 to SRIG 379 – 3 February 1944 in WO 208/4187, TNA.
20 See: 'The Story of MI19'; 'Enclosure I: The History of CSDIC (UK)'; 'Appendix D' in WO 208/4970, TNA.
21 Osti Guerrazzi, *odiare*, 3–5, 10–16. See: Paolo Colacicchi, *L'ultimo fronte d'Africa. Tunisia: novembre 1942 – Maggio 1943* (Milan: Mursia, 1977).
22 Osti Guerrazzi, *odiare*, 297–304; Giovanni Messe, *La mia armata in Tunisia. Come finì la Guerra in Africa* (Milan: Rizzoli, 1960); Giovanni Messe, *La guerra al fronte russo* (Milan: Mursia, 2005); Taddeo Orlando, *Vittoria di un popolo. Dalle battiglia di Tunisia alla Guerra di liberazione* (Rome: Corso, 1946); Paolo Berardi, *Memorie di un Capo di Stato Maggiore dell'Esercito (1943–1945)* (Bologna: ODCU, 1954); Giuseppe Mancinelli, *Dal fronte dell'Africa Settentrionale (1942–1943)* (Milan: Rizzoli, 1970).
23 Harry Miller, *Menace in Malaya* (London: Harrap, 1954), 181–185; Michael Burleigh, *Small Wars, Faraway Places: The Genesis of the Modern World, 1945–65* (London: Pan, 2013), 182.
24 https://www.devere.co.uk/latimer-estate/, accessed 22 December 2018.
25 www.trentparkmuseum.org.uk, accessed 22 December 2018.
26 Osti Guerrazzi, *odiare*; Neitzel and Welzer, *Soldaten*.
27 Schlemmer, *Invasori*; Rodogno *Empire*.

Bibliography

Archives

The National Archives (TNA).
CAB 65/17: War Cabinet, Conclusions, W.M. (41) 1 – W.M. (41) 21, 2 January 1941–27 February 1941.
CAB 121/236: Joint Intelligence Committee, 5 November 1941.
FO 898/325: Treatment and status of Italian prisoners: Correspondence and reports, 1943–1944.
HO 215/201: Home Office; Internment, General Files; Regulations and Enactments; Prisoner of War Camps in the UK: List of Locations and Copies of Administrative Instructions, 1945.
HS 7/58: J Section history: SOE activity in Italy 1941–45, 1945–1946. HW 14/8: Memo on 'List of Summaries, Reports, etc. Received in Hut 3', 28 November 1940.
HW 57/35: Memo from Director of GC&CS to Washington DC, 31 December 1944.
INF 1/920: Propaganda to Italy, December 1940–August 1941.
PREM 3/363/1: Prime Minister's Office; Operational Correspondence and Papers; POWs; Italian Prisoners, December 1940–May 1941.
PREM 3/363/5; Prime Minister's Office; Operational Correspondence and Papers; POWs; Japanese Prisoners, March–October 1943.
PREM 3/364/6: Prime Minister's Office; Operational Correspondence and Papers; POWs; Italian Prisoners of War in India
PREM 3/49: Prime Minister's Office; Operational Correspondence and Papers; POWs; 'Arandora Star' and Huyton Camp Enquiries, July–December 1940.
WO 166/17838: 'Z' Sec. CSDIC (India), April–June 1945.
WO 204/12386: Allied Forces, Mediterranean Theatre; Military Headquarters Papers; Re-organisation of I/CSDIC, September 1945–January 1946.
WO 208/3451: War Office: Directorate of Military Operations and Intelligence, and Directorate of Military Intelligence; Ministry of Defence, Defence Intelligence Staff: Files; POW Section; Future of CSDIC (UK), 1945.
WO 208/3463: CSDIC India, 1944.
WO 208/4184: CSDIC (UK); Interrogation Reports on Italian prisoners of war, I/SRA 1–53, November 1940–January 1943.
WO 208/4185: CSDIC (UK); Interrogation Reports on Italian prisoners of war, SRIG 1–130, May–July 1943.

Bibliography

WO 208/4186: CSDIC (UK); Interrogation reports on Italian prisoners of war, SRIG 131–260, July–September 1943.

WO 208/4187: CSDIC (UK); Interrogation Reports on Italian prisoners of war, SRIG 261–379, September 1943–February 1944.

WO 208/4188: CSDIC (UK); Interrogation Reports on Italian prisoners of war, I/SRM 1–67, June–August 1943.

WO 208/4189: CSDIC (UK); Interrogation Reports on Italian Prisoners of War; I/SRN 1–400, October 1940–July 1942.

WO 208/4190: CSDIC (UK); Interrogation Reports on Italian prisoners of war, I/SRN 401–769, August–December 1942.

WO 208/4191: CSDIC (UK); Interrogation Reports on Italian prisoners of war, I/SRN 770–1130, December 1942–April 1943.

WO 208/4192: CSDIC (UK); Interrogation Reports on Italian prisoners of war, I/SRN 1131–1313, 1 April–31 October 1943.

WO 208/4193: CSDIC (UK); Interrogation Reports on Italian prisoners of war, I/SRX 1–139, 1 November 1940–31 August 1943.

WO 208/4194: CSDIC (UK); Interrogation Reports on Italian prisoners of war, X/SRX 1–8, November 1940–August 1941.

WO 208/4197: CSDIC (UK); Interrogation reports on German and Italian prisoners of war, SR 1–134, April 1941–June 1944.

WO 208/4198: CSDIC (UK); Special extracts from interrogation reports on German and Italian prisoners of war, January 1941–August 1945.

WO 208/4199: CSDIC (UK); Special extracts from interrogation reports on German and Italian prisoners of war, December 1941–May 1944.

WO 208/4200: CSDIC (UK); Special extracts from interrogation reports on German and Italian prisoners of war, December 1942–March 1945.

WO 208/4205: CSDIC (UK); Special extracts from interrogation reports on German and Italian prisoners of war, February 1943–March 1944.

WO 208/4970: War Office: Directorate of Military Operations and Intelligence, and Directorate of Military Intelligence; Ministry of Defence, Defence Intelligence Staff: Files; The Story of MI19, 1941–1945.

WO 208/5507:CSDIC (Africa); Interrogation reports on German and Italian prisoners of war: Middle East and North Africa; MU/3/1–25, 15 April 1943–21 August 1943.

WO 208/5508: CSDIC (Africa); Interrogation reports on German and Italian prisoners of war: AFHQ 1–107, 30 May 1943–27 May 1944.

WO 208/5509: CSDIC (Africa); Interrogation reports on German and Italian prisoners of war: naval and air personnel; AFHQ/X 105–123.

WO 208/5513: CSDIC (Central Mediterranean Forces); Interrogation reports on German and Italian prisoners of war: CMF/X 1–151, 13 March 1944–9 April 1945.

WO 208/5514: CSDIC (Central Mediterranean Forces); Interrogation reports on German and Italian prisoners of war: CMF/Y 3-6 and 10, 24 July 1944–7 November 1944.

WO 208/5516: CSDIC (Central Mediterranean Forces); Interrogation reports on German and Italian prisoners of war: CMF (MAIN)/X 81–114, 28 October 1944–5 January 1945.

WO 208/5518: CSDIC (Middle East); Interrogation reports on German and Italian prisoners of war: ME 359–599, 3 December 1941–19 October 1942.

WO 208/5519: CSDIC (Middle East); Interrogation reports on German and Italian prisoners of war: ME/X 822–825, 26 October 1944–28 October 1944.

WO 208/5574: CSDIC Middle East; Special Reports on German and Italian prisoners of war: CSDIC Middle East Nos 600–813, 20 October 1942–4 June 1944.

WO 208/5621: MI 19: Intelligence – Enemy Prisoners of War; Interrogation of POWs in World War II: expansion of Combined Services Detailed Interrogation Centre UK; justification for Wilton Park Centre, 1 December 1940–31 January 1941.

WO 94/105: Tower of London, Constable's Office: Records; Prisoners of War and Executions; Documents concerning prisoners of war, 1939–1940.

WO 311/632: CSDIC Reports: Use of as Evidence in Court, November 1945–March 1946.

Imperial War Museum, Document Archives (IWM).

K12/1550: Middle East Forces; General Headquarters; Treatment of Enemy Prisoners of War, 15 December 1941.

K12/225: Middle East Forces; General Headquarters; Administration of Prisoners of War, 1st May 1942.

K12/451: Middle East Forces; General Headquarters; Orders for the Administration and Safeguarding of Prisoners of War Whilst on board ships proceeding from the Middle East, October 1942.

K12/744: *Orkney's Italian Chapel*, Chapel Preservation Committee.

K13/1027: POW Accounting October 1941 [amended to June 1943 and subsequently].

K33264: Fifth Divisional Signals; Treatment of Italian Military Forces: a copy of 5 Div Letter 0993 of 17 September 1943.

K77924: Nomi di Alcuni dei 75000 Prigionieri Catturati in Egitto in Libia.

NA 6230: J. West, 'British Soldiers smile at a Viva il Duce slogan on a wall in Reggio, Italy, September 1943'.

NYF 9892, IWM: 'A Badly Defaced Portrait of Mussolini', US Embassy Second World War Photography Library.

Manuscripts and Special Collections, King's Meadow, University of Nottingham (KMMSC) –
THF/C/5/1: Myles Thoroton Hildyard Collection – Material collected by Myles Hildyard relating to his duties as Intelligence Officer, 1942–1945.

THF/C/5/1/1: Printed Intelligence Summaries and Appendices, 7th and 10th Armoured Divisions, 1942–1943.

THF/C/5/1/2: Printed extracts from War Diary of Notts (Sherwood Rangers) Yeomanry, 1942–143.

THF/C/5/1/3: Bundle of Printed Messages to Troops from Army Commanders, 1942–1944.

THF/C/5/1/4: Bundle of Material taken from German and Italian soldiers; 1943.

THF/C/5/1/5/1: General Map of Palestine Illustrating Old and New Testament History According to Palestine Exploration Survey, Edinburgh Geographical Institute, n.d.

THF/C/5/2, 4: Newspaper cuttings relating to Nottingham during the Second World War, 1939–1945, and Newspapers produced by the 8th Army in the Middle East, 1942–1943.

THF/C/5/3: Newspaper cuttings relating to the actions of the 8th Army in the Middle East, 1942–1943.

Center for the Study of Intelligence, CIA.

H. McGaw Smyth, 'The Ciano Papers: Rose Garden', 13/2 (1969), Studies Archives Indexes.

Archivio dell'Ufficio Storico dello Stato Maggiore dell'Esercito (USSME).

Binder H5 r. 34: Report from Admiral Domenico Cavagnari to the Comando Supremo and Undersecretary of War, 16 June 1943.

Published primary sources

Croce, Bendetto, *Il dissidio spirituale della Germania con l'Europa* (Bari: Laterza, 1944).
Longo, Luigi, *Un popola alla macchia* (Milan: Mondadori, 1947).

Memoirs, diaries and autobiographies

Benuzzi, Felice, *No Picnic on Mount Kenya* (London: Kimber, 1952).
Berardi, Paolo, *Memorie di un Capo di Stato Maggiore dell'Esercito (1943–1945)* (Bologna: ODCU, 1954).
Borghese, Valerio, *Sea Devils: Italian Navy Commandos in World War II* (Annapolis: Naval Institute Press, 2009).
Churchill, Winston, *The Second World War, Volume II: Their Finest Hour* (Boston: Houghton Mifflin, 1949).
Churchill, Winston, *The Second World War, Volume III: The Grand Alliance* (Boston: Houghton Mifflin, 1950).
Churchill, Winston, *The Second World War, Volume IV: The Hinge of Fate* (London: Penguin, 2005).
Ciano, Galeazzo, *The War Diaries of Count Galeazzo Ciano, 1939–43* (London: Fonthill, 2015).
Colacicchi, Paolo, *L'ultimo fronte d'Africa. Tunisia: novembre 1942 – Maggio 1943* (Milan: Mursia, 1977).
Corti, Eugenio, *Few Returned: 28 Days on the Russian Front, Winter 1942–43* (Missouri: University of Missouri Press, 1997).
Dönitz, Karl, *Memoirs: Ten Years and Twenty Days* (Barnsley: Frontline, 2012).
Dunlap, Roy, *Ordnance Went Up Front* (Plantersville: SATPC, 1948).
Gobetti, Ada, *Partisan diary: A Woman's Life in the Italian Resistance* (Oxford: Oxford University Press, 2014).
Goebeler, Hans, *Steel Boat, Iron Hearts: A U-Boat Crewman's Life Aboard U-505* (El Dorado Hills: Savas Beatie, 2013).
Kesselring, Albert, *The Memoirs of Field Marshal Kesselring* (London: The History Press, 2007).
Mancinelli, Giuseppe, *Dal fronte dell'Africa Settentrionale (1942–1943)* (Milan: Rizzoli, 1970).
Messe, Giovanni, *La mia armata in Tunisia. Come finì la Guerra in Africa* (Milan: Rizzoli, 1960).
Messe, Giovanni, *La guerra al fronte russo* (Milan: Mursia, 2005).
Miller, Harry, *Menace in Malaya* (London: Harrap, 1954).
Moorehead, Alan, *African Trilogy* (London: Landsborough, 1944),
Newby, Eric, *Love and War in the Apennines* (London: HarperCollins, 2010).
Origo, Iris, *War in the Val D'Orcia: An Italian War Diary, 1943–1944* (London: J. Cape, 1951).
Orlando, Taddeo, *Vittoria di un popolo. Dalle battiglia di Tunisia alla Guerra di liberazione* (Rome: Corso, 1946).
Roatta, Mario, *Otto milioni di baionette* (Milan: Mondadori, 1946).
Sartre, Jean-Paul, 'Paris Under Occupation', *Sartre Studies International*, 4/2 (1998), 1–15.
Steinhoff, Johannes, *The Straits of Messina* (London: Deutsch, 1971).
Stripp, Alan, *Codebreaker in the Far East* (Oxford: Oxford University Press, 1989).
Tarentino, Grazia, *La festa di Muncalè: Storia minore della gente di Milano che qualcuno vorrebbe mettere nella zona grigia senza averne conosciuta la vera natura* (Genoa: Erga, 2005).

Edited collections and works

Caprioli, Maura, ed., *Radio Londra 1940–1945: inventario delle trasmissioni per l'Italia* (Rome: MBCA, 1976).
Delzell, Charles, ed., *Mediterranean Fascism, 1919-1945* (New York: Walker & Company, 1971).
Liddell Hart, Basil, ed., *The Rommel Papers* (New York: Brace, Harcourt & Company, 1953).
Mascellani, Marco, ed., *Vedetta Atlantica: Storie di vita nella base dei sommergibili Italiani a Bordeaux, nelle pagine della rivista di Betasom* (Sarasota: Bianchi Gianni, 2011).

Novels and works of fiction

Calvino, Italo, *The Path to the Spiders' Nest* (London: Penguin, 2009).
Faletti, Giorgio, *Io uccido* (Milan: Baldini & Castoldi, 2014).
Heller, Joseph, *Catch-22* (London: Vintage, 2004).
Linklater, Eric, *Private Angelo* (London: Jonathan Cape, 1946).
Malaparte, Curzio, *Kaputt* (New York: New York Review of Books, 2007).
Moravia, Alberto, *La Ciociara* (Milan: Tascabili Bompiani, 1957).
Stern, Mario Rigoni, *The Sergeant in the Snow* (Evanston: Northwestern University Press, 1998).

Newspaper and magazine articles

Forbes, Charles, 'The Attack on St. Nazaire, 1942', *Supplement to the London Gazette*, 2 October 1947, 4633–4640.
Hughes-Hallett, John, 'The Dieppe Raid', *Supplement to the London Gazette*, 14 August 1947, 3823–3828.
Sereno, Renzo, 'Italian War Propaganda at Home', *The Public Opinion Quarterly*, 3/3 (1939), 468–472.
Twain, Mark, 'Concerning the Jews', *Harper's Magazine*, September 1899, 527–535.
1940 'Mr Churchill Speaks to the Italian People', *The Times*, 24 December 1940, 4.

Unpublished secondary sources

Baldoli, Claudia, 'Italian Fascism in Britain: The Fasci all'Estero, the Italian Communities, and Fascist Sympathisers during the Grandi Era (1932–1939)', PhD Thesis, LSE (London, 2002).
Moeller, Kevin, 'The Italian Submarine Force in the Battle of the Atlantic: Left in the Dark', Masters Thesis, US Army Command and General Staff College (Fort Leavenworth, 2014).
Gould, David, 'Sport and Fascism: A Beautiful Friendship? – A Study of Relations between the State and Elite Sport in Mussolini's Italy', PhD Thesis, the University of Reading (Reading, 2002).

Published secondary sources

'Crimes of the German Wehrmacht: Dimensions of a War of Annihilation, 1941–1944 – An Outline of the Exhibition', The Hamburg Institute for Social Research (Hamburg, 2004).

Bibliography

Aberbach, David, *The European Jews, Patriotism and the Liberal State, 1789–1939: A Study of Literature and Social Pyschology* (London: Routledge, 2013).

Absalom, Roger, 'Hiding history: The Allies, the Resistance and the Others in Occupied Italy 1943–1945', *The Historical Journal*, 38/1 (1995), 111–131.

Addison, Paul, and Calder, Angus, eds., *Time to Kill: The Soldier's Experience of War in the West, 1939–1945* (London: Pimlico, 1997).

Alexievich, Svetlana, *The Unwomanly Face of War: An Oral History of Women in WWII* (London: Penguin Classics, 2017).

Aldrich, Richard, *Witness to War: Diaries of the Second World War in Europe and the Middle East* (London: Corgi, 2005).

Alford, Kenneth, *Allied Looting in World War II: Thefts of Art, Manuscripts, Stamps and Jewelry in Europe* (Jefferson: McFarland & Co, 2011).

Allport, Alan, *Browned Off and Bloody-Minded: The British Soldier Goes to War, 1939–1945* (New Haven: Yale University Press, 2015).

Anderson, Charles, 'Algeria – French Morocco: 8 November 1942–11 November 1942', *The US Army Campaigns of World War II* (Washington: USACMH, 1993).

Anderson, Charles, 'Tunisia: 17 November 1942–13 May 1943', *The US Army Campaigns of World War II* (Washington: USACMH, 1993).

Andrew, Christopher, *Secret World: A History of Intelligence* (New Haven: Yale University Press, 2018).

Annussek, Greg, *Hitlers Raid to Save Mussolini* (Cambridge: Da Capo, 2005).

Anzoletti, Armando, *Il Comandante Salvatore Todaro* (Rome: Giovanni Volpe, 1970).

Appy, Christopher, *Vietnam: The Definitive Oral History told from all sides* (London: Ebury, 2008).

Bailey, Ronald, *Prisoners of War* (New York: Time-Life, 1981).

Bailey, Roderick, *Target Italy: The Secret War against Mussolini, 1940–1943* (London: Faber & Faber, 2014).

Baker, Catherine, *The Yugoslav Wars of the 1990s* (London: Palgrave, 2015).

Baker, David, 'The Political Economy of Fascism: Myth or Reality, or Myth and Reality?', *New Political Economy*, 11/2 (2006), 227–250.

Baldoli, Claudia, and Knapp, Andrew, *Forgotten Blitzes. France and Italy under allied air attack, 1940–1945* (London: Continuum, 2012).

Baldoli, Claudia, Knapp, Andrew, and Overy, Richard, eds., *Bombing, States and Peoples in Western Europe, 1940–1945* (London: Continuum, 2011).

Banti, Alberto, *L'onore della nazione. Identità sessuale e violenza nel nazionalismo europeo dal XVIII secolo alla grande guerra* (Turin: Einaudi, 2005).

Banti, Alberto, *La nazione del Risorgimento. Parentela, santità ed onore alle origini dell'Italia unita* (Turin: Einaudi, 2000).

Banti, Alberto, *Sublime madre nostra. La nazione italiana dal Risorgimento al fascismo* (Rome, 2011).

Barnett, Corelli, *The Desert Generals* (London: Pheonix, 1983).

Barr, Niall, *Pendulum of War: The Three Battles of El Alamein* (Woodstock: Overlook, 2005).

Batey, Mavis, 'Breaking Italian Naval Enigma', in Ralph Erskine and Michael Smith, eds., *The Bletchley Park Codebreakers* (London: Biteback, 2011), 79–92.

Battiglia, Roberto, *Storia della Resistenza Italiana* (Turin: Einaudi, 1970).

Battini, Michele, *The Missing Italian Nuremberg: Cultural Amnesia and Postwar Politics* (Basingstoke: Palgrave, 2007).

Bauer, Eddy, *The History of World War II* (London: Silverdale, 2000).

Bécamps, Pierre, *Bordeaux sous l'Occupation* (Rennes: Ouest France, 1983).
Beevor, Anthony, *Berlin: The Downfall, 1945* (London: Penguin, 2007).
Bell, Falko, "'One of our Most Valuable Sources of Intelligence': British Intelligence and the Prisoner of War System in 1944', *Intelligence and National Security*, 31/4 (2016), 556–578.
Bellina, Elena, 'Theatre and Gender Performance: WWII Italian POW Camps in East Africa', *PAJ: A Journal of Performance and Art*, 40/3 (2018), 80–91.
Benítez, Juan, 'The Italian War in the Mid-Atlantic: Blockade Runners and Submarines in the Canary Islands (1940–1943)', *The Mariner's Mirror*, 100/2 (2014), 186–197.
Bennett, G. H., 'The 1942 Laconia Order: The Murder of Shipwrecked Survivors and the Allied Pursuit of Justice, 1945–46', *Law, Crime and History*, 1 (2011), 16–34.
Berezin, Mabel, *Making the Fascist Self: The Political Culture of Interwar Italy* (Ithaca: Cornell University Press, 1997).
Bernhard, Patrick, 'Colonial Crossovers: Nazi Germany and its Entanglements with Other Empires', *Journal of Global History*, 12 (2017), 206–227.
Bidwell, Shelford, 'The Gentleman versus the Players', *Journal of the RUSI*, 121 (1976), 82–83.
Bierman, John, and Smith, Colin, *Alamein: War Without Hate* (London: Penguin, 2002).
Bishop, Chris, and Warner, Adam, *German Campaigns of World War II* (London: Grange, 2001).
Böhme, Kurt, *Die deutschen Kriegsgefangenen in französischer Hand* (Bielefeld: E&W Gieseking, 1976).
Bonsaver, Guido, *Censorship and Literature in Fascist Italy* (Toronto: University of Toronto Press, 2007).
Borejsza, Jerzy, 'Greece and the Balkan policy of Fascist Italy, 1936–1940', *Journal of the Hellenic Diaspora*, 13/1–2 (1986), 53–70.
Bosworth, Richard, 'Nations Examining Their Past: A Comparative Analysis of the Historiography of the 'Long' Second World War', *The History Teacher*, 29/4 (1996), 499–523.
Bosworth, Richard, '*Per necessità famigliare*: Hypocrisy and Corruption in Fascist Italy', *European History Quarterly*, 30/3 (2000), 357–387.
Bosworth, Richard, 'War, Totalitarianism and 'Deep Belief' in Fascist Italy', *European History Quarterly*, 34/4 (2004), 475–305.
Bosworth, Richard, and Rizzo, Gino, eds., *Altro Polo: Intellectuals and their Ideas in Contemporary Italy* (Sydney: University of Sydney, 1983), 65–86.
Bosworth, Richard, *Claretta: Mussolini's Last Lover* (New Haven: Yale University Press, 2017).
Bosworth, Richard, *Mussolini* (London: Bloomsbury, 2002).
Bosworth, Richard, *Mussolini's Italy: Life under the Dictatorship, 1915–1945* (London: Penguin, 2006).
Botjer, George, *Sideshow War: The Italian Campaign, 1943–1945* (College Station: A&M University Press, 1996).
Broers, Michael, 'Cultural Imperialism in a European Context? Political Culture and Cultural Politics in Napoleonic Italy', *Past and Present*, 170 (2001), 152–180.
Browning, Christopher, *Ordinary Men: Reserve Police Battalion 101 and the Final Solution in Poland* (New York: HarperCollins, 2017).
Bungay, Stephen, *Alamein* (London: Aurum, 2002).
Burgwyn, James, 'General Roatta's war against the partisans in Yugoslavia, 1942', *Journal of Modern Italian Studies*, 9/3 (2004), 314–329.

Burleigh, Michael, *Moral Combat: A History of World War II* (London: HarperPress, 2010).
Burleigh, Michael, *Small Wars, Faraway Places: The Genesis of the Modern World, 1945–65* (London: Pan, 2013).
Burrin, Philippe, *France under the Germans: Collaboration and Compromise* (New York: WW Norton, 1996).
Byford, Jovan, ''When I say 'The Holocaust,' I mean 'Jasenovac': Remembrance of the Holocaust in contemporary Serbia', *East European Jewish Affairs*. 37/1 (2007), 51–74.
Caddick-Adams, Peter, *Monte Cassino: Ten Armies in Hell* (London: Arrow, 2013).
Campbell, Patrick, *Trent Park: A History* (London: Middlesex University Press, 1997).
Capra Casadio, Massimiliano, *Storia della Xa Mas 1943–1945* (Milan: Mursia, 2016).
Casati, Francesco, *Soldati, generali e gerarchi nella Campagna di Grecia. Aspetti e tematiche di una guerra vista da prospettive differenti* (Florence: Prospettiva, 2008).
Cassels, Alan, 'Was there a Fascist Foreign policy? Tradition and Novelty', *International History Review*, 5/2 (1983), 255–268.
Castronovo, Valerio, *La stampa italiana dall'Unità al Fascismo* (Rome: Laterza, 1984).
Cazzola, Franco, *Della Corruzione: Fisiologia e Patologia di un Sistema Politico* (Bologna: Il Mulino, 1988).
Ceva, Lucio, and Curami, Andrea, *Le Meccanizzazione Dell'Esercito Fino Al 1943: Vol. 1 & Vol. 2* (Rome: USSME, 1989).
Ceva, Lucio, *Storia delle forze armate in Italia* (Turin: UTET, 1999).
Chang, Iris, *The Rape of Nanking: The Forgotten Holocaust of World War II* (New York: Basic Books, 1997).
Clark, Martin, *Modern Italy: 1871–1995* (London: Longman, 1996).
Clarke, Joseph, *Russia and Italy against Hitler: The Bolshevik-Fascist Rapprochement of the 1930s* (New York: Greenwood Press, 1991).
Clementi, Marco, *Camicie nere sull'Acropoli: l'occupazione italiana in Grecia (1941–1943)* (Rome: DeriveApprodi, 2013).
Cohen, Jons, 'Fascism and Agriculture in Italy: Policies and Consequences', *The Economic History Review*, 32/1(1979), 70–87.
Cohen, Lenard, *Broken Bonds: The Disintegration of Yugoslavia* (Boulder: Westview Press, 1995).
Collotti, Enzo, and Klinkhammer, Lutz., *Il fascism e l'Italia in Guerra* (Rome: Ediesse, 1996).
Conti, Flavio, *I prigionieri di guerra italiani, 1940–1945* (Bologna: Il Mulino, 1986).
Cooke, Philip, *The Legacy of the Italian Resistance* (New York: Palgrave Macmillan, 2011).
Corner, Paul, *The Fascist Party and Popular Opinion in Mussolini's Italy* (Oxford: Oxford University Press, 2011).
Coverdale, John, 'The Battle of Guadalajara, 8–22 March 1937', *Journal of Contemporary History*, 9/1 (1974), 53–75.
Crociani, Piero, and Battistelli, Pier, *Italian Army Elite Units and Special Forces, 1940–43* (Oxford: Osprey, 2011).
Crociani, Piero, and Battistelli, Pier, *Italian Blackshirt, 1935–45* (Oxford: Osprey, 2010).
Crociani, Piero and Pier Paolo Battistelli, *Italian Navy and Air Force Elite Units and Special Forces, 1940–45* (Oxford: Osprey, 2013).
Cuzzi, Marco, *L'Occupazione Italiana della Slovenia (1941–1943)* (Rome: USSME, 1998).
D'Este, Carlo, *Bitter victory: the battle for Sicily, 1943* (London: Harper Collins, 2008).
De Felice, Renzo, *Mussolini il Duce: II, Lo Stato Totalitario, 1936–1940* (Turin: Einaudi, 1981).
De Felice, Renzo, *Storia degli ebrei italiani sotto il fascismo* (Turin: Einaudi, 1988).

De Grazia, Victoria, *How Fascism Ruled Women: Italy, 1922–1945* (Berkeley: University of California Press, 1992).

De Mauro, Tullio, *Storia linguistica dell'Italia unita* (Rome: Laterza, 2003).

De Ninno, Fabio, *I sommergibili del fascismo. Politica navale, strategia e uomini tra le due guerre mondiali* (Milan: Unicopli, 2014).

De Riso, Carlo, *I Mezzi D'Assalto Nella Seconda Guerra Mondiale* (Rome: USMM, 2013).

Dedijer, Vladimir, *The Yugoslav Auschwitz and the Vatican: The Croatian Massacre of the Serbs During World War II* (Buffalo: Prometheus Books, 1992).

Degli Esposti, Fabio, and Massignani, Alessandro, 'Nuovi documenti sulla Guerra nel Mediterraneo nel 1942: La Logistica dell'Asse', *Italia Contemporanea*, 203 (1996), 305–331.

Del Boca, Angelo, *Gli Italiani in Africa Orientale La caduta dell'Impero* (Rome: Laterza, 1982).

Di Lalla, Fabrizio, *Sotto due bandiere. Lotta di liberazione etiopica e resistenza italiana in Africa Orientale* (Chieti: Solfanelli, 2016).

Diamond, Hanna, *Women and the Second World War in France, 1939–1948: Choices and Constraints* (Harlow: Longman, 1999).

Dimbleby, Jonathan, *The Battle of the Atlantic: How the Allies Won the War* (London: Penguin, 2016).

Duffy, James, *The Sinking of the Laconia and the U-Boat War: Disaster in the Mid-Atlantic* (Lincoln: University of Nebraska Press, 2013).

Duggan, Christopher, *Fascist Voices: An Intimate History of Mussolini's Italy* (London: Bodley Head, 2012).

Duggan, Christopher, *Francesco Crispi, 1818–1901: From Nation to Nationalism* (Oxford: Oxford University Press, 2002).

Duggan, Christopher, *The Force of Destiny: A History of Italy since 1796* (London: Penguin, 2008).

Dunnage, Jonathan, 'Surveillance and Denunciation in Fascist Siena, 1927–1943', *European History Quarterly*, 38/3 (2008), 244–265.

Falasca-Zamponi, Simonetta, *Fascist Spectacle: The Aesthetics of Power in Mussolini's Italy* (Berkeley: University of California Press, 2000).

Ferguson, Niall, 'Prisoner Taking and Prisoner Killing in the Age of Total War: Towards a Political Economy of Military Defeat', *War In History*, 11/2 (2000), 148–192.

Ferrari, Francesco, *Il Regime Fascista Italiano* (Rome: ESL, 1983).

Ferroni, Carlo, *Italian POWs Speak Out at Last: Prisoners of War Break their Silence* (London: Teneo Press, 2013).

Figes, Orlando, *A People's Tragedy: The Russian Revolution, 1891–1924* (London: Pimlico, 1997).

Fioravazo, Giorgio, *'Le Azioni Navali in Mediterraneo dal 1 Aprile 1941 all'8 Settembre 1943* (Rome: USMM, 2001).

Fiore, Massimiliano, *Anglo-Italian Relations in the Middle East, 1922–1940* (Farnham: Ashgate, 2010).

Focardi, Filippo, 'Italy's Amnesia over War Guilt: The "Evil Germans" Alibi', *Mediterranean Quarterly*, 25/4 (2014), 5–26.

Focardi, Filippo, and Klinkhammer, Lutz, 'The Question of Fascist Italy's War Crimes: The Construction of a Self-Acquitting Myth (1943–1948)', *Journal of Modern Italian Studies*, 9/3 (2004), 330–348.

Focardi, Filippo, *Il cattivo Tedesco e il bravo italiano: a rimozione delle colpe della seconda guerra mondiale* (Bari: Laterza, 2013).

Fonio, Chiara, 'Surveillance under Mussolini's Regime', *Surveillance and Society*, 9/1/2 (2011), 80–92.

Fonzi, Paolo, 'The Italian Occupation of Crete during the Second World War', in Emmanuele Sica and Richard Carrier, eds., *Italy and the Second World War: Alternative Perspectives* (Leiden: Brill, 2018), 51–75.

Foot, Michael R.D., *SOE.: An Outline History of the Special Operations Executive, 1940–46* (London: Bodley Head, 2014).

Foot, Michael R. D., *SOE in France: An Account of the Work of the British Special Operations Executive in France, 1940–1944* (London: Frank Cass, 2013).

Ford, Ken, *Battleaxe Division: From Africa to Italy with the 78th Division, 1942–45* (Stroud: Sutton, 2003).

Forno, Mauro, *La stampa del ventennio: strutture e trasformazioni nello stato totalitario* (Catanzaro: Rubbettino, 2005).

French, David, *Raising Churchill's Army: The British Army and the War against Germany, 1919–1945* (Oxford: Oxford University Press, 2000).

Fry, Helen, *The London Cage: The Secret History of Britain's World War II Interrogation Centre* (New Haven: Yale University Press, 2017).

Fry, Helen, *The M Room: Secret Listeners who Bugged the Nazis in WW2* (London: CreateSpace, 2012).

Fry, Helen, *The Walls Have Ears: The Greatest Intelligence Operation of World War II* (New Haven: Yale University Press, 2019).

Fulvi, Luigi, Manzari, Giuliano, Marcon, Tullio, Ottone Miozzi, Ottorini, *Le fanterie di marina Italiane* (Rome: Ufficio Storico della Marina Militare, 1998).

Gambino, Richard, *Vendetta: The True Story of the Largest Lynching in U.S. History* (Toronto: Guernica, 2000).

Gannon, Michael, *Black May: The Epic Story of the Allies' Defeat of the German U-Boats in May 1943* (New York: Naval Institute Press, 1989).

Gentile, Emilio, Corner, Paul, and Duggan, Christopher, 'Two New Books on Fascism: A Review, the Authors' Responses and the Reviewer's Comments', *Journal of Modern Italian Studies*, 19/5 (2014), 665–683.

Ghetti, Walter, *Storia della Marina Italiana nella Seconda Guerra Mondiale: Vol. II* (Rome: De Vecchi, 2001).

Gilbert, Martin, *Churchill: A Life* (London: Pimlico, 2000).

Gildea, Robert, *Marianne in Chains: Daily Life in the Heart of France during the German Occupation* (London: Pan, 2003).

Gillet, Jean-Pierre, *Les Sous-marins Italiens en France: Grandeur et Servitude Italienne Atlantique et Océan Indien, 1940–1943* (Le Vigen: Les Editions Lela Presse, 2002).

Ginsborg, Paul, *A History of Contemporary Italy: Society and Politics, 1943–1988* (London: Penguin, 1990).

Gioannini, Marco, and Massobrio, Giulio, *Bombardate l'Italia: Storia della Guerra di distruzione aerea, 1940–1945* (Milan: Rizzoli, 2007).

Giusti, Maria, *I prigionieri Italiani in Russia* (Bologna: Il Mulino, 2014).

Glei, Dana, and Bruzzone, Silvia, 'Effects of War Losses on Mortality Estimates for Italy: A First Attempt', *Demographic* Research, 13 (2005), 363–388.

Glenny, Misha, *The Fall of Yugoslavia: The Third Balkan War* (London: Penguin, 1996).

Goeschel, Christian, '"*Italia docet?*" The Relationship between Italian Fascism and Nazism Revisited', *European History Quarterly*, 42 (2012), 480–492.

Goeschel, Christian, 'A Parallel History? Rethinking the Relationship between Italy and Germany, ca. 1860–1945', *Journal of Modern History*, 88 (2016), 610–632.

Goeschel, Christian, *Mussolini and Hitler: The Forging of the Fascist Alliance* (New Haven: Yale University Press, 2018).

Gooch, John, *Mussolini and His Generals: The Armed Forces and Fascist Foreign Policy, 1922–1940* (Cambridge: Cambridge University Press, 2007).

Gordon, Robert, *The Holocaust in Italian Culture: 1944–2010* (Stanford: Stanford University Press, 2012).

Gori, Cesare, *Il Savoia Marchetti S.M. 79 nel Secondo Conflitto Mondiale* (Rome: USAM, 2004).

Grampp, Williani, 'The Italian Lira, 1938–45', *Journal of Political Economy*, 54/4 (1946), 309–333.

Greene, Jack, and Massignani, Alessandro, *The Black Prince and the Sea Devils: The Story of Valerio Borghese and the Elite Unites of the Decima MAS* (Cambridge: Da Capo, 2004).

Gribaudi, Gabriella, *Guerra Totale. Tra bombe alleate e violenze naziste: Napoli e il front meridionale, 1940–1944* (Turin: Bollati Boringhieri, 2005).

Grint, Keith, *Leadership: A Very Short Introduction* (Oxford: Oxford University Press, 2010).

Groß, Sebastian, *Gefangem im Krieg Frontsoldaten der Wehrmacht und ihre Welsicht* (Berlin: Be.Bra, 2012).

Osti Guerrazzi, Amedeo, *Noi non sappiamo odiare: L'esercito italiano tra fascism e democrazia* (Milan: UTET, 2010).

Osti Guerrazzi, Amedeo, *The Italian Army in Slovenia* (London: Palgrave and Macmillan, 2013).

Hammond, Bryn, *El Alamein: The Battle that Turned the Tide of the Second World War* (Oxford: Osprey, 2012).

Hastings, Max, *All Hell Let Loose: The World at War, 1939–45* (London: HarperCollins, 2012).

Hastings, Max, *Chastise: The Dambusters Story, 1943* (William Collins: London, 2019).

Hastings, Max, *Overlord: D-Day and the Battle for Normandy* (New York: Simon & Schuster, 1985).

Hastings, Max, *The Korean War* (London: Pan Macmillan, 2010).

Hastings, Max, *The Secret War: Spies, Codes and Guerrillas, 1939–1945* (London: HarperCollins, 2015).

Hellen, J. Anthony, 'Temporary Settlements and Transient Populations The Legacy of Britain's Prisoner of War Camps: 1940–1948', *Erdkunde*, 53/3 (1999), 191–211.

Helstosky, Carol, *Garlic and Oil: Food and Politics in Italy* (Oxford: Berg, 2004).

Henry, Alex, 'Everybody to be Armed': Italian Naval Personnel and the Axis Occupation of Bordeaux, 1940–1943', *The British Journal of Military History*, 6/3 (2020), 23–41.

Herzer, Ivo, ed., *The Italian Refuge: Rescue of Jews during the Holocaust* (Washington DC: Catholic University of America Press, 1989).

Hickman, John, 'What is a Prisoner of War for?', *Scientia Militaria*, 36/2 (2008), 19–35.

Hinsley, Francis, *British Intelligence in the Second World War: Its Influence on Strategy and Operations, Volume One* (London: HMSO, 1979).

Hinsley, Francis, *British Intelligence in the Second World War: Its Influence on Strategy and Operations, Volume Two* (London: HMSO, 1981).

Hinsley, Francis, *British Intelligence in the Second World War: Its Influence on Strategy and Operations, Volume Three, Part One* (London: HMSO, 1984).

Hinsley, Francis, *British Intelligence in the Second World War: Its Influence on Strategy and Operations, Volume Three, Part Two* (London: HMSO, 1988).

Hionidou, Violetta, *Famine and Death in Occupied Greece, 1941–1944* (Cambridge: Cambridge University Press, 2006).

Hof, Tobias, 'Extreme Violence and Military Identity – The Italians on the Balkans (1941–1943)', *Zeitschrift für Genozidforschung. Strukturen, Folgen, Gegenwart kollektiver Gewalt*, 16/1 (2018), 57–84.

Holden-Reid, Brian, 'The Italian Campaign, 1943–45' in John Gooch, ed., *The Decisive Campaigns of the Second World War* (London: Cass, 1990), 129–161.

Holland, James, *Sicily '43: The First Assault on Fortress Europe* (London: Bantam Press, 2020).

Holland, James, *The War in the West: A New History, Volume I: Germany Ascendant, 1939–1941* (London: Bantam, 2015).

Holland, James, *Together We Stand: Turning the Tide in the West, North Africa, 1942–1943* (London: HarperCollins, 2006).

Howe, George, *North West Africa: Seizing the Initiative in the West* (Washington: USACMH, 1993).

Hughes-Hallett, Lucy, *The Pike: Gabriele D'Annunzio, Poet, Seducer and Preacher of War* (London: Fourth Estate, 2013).

Jackson, Julian, *France: The Dark Years, 1940–1944* (Oxford: Oxford University Press, 2003).

Jackson, Julian, *The Fall of France: The Nazi invasion of 1940* (Oxford: Oxford University Press, 2004).

Jackson, Sophie, *Churchill's Unexpected Guests: Prisoners of War in Britain in World War II* (Cheltenham: The History Press, 2010).

Jeffery, Keith, *MI6: The History of the Secret Intelligence Service, 1909–1949* (London: Penguin, 2011).

Jones, Tobias, *The Dark Heart of Italy* (London: Faber & Faber, 2005).

Jowett, Philip, *The Italian Army, 1940–45 (I): Europe, 1940–43* (Oxford: Osprey, 2000).

Judge, Sean, *The Turn of the Tide in the Pacific War: Strategic Initiative, Intelligence, and Command: 1941–1943* (Lawrence: University Press of Kansas, 2018).

Judt, Tony, *Postwar: A History of Europe since 1945* (London: Vintage, 2010).

Katz, Robert, *The Fall of the House of Savoy* (New York: Macmillan, 1971).

Keegan, John, *The Second World War* (London: Pimlico, 1997).

Kershaw, Ian, *The End: Germany, 1944-45* (London: Penguin, 2011).

King, Harry, 'The "O/400" Tradition with the Hampden Bombers', *The War in the Air: 1939–45*, 12 (1990), 25–30. (Originally published in *Flight* on 16 May 1940).

Klinkhammer, Lutz, Osti Guerrazzi, Amedeo, and Schlemmer, Thomas, eds., *Die Achse im Krieg: Politik, Ideologie und Kriegführung, 1939–1945* (Paderborn: Ferdinand Schöningh, 2010).

Knapp, Andrew, 'The Destruction and Liberation of Le Havre in Modern Memory', *War In History*, 14/4 (2007), 476–498.

Knopp, Guido, *Die Wehrmacht - Eine Bilanz* (Munich: Goldmann, 2009).

Knox, MacGregor, 'The Fascist Regime, Its Foreign Policy and Its Wars: An "Anti-Anti-Fascist" Orthodoxy?', *Contemporary European History*, 4/3 (1995), 347–365.

Knox, MacGregor, 'The Italian Armed Forces, 1940–4', in Allan Millett and Williamson Murray, eds., *Military Effectiveness, Volume 3: The Second World War* (Cambridge: Cambridge University Press, 2010), 136–179.

Knox, MacGregor, *Hitler's Italian Allies: Royal Armed Forces, Fascist Regime, and the War of 1940–43* (Cambridge: Cambridge University Press, 2000).
Knox, MacGregor, *Mussolini Unleashed, 1939–1941* (Cambridge: Cambridge University Press, 1982).
Kostornichenko, Vladimir, 'The Export Vector of "Red" Oil: Soviet Oil Exports as the Main Factor Behind Industrialisation in the 1920s and 1930s in the USSR', *Oil of Russia*, 2 (2006). https://bazaarmodel.net/phorum/read.php?1,2341
Lamb, Richard, *War in Italy 1943–1945: A Brutal Story* (London: J. Murray, 1993).
Langeo, Erwan, *Bordeaux 1940–1944: Les Bases de Sous-Marins* (Bordeaux: Association Bunker Atlantique Patrimonie Archéologie, 2017).
Le Gac, Julie, '"Le mal napolitain": les alliés et la prostitution à Naples (1943–1944)', *Genre et Histoire*, 15 (2014/ 2015).
Lepre, Aurelio, *Le illusioni, la paura, la rabbia: Il fronte Italiano, 1940–1943* (Naples: Edizioni Scientifiche Italiane, 1989).
Lett, Brian, *The Small Scale Raiding Force* (Barnsley: Pen & Sword, 2013).
Levine, Alan, *The War Against Rommel's Supply Lines, 1942–1943* (Westport: Praegar, 1999).
Liddell Hart, Basil, *A History of the Second World War* (London: Pan, 2014).
Liddell Hart, Basil, *The Other Side of the Hill* (London: Cassell, 1951).
Linklater, Eric, *The Campaign in Italy* (London: HMSO, 1959).
Lo Biundo, Ester, *London Calling Italy: La Propaganda di Radio Londra nel 1943* (Milan: Unicopli, 2014).
Lomas, Daniel, 'A Tale of Torture? Alexander Scotland, The London Cage and Post-War British Secrecy' in Christopher Moran and Christopher Murphy, eds., *Intelligence Studies in Britain and the US: Historiography since 1945* (Edinburgh: Edinburgh University Press, 2013), 251–262.
Longo, Luigi, *Immagini della Seconda Guerra Mondiale la Campagna in Tunisia (1942–1943)* (Rome: USSME, 2007).
López, Óscar, *Freeing Mussolini: Dismantling the Skorzeny Myth in the Gran Sasso Raid* (Barnsley: Pen & Sword, 2018).
Lormier, Dominique, *Bordeaux sous l'Occupation* (La Crèche: Geste, 2015).
Lukacs, John, *Five Days in London, May 1940* (New Haven: Yale University Press, 2001).
Lupinacci, Pier, *Attivita in Mar Nero e Lago Ladoga* (Rome: USMM, 2003).
Lyttelton, Adrian, *Liberal and Fascist Italy, 1900-1945* (Oxford: Oxford University Press, 2002).
Macdonald, John, and Cimprić, Željko, *Caporetto and the Isonzo Campaign: The Italian Front, 1915–1918* (Barnsley: Pen & Sword, 2011).
Mack Smith, Denis, *Mussolini's Roman Empire* (London: Viking, 1976).
Macksey, Kenneth, *Tank Warfare: A History of Tanks in Battle* (New York: Stein and Day, 1972).
Mafai, Miriam, *Pane Nero: Donne e vita quotidiana nella seconda guerra mondiale* (Milan: Mondadori, 1987).
Mahoney, Patrick, *The Sinking of the Prince of Wales and Repulse* (Barnsley: Pen & Sword, 2014).
Makepeace, Clare, *Captives of War: British Prisoners of War in Europe in the Second World War* (Cambridge: Cambridge University Press, 2017).
Mallett, Derek, *Hitler's Generals in America: Nazi POWs and Allied Military Intelligence* (Lexington: University Press of Kentucky, 2013).

Mallett, Robert, 'The Fascist Challenge Dissected', *The Historical Journal*, 44/3 (2001), 859–862.

Marsan, Mathieu, 'La Base sous-marine de Bordeaux, sous le béton la culture', *In Situ*, 16 (2012), 1–21.

Marsan, Mathieu, 'Bordeaux-Bacalan: Des Bassins à Flot à la Base Sous-Marine', *Aquitaine Historique*, 120 (2013), 2–8.

Marzano, Arturo, 'La <<guerra delle monde>> La risposta inglese e franchese alla propaganda di Radio Bari nel mondo arabo (1938-1939)', *Contemporanea*, 1 (2012), 3–24.

Mason, Timothy, 'Whatever Happened to 'Fascism'?', in Jane Caplan, ed., *Nazism, Fascism and the Working Class* (Cambridge: Cambridge University Press, 1995), 323–331.

Mattesini, Francesco, *BETASOM: La guerra negli oceani (1940–1943)* (Rome: USMM, 2003).

Megargee, Geoffery, White, Joseph, and Hecker, Mel, eds., *The United States Holocaust Memorial Museum Encyclopedia of Camps and Ghettos, 1933-1945: Vol III: Camps and Ghettos under European Regimes Aligned with Nazi Germany* (Bloomington: Indiana University Press, 2018).

Merridale, Catherine, *Ivan's War: The Red Army, 1939–1945* (London: Faber & Faber, 2005).

Michaelis, Meir, *Mussolini and the Jews: German-Italian Relations and the Jewish Question in Italy, 1922–1945* (Oxford: Clarendon Press, 1978),

Miège, Jean, 'I prigionieri di guerra italiani in Africa del Nord' in Romain Rainero, ed., *I prigionieri militari italiani durante la Seconda Guerra Mondiale: aspetti e problemi storici* (Milan: Marzorati, 1985), 171–181.

Migliorini, Bruno, *Storia Della Lingua Italiana* (Milan: RCS Libri, 1994).

Molony, C. J. C., *The Mediterranean and Middle East: Volume V: The Campaign in Sicily 1943 and the Campaign in Italy 3rd September 1943 to 31st March 1944* (London: HMSO, 1973).

Montanari, Mario, *Le Operazioni in Africa Settentrionale, Vol. I: Sidi el Barrani (Giugno 1940 – Settembre 1941)* (Rome: USSME, 2000).

Moore, Bob, 'Enforced Diaspora: The Fate of Italian Prisoners of War during the Second World War', *War in History*, 22/2 (2014), 174–190.

Moore, Bob, 'Turning Liabilities into Assets: British Government Policy towards German and Italian Prisoners of War during the Second World War', *Journal of Contemporary History*, 32/1 (1997), 177 –136.

Moore, Bob, and Fedorowich, Kent, *The British Empire and its Italian Prisoners of War, 1940–1947* (Basingstoke: Palgrave Macmillan, 2002).

Morgan, Philip, *The Fall of Mussolini: Italy, the Italians and the Second World War* (Oxford: Oxford University Press, 2007).

Morison, Samuel, *Operations in North African Wars, 1942 – June 1943* (Boston: Naval Institute Press, 1984).

Morris, Eric, *Circles of Hell: The War in Italy, 1943–1945* (New York: Crown, 1993).

Morselli, Mario, *Caporetto 1917: Victory or Defeat?* (London: Routledge, 2007).

Müller, Rolf-Dieter, Schönherr, Nicole, Widera, Thomas, eds., *Die Zerstörung Dresdens: 13. bis 15. Februar 1945. Gutachten und Ergebnisse der Dresdner Historikerkommission zur Ermittlung der Opferzahlen.* (Göttingen: V&R, 2010).

Müllers, Frederik, *Elite des Führers: Mentalitäten im subalternen Führungspersonal von Waffen-SS und Fallschirmjägertruppe 1944/45* (Berlin: Be.Bra, 2012).

Mulligan, Timothy, *Neither Sharks Nor Wolves: The Men of Nazi Germany's U-Boat Arm, 1939–1945* (Annapolis: Naval Institute Press, 1999).

Neitzel, Sönke, and Welzer, Harald, *Soldaten: On Fighting, Killing and Dying* (London: Simon & Schuster, 2013).
Neitzel, Sönke, *Tapping Hitler's Generals: Transcripts of Secret Conversations, 1942–45* (Barnsley: Frontline, 2007).
Niestle, Axel, *German U-Boat Losses During World War II: Details of Destruction* (Barnsley: Frontline, 2014).
Nützenadel, Alexander, *Landwirschaft, Staat und Autarkie: Agarpolitik im Faschistischen Italien (1922–1943)* (Tübingen: De Gruyter, 1997).
O'Hara, Vincent, and Cernuschi, Enrico, *Dark Navy: The Regia Marina and the Armistice of 8 September 1943* (Ann Arbor: Nimble, 2009).
O'Reilly, Charles, *Forgotten Battles: Italy's War of Liberation, 1943–1945* (Lanham: Lexington Books, 2001).
Ollas, Roberto, *Il Duce and His Women: Mussolini's Rise to Power* (Richmond: Alma Books, 2011).
Othen, Christopher, *Franco's International Brigades: Adventurers, Fascists, and Christian Crusaders in the Spanish Civil War* (London: Hurst, 2013).
Ousby, Ian, *Occupation: The Ordeal of France, 1940–1944* (London: Pimlico, 1999).
Pakenham, Thomas, *The Boer War* (London: Abacus, 1992).
Patriarca, Silvana, *Italian Vices: Nation and Character from the Risorgimento to the Republic* (Cambridge: Cambridge University Press, 2010).
Pavone, Claudio, *A Civil War: A History of the Italian Resistance* (London: Verso, 2013).
Paxton, Robert, *Vichy France: Old Guard and New Order, 1940–1944* (New York: Columbia University Press, 2001).
Pedriali, Ferdinando, *L'Italia nella Guerra Aerea da El Alamein alle Spiagge della Sicilia (4 Novembre 1942 – 9 Luglio 1943)* (Rome: USAM, 2010).
Pedriali, Ferdinando, *L'Italia nella Guerra Aerea dalla Difesa della Sicilia all'8 Settembre* (Rome: USAM, 2014).
Penslar, Derek, *Shylock's Children: Economics and Jewish Identity in Modern Europe* (Berkeley: University of California Press, 2001).
Petersen, Jens, *Hitler-Mussolini: Die Entstehung der Achse Berlin-Rom, 1933–1936* (Tübingen: Max Niemeyer Verlag, 1973).
Petracchi, Giorgio, 'Ideology and Realpolitik: Italo-Soviet Relations, 1917–33', *Journal of Italian History*, 2/3 (1979), 473–519.
Petracchi, Giorgio, *La Russia rivoluzionaria nella politica italiana. Le relazioni italo-sovietiche, 1917–1925* (Rome: Laterza 1982).
Petrella, Luigi, *Staging the Fascist War: The Ministry of Popular Culture and Italian Propaganda on the Home Front, 1938–1943* (Oxford: Peter Lang, 2016).
Piekalkiewicz, Janusz, *Sea War: 1939–1945* (London: Blandford Press, 1987).
Pollard, John, *The Fascist Experience in Italy* (London: Routledge, 2005).
Porch, Douglas, *The Path to Victory: The Mediterranean Theatre in World War II* (New York: Farrar, 2004).
Procacci, Giuliano, *La disfida di Barletta: Tra storia e romanzo* (Milan: Mondadori, 2001).
Quartararo, Rosaria, *Italia-URSS, 1917–1941: i rapporti politici* (Naples: Ed. Scientifiche Italiane, 1997).
Quartararo, Rosaria, *Roma tra Londra e Berlino: Politica estera fascista dal 1930 al 1940* (Rome: Bonacci, 1980).
Quartermaine, Luisa, *Mussolini's Last Republic: Propaganda and Politics in the Italian Social Republic* (Exeter: Elm Bank, 2000).

Quazza, Guido, *Resistenza e Storia d'Italia* (Rome: Feltrinelli, 1976).
Rainero, Romain, *Mussolini e Pétain Storia dei Rapporti tra l'Italia e la Francia di Vichy (10 giugno 1940 – 8 settembre 1943)* (Rome: USSME, 1992).
Rees, Laurence, *Their Darkest Hour: People Tested to the Extreme in World War Two* (London: Ebury Press, 2011).
Reimann, Aribert, *Der Große Krieg der Sprachen* (Essen: Klartext, 2000).
Rein, Christopher, 'Fredenhall's Failure: A Reexamination of the II Corps at the Battle of Kasserine Pass', *Army History*, 108 (2018), 6–21.
Reiss, Matthias, 'Bronzed Bodies behind Barbed Wire: Masculinity and the Treatment of German Prisoners of War in the United States during World War II', *The Journal of Military History*, 69/2 (2005), 475–504.
Revelli, Nuto, *Mussolini's Death March: Eyewitness Accounts of Italian Soldiers on the Eastern Front* (Lawrence: University Press of Kansas, 2013).
Riall, Lucy, *Garibaldi: Invention of a Hero* (New Haven: Yale University Press, 2008).
Ribas-Mateos, Natalia, *The Mediterranean in the Age of Globalisation: Migration, Welfare and Borders* (New Brunswick: Transaction Publishers, 2005).
Ricciotti, Lazzero, *La decima Mas* (Milan: Rizzoli, 1984).
Richards, Denis, *RAF Bomber Command in the Second World War: The Hardest Victory* (London: Penguin, 2001).
Robène, Luc, Dominique Bodin and Stéphane Héas, 'Bordeaux et les Politiques d'Équipement Sportif Durant l'Occupation (1940–1944): Des Enjeux Idéologiques aux Contingences Locales', *Modern & Contemporary France*, 13/2 (2005), 175–192
Roberts, Mary, 'The Price of Discretion: Prostitution, Venereal Disease, and the American Military in France, 1944–1946', *The American Historical Review*, 115/4 (2010), 1002–1030.
Roberts, Mary, *What Soldiers Do: Sex and the American GI in World War II France* (Chicago: University of Chicago, 2013).
Robertson Jr., James, *Soldiers Blue and Gray* (Columbia: University of South Carolina Press, 1998).
Robertson, Esmonde, *Mussolini as Empire-Builder: Europe and Africa, 1932–36* (London: Macmillan, 1977).
Robson, Maria, 'Signals in the Sea: The Value of Ultra Intelligence in the Mediterranean in World War II', *Journal of Intelligence History*, 13/2 (2014), 176–188.
Rochat, Giorgio, *Le guerre italiane, 1935–1943: dall'impero d'Etiopia alla disfatta* (Turin: Einaudi, 2005).
Rodogno, Davide, *Fascism's European Empire: Italian Occupation during the Second World War* (Cambridge: University of Cambridge Press, 2006).
Römer, Felix, *Kameraden: Die Wehrmacht von innen* (Munich: Piper, 2012).
Rossi, Andrea, *Le guerre delle camicie nere: la milizia fascista dalla guerra mondiale alla guerra civile* (Pisa: BFS, 2004).
Sadkovich, James, 'Anglo-American Bias and the Italo-Greek War of 1940–1941', *The Journal of Military History*, 58/4 (1994), 617–642.
Sadkovich, James, 'Of Myths and Men: Rommel and the Italians in North Africa', *The International History Review*, 13/2 (1991), 284–313.
Sadkovich, James, 'Re-evaluating Who Won the Italo-British Naval Conflict, 1940–42', *European History Quarterly*, xvii (1988), 455–471.
Sadkovich, James, 'The Development of the Italian Air Force Prior to World War II', *Military Affairs*, 51/3 (1987), 128–136.

Sadkovich, James, 'The Italo-Greek War in Context: Italian Priorities and Axis Diplomacy', *Journal of Contemporary History*, 28/3 (1993), 439–464.
Sadkovich, James, *The Italian Navy in World War II* (Newport: Greenwood Press, 1994).
Santarelli, Lidia, 'Muted violence: Italian war crimes in occupied Greece', *Journal of Modern Italian Studies*, 9/3 (2004), 280–299.
Santoni, Alberto, *Il vero traditore: Il ruolo documentato di ULTRA nella Guerra del Mediterraneo* (Milan: Mursia, 1981).
Santoni, Alberto, *Le operazioni in Sicilia e in Calabria (luglio – settembre 1943)* (Rome: USSME, 1993).
Sarfatti, Michele, *Gli ebrei nell'Italia fascista: Vicende, identità, persecuzione* (Turin: Einaudi, 2000).
Saunders, Frances, *The Woman Who Shot Mussolini* (London: Faber, 2010).
Sbacchi, Alberto, 'The Price of Empire: Towards an Enumeration of Italian Casualties in Ethiopia, 1935–1940', *Ethiopianist Notes*, 2/2 (1978), 35–46.
Scheck, Raffael, 'Collaboration of the Heart: The Forbidden Love Affairs of French Prisoners of War and German Women in Nazi Germany', *The Journal of Modern History*, 90/2 (2018), 351–382.
Schieder, Wolfgang, *Faschistische Diktaturen: Studien zu Italien und Deutschland* (Göttingen: Wallstein, 2008).
Schieder, Wolfgang, *Mythos Mussolini: Deutsche in Audienz beim Duce* (Munich: Oldenbourg Wissenschaftsverlag, 2013).
Schlemmer, Thomnas, *Invasori, non vittime. La campagna italiana di Russia 1941–1943* (Rome: Laterza, 2009).
Schofield, William, and Carisella, P.J., *Frogmen: First Battles* (Wellesley: Branden, 2014).
Sebag-Montefiore, Hugh, *Dunkirk: Fight to the Last Man* (London: Penguin, 2007).
Sebag-Montefiore, Hugh, *Enigma: The Battle for the Code* (London: Cassell Military, 2004).
Segre, Vittorio, *La guerra private del tenente Guillet* (Milan: Corbaccio, 1993).
Seidl, Tobias, *Führerpersönlichkeiten: Deutungen und Interpretationen deutscher Wehrmachtgenerӓle in britischer Kriegsgefangenschaft* (Paderborn: Schöningh Ferdinand 2012).
Shorrock, William, *From Ally to Enemy: The Enigma of Fascist Italy in French Diplomacy, 1920–1940* (Kent: Kent State University Press,1988).
Sica, Emmanuele, *Mussolini's Army in the French Riviera*, (Chicago: University of Illinois Press, 2016).
Smyth, Denis, 'Duce diplomatico', *Historical Journal*, 21/4 (1978), 981–1000.
Soo, Scott, 'Ambiguities at Work: Spanish Republican Exiles and the Organisation Todt in Occupied Bordeaux', *Modern & Contemporary France*, 15/4 (2007), 457–477.
Spitzer, Leo, *Lettere di prigionieri di Guerra italiani, 1915-1918* (Turin: Boringhieri, 2014).
Stacey, Charles, *The Official History of the Canadian Army in the Second World War, Volume I: Six Years of War: The Army in Canada, Britain and the Pacific* (Ottawa: DND, 1955).
Stargardt, Nicholas, *The German War: A Nation Under Arms, 1939–1945* (London: Vintage, 2015).
Steinberg, Jonathan, *All or Nothing: The Axis and the Holocaust, 1941–43* (London: Routledge, 1991).
Stewart, Andrew, *The First Victory: The Second World War and the East Africa Campaign* (New Haven: Yale University Press, 2016).
Stille, Alexander, *Benevolence and Betrayal: Five Italian Jewish Families under Fascism* (New York: Picador, 1991).

Strang, G. Bruce, ed., *Collision of Empires: Italy's Invasion of Ethiopia and its International Impact* (London: Routledge, 2017).
Streets, Heather, *Martial Races: The Military, Race and Masculinity in British Imperial Culture, 1857–1914* (Manchester: Manchester University Press, 2010).
Sullivan, Brian., 'A Fleet in Being: The Rise and Fall of Italian Sea Power, 1861–1943', *The International History Review*, 10/1 (1988), 106–124.
Sullivan, Brian, 'Fascist Italy's Military Involvement in the Spanish Civil War', *The Journal of Military History*, 59/4 (1995), 697–727.
Sullivan, Brian, 'The Italian Armed Forces, 1918-1940', in Allan Millet and Williamson Murray, eds., *Military Effectiveness, Volume 2: The Interwar Period* (Boston: Allen & Unwin, 1988), 169–217.
Tacchi, Francesca, *Storia Illustrata del Fascismo* (Florence: Giunti, 2000).
Talbot, George, *Censorship in Fascist Italy, 1922–43* (Basingstoke: Palgrave Macmillan, 2007).
Théofilakis, Fabien, *Les prisonniers de guerre allemands: France, 1944–1949* (Paris: Fayard, 2014).
Thomas, Hugh, *The Spanish Civil War* (London: Penguin, 2012).
Thompson, Mark, *The White War: Life and Death on the Italian Front, 1915–1919* (London: Faber & Faber, 2009).
Tooze, Adam, *The Wages of Destruction: The Making and Breaking of the Nazi Economy* (London: Penguin, 2007).
Trifković, Srdjan, 'Rivalry between Germany and Italy in Croatia, 1942–1943', *The Historical Journal*, 36/4 (1993), 879–904.
Tzu, Sun, *The Art of War* (Chichester: Capstone, 2010).
Ubaldini, Mori, *I Sommergibili Negli Oceani* (Rome: USMM, 2002).
USSME, (*Ufficio storico dello Stato maggiore dell'esercito* (USSME)) *La preparazione del conflitto – l'avanzata su sidi el Barrani (ottobre 1935 – settembre 1940)* (Rome: USSME, 1955).
USSME, *La prima controffensiva italo-tedesca in Africa Settentrionale (15 febbraio – 18 novembre 1941)* (Rome: USSME, 1974).
USSME, *Terza offensive Britannica in Africa settentrionale – la battaglia di El Alamein e il ripigamento in Tunisia (6 settembre 1942 – 4 febbraio 1943)* (Rome: USSME, 1961).
Vance, Jonathan, *Unlikely Soldiers: How Two Canadians Fought the Secret War Against Nazi Occupation*, (Toronto: HarperCollins, 2008).
Varley, Karine, 'Between Vichy France and Fascist Italy: Redefining Identity and the Enemy in Corsica During the Second World War', *Journal of Contemporary History*, 47/3 (2012), 505–527.
Varley, Karine, 'Vichy and the Complexities of Collaborating with Fascist Italy: French policy and Perceptions Between June 1940 and March 1942', *Modern and Contemporary France*, 21 (2013), 317–333.
Venuti, Lawrence, ed., *The Translation Studies Reader* (London: Psychology Press, 2000).
Verardo, Fabop, *La campagna di Grecia di Guerrino Bragato alpino della Julia* (Udine: Aviani & Aviani, 2011).
Virgili, Fabrice, *Shorn Women: Gender and Punishment in Liberation France* (Oxford: Berg, 2002).
Voglis, Polymeris, 'Surviving Hunger: Life in the Cities and the Countryside during the Occupation', in Robert Gildea, Olivier Wievorka and Anette Warring, eds., *Surviving Hitler and Mussolini: Daily Life in Occupied Europe* (Oxford: Berg, 2006), 16–41.

Walker, Ian, *Iron Hulls, Iron Hearts: Mussolini's Elite Armoured Divisions in North Africa* (Ramsbury: Crowood, 2006).
Walzer, Michael, 'Prisoners of War: Does the Fight Continue after the Battle?', *The American Political Science Review*, 63/3 (1969), 777–786.
Weinberg, Gerhard, 'Aspects of World War II German Intelligence', *Journal of Intelligence History*, 4/1 (2004), 1–6.
Weinberg, Gerhard, *World War II: A Very Short Introduction* (Oxford: Oxford University Press, 2014).
Whitley, Michael, *Destroyers of World War Two: An International Encyclopedia* (Annapolis: Naval Institute Press, 1988).
Wilcox, Vanda, '"Weeping Tears of Blood": Exploring Italian Soldiers' Emotions in the First World War', *Modern Italy*, 15/2 (2012), 171–184.
Williams, Isobel, *Allies and Italians under Occupation: Sicily and Southern Italy, 1943–45* (London: Palgrave Macmillan, 2013).
Williams, Manuela, 'Mussolini's War of Words: Italian Propaganda and Subversion in Egypt and Palestine, 1934–1939', *Eunomia*, 1/2 (2012), 49–78.
Williamson, David, *The Age of the Dictators: A Study of the European Dictatorships, 1918–53* (London: Routledge, 2007).
Wilson, Perry, *Women in Twentieth-Century Italy* (London: Palgrave Macmillan, 2009).
Zimmerman, Joshua, ed., *Jews in Italy under Fascist and Nazi Rule, 1922–1945* (Cambridge: Cambridge University Press, 2005).

Websites

http://www.jusp-jasenovac.hr/Default.aspx?sid=6711, accessed 19 October 2017.
http://www.marina.difesa.it/storiacultura/storia/medaglie/Pagine/TodaroSalvatore.aspx, accessed 17 July 2018.
http://www.quirinale.it/onorificenze/insigniti/12675, accessed 17 July 2018.
http://www.regiamarina.net, accessed 17 April 2018.
http://www.treccani.it/enciclopedia/lingua-del-novecento_%28Enciclopedia-dell%27Italiano%29/, accessed 1 October 2018.
https://www.devere.co.uk/latimer-estate/, accessed 22 December 2018.
https://www.ushmm.org/wlc/en/article.php?ModuleId=10005456, accessed 19 October 2017.
www.trentparkmuseum.org.uk, accessed 22 December 2018.
www.wrecksite.eu, accessed 9 November 2017.

Films

Captain Corelli's Mandolin (Dir: John Madden, 2001).
Italiani brava gente (Dir: Giuseppe de Santis, 1965).
La linea del fuoco (Dir: Enzo Monteleone, 2002).
Lion of the Desert (Dir: Moustapha Akkad, 1981).
Mediterraneo (Dir: Gabriele Salvatores, 1991).
The Secret of Santa Vittoria (Dir: Stanley Kramer, 1969).

Index

Note: Page numbers in **bold** represent figures/diagrams. Page numbers in *italics* represent tables. Page numbers followed by n and number represent end note and note number respectively.

Abyssinia *see* Ethiopia
Admiralty 8, **25**, 28, 54
Aegean 92, 128, 151
Air Ministry **25**, 54
air raids *see* bombing
Albania, Albanians 96, 151, 155, 161, 177, 186 *see also* Balkans
alcohol 49, 100, 102, 107, 130
Alexander, H. 186
Alexandria 170, 178
Alfieri, D. 79
Algiers 8, 31, 36, 71 *see also* Algiers harbour raid (1942)
Algiers harbour raid (1942) 46, 117, 180
Allegre, Naval Rating (I/N 356) 137–138, 161, 164
Allies 63–78, 176–188; Desert Air Force (DAF) 67, 120; Mediterranean Allied Strategic Air Force 137; Supreme Headquarters Allied Expeditionary Force (SHAEF) 27, 107
Alvisi, Flying Officer (I/A 35) 118, 120, 127, 136, 187–188
American War of Independence (1775–1783) 178
Ancona, Torpedo-Rating (I/N 190) 160
antisemitism 3, 97–100, 196–197
Armistice of Cassibile (1943) 17, 55, 62, 78, 101, 184, 193–194
arrangiarsi 2, 6–7, 116, 136, 196
Athens 56, 92, 155 *see also* Greece
atrocities *see* war crimes
Australia/Australians 36, 43, 84n30, 183, 185

Austria/Austrians 27, 28, 81, 183
Austro-Hungarian Empire 50, 80–81, 179
Axis 1–2, 9, 63, 78, 101, 176–188, 197

Badezzi, Lieutenant (I/N 321) 64, 66, 74, 76, 122, 130–131, 158, 164, 184
Badoglio, P. 100, 193–194
Balbo, I. 70, 126, 163
Balkans 3, 6, 56, 92–97, 183, 196
barbarians, barbarism 65, 80
Bari 62
Bastianini, G. 94
Battle for Grain (1925–1939) 128
Battle of Britain (1940) 66, 177
Battle of Cape Bon (1941) 116
Battle of Cape Matapan (1941) 56, 116
Battle of Caporetto (1917) 178–179
Battle of France (1940) 9, 70, 103, 169, 177
Battle of Guadalajara (1937) 141
Battle of Guadalcanal (1942–1943) 180
Battle of Kasserine Pass (1943) 65, 180
Battle of Midway (1942) 64
Battle of Sidi Barrani (1940) 50, 141, 177
Battle of Stalingrad (1942–1943) 8, 76, 117, 180
Battle of Taranto (1940) 8, 116, 141
Battle of the Atlantic (1939–1945) 6, 8, 43, 122, 124, 196 *see also* combat
Battle of the Falaise Pocket (1944) 40n81
Battle of the Tarigo Convoy (1941) 120–121
Battle of Vittorio Veneto (1918) 179
Battles of El Alamein (1942) 7, 9, 43, 56, 170, 178, 180

beards 107, 117
Belgium, Belgians 29, 61n120, 91, 177
Berardi, General (I/M 4) 70, 74, 79, 151, 156, 183, 186, 194–195
Bergadono, Chief Boatswain (I/N 343) 76, 94, 139, 152
Berlin 44, 73, 79, 90–91, 137, 165
Bernardini Captain (I/N 397) 93
Bersani Sub-Lieutenant (I/N 247) 122, 125, 133–134, 181
black market activity 93, 105, 116, 136
Bletchley Park (GC&CS) 53, 56–57
Bologna 63, 157, 163
bombing 28, 44, 91, 101, 103, 117, 120; of Britain 24, 29; of Germany 138; of Italy 66, 137–141, 166, 180, 182–184
Bordeaux 3, 81, 100–109, 121–122, 132
Borghetti, Boatswain (I/N 280) 131
Boschin, Petty Officer (I/N 176) 63, 66, 78, 90–91, 130, 136, 154, 178
Bottai, G. 70, 168
Botti, Petty Officer (I/N 318) 66, 131, 177
Boyle, A.R. 54
Brenner Pass 81
British Somaliland 11, 178
Brooke, A. 186
Budini, Sub-Lieutenant (I/N 373) 6, 78, 93, 98–99, 137, 154, 159–160, 167, 193–194
Bulgaria, Bulgarians 92
Butcher, H. 186

Cairo 56, 167
Campo Imperatore 193
Canada/Canadians 179, 61n117, 84n30
Cape Bon 185 *see also* Battle of Cape Bon (1941)
Catania 137
Catholic Church 3, 194 *see also* Vatican
Caucasus 75
Cephalonia 193
Churchill, W. 8, 29, 67–68, 77, 148, 180
Ciano, G. 73, 93, 96, 135, 154–156
Colacicchi, Lieutenant (I/M 5) 46, 98–99, 156–157, 168–169, 195
Colombo, Torpedo Rating (I/N 358) 166, 168, 186
Colville, J. 29
combat 117–141, 196; at sea 120–126; in the air 119–120; leadership 129–134; on land 117–119 *see also* partisans
Combined Services Detailed Interrogation Centre (United Kingdom) (CSDIC (UK)) 15–37, 42–57; Anglo-American cooperation at 30–31; cooperation with other intelligence agencies 53; CSDICs outside the UK 31–36; end of Italian operations 194; female staff 30, 40n70; history of 28–37; information gathering 20–25; language and translation 48–49; limitations of 42–47; in numbers 15–17; the 'M' Room 24, 27, 48; post-war 194–195; and the POW experience 49–52; transcript presentation and formatting 17–20; value of CSDIC (UK) 52–57; 'war establishment' of 30–32, 36–37
Commissar Order (1941) 90
communism, communists 62, 75, 77, 82, 95, 194
compassion 70, 95
concentration camps 68, 72, 92, 94, 96, 109 *see also* war crimes
convoys 97, 116, 120–121 *see also* combat
Cooper, A.D. 8
corruption 6–7, 92–94, 107–109, 131, 149, 154–155, 163, 196 *see also* black market activity
Corsica 71, 151, 193
Corvisiero, Warrant Officer (I/N 211) 68, 81–82, 108, 128
courts 58n45, 93–94
Crete 79, 92
Crimean War (1853–1856) 75
Cristini, Lieutenant (I/N 361) 51, 64–65, 73, 130–131, 139, 156
Croatia, Croats 92, 94, 96–97, 99, 122 *see also* Balkans
Crozzi, Torpedo Rating (I/N 196) 125, 163
Czechoslovakia, Czechoslovaks 28, 91, 183

D'Annunzio, G. 51, 134
Dalmatia 94 *see also* Balkans
Dalton, H. 55
D-Day landings *see* Normandy campaign (1944)
de Gaulle, C. 72
De Guigan, Petty Officer (I/N 342) 64, 178–179, 193
De Pasquale, Petty Officer (I/N 212) 184
defeat 3, 180–189, 196–197
democracy 5, 69–70, 83, 196–197
Devescovi, Midshipman (I/N 334) 12n13, 91, 98, 127, 134, 161, 164
Diddi, Torpedo Rating (I/N 191) 104, 135
Dieppe raid (1942) 179

Djibouti 71
Donato Colonel (I/M 26) 128, 135, 151, 186
Dönitz, K. 124, 134
Dresden 138
drugs 106, 109
Duke of Aosta 178
Dunkirk 9, 169

East African campaign (1940–41) 8, 10–11, 54, 129, 165, 177–178, 180
Eastern Front 42–44, 76–77, 108, 116, 132, 151
economy: American 63–64, 150; in Bordeaux 105; Greek 92–94; Italian 126, 128, 135–136, 163
education 53, 58n47, 98
Egypt 50, 56, 180
Eisenhower, D. 186
Enigma *see* Bletchley Park (GC&CS)
equipment and supplies 126–129, 196
Ethiopia 150, 164–165, 68
European Economic Community (EEC) 194

family 6, 24, 47, 51, 96, 104, 135–141, 163
Farinacci, R. 160
fascism *see also* Italian Fascist Party (PNF)
Fascist Militias *see* Italian armed forces (1940–1943)
Fascist Republic *see* Italian Social Republic (RSI)
Ferucci, Sub-Lieutenant (I/N 204) 123, 125, 127, 130
Fiat 91, 137, 140
First World War 9, 67, 80–81
food 66, 105, 145n109, 135–136, 139–141 *see also* black market activity
France, the French 70–74, 100–109, 179–180
Franco, F. 150
Franco, Lieutenant (I/N 248) 131, 183
Franzoni, Quartermaster (I/N 283) 70, 133, 159
fuberia, furbo 2, 6–7, 116, 132, 136, 196

Galliott, Petty Officer (I/N 154) 153–154
Garibaldi, G. 134
Geneva Conventions 28, 49
Genoa 77, 135, 137–139, 159
Germany/Germans 6, 44, 78–82, 107–108, 176–177, 183–185, 188
Gianni, Midshipman (I/N 250) 106, 125, 166–167

Gibraltar 46, 117
Godfrey, J.H. 54
Goebbels, J. 76, 168
Grandi, D. 70, 168
Greece, Greeks 64, 92–94, 106, 155, 183, 195 *see also* Balkans
Gridelli, Midshipman (I/N 378) 51, 69, 71–72, 76, 137–138, 163, 167, 170, 180, 184, 186, 193
Guglielmo, Diver (I/N 206) 121, 123–124, 127, 140–141, 181
Guglielmo, Petty Officer (I/N 89) 68, 71, 80
Guzzoni, A. 186–187

Hague Conventions 94
Haining, R. 53
Hamburg 90, 138
heavy water 61n120
historiography 4–11, 78, 149–150
Hitler, A. 44, 78–79, 107, 149, 159, 167–168, 177
Holocaust *see* antisemitism
Hong Kong 169
House of Commons 178
House of Savoy *see* monarchy
human intelligence (humint) 56–57
Hungary 28

India/Indians 10, 36, 66, 68, 178, 182–183
Indian Mutiny (1857) 68
Ingargiola, Colonel (I/M (Am) 1) 118–119
International Committee of the Red Cross (ICRC) 90–91
Italian 'Civil War' (1943–1945) 168, 192–194
Italian armed forces (1940–1943): *11° Gruppo di Sommergibili* 100; 11th Army Corps 94–95; 206th Coastal Division 118; *Acqui* Division 193; air force 66, 116–117; *Alpini* 77, 95–96; army 8–9, 91, 116, 130, 161; BETASOM *see* Bordeaux; *binario* Italian divisions 9; Blackshirt (MVSN) Militia 44, 150–153; *Carabinieri* 80, 100, 102, 153, 194; *Centauro* Armoured Division 180; *Decima MAS* (*10th Flotilla MAS*) 46, 64, 75, 97, 101, 106, 131, 134, 152, 181; Generals 3, 5, 29, 96–97, 130, 169–170, 194–195; Italian 8th Army 116; Italian battleship *Roma* 192; navy 2, 3, 8, 42, 71, 76, 100, 117, 122, 129, 138, 160; overview of operations 116; OVRA *see* secret police

(OVRA); *Pistoia* Infantry Division 66; San Marco Marines 100, 101, 108, 133; on Sicily *see* Sicily; SIM 55; *X Reggimento Arditi* 117–118; *see also* combat
Italian Armistice Commission 89, 71–72
Italian campaign (1915–1918) 80
Italian campaign (1943–1945) 7, 135, 192
Italian Co-Belligerent Army 193–194
Italian colonies 70
Italian Committee of National Liberation (CLN) 168
Italian Fascist Party (PNF) 98, 135, 148–160
Italian home front 135–140
Italian monarchy 107, 160–162, 168
Italian racial laws 97–98, 160
Italian Social Republic (RSI) 98, 101, 192
Italian surrender *see* Armistice of Cassibile (1943)
Italiani brava gente myth 2, 6–7, 83, 92, 100–101, 118, 141
Italo-Soviet Pact of Friendship, Neutrality and Non-Aggression (1933) 77
Izzi, Second Lieutenant (I/M 22) 64, 66, 70, 79, 156, 170, 179

Japan/Japanese 4, 64, 75, 126, 164, 178, 183
Jasenovac concentration camp 96
Jews *see* antisemitism
Joint Intelligence Committee (JIC) *31*, 37

Kaltenbrunner, E. 53
Kendrick, T. 28, 53
Kesselring, A. 58n45
Kiev 75
Korean War (1950–1953) 50

La Spezia 101, 106
Laconia Order 124
Lampedusa 93
Latimer House 11n4, 22, 29–30, 53, 195 *see also* Combined Services Detailed Interrogation Centre (United Kingdom) (CSDIC (UK))
Leghorn 99, 152
Lend-Lease Agreement 64
Leningrad 75
Leonardi, Rear-Admiral (I/N 402) 79, 163–164
Libya 56, 80, 116, 151, 164, 170, 178–179, 181–182 *see also* North African campaign (1940–1943)
Lingfield *23*

Livorno *see* Leghorn
Lombardy 140
London 28, 30, 51, 177, 185
London Cage 49
London Reception Centre (LRC) 29
Longobardo, P. 43, 125
Losi, Petty Officer (I/N 239) 66, 136, 158, 184
Luciani, Chief Boatswain (I/N 235) 139

Malaparte, C. 76
Malaya 195
malnutrition *see* food
Malta 8, 55, 68, 117, 119, 131, 140, 178, 184, 196
Manisco, Midshipman (I/N 297) 46, 106, 121, 131
maps 128, 156
Marchiol, Petty Officer (I/N 177) 90, 98, 101, 103, 108, 183
Mare Nostrum 178
Mareth Line 181
Marinetti, F. 163
massacres *see* war crimes
Mazzinghi, Sub-Lieutenant (I/N 249) 65, 71, 75, 131, 133–134, 140, 154, 161, 166–167, 181
Menzies, S. 53
merchant navy 67, 124, 183 *see also* combat
Messe, Field Marshal (I/M 2) 4, 42, 91, 98, 156, 160–161, 168–170, 185–186, 194–195
Messina 132, 137, 186
MI19 5, *23*, *25*, 29, 37, 49, 194
MI1H 28
MI6 *see* Secret Intelligence Service (SIS)
MI9 29, 31
Milan
militias *see* Italian armed forces (1940–1943)
Montaldo, Seaman (I/N 207) 160, 182
Montenegro 94–95, 151 *see also* Balkans
Montgomery, B. 53, 107, 181, 186
Moorehead, A. 185
Morello, Sub-Lieutenant (I/N 329) 131, 134, 167
Morocco 67, 72, 179–180
Morone, Lieutenant (I/N 375) 51, 138
Mussolini, B. 3, 149, 162–171
Mussolini, E. 81, 155, 170
Mussolini, R. 163

Naples 137, 138, 158
NATO 194

Nazism/Nazis *see* Germany, Germans
Netherlands, the Dutch 73–74, 177
neutral countries 24, 91, 92, 165, 167
New Zealand, New Zealanders 52, 84n30
newspapers 29, 51, 65, 104, 160
NKVD 58n42
Normandy campaign (1944) 5, 36, 65
North African campaign (1940–1943) 8–11, 36, 43, 65, 67, 116, 126, 128, 170, 179, 180–181, 184–185
Norway 61n120, 84n4, 177
Nuremberg War Crimes Trials 2

Odessa 75
onions 128
Operation *Achse* (1943) 93, 193
Operation Barbarossa (1941) 74, 77
Operation Flax (1943) 184
Operation Foxley 167
Operation Husky (1943) *see* Sicily
Operation Overlord *see* Normandy campaign (1944)
Operation Torch (1942) 179–180
oranges 128
Organisation Todt 102
Orlando, General (I/M 3) 96, 151, 156, 163, 166, 182, 194–195

Pacelli, Petty Officer (I/N 367) 74, 193
Pacific war (1940–1945) 40n83, 64–65, 178
Padua 136
Paladini, Lieutenant (I/N 298) 74–75, 80, 94, 131, 136, 158, 183
Palazzo Venezia 164
Palermo 117, 137, 139–140, 195
Paoli, Petty Officer (I/N 175) 104–105, 107, 133, 182
paratroopers 79, 92, 94, 116–118, 120, 127, 187, 192
partisans: in Balkans 92, 95, 151, 196; in Italy 168, 192
Pavelić, A. 96–97
Pedala, Lieutenant-Colonel (I/M 13) 20, 44, 80, 119, 139–140, 151–152, 158–159, 162, 182
Piedmont 139, 140, 152
Pietromarchi, L. 79
Pirzio Biroli, A. 94
Poland, Poles 45, 61n120, 73–74, 81, 91, 98, 177,196
Pontone, Chief Boatswain (I/N 254) 66–67, 69, 77, 103, 107–108, 154, 177–178, 181, 186–187

Portugal 56, 73–74
Post Office Research Station (PORS) 22, 28–29
Postal and Telegraph Censorship Department (Liverpool) 55
potemkinism 128, 159
Predappio 163
Prisoners of War Interrogation Service (PWIS) 20, 29, 47
propaganda 10–11, 44, 64–65, 69, 77, 103, 159–160, 182, 194
prostitution 58n42, 105–107, 108, 161

racism 6, 95–96, 97, 196
see also antisemitism
radar 120, 131, 139
radio 29, 56, 64, 69, 104, 160
rationing *see* food
Ravazzoni, Lieutenant-Colonel (I/A 32) 63, 68, 77, 81–82, 119, 140, 156, 159–160, 162, 193, 197
re-education 195
Reggio 162
Regia Aeronautica (Royal Italian Air Force) *see* Italian armed forces
Regia Marina (Royal Italian Navy) *see* Italian armed forces
Regio Esercito (Royal Italian Army) *see* Italian armed forces
Ribbentrop, J. 53
Rigoni Stern, M. 77
Rizzi, Second Lieutenant (I/M 14) 20, 45, 70–71, 161–162, 182–183, 197
Rizzo, Second Lieutenant (I/M 45) 51, 117–118, 120, 127, 136, 187–188
Roatta, M. 94–96
Robotti, M. 94–95
Rome 9, 77, 98, 103, 127, 129–130, 140, 151, 156, 166, 170, 192
Rommel, E. 7, 80, 181, 184
Roosevelt, F.D 64
Rosali, Midshipman (I/N 340) 76, 167, 193
Russia *see* Soviet Union

Salò Republic *see* Italian Social Republic (RSI)
Salza, Captain (I/M 52) 157–158
Sardinia 56, 192
Sauro, Signalman (I/N 198) 136, 182
Seattini, General (I/M 18) 168
Second Boer War (1899–1902) 28, 68
Second Front delays 76

Secret Intelligence Service (SIS) 23, 26, 39, 54–56
secret police (OVRA) 47, 56
Serbia, Serbs 96–97 see also Balkans
sex 93, 105–107, 163–164
Sexually Transmitted Diseases (STDs) 106–107
Sfax 120–121
Sicily 55, 117, 130, 158–159, 184; Allied invasion of (1943) 117–119, 186–188, 192–194
signals intelligence (signint) 53, 55, 57
Singapore 169, 178
Slovenia 94–95, 128 see also Balkans
Sousse 120
South Africa 50, 68, 84n30
Soviet Union (USSR), Soviets 74–78
Spain 1, 91, 102–103, 133, 150, 152, 164–165, 183, 193
Spanish Civil War (1936–1939) 104, 132, 152, 165
Special Operations Executive (SOE) 27, 55–56, 102, 167
St Nazaire 102; raid (1942) 65, 180
Stalin, J. 75, 76, 148
Stefanelli, Petty Officer (I/N 387) 186
Stefanni, Seaman (I/N 131) 1, 43, 67, 79, 102, 104–106, 107–108, 120, 122, 124, 133, 155, 158, 197
stool pigeons 27, 44, 46
strikes 140
Student, K. 79
Switzerland 56

Taranto 63, 94, 116, 141, 160, 178
Tebessa 65
Thessaloniki 92
Tobruk 72, 116, 120, 169, 178
Todaro, S. 132–134
torture see war crimes
Tower of London 28, 37 see also Combined Services Detailed Interrogation Centre (United Kingdom) (CSDIC (UK))
Trent Park 5, 11n4, 22, 27, 28–29, 44–45, 195 see also Combined Services Detailed Interrogation Centre (United Kingdom) (CSDIC (UK))
Trieste 80

Tripoli 164, 181
Tunisia 10, 20, 42, 68, 71–72, 75, 80, 120, 127, 151, 158, 179, 181, 183–185, 186–187 see also North African campaign (1940–1943)
Turin 66, 78, 121, 137–138, 139

U-boats see combat
ULTRA see Bletchley Park (GC&CS)
Umberto of Savoy, Prince see monarchy
United Kingdom (UK), 'the English'/ British 66–70, 82–83 see also Allies
United Nations (UN) 50
United States of America (USA), Americans 63–65, 82–83 see also Allies
USSR see Soviet Union (USSR)

Varini, Petty Officer (I/N 294) 139
Vatican 12n13, 91, 194 see also Catholic Church
Venice 56, 163
Vertua, Artillery Lieutenant (I/M 20) 67, 71, 75, 120, 128, 148, 185, 193
Victor Emmanuel III, King see monarchy
victory 176–180, 188
Vienna 134
Vietnam War (1955–75) 50
Villosio, Petty Officer (I/N 188) 64, 75, 106, 130, 133, 154, 181, 184
Vincenzi, Able Seaman (I/N 197) 182

war crimes 90–97, 100–109
War Office 20, 23, 25, 30, 37, 55, 72
Washington DC 27, 31
weaponry see equipment and supplies
Wilton Park 11n4, 22, 27, 29, 39n43, 53–54, 161, 194–195 see also Combined Services Detailed Interrogation Centre (United Kingdom) (CSDIC (UK))

Yalta 58n42
Yugoslav Wars (1991–2001) 97
Yugoslavia, Yugoslavs 69, 90, 91, 94–97, 109, 117, 151–152, 183 see also Balkans

Zhukov, G. 58n42
Ziccardi, Engineer Lieutenant (I/N 295) 183